THE WORLDS OF
THE EAST INDIA COMPANY

Detail from *The European Factories at Canton* by William Daniell.
National Maritime Museum (neg. PZ7195)

THE WORLDS OF
THE EAST INDIA COMPANY

EDITED BY

H.V. Bowen, Margarette Lincoln and Nigel Rigby

THE BOYDELL PRESS

in association with the

and

First published 2002
Reprinted 2003
Reprinted in paperback 2004, 2006, 2015
The Boydell Press in association with the National Maritime Museum
and the University of Leicester

ISBN 0 85115 877 3 hardback
ISBN 1 84383 073 6 paperback
ISBN 978 1 84383 073 3

Published by The Boydell Press
an imprint of Boydell & Brewer Ltd
PO Box 9, Woodbridge, Suffolk IP12 3DF, UK
and of Boydell & Brewer Inc.
668 Mt Hope Avenue, Rochester, NY 14620, USA
website: www.boydellandbrewer.com

A catalogue record for this book is available
from the British Library

This publication is printed on acid-free paper

CONTENTS

ILLUSTRATIONS

Frontispiece

Colour Plates (between pages 110 and 111)

Black and White Plates

FOREWORD

This volume is the latest in a succession of works that have resulted from conferences held at the National Maritime Museum. The majority of these conferences have been held jointly with universities, illustrating the potential of such collaboration and the effectiveness with which resources can be pooled to mutual benefit when the aim is to reach a wider audience. The subject of this publication, the East India Company, is so multi-faceted as to be of enduring interest. The maritime aspect, strangely neglected in the past, is emphasized with contributions from internationally renowned scholars whose writing helps to redress the balance and point the way for further research.

I am most grateful to the sponsors of the conference, the University of Leicester and the British Academy, whose generous contributions have allowed us to address this subject to such good effect. I would like to thank the conference advisory committee, drawn from the Museum, the University of Leicester and the India Office Records. Finally, very warm thanks are due to all those museum staff who ensured that the event ran smoothly on the day.

Roy Clare
Director, National Maritime Museum

CONTRIBUTORS

Dr H.V. Bowen
Huw Bowen is Senior Lecturer in Economic and Social History at the University of Leicester. Among his published works are *Revenue and Reform: the Indian Problem in British Politics, 1757–1773* (1991) and *Elites, Enterprise and the Making of the British Overseas Empire, 1688–1775*. He has also written a number of articles about the East India Company, and is currently preparing a book-length study of the Company between 1750 and 1813.

Dr Andrew S. Cook
Andrew Cook has been Map Archivist, India Office Records at the British Library since 1974. He is currently preparing for publication a catalogue of Alexander Dalrymple's charts and sailing directions, and editing Dalrymple's hydrographic correspondence. He is also completing a bibliography of Admiralty sailing directions 1799–1999, and compiling a cartobibliography of Admiralty charts of British Columbia. Andrew Cook has been a regular contributor to *Imago Mundi* and other journals, and has given a number of papers to academic conferences.

Anthony Farrington
Anthony Farrington joined the India Office Records in 1964 and spent 35 years working on the archives of the English East India Company and its successors, serving as the Deputy-Director of the India Office Collections (the former India Office Library and Records) at the British Library from 1989 until retirement in 1999. Publications include: *The Records of the East India College Haileybury* (1976), *British Policy in Asia: Tibet, Burma and Indio-China, 1862–1840* (1980), *Guide to the Records of the India Office Military Department* (1982), *The English Factory in Japan, 1613–1623* (1991), *The English Factory in Taiwan, 1670–1685* (1995), *Catalogue of East India Company Ships' Journals and Logs, 1600–1834* (1999), and *A Biographical Index of East India Company Maritime Service Officers, 1600–1834* (1999). He is currently working on a fiche edition of the surviving files (c.58,000 pages) of the India Office's secret intelligence organisation, and preparing *The English Factory in Siam, 1613–1688* for publication next year.

Dr Femme S. Gaastra
Femme Gaastra is Lecturer in History at the University of Leiden. He is currently working on a study about the private trade and fortunes of servants of the Dutch East India Company during the eighteenth century. His publications include: with J.R. Bruijn and I. Schöffer, *Dutch-Asiatic Shipping in the 17th and 18th Centuries* (1979–1987), *De Geschiedenis van de VOC* (The History of the VOC) (1999), *Bewind en beleid bij de VOC. De financiële en commerciële politiek van de*

bewindhebbers, 1672–1702 (1989), J.R. Bruijn, F.S. Gaastra (eds), *Ships, Sailors and Spices: East India Companies and their Shipping* (Amsterdam 1993). He has also written a range of articles, including: 'Dutch, French and English Rivalry in Asia, 1688–1714', in *Guerres Maritimes, 1688–1713. IVes Journées franco-brittaniques d'histoire de la marine* (1996), and 'British Capital for the VOC in Bengal', in Om Prakash and Denys Lombard (eds), *Commerce and Culture in the Bay of Bengal, 1500–1800* (1999).

Professor David Hancock

David Hancock is Associate Professor of American History at the University of Michigan in Ann Arbor. He is the author of *Citizens of the World: London Merchants and the Integration of the British Atlantic Community, 1735–1785* (1995), and the editor of *The Letters of William Freeman, 1678–1685* (2002). He is currently working on a study of the emergence and self-organisation of the Atlantic economy between 1640 and 1815.

Dr Shompa Lahiri

Shompa Lahiri is Harry Weinrebe Research Fellow at the Centre for the Study of Migration, Queen Mary, University of London. She is author of *Indians in Britain: Anglo-Indian Encounters, Race and Identity, 1880–1930* (1999), based on her doctoral thesis completed at the School of Oriental and African Studies. She has also published articles in journals and edited volumes on various aspects of the South Asian Diaspora in Britain during the imperial era. Her current research focuses on constructions of colonial migrants/sojourners in nineteenth- and early twentieth-century Britain.

Professor Andrew Lambert

Andrew Lambert is Laughton Professor of Naval History in the Department of War Studies at King's College, London. Recent publications include *The Crimean War: British Grand Strategy against Russia, 1853–1856* (1990), *The Last Sailing Battlefleet: Maintaining Naval Mastery, 1815–1850* (1991), and *The Foundations of Naval History: Sir John Laughton, the Royal Navy and the Historical Profession* (1998). He is currently Honorary Secretary of the Navy Records Society, a Fellow of the Royal Historical Society and Honorary Research Consultant on the New Dictionary of National Biography Project. His current research interests concern the development of the British Empire as a strategic unit, 1815–1914.

Professor Bruce P. Lenman

Bruce Lenman is currently Professor of Modern History in the University of St Andrews. He wrote several books on the internal colonial problem posed by the Jacobite risings before returning to his original interest in colonial wars. He has written many articles in the field, and recently completed his two-volume *England's Colonial Wars 1550–1688: Conflicts, Empire and National Identity (Modern Wars in Perspective)* (2001). His current research is on the cartography and cultural development of early-modern colonial entrepôt port-cities, and, as befits a military historian, on attacks on those cities, especially Manila, Havana and Cartagena de Indias.

Professor P.J. Marshall

P.J. Marshall, FBA, is Professor Emeritus, King's College, London, and author of numerous publications, including *East India Fortunes* (1976), *Bengal: The British Bridgehead* (1987), and is editor of *The Oxford History of the British Empire, II, The Eighteenth Century* (1998). He edited the three volumes concerned with India of *The Writings and Speeches of Edmund Burke* and was President of the Royal Historical Society, 1996–2000

Dr Jeremy Osborn

Jeremy Osborn's doctoral research investigated the impact of India and the East India Company on the British public sphere in the late eighteenth century. The full title of his thesis, which is deposited in the Bodleian Library and which is also available on microfilm in the British Library, is 'India, Parliament and the Press under George III: A Study of English Attitudes Towards the East India Company and Empire in the Late Eighteenth and Early Nineteenth Centuries'. Jeremy was the Senior Scholar at Lincoln College, Oxford. He now works as a commercial manager for Unilever, through whom he hopes to continue pursuing his passion for India from new perspectives.

Professor Om Prakash

Om Prakash has been Professor of Economic History at the Delhi School of Economics, University of Delhi, since 1983. He has published widely and his main publications include: *The Dutch Factories in India, 1617–1623* (1984), *The Dutch East India Company and the Economy of Bengal, 1630–1720* (1985), *Precious Metals and Commerce: The Dutch East India Company in the Indian Ocean Trade* (1994), *European Commercial Enterprise in Pre-Colonial India* (1998). He has also edited *European Commercial Expansion in Early Modern Asia* (1997) and, with Denys Lombard, *Commerce and Culture in the Bay of Bengal, 1500–1800* (1999).

Dr Geoff Quilley

Geoff Quilley is currently Lecturer in History of Art at the University of Leicester, where he teaches courses on eighteenth- and nineteenth-century British and French art. His principal research interest is the role of visual culture in the articulation of Britain as an imperial nation in the eighteenth century, and more particularly as a nation with a manifest maritime destiny. Works already published or forthcoming include articles on art and the image of the maritime nation, the representation of the sailor in the 1790s, the representation of the slave trade, and the place of the maritime in British visual culture. He is currently working on a book based on his PhD (Warwick), on art and the maritime nation, c.1770–1810.

Professor Sanjay Subrahmanyam

Sanjay Subrahmanyam is Directeur d'études (Research Professor) at the Ecole des Hautes Etudes en Sciences Sociales, Paris, where he has taught since 1995, and where he holds a Chair in the Social and Economic History of India and the Indian Ocean, fifteenth to eighteenth centuries. Earlier, he was Professor of Economic History at the Delhi School of Economics, University of Delhi. His main publications include: *The Political Economy of Commerce: Southern India, 1500–1650* (1990), *The Portuguese Empire in Asia, 1500–1700* (1993), *The Career and Legend of Vasco da Gama* (1997), and *Penumbral Visions: Making Polities in Early Modern South India* (2001). He has also edited *The Mughal State, 1526–1750* (1998), with Muzaffar Alam. He is currently completing a joint work for Cambridge University Press with Muzaffar Alam on Indio-Persian travel-accounts of the early-modern period, as well as a history of early-modern Asia.

Dr James H. Thomas

James Thomas is Principal Lecturer in History at the University of Portsmouth, where he has taught since 1968. Since 1985 he has been researching the relation-ship between the East India Company and the provinces, the fruits of his labours appearing as a number of articles and papers and, in 1999, Volume 1 of his Company trilogy entitled *Portsmouth and the East India Company, 1700–1815*. He has published three other books, three *Portsmouth Papers* and over 50 arti-cles. Elected a Fellow of the Royal Historical Society in 1983, he has served on a number of bodies at local, regional and national level. Currently Chairman of the Portsmouth branch of the Historical Association, he is also a member of the Portsmouth Historical Publications Advisory Panel.

ABBREVIATIONS

Add. MSS	Additional Manuscripts, British Library, London
ARA	Algemeen Rijksarchief
BL	British Library, London
BPP	British Parliamentary Papers
Cal. T.B. and P.	*Calendar of Treasury Books and Papers*
CSP	Calendar of State Papers
EIC	East India Company
GM	*Gentleman's Magazine*
GSH	Goldsmith's Storehouse
HRB	Hooge Regering Batavia
HSP	Historical Society of Pennsylvania
NC	*Naval Chronicle*
OIOC	Oriental and India Office Collections, British Library, London
PHSL	*Proceedings of the Huguenot Society of London*
PRO	Public Record Office, London
VOC	Verenigde Oostindische Compagnie (United East India Company)

INTRODUCTION

The history of the English East India Company is central to the interlinked histories of Britain and Asia. For two and a half centuries, the Company lay at the very heart of British commercial, maritime and imperial activity, and its power and influence was felt widely across a trading world which long centred on the Indian Ocean but was always defined by contacts and interactions with other seas and regions, both near and far. Most important of all, the Company laid the foundations of a large territorial empire in South Asia, and because of this it has left an especially deep imprint on the history and historiography of India. As a result, and not surprisingly, the evolution and workings of the Raj have tended to dominate histories of British India, particularly popular histories. A significant side effect of this preoccupation, however, has been that the relationship between Britain and Asia has often been represented, rather narrowly, as a land-based, imperial history. What has become somewhat obscured is that the East India Company was founded in 1600 as a maritime trading company, and it survived as such until it lost its India and China trade monopolies in 1813 and 1833 respectively. A primary aim of this volume is to redress that imbalance and to explore the origins, operation and influence of the East India Company as a trading organization, one which remained firmly engaged in maritime commercial activity even as it began to act as the powerful agent of British territorial expansion on the Indian subcontinent. Consequently, while duly acknowledging the Company's importance to the history of Britain's Indian empire, many of the contributions seek also to explore some of the other worlds touched, created, or influenced by the Company during its long and ever-changing existence.

The study of British India has been subject to a constant stream of influences, transformations and revisions since the learned Asiatic societies began to study Indian culture and society in the late eighteenth century. Arguably, the most profound of these influences were the 'Indian Mutiny' of 1857 and the dissolution of Britain's Indian empire immediately after the Second World War. The fallout from the Mutiny saw the effective end of the Company period of control, the introduction of direct British rule, and an undoubted hardening of British attitudes to India – both popular and scholarly – that was itself part of a broader European movement towards racialized interpretations of history during the nineteenth century. While the scholarly fascination with all things Indian that had flourished among the Asiatic societies and 'orientalists' of the late eighteenth and early nineteenth centuries never disappeared, British historians became more interested in explaining Britain's rise to imperial power. These conquest narratives were seldom alive to the influence of local political and economic forces and cast the growth of the Raj as a coherent imperial strategy, as an inevitable imperial destiny.

On the one hand, the loss of the Indian empire nearly a hundred years after the Mutiny undoubtedly increased nostalgia for the Raj – a tendency that can be seen in the continuing popularity of television and film adaptations of novels such as E.M. Forster's *A Passage to India* and Paul Scott's *The Jewel in the Crown*, novels whose often profound criticisms of imperialism and imperial attitudes are strangely dissipated by the visual splendour of British India. On the other hand, the comfortable 'grand narratives' of imperial destiny that had 'naturalized' Britain's Indian empire sat uneasily with the fact of its rapid decline. Increasingly, modern writers, and indeed post-modern writers, have come to very different conclusions: Frantz Fanon's *Black Skin, White Mask*, Edward Said's *Orientalism*, the Subaltern Studies School, and many others have all played significant roles in challenging the assumptions of empire, but more importantly, perhaps, in helping to redefine and reinvigorate imperial studies.

One aspect of imperial rule that has received particular attention is that of power. At one time, the power of the imperial centre was considered to be both absolute and unchanging: Britain's imperial strategy was decided centrally and carried through coherently on the ground; British civilization and morality were planted firmly in all quarters of the empire; Britain's military power was invariably dominant and used judiciously. Today we recognize that imperial power was rarely absolute and varied enormously across geographical space and time, as several of the essays in this collection illustrate extremely well. The models of empire that are generally more persuasive now are ones of interaction, of exchange, of local difference rather than centralized uniformity, of micro-narratives contradicting the stately progression of the grand sweep, and these shifts have had the effect of producing a renaissance of interest in the early forms of imperial contact. It is in this context that imperial maritime trade – which, through cultural contact, commercial exchange and the political and economic realities of trade, exemplifies some of the new areas of imperial studies - has begun to take on a new significance.

This volume results from a conference of the same name held at the National Maritime Museum, in association with the University of Leicester, in July 2000 to commemorate the four-hundredth anniversary of the founding of the Company of London Merchants Trading to the East Indies. Included are essays by historians of art, culture, cartography, empire, economics, politics and the sea, all of whom were drawn together by their interest in the East India Company. They are set in context by the first two contributions, which offer overviews of the Company, and an 'afterword' which reflects on the essays as mirrors of changing perceptions of the legacies of the Company, both in Britain and Asia. The essays are not ordered chronologically, but reflect instead the four main organizational 'worlds' of the conference – the Company in Britain and Europe; the Company in Asia; the maritime commerce of the Company; and the cultural influences and legacies of the East India Company. In reality, of course, these worlds all overlapped and interacted with one another to a lesser or greater degree, and in many different ways this is evident in each of the essays.

The chosen structure of the volume also allows for the integration of maritime history with some of the recent developments in imperial and Indian history, and the essays clearly demonstrate how each sub-discipline is enriched by this approach. There are gaps, inevitably; no book can hope to cover comprehensively a subject as large as that offered by the history of the East India Company. The effects of the 'Eastern trade' on literature, and the consumption of Asian goods and culture in Britain are unfortunate omissions in this book, for example, but these are due more to the sort of problems that will be familiar to all editors of collected essays than to any decision to exclude the subjects. The 'China trade' and the projection of Company influence into the Persian Gulf, both of which were so important to the Company's fortunes, are only touched upon here. But it is also important to recognize that the full integration of maritime and East India Company history is still in its early days, and such gaps are also reflections of scholarly work that is either still in progress or that has yet to be started; it is not a problem, but an opportunity, so to speak. It is, perhaps, useful to see the essays in this volume as carefully focused studies in their own right, as showing the way forward to new research on the East India Company and as indicating the real and exciting possibilities that exist for closer collaboration between museums and academic institutions in the future.

Neither the conference nor the book would have been possible without the generous support of the University of Leicester, the National Maritime Museum and the British Academy, and it gives us particular pleasure to be able to thank them here. Many other people and institutions have helped, but in particular we would like to thank Dr Andrew Cook of the India Office Records, British Library, and Dr Geoff Quilley of the University of Leicester who gave unstintingly of their time, energy and experience in helping to plan the conference. Helen Jones organized the conference at the National Maritime Museum and ensured its smooth and efficient running; Alasdair Macleod and Jane Ace of the Museum's Publication Department have worked closely and harmoniously with Peter Sowden of Boydell & Brewer to see the book through publication. Finally, we would also like to thank the contributors to this volume who made our work as editors considerably easier by producing their essays to tight deadlines and to a high standard.

H.V. Bowen
Margarette Lincoln
Nigel Rigby

The English East India Company and India

OM PRAKASH

It was on the last day of the year 1600 that a charter granted by Queen Elizabeth I incorporated some 219 members under the title of 'The Governor and Company of Merchants of London Trading into the East Indies': this was the body that came to be known as the English East India Company. Along with its rival organization in the Netherlands, the Dutch East India Company chartered just over a year later, it stood out as the most remarkable contemporary edifice of commercial capitalism. The process which had culminated in the establishment of these two organizations which dominated trade between Asia and Europe during the seventeenth and the eighteenth centuries had indeed started with the discovery by the Portuguese at the end of the fifteenth century of the all-water route to the East Indies via the Cape of Good Hope. Among the historic consequences of the discovery was the overcoming of the transport-technology barrier to the growth of trade between Asia and Europe. The volume of this trade was no longer subject to the capacity constraint imposed by the availability of pack animals and riverboats in the Middle East. Both the old and the new routes were in use throughout the sixteenth century, but by the early years of the seventeenth, when the English and the Dutch companies had successfully challenged the Portuguese monopoly of the all-water route, the new route had almost completely taken over the transportation of goods between the two continents. In addition to transportation, the procurement of Asian goods was also organized from the sixteenth century onward by the Europeans themselves, who were then arriving in the East in significant numbers. The goods procured had to be paid for overwhelmingly in precious metals. This was essentially an outcome of the inability of Europe to supply goods that could be sold in Asia in reasonably large quantities at competitive terms. The new vistas of the growth of trade between the two continents opened up by the overcoming of the transport-technology barrier could have been frustrated by the shortage of silver for export to Asia that the declining, or at best stagnant, European output of this metal might have occasioned, but fortunately, the discovery of the Cape route had coincided with that of the Americas. The working of the Spanish American silver mines had tremendously expanded the European silver stock, a part of which was available for diversion to Asia for investment in Asian goods. A continued expansion in the volume and the value of the Euro-Asian trade could now take place.

In the last quarter of the sixteenth century, the Portuguese Crown faced a growing range of problems in its Euro-Asian pepper trade. These, coupled with the loss in 1585 of Antwerp's position as the staple market for Asian spices in north-western Europe as a result of the blockade of the Scheldt, gave the merchants from the northern Netherlands a strong incentive to challenge the Portuguese monopoly of the Cape route and to participate directly in the Euro-Asian spice trade. In April 1595, the Amsterdam based 'Company of Far Lands', which was the first among the so-called Dutch 'precompanies', sent out four ships to the East Indies under the command of Cornelis de Houtman. One of the ships was lost but the remaining three came back in August 1597 with a cargo of pepper, nutmeg and mace. In the meantime, a number of new 'precompanies' had been organized for trade with the East Indies. One of these was in Amsterdam, two in Zeeland and another two in Rotterdam. The two Amsterdam companies were merged in 1598 and came to be known as the 'Old Company'. It was on the account of this Company that eight ships were sent out to the East in the spring of 1598. The ships returned safely in 1599, and the profit on the voyage was estimated at around 400 percent. This caused great consternation among the English merchants engaged in the spice trade from the Levant where supplies of Asian spices were brought in regularly via the water-cum-land route passing either through the Red Sea and Egypt or through the Persian Gulf, Iraq and the Syrian desert. The fear of Dutch domination of the spice market in north-western Europe thus served as the catalyst that led a group of London merchants to apply to the Crown for a monopoly charter for the East India trade. The birth of the English East India Company on 31 December 1600 was followed by that of the Dutch East India Company on 20 March 1602 on the strength of a charter granted by the States-General, the national administrative body of the Dutch Republic. In so far as this Company brought the existing 'precompanies' together under one umbrella, it was christened the United East India Company (Verenigde Oost-Indische Compagnie).

Between 1601 and 1612, the 12 voyages organized by the English East India Company to the East were on separate and terminable account. The period between 1613 and 1642 witnessed the operation of three successive joint stocks. In the meantime, in 1637, Charles I had granted a patent to the so-called Courteen's Association to trade to those parts of the East Indies where the Company had not established a factory. But the Association turned out to be a dismal failure and constituted no real threat to the monopoly of the Company. The outbreak of the civil war in the 1640s caused a certain amount of dislocation for the Company's trade, but matters improved considerably after the charter of 1657 which provided for a permanent joint stock. The monopoly privileges of the Company were threatened yet again in July 1698 when a rival body – usually described as the New English East India Company – received a charter from the Crown. But in April 1702, the two companies agreed to have a joint Board of Directors, the final amalgamation coming in 1709 under an award by the Earl of Godolphin. From this point on there was no further challenge to the Company's monopoly until 1813, when the new charter legalized the entry of private traders into the East Indian trade. Twenty years later, the Company ceased to be a trading body and was entrusted solely with the running of the colonial administration of India, a process that had started in 1765 with the Company wresting from the Mughal Emperor Shah Alam the *diwani* (revenue collection) rights in the province of Bengal. The Company was liquidated in 1858 following the assumption by the British Crown of direct responsibility for Indian affairs.

Like other Europeans, the principal interest of the English in the East, initially at least, was in the procurement of pepper and other spices for the European market. The first two voyages were directed at Bantam in Java where a factory was established in 1602. From 1613, Sumatra became the chief supplier of pepper to the Company. The crucial importance of the Coromandel textiles in facilitating this trade and making it more profitable had also been brought home to the Company quite early. A factory was established at Masulipatnam in 1611, though the first Company voyage to the Coromandel coast was not organized until 1614. In the meantime, given the Dutch monopsonistic designs in the Indonesian archipelago in the matter of the procurement of spices such as cloves, nutmeg and mace, a situation of armed conflict with the VOC was becoming inevitable. The hostilities erupted in 1618, and the English emerged distinctly the worse of the two. The London agreement of 1619 provided for an English share of one-third in the trade of the Spice Islands, and of one half in the pepper trade of Java subject to the English contributing one-third of the cost of maintaining the Dutch garrisons in the area. The English headquarters in the region were moved to Batavia in 1620, and the two companies shared garrisons in Banda, Moluccas and Amboyna, but due both to Dutch hostility as well as the English shortage of resources, the arrangement did not quite work. The 1623 incident at Amboyna led to a recall of the English factors from the shared centres in the archipelago to Batavia, and hastened the process of the English withdrawal from the Spice Islands.

While the English had come to Coromandel in search of textiles for the south-east Asian markets, their attempts to penetrate the Gujarat trade were linked directly to their Euro-Asian trade. Because of the possibility of a military engagement with the Portuguese and/or the Dutch, each of the English voyages to the East consisted of a certain minimum number of ships. But on the return voyage, a cargo consisting of pepper and other spices alone would fill perhaps only one of these ships. Hence the urgent need to diversify the return cargo by including in it items such as Indian textiles and indigo. Gujarat textiles could, of course, also be used for the south-east Asian trade to the extent necessary. The third voyage sent out in 1607, therefore, carried instructions to explore the commercial possibilities of the western coast of India. William Hawkins reached Surat in 1608 and went on to Agra the following year but was unable to obtain formal trading rights. Henry Middleton, the Commander of the sixth voyage, was also refused permission to trade at Surat. Thomas Best, the Commander of the tenth voyage, who reached Surat in September 1612, however, finally managed to obtain an imperial edict conferring formal trading rights on the Company. A factory was established at Surat in 1613, and regular trade started there and at Ahmedabad, Burhanpur and Agra, with a ship being sent back directly from Surat for the first time in 1615. Between 1616 and 1617, while only four small ships were dispatched directly to Bantam from London, nine ships of large tonnage were sent to Surat. The President at Surat was also placed in charge of the Company's trade in Persia. The Crown leased Bombay to the Company in 1668, and in 1687 Bombay superseded Surat as the headquarters of the Company in western India. In the meantime, the Company's trade had extended into Bengal in the early 1650s with the establishment of a factory at Hugli.[1]

Though items such as indigo and saltpetre figured in the Company's exports from India, the most important commodity the Company procured there was textiles. Initially, a part of these textiles was carried to the Indonesian archipelago to pay for the pepper and spices bought there. After 1624 when the Company's procurement of cloves smuggled by Asian merchants into Makassar became important, the volume of Coromandel textiles carried to Makassar via Batavia and later Bantam became fairly large. But this trade declined rather sharply from 1643 as Dutch efforts to plug the smuggling into Makassar became increasingly more successful. The only other Asian market to which the Company carried Coromandel textiles was Persia, but the quantities involved were never large. In view of the continuing poor performance in this area, the Company decided in 1661 to withdraw from participation in intra-Asian trade and concentrate its energies and resources on Euro-Asian trade.

From about this time onward, the English participation in intra-Asian trade was confined to private traders, and these included senior Company employees engaged in this activity on their private account. Among the important private English traders operating from Coromandel during the second half of the seventeenth century were the governors of Madras. Two of these, Elihu Yale and Thomas Pitt, were particularly active and are known to have amassed huge fortunes, estimated in the case of Yale at a massive £200,000. Other governors with significant private trading interests included Edward Winter, William Langhorn, Streynsham Master, Gulston Addison, Edward Harrison and Joseph Collet.[2] Most, if not all of these individuals were also diamond commissioners. Diamonds were an important item of trade not covered by the Company's monopoly and figured prominently in English Euro-Asian trade on private account. The diamond trade was controlled basically by Jewish merchants, many of whom had migrated from Portugal to England around the middle of the seventeenth century. This migration had led to a shift in the axis of the diamond trade from Goa–Lisbon to Madras–London. The diamond merchants operated mainly by appointing commissioners in India to whom funds were dispatched regularly and who looked after the procurement and shipment of the rough stones. In recompense for their labours, the commissioners were entitled to a 7 percent commission on the value of the investment. The accounts of a leading

1 K.N. Chaudhuri, *The English East India Company: The Study of an Early Joint-Stock Company 1600–1640* (London, 1965); K.N. Chaudhuri, *The Trading World of Asia and the English East India Company, 1660–1760* (Cambridge, 1978).
2 P.J. Marshall, 'Private British Trade in the Indian Ocean before 1800', in *India and the Indian Ocean, 1500–1800*, eds Ashin Das Gupta and M.N. Pearson (Calcutta, 1987).

diamond merchant in London, John Chomley, provide for some years information on the total amount of funds remitted annually from London to Madras for investment in rough diamonds. While this amount fluctuated a great deal between one year and another, an exceptionally good year such as 1676 witnessed the remittance of as much as £100,000 on this account.[3] There ordinarily was a gap, sometimes as long as six months, between the receipt of the funds by the commissioner in Madras and their actual investment in the purchase of the diamonds. The resultant additional liquidity available at no extra cost often constituted a major contributory element to the commissioner's success in the trading ventures he carried on on his private account. The group of Company servants engaged in private trade, of course, also included many who did not occupy senior positions in the Company's hierarchy. In addition, there were the so-called free merchants settled in India who were an important constituent of the group of English private traders engaged in intra-Asian trade.

The trading strategy followed by the Company's principal rival, the Dutch East India Company, was quite different. By far the most distinctive characteristic feature of this strategy was a large-scale participation in intra-Asian trade as an integral part of the Company's overall trading operations. By the middle of the seventeenth century the range of the Company's intra-Asian trading network covered practically all major points along the great arc of Asian trade extending from Gombroon in the Persian Gulf to Nagasaki in Japan. The two principal factors contributing to the great success achieved by the Dutch East India Company in this endeavour were the spice monopoly in the Indonesian archipelago and the exclusive access amongst the Europeans to the Japan trade following the closure of the country to the rest of the world in 1639. It should also be realized that the extensive as well as highly profitable participation in intra-Asian trade, which contributed a great deal to the Company's dominant position in Euro-Asian trade through at least the seventeenth century, would have been impossible without the coordinating role played by the office of the Governor-General and Council at Batavia, the intermediate high-ranking agency in Asia with extensive decision-making powers. But at the same time it must be recognized that there were other dimensions of Batavia's intermediate role, all of which were not necessarily to the Company's advantage in the long run. Take, for example, the procurement of Indian textiles for the European market following the fashion revolution of the last quarter of the seventeenth century, when trade in these textiles became the single most important component of the English and the Dutch East India companies' Euro-Asian trade. By the turn of the eighteenth century, Bengal emerged as the single largest provider of these textiles. The Bengal Europe trade in textiles was essentially a luxury trade in which exclusiveness and novelty in designs and patterns mattered a great deal. In 1681, for example, the English Court of Directors had written to their factors in Bengal:

---

[3] Sren Mentz, 'English Private Trade on the Coromandel Coast, 1660–1690: Diamonds and Country trade', *Indian Economic and Social History Review*, 33 (1996), 155–74.

Now this for a constant and generall Rule, that in all flowered silks you change ye fashion and flower as much as you can every yeare, for English Ladies and they say ye French and other Europeans will give twice as much for a new thing not seen in Europe before, though worse, than they will give for a better silk for [of] the same fashion worn ye former yeare.[4]

Later the same year, they wrote: 'Of all silk wares, take it for a certain rule that whatever is new, gaudy or unusual will always find a good price at our candle.'[5] This exclusiveness, coupled with the intense competition among the Europeans for limited supplies, put a large premium on quick decisions by the local European factors. Such a decision might pertain to the purchase of a textile with a new pattern or a colour combination or a textile whose quality or size specification was substantially different from that stated in the relevant orders list. In this kind of a situation, the English factors were able to score a great deal over their Dutch counterparts. Given the distance between England and India, the English Directors really had no option but to allow a considerable amount of discretion in such matters to factors in Calcutta and elsewhere on the subcontinent. The result was a constant flow of new varieties, colour combinations and patterns in the textiles sent by Calcutta to London, though in the process the prices paid for these textiles continuously went up. The Dutch factors, on the other hand, were systematically denied such discretionary powers. The reason was the belief that, considering that Batavia was only a few weeks away from Hugli or for that matter any other Asian chief factory, such discretion was best left only to the Governor-General and Council. But the fact of the matter was that Batavia was never really able to help the Bengal factors effectively in deciding what to buy. The net result was that the Dutch factors in Bengal were at no time able to match the initiative and drive of their English counterparts. It was this more than anything else that enabled the English Company to almost catch up with the VOC by the turn of the eighteenth century in the matter of the average annual value of its imports from Asia. This process continued in the eighteenth century, and by 1740 the English had actually forged ahead of the Dutch.

The increase in the output of textiles and other export goods in the subcontinent in response to the secularly rising demand for these goods by the English and the Dutch East India companies would seem to have been achieved through a reallocation of resources, a fuller utilization of existing productive capacity and an increase over time in the capacity itself. A reallocation of resources in favour of the production of export goods such as raw silk and particular varieties of textiles would have been signalled, among other things, by a continuous rise in the prices of these goods in the markets where they were procured. Evidence regarding such a rise is available in plenty in the European company documentation. The available evidence also suggests both a fuller utilization of existing capacity as well as expansion thereof over time. In the case of textile

---

4   Quoted in V. Slomann, *Bizarre Designs in Silks* (Copenhagen, 1953), p. 114.
5   Quoted in Slomann, *Bizarre Designs in Silks*, p. 114.

manufacturing, for example, artisans engaged in the activity on a part-time basis seem to have increasingly found it worth their while to become full-time producers and to relocate themselves in the so-called *aurungs* – localized centres of manufacturing production, where the Europeans were increasingly concentrating their procurement through the intermediary merchants. Among the other factors of production required, land was clearly in abundant supply practically all over the subcontinent at this time. As far as the necessary capital resources needed for the production of new spindles, wheels and looms etc. were concerned, given the extremely small amounts involved and the fact that the European companies were ever willing to advance the necessary sums, the availability of funds also is highly unlikely to have been a constraining factor. It need hardly be stressed that across a country the size of the Indian subcontinent there are likely to have been regional variations with regard to the degree of dynamism, flexibility and potential for continuing expansion in the scale of production that this scenario envisages. However, evidence available at least in respect of a region such as Bengal, which was by far the most important theatre of company activity on the subcontinent, would generally seem to confirm the presence of such attributes in ample measure.

In this scenario, the English and other European companies' trade would have become a vehicle for an expansion in income, output and employment in the subcontinent. As far as additional employment generated in the textile manufacturing sector as a result of European procurement is concerned, a recent study of the trade of the English and the Dutch East India companies in the early years of the eighteenth century, estimated the number of additional full-time jobs created at approximately 100,000, accounting for around 10 percent of the total workforce in the sector.[6]

Our information on the distribution of the gains accruing from a growing foreign trade among the various sections engaged in productive activity is extremely limited. The two major groups directly affected by the growth in the volume of the European trade were the merchants dealing with the companies and the artisans who manufactured the export goods. The intense and growing competition among the English and the Dutch for goods such as textiles and raw silk increasingly created a sellers' market. This was reflected in the growing bargaining strength of the merchants vis-à-vis the companies. The position is somewhat less clear in relation to the textile weavers and other producing groups supplying to the merchants where, in principle, one would expect that at least a small part of the gain would have been transmitted to the producers in the form of increased employment and better returns, and there is some evidence that this indeed happened. On the whole, then, there can be very little doubt that the English East India Company and other European trading companies' commer-

6 Om Prakash, *The Dutch East India Company and the Economy of Bengal, 1630–1720* (Princeton, 1985), Chapter 8.

cial operations in the subcontinent represented a distinctly positive development from the perspective of the Indian economy.[7]

This scenario, however, underwent a substantive modification during the second half of the eighteenth century. The starting point was the assumption of political leverage by the English East India Company in different parts of the subcontinent. The process began in south-eastern India where the English and the French became allies of contestants for the succession of the Nawab of Arcot and the Nizam of Hyderabad. War ebbed and flowed across southern India with little intermission from 1746 until complete English victory brought the fighting to an end in 1761. British victory meant that the territories of the English-backed Nawab of Arcot became a client state of the English East India Company. Much more fundamental in importance was the incorporation of Bengal as a province under actual British rule. The 1765 Treaty of Allahabad was an outcome of the battle of Plassey in 1757 and that of Buxar in 1764. According to this treaty, the Mughal emperor conferred on the East India Company the *diwani* or the responsibility for the civil administration of Bengal; at the same time the *wazir* of Awadh accepted a British alliance and a British garrison. This settlement gave the British rule over some 20 million people in Bengal together with access to a revenue of about £3 million, and it took British influence nearly up to Delhi.

What the availability of substantive political leverage to the English East India Company in a province such as Bengal did was to bring to an end the level playing field that the intermediary merchants and artisans doing business with it had hitherto enjoyed. The relationship between these groups and the European companies had generally been free of coercion and determined by the market forces of supply and demand. That was now a thing of the past. Through an extensive misuse of its newly acquired political power, the Company subjected suppliers and artisans to complete domination, imposing upon them unilaterally determined terms and conditions which significantly cut into their margin of profit. For the procurement of textiles, for example, the province was divided into a number of segments each under the authority of a Commercial Resident. This Resident then arranged for information to be collected regarding the number of weavers, looms, pieces of textiles of different kinds manufactured in each *aurung* in his area in a year, the number ordinarily procured by rival European trading companies as well as private merchants each year, and so on. Since the Company's textile requirements took precedence over everyone else's, individual suppliers of the Company were allotted weavers who were banned from working for anyone else till such time as they had met their contractual obligations towards the Company. The terms offered by the Company to the suppliers, and in turn, by the latter to the weavers, were extraordinarily poor. The perennial complaint of the weavers was that the price allowed them by the Company hardly enabled them to cover the cost of the raw materials. In 1767, the weavers of the Khirpai division went so far as to send a delegation to Calcutta with a peti-

---

[7] Prakash, *The Dutch East India Company and the Economy of Bengal*, Chapter 8.

tion requesting that the prices offered to them be increased by at least so much as to afford them a subsistence wage. They did manage to obtain an order directing the Commercial Resident, identified as one John Bathoe, to do the needful. But this evidently was no more than eyewash because Bathoe not only openly disregarded the order but indeed threatened to have the weavers arrested in the event that they continued with their claims.[8]

The woes of the intermediary merchants and the artisans were further aggravated by the complete marginalization of the rival European trading companies by the English. Indeed, within a few months of the takeover of the province after the battle of Plassey, the English factors were reported to be forcibly taking away pieces woven for the Dutch. In the early 1760s, the Commercial Residents at Malda and Midnapur were instructed to ensure that the best weavers of Jagannathpur, Olmara and the neighbouring *aurungs* worked exclusively for the English. This was at complete variance with the public posture that the English East India Company took. A Fort William public notification dated 28 April 1775, for example, asserted

> that the weavers of the province of Bengal and Bihar should enjoy a perfect and entire liberty to deal with any persons whom they pleased and that no person should use force of any kind to oblige the weavers or other manufacturers to receive advances of money or to engage in contracts for the provision of clothes against their will, and that all persons offending against this order should suffer severe punishment.[9]

The charade was continued in the English response dated 8 September 1785 to a Dutch memorandum:

> Under your agents, they [the weavers] may work more freely perhaps than under our own, and you may rest assured that we shall not countenance the servants or gomastahs of our own Board of Trade in any attempts that they may make to oppress the natives who work for you and not us, or prevent your employment of their industry. The weaver who works for your Company contributes equally to pay the revenue with the weaver who works for our own Board of Trade, and perhaps more so. And an extension to the sale of Bengal manufacture is more profitable to Great Britain than a monopoly in the purchase of such goods as would restrain the manufacture.[10]

The truth, however, was otherwise. The marked decline in the relative share in the total value of the output produced as far as the Bengali artisanal and the mercantile groups engaged in business with the English East India Company were

---

8   Algemeen Rijksarchief (ARA), J.M. Ross at Khirpai to Directors at Hugli, 16 May 1767, Appendix C2, Hooge Regering Batavia (HRB), 247.
9   ARA. The notification was signed by J.P. Auriol, Assistant Secretary, HRB 253.
10 ARA. The English Company reply dated 8 September 1785 to the second Dutch memorandum, Macpherson and Council to Eilbracht and van Citters, HRB 211.

concerned might, in turn, have introduced distortions in the structure of incentives in the domain of manufacturing and other production in the province.

Totally unjustified and distressing as such an erosion into the relative share of the mercantile and artisanal groups in the total output produced was, it is nevertheless important to distinguish between this range of implications of the altered status of the English East India Company as a trading body and the changes, if any, in the broad macroeconomic implications of its trading operations. There is a strong likelihood that the structure of manufacturing production in the province continued to be marked by a reasonable degree of vitality and capacity to deliver. An important, though by no means conclusive, index suggesting this scenario is the continuing growth of both the Euro-Asian and the intra-Asian trade from the province. It is true that under the pressure of the increasingly monopsonistic policies adopted by the English Company, the trade of their rival companies operating in the region was on the decline. But such a decline was much more than made up for by the English Company's own total exports to Europe going up from an annual average of under £700,000 during 1758–60 to as much as £1.92 million during 1777–79. Bengal accounted for as much as half of this value.[11] In intra-Asian trade, the decline in the Dutch Company exports as well as in those by the Indian merchants engaged in this trade was similarly much more than made up for by the spectacular rise in the English private merchants' trade with China.

Seemingly paradoxically, while the English East India Company's exports from India were undergoing a substantial increase during the second half of the eighteenth century, the import of bullion by the Company into the subcontinent was practically coming to an end. Thus against the annual average of £650,000 for the decade of 1751–60 as a whole, the annual average for the last two years of the decade was under £160,000. Such detailed information is unfortunately not available for the post-1760 period, but an appendix to the Ninth Report from the Select Committee of the East India Company entitled 'An account of the quantity of silver exported by the East India Company to Saint Helena, India and to China' from 1758 to 1771 lists only Mocha and Benkulen under India.[12] There is some evidence, however, which suggests that the import of treasure into India was resumed on a limited scale and on an occasional basis from 1784 onward.

Before we go into the question of how the export of goods was financed in the absence of the import of treasure, a comment on the resultant perceived shortage of circulating medium in the province would seem to be in order. The classic statement drawn upon in this context is the one made by James Steuart in 1772: 'the complaints of a scarcity of coin in Bengal, once so famous for its

---

[11] Om Prakash, *European Commercial Enterprise in Pre-Colonial India*, vol. II, no. 5, in the *New Cambridge History of India* series (Cambridge, 1998), p. 348.

[12] This statement is available in Appendix 5 to the 'Ninth Report from Select Committee appointed to take into consideration the state of the administration of justice in the provinces of Bengal, Bihar and Orissa', 25 June 1783, BL, OIOC, L/Parl/2/15.

wealth, are so general that the fact can hardly be called into question.[13] Considering that there is no evidence on the stock of coined money or the amount of *sicca* rupees in circulation in the province at any point in time during the eighteenth century, there is no way the fact of shortage of money can be established or disputed in an objective manner. However, the relatively low rate of agio (*batta*) that was charged on Arcot *sicca* rupees at Dhaka between 1769 and 1773 would strongly discount the likelihood of any serious shortage of money being there in the region at this time.[14]

That still leaves the question of how the Company managed to increase its exports from India significantly during this period in the context of the virtual stoppage of the import of bullion unanswered. The explanation lies in good measure in the substantial quantities of rupee receipts obtained by the Company locally against bills of exchange issued to English and other European private traders payable in London and other European capitals. In so far as this procedure provided a safe channel to a whole host of European individuals to remit home savings made in India by participation in private trade and through other means, the amounts available under this arrangement were usually quite large. Even the procurement of tea at Canton was organized partly on the basis of the funds made available at Calcutta by Englishmen in exchange for bills to be issued at Canton on London.[15] Between 1757 and 1784, the value of the bills issued on the East India Company headquarters in London, including those drawn at Canton, has been estimated at a little over £11.8 million.[16] For the period between 1785 and 1796, the figure suggested is £5.7 million.[17] From the perspective of the Company as a corporate enterprise, the financing of the procurement of the export goods in India through rupee receipts obtained against bills of exchange payable in London or elsewhere as against through bullion shipped from home only represented a change of form, but from the perspective of the economy of the regions in which the Company functioned, this represented a substantive change.

Another source of funds for investment in export goods that the Company had access to after obtaining the *diwani* of the province of Bengal in 1765 was the surplus from the provincial revenue that it now collected. Such a diversion of the revenue was obviously unethical, and indeed the Parliamentary Select Committee of 1783 indicted the Company in no uncertain terms for having done this. The Committee observed that:

---

13 'Memoirs of Coinage in Bengal', 1772, OIOC, Home Miscellaneous, vol. 62, p. 163.

14 Rajat Datta, *Society, Economy and the Market: Commercialization in Rural Bengal, c.1760–1800* (Delhi, 2000), pp. 348–50.

15 For an example of this kind of transaction, see a Company advertisement from Fort William dated 30 July 1781, Appendix 12 to Ninth Committee Report, OIOC, L/Parl/2/15.

16 Calculated from P.J. Marshall, *East Indian Fortunes: The British in Bengal in the Eighteenth Century* (Oxford, 1976), p. 255.

17 Rajat Datta, *Society, Economy and the Market*, p. 353.

In all other Countries, the Revenue following the natural Course and Order of Things, arises out of their Commerce. Here, by a mischievious Inversion of that Order, the whole Foreign, Maritime Trade, whether English, French, Dutch or Danish arises from the Revenues; and these are carried out of the Country, without producing any Thing to compensate so heavy a Loss.[18]

But ethics had never been the weakness of the likes of Robert Clive who predicted to the Directors in September 1765 that in the forthcoming year there would be a 'clear gain' to the Company of £1.65 million which would serve to 'defray all the expense of the investment [in goods for export], furnish the whole of the China treasure, answer the demands of all your other settlements in India, and leave a considerable balance in your treasury besides'.[19] Such extravagant hopes were in fact never realized because a large part of the Bengal revenues had to be diverted to wars and other uses. With the return of peace in the 1780s and the 1790s, hopes were raised yet once again, and in 1793 Henry Dundas produced figures to show that a clear £1.4 million a year would be available for investing in goods for Europe.[20] His prophecies, like those of Clive and his contemporaries in 1765, were again brought to nothing by war. A Select Committee of the House of Commons reviewing the years 1792 to 1809 was obliged to point out that instead of the surpluses promised by Dundas, there had indeed been an overall deficit in India of some £8 million.[21] This, of course, does not mean that a part of the Bengal revenues would not have been diverted to the procurement of goods for export to England and there would clearly have been years when the sums so diverted would have been substantial. But it would seem impossible to work out on a systematic basis what proportion of the total exports of the English East India Company in the post-1765 era would have been financed from the Bengal revenues and qualifying for the category of 'unrequited' exports.

'Unrequited' exports represented the principal constituent element in the rubric of 'drain' of resources from India to Britain by the English East India Company in its corporate dimension. But there was in addition a private dimension to this phenomenon effected partly through the purchase of bills of exchange issued by the Company. The practice was by no means confined to the English Company. The Dutch East India Company was an equally important channel used for the transmission of private savings to Europe. Indeed, from about 1770 onward the process of raising resources in Bengal by the Dutch East India Company for investment in goods for export was marked by an important innovation. In addition to the usual mechanism of funds being collected in Asia through bills of exchange issued locally, the Directors of the Company now also began operating at the European end. This was done by negotiating in Amsterdam the procurement of bills of exchange drawn by Englishmen resident

---

[18] Ninth Report from Select Committee, OIOC, L/Parl/2/15.
[19] *Fort William–India House Correspondence and Other Contemporary-Papers Relating Thereto*, IV (Public Series), ed. C.S. Srinivasachari (New Delhi, 1962), pp. 338–9.
[20] P.J. Marshall, *Problems of Empire: Britain and India, 1757–1813* (London, 1968), p. 84.
[21] Marshall, *Problems of Empire*, p. 84.

in England on their correspondents in Calcutta, directing the latter to pay the local Dutch Company factors the sum of money specified in the bill. Many of these Englishmen had earlier bought bills from the Dutch Company factors in Bengal and were now on the other side. The transactions in these bills were inter-mediated by some of the leading Anglo-Dutch banking firms such as Hope & Co. and Pye Rich & Wilkieson who guaranteed timely payment against them. During the 1770s, this particular method became an important avenue for raising resources in Bengal. In a transaction entered into with Pye Rich & Wilkieson in 1773, for example, the Directors bought four such bills, each of the value of a little over £10,000. In the event of the bills not being honoured in Bengal, the banking firm was liable to pay a 12 percent compensation to the Company. The payment due to the firm against the bills was to be made only after the receipt of information that the money had in fact been collected in Bengal.[22] The Directors were evidently able to negotiate such a favourable package because of the large sums of money waiting in Calcutta to be remitted home. The parties interested in effecting the remittances were not particularly keen to use the offices of the English East India Company for the purpose, because the savings sought to be remitted home often contained a part – at times a rather large part – that the person concerned would be hard put to justify as legitimately made through participation in private trade or other authorized avenues of earning money.

In his *John Company at Work* published more than half a century ago, Holden Furber was the first professional historian to try to quantify the size of the annual drain of wealth from India to Britain. For the years between 1783 and 1793, he put this figure at £1.8 million.[23] For Bengal alone, which was by far the most important single Indian region to contribute to this phenomenon, a recent study puts the figure at £1 million for the years between 1757 and 1794.[24] Given the nature of the data, it is indeed quite impossible to attach any degree of preci-sion to such estimates. All that one can say is that Bengal revenues provided an indirect subsidy to the British exchequer, and the enormous opportunities for private gain now available to the Company servants in their personal capacity created a whole new class of new-rich 'nabobs' returning to England with fortunes unheard of before. It is, however, highly unlikely that these private fortunes constituted an element of any importance in the financing of the Indus-trial Revolution in Britain which was then getting under way.

The rise of the China trade, which was by far the most important source of private trading fortunes, led to what Holden Furber has termed a 'commercial revolution' involving a clear domination of trade in the Indian Ocean and the South China Sea by the private English traders. Such a domination would almost certainly have had a certain amount of adverse impact on the trading operations

22 Femme Gaastra, 'British Capital for the VOC in Bengal', in *Commerce and Culture in the Bay of Bengal, 1500–1800*, eds Om Prakash and Denys Lombard (Delhi, 1999).
23 Holden Furber, *John Company at Work, A Study of European Expansion in India in the Late Eighteenth Century* (Cambridge, Mass., 1948), p. 310.

of the Indian merchants engaged in trade in the Eastern Indian Ocean. It is, however, important to keep the matter in perspective. The overall adverse impact on the fortunes of the Indian merchants engaged in intra-Asian trade would not seem to have been anything like catastrophic. The direct involvement of the Indian merchants in the China trade had never been of any significance, and to that extent, a growth in the English private trade in the sector had no specific and immediate implication for these merchants except that English ships also did a fair amount of business in south-east Asia on the way to and from China. It would seem that initially the increased competition by the English was injurious to the Indian merchants engaged in trade with this region. But over time the volume and value of trade on the India–south-east Asia sector would in fact seem to have registered a significant increase, with the Indian merchants getting their due share in the rising volume of trade.

As far as the English East India Company in its corporate dimension was concerned, an analysis of the implications of the grant of the *diwani* to the Company for the prosperity or otherwise of the agricultural sector of the province is perhaps more promising than trying to work out what part of the total Bengal revenues drained away to Britain.

The agrarian counterpart of the aggrieved Bengal textile weaver was the opium peasant who was similarly subjected to significant non-market pressures by the English East India Company, as well as by its employees operating in their private capacity. Soon after the takeover of the province, Company servants tried to establish private monopolies in the drug. These individuals generally did not engage in internal or international trade in the item on their own but would sell it on a monopoly basis to the prospective traders in the drug who would include Indian merchants, other private English traders and the Dutch East India Company. The gross profit earned in the process has been estimated to be quite high. This situation was altered radically in 1773 when the English Company decided to assume monopoly rights in the drug for itself. The arrangement was for the Company to organize the procurement of the drug on an exclusive basis and then arrange for its sale to prospective traders through public auctions held at Calcutta. In principle, the monopoly implied that the entire output of the drug would have to be handed over to the Company through a contractor at a price determined unilaterally for the year. In 1797, the contract system was abolished in favour of an agency system involving direct control by the Company of the cultivation of opium. If a peasant decided to be in the business of producing opium, he had no option but to deal with the Company. But in principle, he had the right not to be in the business of producing opium and to reject the offer of a cash advance in return for pledging his crop to the English Company agent.[25]

The opium enterprise was clearly of great advantage to the English East India Company, the contractors and other intermediaries participating in the enter-

[24] Datta, *Society, Economy and the Market*, p. 57.
[25] Extract, Bengal Revenue Consulations, 23 November 1773, Appendix 57, Ninth Committee Report, OIOC.

prise as well as to the private English traders engaged in the opium trade. As for the peasants participating in the opium enterprise, the position was more complex. There can be no question that the opium monopoly involved a certain amount of coercion over the peasants, and it is likely that the degree of this coercion exceeded the officially stipulated limits. What can one say about the overall implications of the English Company's opium monopoly? Was the expansion in output over time solely a function of the coercion to which the peasant was subjected? Or is it possible that the peasant found even the monopoly price, particularly after it was periodically increased between 1823 and 1838, preferable to the option of growing alternative crops? While no definitive answers to these questions are as yet possible, certain tentative suggestions may be made. The cultivation of opium did involve a four- to five-month commitment to demanding arduous work. The reason the acreage still went on increasing was because of the liberal policy the government followed in the matter of giving advances to the actual and prospective opium growers. These advances came in handy for meeting the peasants' land rent obligations and were extremely welcome. The fact that the government monopoly provided an assured market for the peasants' output at a predetermined price not subject to alteration by the size of the crop also worked as a positive factor. The cash advances involved the injection of fairly large sums of money into the commercial agricultural sector of the region directly through the peasants. The crop that this helped the expansion of was both of high value as well as being intended entirely for the market.

At a more general level, how did the functioning of the Company as the *diwan* affect the state of the agricultural sector in the province? The most basic element of state policy, of course, was the size and the pattern of land revenue demand made on the sector. On an average, 40–45 percent of the agricultural output was collected as land revenue. There was an almost continuous increase in both the amount of revenue assessed as well as that collected. With 1755 as base equal to 100, the index of the amount assessed stood at 135 in 1770, 155 in 1778 and 168 in 1783. The amount of revenue collected also went up but by a somewhat smaller margin. The collection was made exclusively in cash, significantly furthering the process of monetization in the province. There is evidence, for example, that in 1769 even sharecroppers in an extended *zamindari* of Burdwan were obliged to sell the crop and then pay the *zamindar* in cash, a process which seems to have intensified in subsequent years. During periods of price slumps, the Mughal revenue officials often used to accept payment of revenue in kind in order that the real burden on the peasantry was reduced. That element of flexibility was now done away with altogether.[26]

The major famine that hit the province in 1769–70 is conventionally believed to have caused as many as 10 million deaths, accounting for a third of the total population. Recent research, however, suggests that devastating as the famine was, the death toll is unlikely to have been anywhere near this figure. The dura-

---

26 Datta, *Society, Economy and the Market*, pp. 333–4.

tion of the famine at its peak was a maximum of six months, and the worst affected were six districts in western and north-eastern Bengal. It is nevertheless true that the role of the English East India Company in alleviating the misery caused by the famine was practically nil. The collection of revenue was strictly enforced throughout the famine: indeed, more revenue was collected at its height than in the subsequent year. Also, the Company failed to provide any form of institutional relief. Up to April 1770, the Company had advanced only Rs100,000 'for the purchase of rice on account of a charitable distribution made to the poor in and around Murshidabad'. An amount of Rs400,000 was all that was provided by way of financial aid from the Murshidabad treasury between April 1769 and May 1770 to help the cultivators to organize production during the ensuing agricultural season.[27]

An area in which the Company was more effective was in intervening in the market as a device to free it of the major internal restrictions imposed by *zamindari* control during the period of the *nizamat*. The fact that merchants were able to carve out petty domains of privileged trade, and that *zamindars* and other landed proprietors were the prime agents for the establishment of these markets, jointly militated against the development of an unfettered system of markets in the province. What this had involved was the proliferation of *zamindari* outposts (*chowkies*) to collect tolls at various rates dictated by the financial predilections of an individual *zamindar* and continuous conflicts between merchants and *zamindars* over the rate of tolls, over market jurisdictions and the movement of commodities. What the East India Company was able to do was to take a body of steps between 1773 and 1790 to rectify this situation. These included the abolition of all duties levied upon grain while being transported from one place to another. It was only at the final point of destination that a duty was to be charged. The management of such duties was to be under five customs houses to be established at Calcutta, Hugli, Murshidabad, Dhaka and Patna. The other problem, of the control exercised by the *zamindars* and the *talluqdars* over markets, was found more difficult to address. Finally in 1790 the Board of Revenue decreed a separation between rent collected in the markets so controlled and the taxes collected there on trade. While rent could continue to be collected on a private basis, the right to tax was henceforth to be vested in the Company. The combined result of these policies was a proliferation of market places all over Bengal. The increase in their numbers or their establishment in previously deficient areas enabled the peasantry to relate more easily to wider commercial networks.[28]

This profile of a reasonably vibrant agricultural sector and rural economy in the second half of the eighteenth century seeks to revise substantially the orthodoxy in the historiography on the subject. It has traditionally been held, for

---

[27] Datta, *Society, Economy and the Market*, Chapter 5.
[28] Datta, 'Markets, Bullion and Bengal's Commercial Economy: An Eighteenth-Century Perspective', in *Commerce and Culture in the Bay of Bengal, 1500–1800*, eds Om Prakash and Denys Lombard (Delhi, 1999).

example, that because of the revenue policy of the East India Company, there was a large-scale distress sale of *zamindaris* in the province which had rendered the land market highly depressed. Specific evidence now available regarding the generally buoyant state of the land market during this period suggests the strong need of giving up such stereotypes and having a fresh look at this phase in the history of Bengal. Such an enterprise will fit in quite well with the work that has now been under way for two decades or more seeking to view Indian history in the eighteenth century in a new light.

'No Longer Mere Traders': Continuities and Change in the Metropolitan Development of the East India Company, 1600–1834

H.V. BOWEN

As the contributions to this volume demonstrate in many different ways, the overseas activities of the East India Company changed substantially over the course of its 250-year history. The Company did not long restrict itself to one sphere of operation or one type of endeavour; rather the restless search for commercial advantage and profit ensured that it sought constantly to exploit new opportunities and openings. Hence, over time, trading patterns and structures changed as the Company's geographical focus of attention shifted, as new markets were entered, as new commodities were traded, and, eventually and perhaps most importantly, as new possessions and territories were acquired. The Company became much more than a maritime commercial organization as it evolved into a powerful imperial agency, and by 1800 its imprint on the east was quite profoundly different from that envisaged by its founding fathers in 1600. As one contemporary, Joseph Hume, declared to the assembled stockholders in 1813, the directors of the Company now 'acted as the ministers of a state, or as monarchs of an empire, greater in extent and population, if he excepted China, than any other in the world'.[1]

The transformation of the Company from trader to sovereign is, of course, quite clearly discernible from even the most cursory examination of the military and political events that unfolded in India after 1740. Far less obvious is the extent to which the Company's domestic history was also characterized by ongoing processes of institutional adaptation, reinvention, and reorientation. Yet in Britain, too, the Company by 1800 had also moved a considerable distance from its origins in terms of its organization, function, external relationships, and perceived utility to the nation. No longer simply a private trading organization dedicated to the narrow pursuit of commercial profit, the Company had since the middle of the eighteenth century assumed many of the characteristics associated with the government of empire. As one observer recalled during the 1840s, over time the Company had become 'a compendium of all the offices of government, including a department for the transfer of stock, and was in addition a

---

[1] *The Speech of Mr Joseph Hume at the East India House on the 6th October 1813*... (London, 1813), p. 10.

great mercantile establishment'.[2] This reflected the fact that, beyond its continuing core commercial and maritime activities, the Company had developed a
range of measures and policies believed to be suitable for the support of a
powerful military machine, the control of new peoples and territory, the administration of justice, the collection of revenue, and the advancement of science
and knowledge. Accordingly, the Company eventually embraced an entirely new
set of responsibilities that served to redefine its metropolitan position within the
wider British polity. By the end of its days in the 1850s, when it had long since
lost its commercial privileges, the Company had become, to all intents and
purposes, an office or department of state.

The processes of change and expansion that underpinned the Company's
transformation from trader to sovereign in India have understandably received
considerable attention from successive generations of scholars, but by comparison relatively little work has been devoted to institutional change at the metropolitan heart of the East Indian empire. In part, this is a reflection of the subject
and geographical boundaries that exist within the historical discipline, but it also
stems from an implicit assumption in much of the literature on the empire that,
despite the occasional political or financial crisis, the Company's domestic experience was characterized by underlying continuity and strength. In such a
scheme of things, an often turbulent, fluctuating, though generally expanding,
overseas empire was anchored to a metropolitan core in London by a Company
whose chief characteristics are believed to have been those of stability and
permanence. At the most basic of levels, this is reflected in the way that historians often refer rather loosely and indiscriminately to *the* Company as though
it had one single unbroken span of existence. There are indeed many grounds on
which to support a continuity thesis, but it is possible to overlook the extent to
which domestic factors, as well as the acquisition of overseas territories, acted as
motors of organizational change and reconfiguration throughout the entire
250-year life of the Company.

While it can be argued that direct metropolitan influences or impulses were
often only very faintly felt within the expansionist process in the East, the
Company in Asia always represented, to a lesser or greater degree, a semi-formal
extension of the State that created it in the first place and then sought over
two-and-a-half centuries to sustain and protect it. From the very beginning, the
Company was dependent upon the Crown and Parliament for the periodic
renewal of the trading privileges and military powers that it exercised beyond the
Cape of Good Hope, and as an organization it always relied heavily upon the
official seal of sanction and approval. If this helped to draw the Company close
to the State, it also meant that the Company acted as a vehicle for the simultaneous promotion of private and public interest. Considerable local autonomy
was devolved to the Company by a state that could not itself extend any
'national' influence to the east but nonetheless recognized the importance of

---

[2]   J.C. Platt, 'East India House', in Charles Knight, ed., *London*, 6 vols (London, 1841–3), v, 59.

establishing some form of English presence in Asia.[3] As a result, although State-Company relations were always primarily determined by the narrow practical day-to-day concerns of politics, trade, and finance, prevailing ideas, attitudes, and assumptions about the purpose and organization of commercial endeavour and imperial activity also bore heavily upon the development of the Company as an institution. None of these wider influences remained unchanging, of course, and as they altered over time then so too the metropolitan framework supporting Britain's Asian empire was re-cast, and the Company's domestic position was modified accordingly. To ignore these changing circumstances is thus to run the risk of ignoring factors that helped to shape the emergence of the Company as an organization that could appear outwardly unaltered in form, but which at the same time took on a series of quite new and different non-commercial roles and responsibilities.

The view that the Company had enjoyed long-term stability and continuity was certainly shared by many of those who, from the vantage point of the late eighteenth century, reflected upon the Company's history and achievements at a time when memories of deep political and financial crises experienced during the 1760s and 1770s were beginning to recede, and when rival European companies were falling by the wayside. The Company's very obvious advances in Asia, together with its contribution to the well-being of the nation as a whole, allowed some contemporaries to suggest that it had arrived at a point where its successes had created a position of influence that was considerably greater than that achieved by any other commercial organization in history. In the words of the political economist David Macpherson, who was writing at the beginning of the nineteenth century, the Company was now 'the most illustrious and most flourishing commercial association that ever existed in any age or country'.[4]

Part of the explanation offered by contemporaries for this happy state of affairs was that in term of its management and methods the Company had risen to heights far greater than those that could be achieved by individuals or other types of organization. As an earlier political economist, Thomas Mortimer, had put it, the East India Company, together with the Bank of England, had

> brought the commerce and mercantile credit of Great Britain to such a degree of perfection, as no age or country can equal, and to suppose that this national success could have been accomplished by private merchants, or even by

---

3   For the role of the state in overseas enterprise and the development of 'government by licence' in the east, see Michael J. Braddick, 'The English government, war, trade, and settlement, 1625–1688', *Oxford History of the British Empire*, Vol. 1: *The Origins of Empire*, ed. Nicholas Canny (Oxford, 1998), pp. 286–308.

4   David Macpherson in his dedication to the directors of the East India Company, printed at the beginning of *Annals of Commerce, Manufactures, Fisheries and Navigation, with Brief Notices of the Arts and Sciences Connected with Them*, 4 vols (London, 1805).

companies not trading on a joint stock, is an absurdity that does not deserve serious consideration.[5]

This belief that the Company's organizational form was the most appropriate for the management of long-distance enterprise was, of course, hotly contested by those who took an increasingly hard anti-monopolist line against the Company during the second half of the eighteenth century. Nevertheless, the members of the merchant and business community who did endorse a positive view of the Company were inclined to suggest that its institutional strength had been considerably reinforced by a strict adherence to the routine and rhythm that had long driven its internal practices and systems. In the words of one contemporary, 'Regularity and order were the soul of business; and they were the more necessary in an establishment like the East India Company, so multifarious and complex as it was in its arrangements.'[6] Long-established systems had been refined over the years in such a way as to draw from one director, Sir Joseph Cotton, a comparison with the development of the British constitution. Cotton, when defending the Company's shipping system against charges of inefficiency and favouritism, declared that 'Innovations in an established system are at all times dangerous', and he commended the Company for its attitude to modification and reform by writing that 'Like the constitution of our country, it [the shipping system] has been improved by the hand of time, and abuses corrected as they arose.'[7] This whiggish view of the Company's past, which was also applied to contemporary analyses of 'improvement' in the Company's government of India, helped to ensure that from the perspective of the late eighteenth century it could appear that the Company had made an almost seamless transition from one phase of its development to another, with the long-run continuities established by internal practice and procedure helping to create the impression of uninterrupted growth from a single organizational seed planted during the early seventeenth century.

At the same time, a rather different and far from positive emphasis upon institutional continuity was evident among critics who argued that the Company had, in its domestic world, entirely failed to come to terms with the marked change in circumstances that accompanied the transition from trade to empire in Bengal during the third quarter of the eighteenth century. Those seeking to breach the Company's monopoly were vociferous in their condemnation of the

---

5   Thomas Mortimer, *The Elements of Commerce, Politics and Finance in Three Treatises on Those Important Subjects* (London, 1780), p. 130.
6   Alderman Atkins speaking at the Company's General Court on 1 Sept. 1813, as reported in *Debates at the East India House . . .*, III (London, 1814), 78. Of course, critics argued that the Company's strict adherence to 'regularity' served only to stifle innovation and entrepreneurial spirit. See, for example, William Playfair, *Strictures on the Asiatic Establishment of Great Britain: With a view to an enquiry into the true interests of the East India Company* (London, 1799), p. 57.
7   Joseph Cotton, *A Review of the Shipping System of the East India Company . . .* (London, 1798), p. 15.

Company as an institution so fatally wedded to outmoded and uncompetitive commercial practices that it was damaging the national interest by failing to manage the East India trade efficiently and profitably. Others, including influential insiders such as Lord Clive, Laurence Sulivan, and Warren Hastings, argued that the Company's unreformed administrative structures and decision-making processes were ill suited to the demands of managing an expanding territorial empire. These critics had various axes to grind, and they approached the issue of Company reform from often radically different standpoints, but all were agreed that the internal guidelines for the conduct of Company business established in the charters and by-laws of the late-seventeenth and early-eighteenth century had been cast in stone to such a degree that they no longer accurately reflected what the Company had now become. Veteran Company politician Laurence Sulivan was moved to complain in 1784 that 'the rules and ordinances of the Company at home are exactly upon the same scale as they stood in 1707, when the Company thought only of trade'.[8] This was far from accurate – the by-laws had been entirely re-cast in 1774 – but words such as these helped to underpin a widespread contemporary belief that the Company was an unchanging institution seemingly incapable of undertaking deep-rooted internal reform.

Not only contemporaries cast the Company's history within a framework of organization or interpretation defined by the existence of continuities. In recent years business and economic historians have endeavoured to seek in the Company (and other early-modern chartered companies) the origins and development of the present-day multinational or transnational firm, and they have been inclined to emphasize long-run continuities and the existence from the seventeenth century of a range of recognizably 'modern' organizational characteristics. Focusing in particular (and it should be said almost exclusively) upon the years between 1660 and 1760, they have identified, among other features, the early emergence of management hierarchies and systems, a multidivisional form, effective information gathering and processing procedures, reasonably reliable methods of control over employees, and well-developed accounting and bookkeeping practices.[9] These characteristics are considered to have underpinned the Company's long-term survival, but it is also held that the East India

---

[8] Quoted in C.H. Philips, *The East India Company 1784–1834* (Manchester, 1940), p. 44.

[9] See, for example, G.M. Anderson, R.E. McCormick and R.E. Tollison, 'The economic organization of the English East India Company', *Journal of Economic Behavior and Organization*, 4 (1983), 221–38; A.M. Carlos and S. Nicholas, ' "Giants of an earlier capitalism": the chartered trading companies as modern multinationals', *Business History Review*, 62 (1988), 398–419; K.N. Chaudhuri, 'The English East India Company in the 17th and 18th centuries: a pre-modern multinational organization', in L. Busse and F. Gaastra, eds, *Companies and Trade* (Leiden, 1981), pp. 29–46; K.N. Chaudhuri, 'The "new economic history" and the business records of the East India Company', in P.L. Cottrell and D.H. Aldcroft, eds, *Shipping and Commerce: Essays in Memory of Ralph Davis* (Leicester, 1981), pp. 45–59; K.N. Chaudhuri, 'The English East India Company and its decision-making', in K. Ballhatchet and J. Harrison, eds, *East India Company Studies: Papers presented to Professor Sir Cyril Philips* (Hong Kong, 1986), 97–121.

Company represents the precursor of the modern firm, and thus provides an important point of institutional contact between the early-modern and modern business worlds. These are bold claims and, up to a point, they can be endorsed, as anyone familiar with K.N. Chaudhuri's distinguished book-length studies of the Company can testify.[10] They should not be allowed, however, to obscure the fact that for a considerable part of its lifespan (especially the part following the period covered by Chaudhuri's studies) the Company was an organization pursuing aims and objectives that are difficult to place within a framework of interpretation defined by conventional terms of business or commercial analysis, historical or otherwise. The trader became sovereign, and after the acquisition of the territorial revenues of Bengal in 1765 this required a fundamental resetting of primary aims and objectives, all of which disrupted, if not destroyed, long-established established patterns of commercial activity and thought. The directors were now motivated primarily by a desire to use the trade with India and China as a 'vehicle for tribute', and contemporaries such as Edmund Burke were inclined to use the word 'revolution' when they considered the effect that the acquisition of empire had upon the Company's commercial assumptions, methods, and outlook.[11] This break with its own past, a change in 'character and function' during the 1760s as Chaudhuri puts it,[12] obliges us to consider how the Company came to terms with the simultaneous management of both trade *and* empire; and whether, within its metropolitan world, it was indeed unresponsive to change so that it was unable to reconcile a fundamental recasting of its role and purpose with an enduring commitment to long-standing practices and procedures. Addressing these questions can help to establish how a joint-stock organization originally established and organized with narrow trading aims and objectives in mind could eventually end its days tackling a set of quite different non-commercial priorities.

It must be stressed that the identification of organizational continuities is not unimportant to our understanding of how the Company survived for so long – indeed in many ways it is crucial – but rather it is suggested that perhaps more emphasis than has hitherto been the case needs to be placed upon the extent to which the Company over many years was able successfully to adapt and reinvent itself in response to changing external circumstances at home and abroad. Even the most superficial review of the Company's domestic chronology reveals that from 1600 onwards the Company moved through several distinct phases of

---

10 K.N. Chaudhuri, *The English East India Company: The study of an early joint-stock Company, 1600–1640* (London, 1965); idem, *The trading world of Asia and the East India Company, 1660–1760* (Cambridge, 1978).

11 For Burke's trenchant analysis of the changes that occurred to the conduct of Company trade after 1765, see the appropriate section of the *Ninth Report from the Select Committee, Appointed to Take Into Consideration the State of the Administration of Justice in the Provinces of Bengal, Bahar and Orissa* (1783), reprinted in P.J. Marshall, ed., *The Writings and Speeches of Edmund Burke Vol. V: Madras and Bengal* (Oxford, 1981), 222–31.

12 Chaudhuri, 'The English East India Company and its decision-making', p. 97.

development, all of which saw profound change in terms of both institutional reorganization and the nature of its relationships with the Crown or State.[13] These phases help to establish some of the major punctuation marks in the Company's domestic history, but they also serve as a reminder that beneath the term 'East India Company' is to be found a number of quite different meanings and associations. From its founding on the last day of 1600 until 1613 the Company's trade was based upon the funding of separate voyages to the east. Thereafter, three successive joint-stock ventures were established, and it was not until 1657 that Company finances and organization were consolidated by the Cromwell regime's endorsement of the creation of a permanent joint stock. The founding of a 'new' Company in 1698 saw the uncomfortable co-existence of two rival East India Companies until a merger effected between 1702 and 1709 created the United Company of Merchants of England trading to the East Indies. Until the 1750s the United Company not only successfully expanded its overseas commerce but it also became firmly embedded at the heart of the British State and the system of public credit. The period between 1756 and 1765 saw military and political advances transform the Company's position in Bengal, a process that prompted metropolitan concerns and anxieties that led ultimately to far-reaching parliamentary reform and regulation of the Company at home and abroad during the 1770s and 1780s. Under mounting pressure from free traders, the Company then gradually lost its commercial privileges between 1793 and 1833, and it saw out its last 25 years as an agency charged with purely adminis- trative and military duties in India. There are few clean chronological breaks between these different phases, and indeed in some cases there are considerable overlaps. Nevertheless the phases are sufficiently distinct as to raise important questions about long-term stability and continuity, and about which, if any, of these periods is best representative of the Company's history as a whole.

In addition to some obvious consequences of events in the East, what general domestic factors determined this particular pattern of development? Perhaps the most important were those determined by the changing nature of the Company's relationship with the State and Crown. Because in its early years the Company was heavily dependent upon royal favour, approval, and support, it was at times only as stable as the regime itself. Not surprisingly, during the seventeenth century it had to chart a course through dangerous political waters. At times it found itself, despite its monopoly, engaged in fierce competition with domestic rivals encouraged by a hard-pressed monarch keen to exploit all the financial opportunities offered by the sanctioning of commercial privileges, such as was the case when the short-lived Courteen Association was backed by Charles I during the late 1630s. This state of affairs was such, of course, that after a period of relative stability and prosperity following Cromwell's establishment

---

[13] For the details of the changes underlying these different phases of the Company's existence, see the overview of the Company's history offered in Philip Lawson, *The East India Company: A history* (London, 1994).

of the permanent joint stock in 1657, East Indian affairs were plunged back into a deep political crisis by the debilitating co-existence of the original Company and a new Company granted privileges by William III in 1698. From the 1720s, however, the United Company was increasingly to reflect the permanence and resilience of the recently established Hanoverian state which proved capable of overcoming serious internal and external threats to its own existence. Indeed, all the statistical indicators of economic and political activity within the Company point to the years 1720–60 as being a period of unprecedented, and not to be repeated, calm and stability.

The nature of the Company's accommodation with the post-settlement regime of 1688 saw regular and routine expression given to a pragmatic and mutually beneficial compact between State and Company.[14] The Crown offered repeated extensions or enlargements of Company privileges in return for the Company helping to oil the wheels of a state often at war with its European rivals. In one sense this served only to lock the Company into a series of arrangements based upon short-term renewals or enlargements of its chartered rights in 1708, 1712, 1730, 1744, 1766, 1780, and 1793. If this appears to have offered the Company little by way of permanence or security during the eighteenth century, it should be stressed that the revocation of the charter was never a matter for serious debate, and any potential threat to its continued existence was more than offset by the extent to which the Company's substantial financial resources had been exploited by a hard-pressed state after the 'Glorious Revolution' of 1688. In 1698 the new Company's entire paid-up share capital of £2 million had been loaned to the state at 8 percent, and ministers drew upon the United Company on several further occasions when the permanent East India debt was increased and other loans and gifts were solicited. As a consequence of this, the Company, together with the Bank of England and the ill-fated South Sea Company, became an institutional manifestation of the influential 'monied interest'; and the growth of a market in transferable securities that lay at the heart of the financial revolution saw Company stocks and bonds become the most sought-after investments in London. These financial developments were endorsed by Parliament, and with interest payments from the state representing an income stream linked to specific taxes, the Company came to be regarded as an institution of unimpeachable credit after 1720. This financial reputation was only enhanced by a sound trading performance characterized by solid growth that ensured that annual stock dividend payments did not fall beneath six percent per year after 1709.[15]

---

[14] For a general discussion of this relationship in its domestic and overseas context, see H.V. Bowen, 'Company, state, and empire: Government and the East India Company during the eighteenth century', *Poteri economici e poteri politicii secc.xiii–xviii. Instituto internazionale di storia economica 'F. Datini' Prato*, serie II, 30, 677–87. For the place of the East India Company in eighteenth-century politics, see the classic study by L.S. Sutherland, *The East India Company in Eighteenth-Century Politics* (Oxford, 1952).

[15] For the central position of the East India Company within the emerging system of public

Over time, the financial health of the Company began to act as a barometer for the condition of the City of London and even the nation as a whole, and because of this no government could afford to allow the Company to run into difficulties. This partly explains why a hard-pressed Company received so much financial support from the state as post-conquest difficulties began sharply to bite after 1770 when military and civil costs in India spiralled and the Company failed fully to put its Bengal revenue surplus sufficiently 'in train' via an expanding China tea trade. A range of commentators noted how tightly inter-woven national and Company finances had become, but few pinpointed the important shift in the relationship between state and Company that occurred in 1772–73 when the Company first defaulted on revenue and customs payments to the Treasury and then required a loan of £1.4 million to stave off rapidly approaching bankruptcy.[16] This represented a reversal of long-established cred-itor–debtor roles, and it marked the beginning of a heated period of debate about the Company's methods, strategy, and general worth to the nation. No longer a commercial Company in the narrowest sense, many believed that the Company had sacrificed steady sustainable profit in the forlorn pursuit of a role for which it, together with its London-based directors and managers, was entirely ill suited.

The problems and difficulties of the period 1760–80 were accompanied by altered perceptions of what the Company was and what role it was attempting to fulfil in both India and Britain, and these have to be accommodated in any consideration of long-term institutional change. Some commentators, as noted earlier, continued to place the Company within familiar and straightforward commercial terms of reference. Others, however, fully acknowledged that the Company had evolved rapidly into an organization capable of wielding great military power, and they lay emphasis on the Company's role as kingmaker and territorial ruler in India. Thus to Lord Clive's aide and friend Luke Scrafton, as early as 1758 the Company were 'No longer considered as mere merchants, they were now thought the umpires of Indostan.'[17] As one writer declared in 1772, the Company had risen from 'very slender beginnings to a state of the highest importance; their concerns simple at first, are grown extremely complex and are immensely extended. They are no longer mere traders, and confined in their privileges; they are sovereigns over fertile and populous territories.'[18] Such descriptions of the Company were of course being written in response to the dramatic events that had unfolded in Bengal, but the transformation of the Company's fortunes in the East had important consequences for those who gave

---

finance, see P.G.M. Dickson, *The Financial Revolution in England: A study in the develop-ment of public credit, 1688–1756* (London, 1967), passim.

[16] For a detailed discussion of this, see H.V. Bowen, *Revenue and Reform: The Indian Problem in British politics, 1757–1773* (Cambridge, 1991), pp. 103–86.

[17] Luke Scrafton, *Reflections on the Government of Indostan . . .* (London, 1763, reprinted 1770), p. 120.

[18] *Monthly Review,* 46 (1772), 236.

any considered thought to changing patterns of State–Company relations in Britain itself.

Beyond the narrow issues of reform and regulation, it is possible to discern a growing awareness of a situation in which the Company was now managing an important economic asset not simply for the benefit of its stockholders but for the nation as a whole. At a time when it was being acknowledged that parts of India now belonged to a wider British empire, this helped more sharply to define the Company as a vehicle for public as well as private interest.[19] Accordingly, much more than the domestic 'monied' connection forged the relationship between the State and the Company after 1760, and the Company found itself established ever more firmly as an overseas economic and administrative arm of the British state. As Lord North put it in 1773 when discussing the collection of the Bengal land revenues acquired by the Company in 1765, the Company had become 'farmers to the publick'.[20] A quarter of a century later the commentator William Playfair was able to suggest that the Company was cultivating India as 'stewards of the state', while in a rather different context the Crown's law officers Lord Kenyon and Mr Justice Lawrence referred to the Company as a 'limb of the government of the country'.[21] In these terms, the Company might be regarded as having become, *de facto*, a department of state – one to be closely monitored by the Board of Control established in 1784 – but of course the Company continued simultaneously to operate as a commercial company, although one now dedicated to the transfer of revenue surplus or 'tribute' rather than simply to the pursuit of trade for trade's sake. Even as it was translating itself into an imperial agency, the Company still dispatched annual fleets with goods for export; it still sold vast quantities of imports, notably China tea; and it still declared an annual dividend for its stockholders. It was this that allowed some in Britain to give primacy to the Company's commercial functions even as millions of Indians were being brought under British rule after 1760.

It is of course this duality of function and purpose – the commercial alongside, and interacting with, the imperial – that helps to explain the co-existence of continuity and change, and this was reflected in the way that the Company conducted its business in Britain. Outwardly, the Company retained all the

---

[19] For manifestations of the 'public interest' in discussions about reform of the Company during the 1780s see Susan Staves, 'The construction of the public interest in the debates over Fox's India Bill', *Prose Studies: History, theory, criticism*, 18 (1995), 175–98. For the position of India within a wider, global, British empire see H.V. Bowen, 'British conceptions of global empire 1756–1783', *Journal of Imperial and Commonwealth History*, 26 (1998), 1–27.

[20] Lord North's speech in the House of Commons of 9 March 1773, as reported in British Library, Egerton MS 244, p. 288.

[21] Playfair, *Strictures on the Asiatic Establishment*, p. 65; views of Kenyon and Lawrence, as quoted in Peter Auber, *An Analysis of the Constitution of the East-India Company, and of the Laws Passed by Parliament for the Government of Their Affairs, at Home and Abroad; to which is prefixed, a brief history of the Company, and of the rise and progress of the British power in India* (London, 1826), p. vii.

essential features and characteristics of a transoceanic trading organization, and it continued to do so long after it embarked on the process of expansion and annexation. This was quite unlike the situation in Bengal where the separation of commercial and 'political' functions and departments resulted in the Company's administrative structure being recast after 1760.[22] The Company as organized in Britain in 1785, however, had most of the committees, offices, and departments it had possessed a century earlier, and few concessions had been made to the acquisition of empire.[23] Some attempts had been made to improve the storage and retrieval of the ever-expanding amount of paperwork circulating around East India House, but the only recent major innovation had been the appointment in 1769 of an Examiner of Indian Correspondence whose task it was to scrutinize the increasing number of incoming dispatches and collect information on the increasingly varied subjects that they contained. In the following year the short-lived post of Compiler and Writer of Indian correspondence was established, but after 1782 the Examiner and his small staff acted as the main channel of communication between India House and the Company's Presidencies, and it was in their office that corporate instructions were drafted following consultations with the Court of Directors and its Committee of Correspondence.[24] Although these, and later, administrative adjustments were undoubtedly important, they essentially represented attempts to improve the processing of information and the response time to developments in India. They did not amount to the establishment of any new decision-making machinery designed specifically to deal with the problems of empire, and the Company's structures and systems remained essentially those of a commercial organization.

Those structures and systems were reinforced in a number of different ways, each of which helped to sustain the impression of continuity and permanence in the Company's affairs, and enabled the Company to survive periods of domestic instability. The Company moved, for example, to an institutional rhythm determined by adherence to a timetable structured around annual elections, half-yearly dividend declarations, quarterly meetings of stockholders, and

---

22 B.B. Misra, *The Central Administration of the East India Company, 1773–1834* (Manchester, 1959), pp. 64–107.

23 In 1785 a detailed analysis of the Company's home establishment was compiled by the Secretary, Thomas Morton, in response to a request for information from the Board of Control (Thomas Morton to Charles William Boughton Rouse, 28 Apr. 1785, BL, OIOC, H/362, pp. 5–77 [including appendices]). The information eventually provided by Morton was based upon returns made by all the departmental heads, and it included job descriptions, details of salaries, and the number of employees. This is the only surviving description of each administrative unit, and it allows a detailed reconstruction of the Company's inner workings to be made. For a detailed modern description of the Company's metropolitan administrative structure, see Martin Moir, *A General Guide to the India Office Records* (London, 1996), pp. 14–45.

24 For the development of the Examiner's Office, see Martin Moir, 'The Examiner's Office: the emergence of an administrative élite in East India House (1804–58), *India Office Library and Records: Report for the Year 1977* (London, 1979), pp. 25–42.

weekly meetings of directors. Similarly, commercial transactions were conducted according to dates fixed by the need to assemble cargoes, dispatch ships, and sell goods at particular times of the year, and these varied hardly at all over time. As far as Company personnel were concerned, career patterns within the administrative hierarchy saw many individuals work in departments over several decades, and a rise to the very top could result in senior officials recording over 50 years of Company service. Thus Charles Cartwright who was Accountant General between November 1798 and March 1822 had first entered the Accountant's department in August 1773. William Sibley, the Treasurer, had been employed by the Company for 62 years when he died in office in 1807, while Peter Corbett, the Bengal Warehousekeeper, had given 59 years of service by the time he retired in 1802.[25] While these individuals might be regarded as representing atypical cases, officials with 20 or 30 years experience were quite commonplace, and it can be calculated that the 167 established officials on the Company's payroll in 1801 each had an average of almost 16 years of service to their name.[26] This state of affairs helped to ensure that internal working practices remained strongly rooted in precedent and tradition, and many within the Company proclaimed this to be a great strength and virtue. Further core strength was established by the commercial bookkeeping and accountancy practices changed little over a century or more, so much so that a clerk of 1670 would have been almost entirely familiar with the ways in which his successors were working over a century later. It was these characteristics that caused contemporaries to comment both favourably and unfavourably upon the ways in which the Company's domestic affairs were handled.

The cautious approach to administration that was so characteristic of the eighteenth century helped to ensure that the Company's metropolitan offices and departments were largely undisturbed by events and transformations in India. Few insiders saw any need to reshape the Company's commercial bureaucracy in London. Where change is clearly evident, however, is in the way that business was handled internally by directors and officials within that unreconstructed system. Over time, those who had to tackle the problems of administration and revenue, as well as trade, were obliged to reformulate working practices, principles, and procedures. Barely visible to the outside world, these changes all represented significant extensions to, and modifications of, the Company's position as it had stood before 1760. Only two such changes are noted here, but they both reflect ways in which the Company was obliged to come to terms with the transition from trade to empire.

As far as the directors' Committee of Correspondence was concerned, for example, attempts were made to rationalize the organization of material contained in Company despatches, minutes, and records. If convention dictated that the overall structure of many different classes of document remained largely

---

[25] BL, OIOC, L/AG/30/3/24, p. 143.
[26] *Ibid.*, H/67, pp. 161–65.

unaltered, there were nevertheless shifts of emphasis that reflected important changes in official Company concerns and attitudes. Thus, although the directors' detailed instructions to the Company's overseas employees had always contained much more than commercial information and intelligence, a great deal more space was devoted after 1765 to the guidelines that were being established to define the Company's new role as a territorial power. This meant that there was often an intermingling of different types of information and instruction within despatches, and paragraphs containing commercial information were often to be found alongside instructions relating to foreign policy, revenue collection, the administration of justice, and so on. During the mid- to late-1780s, however, an attempt was made to formalize a logical division within the correspondence with each Presidency in order to improve the consideration and analysis of different types of problems. In 1785 it was decided that despatches to and from India should be arranged under five headings - commercial, military, public, revenue, and secret – which would correspond with the organization of administrative affairs in India. The new system came into effect in 1789 when a sixth, political, heading was added, but it was not always easy or practical to allocate subject matter to the available categories. The system took some time to become well established, and even then it was never possible to draw firm lines of demarcation between the headings, or 'departments' as they were known, in the correspondence. Although the formal separation of different Company functions was not being effected through the establishment at India House of specialist administrative machinery, those who were dealing with the problems of the east were beginning to draw a distinction between different types of overseas functions and responsibilities. They arranged their business, and formulated their responses, accordingly.

Those who handled and analysed the Company's financial affairs were also obliged to change their outlook, not least because their traditional working practices and constructions of balance sheets were rendered obsolete during the 1760s. This applied to those in the Accountant's Office who endeavoured to form up-to-date estimates of the Company's overall commercial and financial position, and those in the Auditor's Office who monitored trade, revenue collection, and expenditure in India. Their conceptual approach to the Company's finances was revolutionized by a rapid expansion of the Company's armed forces after 1750 and by the acquisition of the *Diwani* in 1765 because any attempt to assess the Company's current or future economic performance now required much more than the construction of a traditionally formulated trading account. Instead, the analysis and presentation of statistical data had to be placed within an accounting framework in which due emphasis had to be given to important non-commercial variables, such as income from revenue collection or outgoings in the form of considerable civil and military expenditures.[27] As just one

27 It was only after the passage of the Charter Act of 1813, however, that the Company was formally required to separate territorial and 'political' details from the commercial information in its accounts.

example of this, adjustments were made to the items noted under the overseas 'quick stock' and 'dead stock' headings in the annual balance sheets, as attempts were made to assess more accurately the Company's financial position in India.[28] Internal briefing papers and balance sheets, the calculations of senior finance officers, and information passed by the directors to Parliament or the government all reflect these and other changes and indicate how far the Company moved from being a straightforward commercial concern after 1765.

The organizational framework adopted for this volume locates the Company in a number of different contexts, described as the 'worlds' of the East India Company. None of these worlds was unchanging or stable, and this applies as much to the domestic world in which the Company was rooted as it does to any of those in Asia or elsewhere. While clearly many of the developments discussed in this chapter took the form of responses to events overseas, domestic factors also exerted a profound influence upon the shaping of the Company. In particular, stress has been placed upon the emergence of two forms of metropolitan development. One, operating in the short term and often driven by crisis and change in the wider English or British state helped to define external relationships and different institutional and financial arrangements. The other, much longer run and defined by internal operational continuities, determined the emergence of systems and procedures that were able, with varying degrees of success, to accommodate overseas changes of an often wide-ranging nature. Always a product of changing times, the Company was obliged constantly to reinvent and reform itself, and it was its capacity to do this, without ever entirely recasting its domestic foundations, that enabled it to survive for so long.

---

[28] Changes to the annual balance sheets can be traced in the annual 'stock computations' produced between 1758 and 1778 (BL, OIOC, L/AG/18/2/24).

East India Company Agency Work in the British Isles, 1700–1800

JAMES H. THOMAS

During the 'long' eighteenth century in particular, the East India Company established, fostered, administered and encouraged a complex organisation, among whose valuable properties were representative agents stationed both abroad and at home. As a result, by 1815 agents were retained in at least 11 overseas locations, including Aleppo, Basra and Rio de Janeiro. Nearer home, both Venice and Vienna were valued locations for agents from 1760 onwards. Whether in these communities, or on strategically important islands such as Malta and Mauritius, particularly during the Revolutionary and Napoleonic Wars, individuals or business houses acted on the Company's behalf, keeping a vigilant eye upon its manifold interests. Whether it was Smetmers in Vienna or Cliffords in Amsterdam,[1] they were each doing the same thing – protecting John Company's far-flung, ramified and very valuable interests.

In Great Britain 17 ports, 14 in the southern half of England and Wales and three in Ireland, enjoyed the services of a Company agent. The establishment of agencies reflected particular communities' growing importance, especially as far as maritime life was concerned, as well, of course, as increasing penetration by the Company into provincial life. Thus Milford in Pembrokeshire, which was deliberately developed as a naval town in the late eighteenth century, had an agent from 1812 onwards. The increasingly fashionable seaside community of Margate had one from 1810. Weymouth, the growing seaside community that wallowed in royal patronage, had an agent from 1815 onwards. Irish agencies at Cork and Kinsale, by contrast, had a much longer lineage, being established in 1706 and 1708 respectively. Changing over time in terms of both locations and personnel, agencies carried out sterling work on the Company's behalf. One fact is particularly clear. Much, if not most, of the Company's success and influence in particular communities was directly attributable to the local agent's applica-

The research was supported by grants from the British Academy, the Nuffield Foundation and the University of Portsmouth. I am obliged to the many archivists and librarians who facilitated the work and to Paula Heiron who kindly produced the final version of this chapter.

Unless otherwise stated, manuscript references are taken from the Oriental and India Office Collection, the East India Company's voluminous archive now lodged in the British Library.

[1] For the information regarding Cliffords, I am obliged to Dr Huw Bowen of the University of Leicester.

tion, flair and effort. About such work there are five key questions that suggest themselves. Where were the Agencies maintained? Who were the agents? How were they appointed? What were their duties and responsibilities? What were their rewards?

I

As to the first of these questions, Table 1 provides the initial answer. Certain trends and features are apparent from the Table, one being the impact of war. The early establishment of an agency at Portsmouth, for example, was a clear reflection of that community's vital and growing significance in the context of both Company and mainstream defence developments. Similarly, as Plymouth provided the solution to the quest for a western naval yard, especially after Bantry Bay,[2] so the rising town acquired a Company agent in 1695. By the same token, it is by no means coincidental that five agencies were established during the War of the Spanish Succession and that seven more were created during the long struggle against Revolutionary and Napoleonic France. War, as in so many other key economic and social developments, especially provincial ones, was the underlying force behind Company decisions to retain an agent at many of the ports indicated in the Table. With immensely valuable cargoes at risk in fleets returning from the East, and with increased economic dependence on those cargoes, such concern was appropriate.

When the communities where agencies were established are examined more closely, however, a number of other common characteristics become evident. While war clearly had a very significant part to play, it was by no means coincidental that some of the selected communities enjoyed an increasing naval presence. By the same token, all of the communities where Company agencies were established were of both strategic and commercial significance.

In southern Ireland the East India Company established and retained agencies in three communities – Limerick, Kinsale and Cork. When Arthur Young visited Limerick in the 1770s, he was mightily impressed. Built partly on an island formed by the river Shannon, Limerick, with its population of c.32,000, bore all the hallmarks of success and affluence. Its export and import capacity was stretched to the limit. Social life was a whirl, the community boasting a theatre, and the main thoroughfare was always busy, helped along by the presence, on a regular basis, of free-spending troops.[3] That the Company agency was established in 1758 could well have been explained by the exigencies of the Seven Years War. The port of Kinsale, away to the south-east, the abortive landing place

---

2   M. Duffy et al., eds, *The New Maritime History of Devon*, 2 vols (London, 1992–4), I, 83.
3   A. Young, 'A Tour in Ireland; . . . with General Observations . . . made in 1776, 1777 and 1778, and brought down to the end of 1779', in J. Pinkerton, ed., *A General Collection of the Best and Most Interesting Voyages and Travels in all Parts of the World*, 17 vols (London, 1808–14), III, 831–3.

Table 1   East India Company Agencies in Britain 1640–1820

Community	Span
Appledore	1796
Bristol	1802–17
Cork	1706–1815
Cowes	1709–?
Dartmouth	1803–17
Deal	1704–1817
Dover	1802
Falmouth	1765–1817
Gravesend	1703–1802
Kinsale	1708
Limerick	1758–1817
Margate	1810–17
Milford Haven	1812–17
Plymouth	1695–1815
Portsmouth	1640–1815
Torbay	1796–1817
Weymouth	1815–18

Sources: E.B. Sainsbury, ed., *A Calendar of the Court Minutes of the East India Company 1640–1643* (Oxford, 1909), p. 257; B/41, 44, 47–8, 66, 76, 122, East India Company Court Minutes April 1695 – April 1796, passim; E/1/3, 41, 44, 50, 73, Miscellaneous Letters Received 1711, 1758–9; 1762, 1768, 1783, passim; *The East India Register and Directory* (1803–16), passim.

of Spaniards in the early seventeenth century and of James II in 1689, had become particularly useful to the East India Company by the early eighteenth century. With its fort in Castlenye Park, garrison and Governor, it was strategically important. With small store and victualling depots under a naval agent,[4] Kinsale could be useful for replenishing Indiamen. During 1706, for example, four Company vessels were supplied in this fashion with nearly £500 worth of stores.[5] The port could also carry out light refit work, though a shoal across the harbour mouth prevented Kinsale from realising its full potential in this regard. The community's greatest asset, however, was its strategic location for cruising in the Channel Approaches and as a port to which returning Indiamen could be diverted in the event of either bad weather or preying French, Jacobite and Dutch privateers or rapacious North African corsairs.[6] Cork, the third Irish port where

[4] *Cal(endar of) T(reasury) B(ooks) 1709*, pp. 117, 120; R.D. Merriman, ed., *Queen Anne's Navy* (London, 1961), p. 102. In 1714 John Hayward and Joseph Griffin were Master Shipwright and Storekeeper and Clerk of the Cheque respectively at Kinsale: *ibid.*, p. 374.

[5] Vessels supplied and amounts involved were: *Josia* £93 14s ½d; *Macklesfield Galley*: £134 19s 3¼d; *Eaton Frigot*: £194 11s 5¼d; *Donnegall*: £71 9s 9¾d: B/48 East India Company Court Minutes 24 April 1705–23 April 1708, pp. 444–5.

[6] Merriman, pp. 102–3.

the Company retained an agent, possessing 'one of the safest and most commodious harbours in the world', exuded an air of constant activity, excitement and wealth.[7] A departure point for shipping provisions to Spithead and Southampton for onward transfer to New World garrisons and for troops bound for Bristol and Mediterranean destinations,[8] Cork enjoyed a thriving trade. Arthur Young observed in the 1770s that there were 700 coopers alone working in the community, and that there was a new manufacture for military clothing. With its canals, quays and houses it must, he felt, 'resemble a Dutch town'. Tumult, clatter and noise prevailed.[9] Nor was it simply a matter of the generation of wealth. Cork's merchants ploughed much of their new-found wealth into public buildings, church building and cathedral refurbishment, into street widening and improvement schemes. As a result, by 1800 Cork was busy, rich and aesthetically pleasing, being accounted by one historian as one of the 'handsomest seaport towns in the British Isles'.[10] What could be more natural, therefore, than to retain a Company agent there?

Across the Irish Sea lay the ports of Milford Haven, Bristol and Appledore. Totally different in socio-economic structure and significance, each had something to offer the East India Company. Milford Haven, the youngest of them, possessed an impressive, seemingly landlocked, harbour,[11] and had much to offer the eighteenth-century mariner. It was the area's natural features and location which had led the Admiralty to foster and encourage its growth as a naval facility in the eighteenth century. Loud, colourful and wealthy, Bristol, by 1800, was easily the metropolis of the West, aping London in as many ways as possible.[12] As a communications centre it excelled, while as port, commercial and industrial centre, Bristol had much to offer. Sea captains rubbed shoulders with clockmakers who did business with gold- and silversmiths while, for obvious reasons, the merchants and bankers formed a close, powerful, coterie in the community. Grocers and tea dealers, maltsters and mariners, peruke- and pipemakers could all be found in eighteenth-century Bristol.[13] Visitors were certainly impressed, Louis Simond observing, 'There is a look of comfort and neatness in the inside of houses, which is very striking; every thing is substantial

---

7   Young, 'A Tour in Ireland', p. 835.
8   On 22 December 1775 the *Marquis of Rockingham* transport, *en route* from Portsmouth to Cork with part of the 32nd Regiment aboard, was wrecked between Cork and Kinsale. Two officers, 100 soldiers, the vessel's captain, nearly all the crew and 'all the Women and Children on board' were drowned: Guildhall Library MS 14931/3, Lloyds Subscription Book 1776, n.p.
9   Young, 'A Tour in Ireland', pp. 831–3.
10 J.C. Beckett, *The Anglo-Irish Tradition* (London, 1976), p. 71.
11 H. Skrine, *Two Successive Tours throughout the whole of Wales . . . in 1795* in Pinkerton, II, 597. Skrine (1755–1803) is noted in *DNB*.
12 See W. Minchinton, 'Bristol – Metropolis of the West', *Transactions of the Royal Historical Society* 5th series, 4 (1954), 69–89 for further details.
13 *Bath and Bristol Guide* (Bath, 1755), passim; *Sketchley's Bristol Directory of 1775* (Bath, 1971, reprint), passim.

and good.' What could be more natural, therefore, than for the East India Company to retain an agent, albeit for a short time only, in such a thriving, dynamic community? A world away from Bristol, in many respects, was the North Devon port community of Appledore, where the Company retained an agent in the 1790s. Both port and shipbuilding centre in the eighteenth century, and possessing an expanding economy,[14] Appledore was a useful community for agency work.

Totally different, yet again, was the thriving Cornish port of Falmouth, described in the early 1730s by Portuguese merchant Don Manoel Gonzales as:

> by much the richest and best trading town in . . . Cornwall. 'Tis so commodious an harbour, that ships of the greatest burden come up to its key. 'Tis guarded . . . and there is much shelter in many creeks belonging to it, that the whole royal navy may ride here safe, whatever wind blows.

The keys to Falmouth's success were its location and its participation in the Portuguese and packet trades. Defoe was of the view that Falmouth Haven 'is certainly next to Milford Haven in South Wales, the fairest and best road for shipping that is in the whole of Britain'.[15] The safe anchorage and navigable creeks made it incomparable. As a potential final and first port of call for Indiamen, and with its ability to provide repair facilities, Falmouth was a 'natural' community for the Company.

Similar traits were discernible in the three south Devon ports that the Company utilised from time to time – Plymouth, Dartmouth and Torbay. Defoe pinpointed Plymouth's significance when he observed that its 'excellent harbour' made it the first port for shipping 'to put in at for refreshment, or safety, from either weather or enemies', adding that the 'populous and wealthy' community included considerable merchants and an 'abundance of wealthy shop-keepers, whose trade depends upon supplying the sea-faring people'. Plymouth, moreover, had early links with the Company, most notably in the form of the Gayer family. While one member was mayor in 1592, two moved to London, one of whom, John (d.1649), became a prominent director of the East India Company, Sheriff and Lord Mayor. Later in the century Plymouth-produced woollen goods would be shipped to London for the Company.[16] With its rising prominence, affluence and convenient location, Plymouth was ideal as far as the Company was concerned. Dartmouth's great asset was its capacious harbour. In Defoe's opinion, it was 'a town of note', while 'the channel [was] deep enough for the biggest ships in the royal navy', leading to a harbour capable of receiving '500 sail

---

[14] C. Hibbert, ed., *An American in Regency England* (London, 1968), p. 18; Duffy et al., I, 130; II, 264; J.A. Goldenberg, 'An Analysis of Shipbuilding Sites in *Lloyd's Register* of 1776', *The Mariner's Mirror*, 59 (1973), 429.

[15] 'The Voyage of Don Manoel Gonzales' in Pinkerton, II, 26; Hibbert, pp. 13–15. Daniel Defoe, *A Tour through the Whole Island of Great Britain*, 2 vols (London, 1966), I, 236–8.

[16] Defoe, I, 231. C. Gill, *Plymouth: A New History*, 2 vols (Newton Abbot, 1979), II, 7, 65. Sir John Gayer is noted in *DNB*.

of ships of any size'. Wartime exigencies and local shipbuilding and repair facilities certainly helped the Company decide to retain an agent there between 1803 and 1817. Slightly longer usage was made by the Company of the port of Torbay, where an agent was retained from at least 1796. In some respects, however, this was a curious decision given the nature of Torbay, as a contemporary made clear in 1799:

> This spacious Bay, which is formed by two capes, called Berry Head and Bob's Nose, though it affords an excellent roadstead during the summer months, yet afterwards, owing to the prevalence of easterly winds, becomes particularly dangerous. It has often been a subject of surprise to naval men, that no attempt has yet been made by this country, to render the Bay perfectly secure at all seasons of the year.[17]

While Dorset had just the one agency at Weymouth, whose 'substantial merchants' drove 'a considerable trade', particularly in corn, rum and salt,[18] Hampshire with its extensive, heavily indented, coastline had two – at Cowes and Portsmouth, the former being of short duration only. While the port was of major significance in terms of eighteenth-century entrepôt activity with New World colonies, the Company made comparatively little use of its facilities. To defuse a wrangle between Cowes and Portsmouth regarding agency work, the Company resolved, early in 1709, to retain an agent in the Isle of Wight only as and when the need arose.[19] Richard Loving was the agent appointed, doing, in consequence, very little and thus it should come as no surprise to learn that little or nothing is heard of the agency after the War of the Spanish Succession, 1702–13. Indicative of Portsmouth's use as the Company's leading provincial outport, was the fact that agency work there was long-standing, vital and thorough. Despite Portsmouth's contemporary reputation for corruption, no agent was ever sacked or asked to resign by the Company. Furthermore, by comparison with other communities, Portsmouth was 'early in the field' with regard to agency work, the first agent there being noted in 1640.[20]

While the Company was to retain an agency in Dover for only a short period during the Napoleonic Wars, usage of Deal in this fashion was to be much longer, dating back to the War of the Spanish Succession. Adjacent to the Downs anchorage, 'so well known all over the trading world', Deal was of vital importance. Peter Kalm commented upon the community's significance, succinctly observing early in August 1748:

---

[17] Defoe, I, 225; N(aval) C(hronicle), I (January–June 1799), 330, 328.

[18] Defoe, I, 211, 212; Cal(endar of) T(reasury) B(ooks) and P(apers) 1739–41, p. 97; ibid., 1742–5, pp. 579, 590, 766.

[19] For further details, see J.H. Thomas, Portsmouth and the East India Company, 1700–1815 (New York, 1999), Chapter 4 and idem, 'The East India Company and the Isle of Wight, 1700–1840: Some Connections Considered', The Local Historian, 30 (2000), 4–22.

[20] E.B. Sainsbury, ed., A Calendar of the Court Minutes of the East India Company, 1640–1643 (Oxford, 1909), p. 257.

Here commonly the outward-bound ships provide themselves with greens, fresh victuals, brandy, and many more articles. This trade, a fishery, and in the last war the equipping of privateers, has enriched the inhabitants.[21]

Deal possessed a multi-faceted economy, to which could be added income generated from local smuggling. Thus late in May 1745 George Brice of Deal proposed to the Treasury that he compound 'for receiving prohibited East India goods'.[22]

For a short while during the Napoleonic Wars the increasingly fashionable resort of Margate, along the coast from Deal, also retained the services of a Company agent. Location at the lower end of the Thames estuary counted for much. While dealing with Spanish and other prize vessels created more work,[23] Margate was developing an increasingly fashionable face and demonstrating considerable potential.[24]

The final community retaining an agent in Southern Britain was Gravesend, but a stone's throw from London. It was also the third earliest, appointment dating from 1703, an arrangement clearly caused by wartime pressures. At least one visitor was impressed:

> The prospect towards Gravesend is particularly beautiful. It is a clever little town, built on the side of an hill; about which there lie hill and dale, and meadows, and arable land, intermixed with pleasure grounds and country seats; all diversified in the most agreeable manner.

While the German Moritz might have found its windmill 'a very good object', Gravesend was not all fashionability. Considerable quantities of coffee and gold coinage were seized by local customs officers in the years before 1720 as people sought to evade duties there.[25] Indeed, Defoe was of the opinion that 'having been often in the town, I know enough to be able to say, that there is nothing considerable in it'. Its significance lay, however, in its principal activity, which he outlined thus:

> all the ships which go to sea from London, take, as we say, their departure from hence; for here all outward-bound ships must stop, come to an anchor, and suffer what they call a second clearing, (viz.) here a searcher of the customs comes on board, looks over all the coquets or entries of the cargo, and may, if

---

[21] Defoe, I, 120; Pinkerton, XIII, 377.

[22] George Brice to Treasury, 23 May 1745: *Cal.T.B. and P. 1742–5,* p. 764.

[23] In December 1739, J. Scrope approached the Secretary at War 'for sufficient forces to be marched to the sea coast at Westgate Bay, near Margate, to assist the officers of the customs engaged in lightening the Spanish prize *St. Joseph* of part of her loading': *Cal.T.B. and P. 1739–41,* p. 69.

[24] In 1770, for example, Joseph Hall had published *The Margate Guide* at his 'Circulating Library and Toy-shop under the New Assemble Room': J. Vaughan, *The English Guide Book c.1780–1870* (Newton Abbot, 1974), p. 109.

[25] C.P. Moritz, 'Travels, Chiefly on Foot, through Several Parts of England, in 1782 . . .' in Pinkerton, II, 677; *Cal.T.B. 1712,* pp. 349, 431; *Cal.T.P. 1714–19,* p. 328.

he pleases, rummage the whole loading, to see if there are no more goods than are enter'd.[26]

As Indiamen were also victualled at Gravesend, it was essential that the Company retain an agent there.

Evidence for agency work elsewhere in Britain, however, is, to say the least, somewhat sketchy. While the substantial northern communities of Durham and Newcastle included tea dealers amongst their inhabitants in the 1790s,[27] of Company agents there appear to have been none. While Scotland produced nabobs such as John Johnstone, Alexander Brodie and Sir John Macpherson, Company agents in Scotland have, to date, proved rather elusive. Glasgow, Leith and Edinburgh were all replete with tea dealers in the early nineteenth century, but it was only Edinburgh that could boast Company agency work in the form of Patrick McGregor at South Bridge who described himself as 'merchant, army, navy and East India agent',[28] albeit an agent of a rather different type. By the same token, although Channel Island residents, including merchants such as Peter Dobree (jun.) of Guernsey in 1767, invested in Company stock,[29] none of them converted their financial involvement into tangible agency work.

II

Having identified and commented upon the locations for Company agencies, who was doing the work as agents, and how were they appointed? To date, some 60 individuals have been identified as working as East India Company agents in Britain, sometimes as part of a consortium and sometimes alone. Their identities and spans of service are set out in Table 2. Prosopography and multi-record linkage demonstrate that while a range of individuals undertook agency responsibilities there was a common strand connecting them. They were nearly all, in some way or other, engaged in business. Such an arrangement, given the Company's high and exacting standards, was only to be expected. In terms of occupation, the majority were merchants. Thus Richard Carne at Falmouth, Andrew Lindegren at Portsmouth, Charles Anderson at Bristol, Dennis Lyons and Ralph

---

26 Defoe, I, 101.
27 *Universal British Directory*, II, 872–3; IV, pp. 30–42.
28 B. Lenman, *Integration, Enlightenment, and Industrialization: Scotland 1746–1832* (London, 1981), pp. 81–2; G.J. Bryant, 'Scots in India in the Eighteenth Century', *Scottish Historical Review*, 64 (1985), pp. 22–41; *Holden's Annual London and County Directory 1811* (Norwich, 1996 facsimile), II, passim.
29 BL, OIOC, L/AG/14/5/16 Stock Ledger January 1767–July 1796, p. 244. Other Guernsey investors included Captain James Graham (p. 318). Those from Jersey included Paul Griffon and from Alderney John and Peter Le Mesurier, the latter serving as the island's Governor between 1793 and 1803: L/AG/14/5/18 Stock Ledger July 1769–January 1774, p. 340; BL, OIOC, L/AG/14/5/21 Stock Ledger January 1774–April 1783, pp. 519, 522; A.G. Jamieson, *A People of the Sea: The Maritime History of the Channel Islands* (London, 1986), p. 178.

Table 2 East India Company Agents in Britain

Set out below are the identities of agents appointed by the East India Company in British communities. The lists do not claim to be exhaustive; rather are they the reflection of research findings to date.

1. **Appledore**
1796	Thomas Hogg

2. **Bristol**
1802–7	Charles Young
1808–17	Charles Anderson

3. **Cork**
1706–?	Robert Hill
1779–81	Paul Benson
1790	Patrick O'Conor (?)
1802–4	Marcus Lynch
1804–5	Michael Wood
1805–16	Gerard Byrne
1816–17	Daniel Callagan (jun.)

4. **Cowes**
1709–?	Richard Loving

5. **Dartmouth**
1803–17	William Newman

6. **Deal**
1704–9	Richard Knight
1740s	William (?) Bell
1760–3(?)	George Brooks
1764–84	George Hudson
1784–1807	John Iggulden
1807–17	John and Edward Iggulden

7. **Dover**
1802	Messrs Fector and Minet

8. **Falmouth**
1765	Daniel Hoissard
1768	Mr Bell
1773–8	Richard Carne
1786–1817	John Carne

9. **Gravesend**
1703	Mr Roe
1793–96	John Scafe
1796	John Hezey
1796	John Nixon

1802	'The Company's Inspectors for the time being'

10. **Kinsale**
1708	William Roth

11. **Limerick**
1758	Edmond Tierney (?)
1780	Captain James Lyons
1795–1809	Dennis Lyons (jun.)
1809–17	Ralph and Thomas Westropp

12. **Margate**
1810–17	Messrs Cobb and Co.

13. **Milford**
1812–17	Captain John Hearding

14. **Plymouth**
?–1702	William Addis
1702–5	George and John Lapthorne
1705–7	John Addis
1707	John Lapthorne
1711	William and John Addis
1760–7(?)	William Hambly
1772–84	Christopher Harris
1796–8	Richard Birdwood
1798–1810	Richard and Peter Birdwood
1810–17	Peter Birdwood

15. **Portsmouth**
1650–61	Josiah Child
1661–80s(?)	Richard Norton
1695–1709	William Cooper
1709–21	Thomas Blackley
1721–23	John Mellish
1723–26	James Harman
1726–31	James Blackley
1731–46	George Huish (sen.)

1746–88	George Huish (jun.)	**17. Weymouth**		
1788–1805	Andrew Lindegren	1815–17	Samuel Weston
1805–25	Andrew and John Lindegren	1817–18	Robert Penny

16. Torbay

1796–1812	George Sa(u)nders
1814–17	John Colley

Sources: *East-India Registry and Directory 1803–1818,* passim; *Holden's Annual London and Country Directory . . . 1811* (1996 facsimile reprint), passim; C. Hardy, *Register of Ships 1707–60 Employed in the Service of the Hon. the United East India Company* (1799), 152 and Appendix, n.p.; Court Minutes, passim; Miscellaneous Letters Received, passim.

and Thomas Westropp at Limerick and Samuel Weston at Weymouth, a timber merchant who also doubled as Swedish consul,[30] were all established merchants who took on Company agency work in addition to their commercial activities. If Lindegren's experiences at Portsmouth are anything to go by, there may have been the added bonus of other Company links, additional commercial connections and a wide net of allied business connections. 'Networking', though not employed as a term in the eighteenth century to describe extensive personal and business friendships, was nevertheless significant and extensive.

To this could be added, in some cases, the important thread of civic service. Thus Richard Carne, Falmouth agent in the 1770s, served as the community's mayor some two decades later, while in Weymouth agent Samuel Weston's brother William was an Alderman for many years.[31] Other agents, albeit businessmen on a smaller scale, exhibited a similar trait. Richard Birdwood, Plymouth agent at the tail end of the eighteenth century, was a linen draper, gentleman and local Alderman. Company agent at Deal for over two decades after 1784 was John Iggulden, a local brewer and jurat. While confirming the trait of civic service, Iggulden reinforced another – membership of an extensive and influential family network. Two other family members who resided at Deal in the 1790s were naval Captain John Iggulden and butcher Joseph Iggulden.[32] But Iggulden was not alone in belonging to an extensive family network. Ralph and Thomas Westropp, the agents at Limerick, belonged to an even more extensive family. While they were merchants and while Ralph served as a local Alderman and a Royal Limerick Volunteer Captain, three other family members, Mount, John Thomas and Henry, styled themselves 'Esquires', and a fourth was a cleric.[33]

---

[30] *Holden's Annual London and County Directory, 1811* (Norwich, 1996, facsimile), II, n.p. Carnes had lived at Falmouth since at least the 1660s: *Devon and Cornwall Record Soc.,* Pt VII (1908), passim.

[31] *University British Directory,* III, 98, IV, 728. William Weston was also Collector of Customs: *ibid.,* IV, 730.

[32] *Ibid.,* IV, 264, 266, 819–20.

[33] *Holden's Annual London and County Directory, 1811,* II.

A link with the armed forces, however, extended beyond the Iggulden experience at Deal. In Limerick there was Captain James Lyons, agent between 1780 and 1795; in Milford, Captain John Hearding was the agent between 1812 and 1817. Both men were military officers. George Hudson, agent at Deal for two decades after 1764, was a Captain who died, aged 92, in early 1784, being described as 'many years agent to the East India Company'.[34] Early in the eighteenth century, Company agents at Plymouth were appointed from two leading local dynasties – the Addis and Lapthorne families. The former were synonymous with wealth, exemplified in Samuel Addis who died 3 April 1741, 'a Batchelor, worth £100,000'.[35] The Lapthornes, George and John, were, in all probability, the sons of Richard. Of Devon origins, he resided in Hatton Garden in the 1680s and 1690s and acted as London agent for Richard Coffin of Portledge near Bideford between 1683 and 1698.[36] In many respects, therefore, there was a readily discernable trait of agency work within the family. The Lapthornes also belonged to the group of agents who were appointed during the War of the Spanish Succession.

Given that the appointment at Cowes of agent Richard Loving was indicative of that port's rising status and the result of exerting Company patronage, a further key question is raised – just how were agents appointed? In some cases, it was simply a matter of Company employees assuming additional responsibilities. At Gravesend John Scaife was already the Inspector of Indian Shipping when he assumed the additional duties of Company agent. In similar fashion William Cooper was Yard Storekeeper at Portsmouth before being appointed as Company agent in 1695. At Milford Captain John Hearding was Quaymaster before becoming agent in 1812, while Peter Birdwood served as navy agent at Plymouth prior to being Company agent there in 1810. In his case, however, and that of three Company agents in Portsmouth, other forces came into play as well. Part of the reasoning behind Birdwood's appointment was that the Company, pleased with his father Richard's service, were only too delighted to appoint him as agent in his place. In the case of the Huish and Lindegren families at Portsmouth it was certainly family influence, as well as long-term involvement, which helped to swing the balance in their favour.[37]

34 *(The) G(entleman's) M(agazine)*, LIV (1784), Pt I, 316. The same periodical carried obituaries for George Hudson, 'an Eminent Merchant' and possibly the agent's father, in May 1737, and for two men called Robert Hudson. The first died 15 January 1735 and was one of the Directors of the East India Company. The second, perhaps his namesake son, died 9 August 1779 and was described as 'Advanced in years' and 'for many years an East India captain and director': *ibid.*, VII (1737), 316; IV (1735), 51; XLIX (1779), 470.

35 *GM*, XI (1741), 221.

36 R.J. Kerr and I.C. Duncan, eds, *The Portledge Papers* (London, 1928), passim.

37 B/41, East India Company Court Minutes April 1695–April 1699, f. 66; *NC*, XXVIII (July–December 1812), p. 174; *The East India Register and Directory for 1812*, p. liv; *N.C.*, XXV (January–June 1811), p. 84; . . . *for 1809*, p. xiv; . . . *for 1810*, xlvi; J.H. Thomas, *Portsmouth and the East India Company, 1700–1815* (New York, 1999), Chapter 4.

III

Having been appointed in the various ports, what did agents do? Their duties, to say the least, were many, demanding and various, requiring substantial reserves. 'Inter-personal', numerical and literary skills were required as agents had to submit accounts to the Company regarding their expenditure and write copious missives about anything and everything going on in the port which might affect Company interests. With duties that could perhaps best be termed onerous, the Company placed great trust in its many agents.

The activities of agents at Portsmouth, Plymouth and Falmouth may be taken as typical of what was required. Surveillance over provisions, collection and distribution of Company mail, and correspondence with the Court of Directors were just some of the responsibilities. Thus when the homeward-bound Indiaman *Nile* put in at Plymouth in January 1803, Mr Heanstop, one of the ship's officers, set off overland for London 'with dispatches for the Honourable East India Company from Messrs. Birdwood and son, Agents to the Company at this port'.[38] While large sums of money had to be handled scrupulously, Company agents were also expected to be good correspondents. Thus Company agent at Portsmouth Andrew Lindegren (c.1753–1827), of Swedish descent, wrote to the Company 53 times between November 1795 and March 1796 alone. The one responsibility which gave Portsmouth agents most sleepless nights was despatch of silver. Required in India for three main reasons – use by diamond merchants, for direct use by the Company itself, and for the various Company mints operating in the sub-continent – silver was sent out through Portsmouth. The absence of banks in the town until October 1787, however, made retention of substantial sums of silver a real problem for the local agent. In 1708 bullion was lodged in the house of Captain Jeyes Seawell, or Sewell, who was rewarded with ¼ percent of the value as a thank you.

Extant accounts for Portsmouth agent George Huish (1710–88) show that he spent £262 1s 10d on East India Company business between 16 December 1782 and 20 August 1787. Letters and packages had to be taken to and from waiting Indiamen, clothing and drugs had to be got aboard. In January 1783 he charged 1 guinea for delivering 561 hammocks to East Indiamen – 150 to the *Earl of Oxford*, 140 each to the *Atlas* and the *Lord Macartney* and 131 to the *Duke of Kingston*. Natives seeking repatriation, and lascar seamen had to be cared for. Huish charged 15s for putting St Helena-bound stonemason William Gray aboard the *Raymond* in March 1783. That August a discharged Company recruit, Philip Nourse, received 5s travelling charges and a local waggoner given 1s 'to take Care of him to London'. For the previous 25 weeks Nourse had been in the Portsmouth workhouse, a sojourn for which Huish paid £3 15s. In February

---

[38] *NC*, IX (January–June 1803), 161.

1787 he spent 6s on the burial of a soldier from the *Rodney*. On a rather happier note, the postmaster's clerk always received a Christmas box of 2s 6d.

Never one to miss a promising opportunity, Huish also extended his letter-writing and responsibilities to act for Robert, Lord Clive and Warren Hastings. In June 1764 he sent to London by wagon Lady Clive's 'Baggage Plate and c. consisting of Nineteen Packages or Parcels all directed to yourself at Lord Clives in Berkley Square', as he explained to Mr Kelsall. Huish also acted as an interme-diary to facilitate correspondence with Warren Hastings in India, agreeing to forward a letter for him by the *Stafford* Indiaman, then detained in Portsmouth by contrary winds. In every way possible, Huish was always anxious to please. His reliability, competence and responsibility are attested to amply by his service as Company agent in Portsmouth for a 42–year period.[39]

In the case of Plymouth, the agent appears only to have been responsible for postal payments, as agent William Hambly explained in October 1767 when presenting his accounts for the previous five years, which amounted to the princely sum of £6 3s:

> I have not charged in the enclosed Account any Disbursement paid for freight of Anchors, Cables &c. or Disbursements on Shipping as I humbly presume you would chuse those Charges should be sent to the Committee of Shipping.

Should the Court be thinking of a salary for an agent, he noted, perhaps they would remember him! Plymouth agent Christopher Harris did not enjoy the ex-perience, as he explained to the Court in mid-July 1774, when submitting his expenses bill for the period since 24 March 1772. They totalled just £3 2s 10d 'To sundry postages', Harris adding by way of explanation:

> You will observe the Acc[oun]t is Very Small and that I have been Very Partic-ular not to be at any unnecessary expence.

He listed the Company's vessels that had called in since his appointment, while also alluding to frustration that he had experienced:

> I have been constantly obliged to Apply to Commiss[ione]r Rogers and Attend on the Master Attendants to get the liberty for the Ships taking in the Kings Moorings, who have been always Ready to grant them, I have given all the ships the Necessary Assistance in my power, The Nottingham had a New fore Mast made in the Kings Yard where I was Obliged to Attend Every day to get the Mast Expedited.[40]

His expenses for midsummer 1774 to midsummer 1776 were equally frugal, amounting to only £5 13s 8d. From Falmouth, agent Richard Carne explained,

---

39 Thomas, Chapter 4.
40 William Hambly to Robert James, 16 October 1767: BL, OIOC, E/1/49, Miscellaneous Letters Received 1767, ff. 108–108b; Christopher Harris to Peter Mitchell, 19 July 1774: E/1/58, Miscellaneous Letters Received 1774, ff. 176–176a.

when submitting his expenses claim, that he had spent only £12 on the Company's behalf during the year after July 1777:

> I have had very little to do for their Service since August 1776 when the Ankerwyke, Capt. Barwell put in here, except Acknowledging receipt of Lists, and Standing orders of the Court – forwarding a Letter from Capt. Larkins of the Lioness and painting the Anchors to prevent their getting rusty. Had opportunitys presented I should readily have done more.[41]

The recurring theme, with all agents whose correspondence has been examined, is one of extreme willingness to help.

IV

Lastly, what of the emoluments enjoyed by eighteenth-century Company agents? The East India Company did not pay a formal salary. Rather were agents paid by a combination of commission, reimbursement of initial outlay and a judicious system of gratuities as and when occasion demanded. The experiences of Richard Knight at Deal, Robert Hill at Cork and of William Cooper at Portsmouth may be taken as typical of rewarding early-eighteenth-century agents. Early in June 1705 the Company agreed to retain Knight at Deal on £30 per annum 'for his Service there', subsequently ensuring that he was paid £26 14s 3d for the 'Ballance of his account of Disbursements from 22d Novem[be]r to 14th January last'. In August 1706, feeling he had been put to extra trouble, Knight pressed for increased payments 'on account of his service relating to the Annandale'. To Robert Hill payment was made early in April 1706 of £9 3s 6d 'in full for a bill of £5 19s and a gratuity for his pains'. At Portsmouth agent Cooper had much more to do, receiving reimbursement and a gratuity in August and October 1706. On the first occasion the gratuity was £40, 'for his pains during the said time'; two months later he received an additional 30 guineas 'in consideration of his extraordinary trouble of late in the Companys affairs'. On occasion agents would write to the Court of Directors, as John Lapthorne did from Plymouth in October 1707, 'touching his allowance for being the Company's Correspondent there'. At the same time there is evidence to suggest that surrendered accounts were scrutinised quite sharply before reimbursement took place. Thus the Committee of Accounts looked at the sums spent by George and John Lapthorne 'in Postage of Letters, Boatage &c. according to the particulars by them given in writing'.[42] And when an agent had died before reimbursement had

---

[41] The accounts are contained in Christopher Harris to Peter Mitchell, 30 August 1776: BL, OIOC, E/1/60, Miscellaneous Letters Received 1776, ff. 120–121; Richard Carne to same, 6 July 1778: E/1/63, Miscellaneous Letters Received 1778, f. 2.

[42] BL, OIOC, B/48, East India Company Court Minutes 24 April 1705–23 April 1708, ff.7, 19, 156, 283, 320, 721; B/44, East India Company Court Minutes 28 April 1702–18 April 1705 (Old Company), f. 319b.

been completed, the Company would deal with his next of kin, so that in March 1727 widow Sarah Harman received the 20-guinea balance of the fee due to her husband James, Company agent in Portsmouth between 1723 and his death in 1726. The Directors clearly took agent activity and wartime circumstances into account. On 23 February 1796 the Company resolved to pay Portsmouth agent Lindegren £668 18s 6d that he had spent in the previous two years 'and that in consideration of the great increase of the Company's business Mr. Lindegren be allowed £400 as a Gratuity for the last two Years, making together the sum of £1068 18s 6d'. Agent Huish did not worry excessively about Company reimbursement, returning his accounts in December 1787 for the previous 4½ years. That the pressures and demands of the Revolutionary and Napoleonic struggles were taking their toll was demonstrated in that Lindegren spent nearly twice Huish's outlay as agent in a quarter of the time. Where Huish spent £29 p.a. on Company business, Lindegren spent £179. This included, in 1792, a £7,100 advance to Lord Macartney preparing for his Embassy to the Chinese Emperor Ch'ien Lung, in which Lindegren charged him 'the usual Commissions' of 2½ percent – £177 10s.[43]

V

At the very least Company agency work required alertness, commercial awareness, literacy, numeracy and inter-personal skills. Agents dealt with a range of people from Company directors and genteel ladies to sea-captains; from lascars, Chinese and Malays to nervous passengers; from Highland troops to awesome Hessian and Swiss soldiers. Furthermore, because the Agent was paid retrospectively, he had to be sound financially in order to make the initial outlay. Thus the agent at Deal in the 1790s was prosperous local brewer John Iggulden. Talent, ability, skill and sheer industry were all there, ably demonstrated in Thomas Hogg, Company agent at Appledore who was also the Swedish Vice-Consul at the port.[44] No finer exemplar of this could be found than in George Huish. A vigorous and conscientious agent, he also served Portsmouth as Town Clerk, was a Master Extraordinary in Chancery, consul for the Dutch government and agent for the Dutch East India Company in the town from at least 1749 onwards.[45] Quite clearly, idleness was not his forté. And for all the other Company agents, whether in Scotland, Ireland or Wales, this was equally true.

[43] Thomas, Chapter 4.
[44] Claes Grill to Thomas Hogg, 8 January 1805: NC, XIII (January–June 1805), 116.
[45] GM, LVIII (1788), 1129.

War, Competition and Collaboration: Relations between the English and Dutch East India Company in the Seventeenth and Eighteenth Centuries

FEMME S. GAASTRA

On 10 March 1701, the Gentlemen Seventeen, who formed the central governing board of the Dutch East India Company, held a special meeting. Pieter van Dam, who had acted for more than 50 years as secretary (*advocaat*) of the directors and who had an intimate knowledge of the Company's affairs, presented his 'Description of the Dutch East India Company'. This voluminous manuscript, in five books and published in a modern text edition of seven volumes, was kept secret from the outside world. Van Dam gave an extensive survey of the Company's organization at home and overseas, presenting a wealth of facts and figures on the Dutch presence in Asia. It is nowadays an important source for historians. However, one book is missing and that is the book devoted to the rivalry – the '*questiën en differentiën*' – between the Dutch and English East India companies. It has been suggested that the book went missing at the beginning of the nineteenth century, when diplomats of the new kingdom of the Netherlands were deliberating with the British over the colonial disputes that were settled with the first Singapore treaty in 1824.[1]

Until this book is found in a (British?) archive or library, we will have to deal with the Anglo-Dutch rivalry in the East without the help of Pieter van Dam. The fact that van Dam devoted a whole book to the subject indicates the importance of Anglo-Dutch rivalry to him, and also perhaps, that he thought that lessons could be learned for the future from the way in which the directors had handled these conflicts in the past.

It is, however, notable that the nature of Anglo-Dutch rivalry changed substantially during van Dam's term of office. It is general practice to divide the history of the European-Asian trade during the time of the East India Companies into three periods: from 1600 up to the 1680s, from around 1680 to the middle of the eighteenth century, and a final period from about 1750 or 1760

---

1 Pieter van Dam, *Beschryvinge van de Oostindische Compagnie*, eds F.W. Stapel and C.W.Th. Van Boetzelaer (The Hague, 1927–54; reprint in 1977), pp. 63, 68, 74, 76, 83, 87, 96. See the introduction by F.W. Stapel, 1, xx, xxii.

to the end of the eighteenth century.[2] Anglo-Dutch rivalry in the East fits this pattern and has the same caesura. The first period is one of an aggressive Dutch East India Company. The Dutch Company was expanding its influence in the Indonesian Archipelago in an effort to control the spice trade. It attacked the Portuguese positions in Malacca, Ceylon and other places and used military force to exclude other nations from trade and shipping in areas that the VOC wanted to keep for itself. The second period is characterized by a more pure commercial competition, when the VOC became reluctant to use its military power. The theatre of European rivalry shifted to India, where the French disputed the rising influence of the British while the VOC could only try to minimize the negative effects of this encounter as much as possible. The third and last period is one in which the EIC took the lead in the European–Asian trade. It was during this period, more than ever before, that servants of both the companies were pursuing their own private fortunes and working closely together, no matter the national interests and Company policy.

I. 1602–84: Dutch domination

There is no one single explanation for the success of the Dutch Company in the first decades of its existence that led to the Dutch domination of European Asian trade in the seventeenth century. The Dutch Company was founded in 1602 as result of a unification of six smaller companies that had been trading to the East since 1594. It was decided that this United East India Company or *Verenigde Oostindische Compagnie* (VOC) should have a temporarily joint stock for ten years. Moreover, the shareholders or participants were promised that they would receive a dividend on the sales of the Asian commodities when a return of 5 percent on the original capital had been realized. The disappointing results and the need for investments in Asia during the first years made the directors or *bewindhebbers* realize that it would be impossible to wind up the capital after the ten-years' term and that the promise of a quick dividend could not be kept. The Company thus became based on a permanent share capital and could, instead of paying back the capital and issuing dividends to the shareholders, invest its money in shipping and trade in Asian waters. But the directors learned more during the first decade of VOC trade. The Portuguese example taught them the need for a centre of shipping, trade and governance in the East. Moreover, they came to the conclusion that a monopoly in spices was a necessity for profitable trade in these commodities.

Some historians have stressed the importance of the institutional changes created by the Charter of 1602 as a key factor behind the success of the VOC. The Charter not only reduced the influence of shareholders (as compared to the situ-

---

[2] See, for instance, Om Prakash, 'European Commercial Enterprise in pre-colonial India', *The New Cambridge History of India* (Cambridge, 1998), vol. 2, chapter 5.

ation in the pre-companies before 1602 or, for that matter, within the EIC), but also gave the directors interests other than the realization of high dividends, which was the primary reason for the participants to invest their money. The remuneration by provision over the investments as well as over the sales provided them, as the Danish historian Niels Steensgaard has remarked, with an incentive to maximize the turnover of the Company, even at terms that were not advantageous to the participants.[3] The economist Douglas Irwin, who compared the Dutch and English East India pepper trade around 1620 to conclude that the Dutch trade policy generated higher profits, sees this managerial incentive scheme as an important factor in giving the Dutch a lead over their English competitors.[4]

The story of how the directors of the VOC realized their goals is a long one and need not to be told here. Batavia became, in 1619, the central rendezvous and seat of the Governor-general and Council of the Indies (also called *Hoge Regering* or 'High Government'). The VOC indeed achieved a monopoly in fine spices: cloves from Ambon, nutmeg and mace from the Banda islands, and cinnamon from Ceylon. Finally, around the 1630s, the Dutch succeeded in creating a profitable intra-Asian trade network. This intra-Asian trade was based upon the exchange of a number of important commodities: Japanese silver and copper for Indian textiles and Chinese gold, Indian textiles for pepper and spices, pepper and spices for precious metals from the Middle East, or Bengal or Chinese silk for Japanese silver.

The Dutch policy led to fierce and sometimes violent competition with the EIC. Such a competition is unremarkable, of course, during a century when three wars were fought by the two nations, wars in which commercial rivalry played a major part. But an explanation for the intense and violent rivalry in the early seventeenth century can also be found in the characteristics of European–Asian trade during this time. It was well understood by the directors of both the Companies that the market for spices in Europe was a limited one. Huge profits could be gained, but only if the imports from Asia were kept in balance with demand in Europe. If the European market were flooded with spices, prices would fall dramatically and profits would drop accordingly. In case of shortages, prices would raise sky high. It is true that large profits could be made in such a situation, but the directors feared that the profits should primarily go to merchants buying spices from the Company. These merchants could easily drive up the prices. That could lead to a shrinking market and declining consumption. On the other hand, high prices could also induce competitors to bring more spices on the market, turning the tables very quickly

---

3 Niels Steensgaard, 'The Dutch East India Company as an Institutional Innovation', *Dutch Capitalism and World Capitalism*, ed. Maurice Aymard (New York and Cambridge, 1982), p. 243.
4 Douglas A. Irwin, 'Mercantilism as Strategic Trade Policy: The Anglo-Dutch Rivalry for the East India Trade', *Journal of Political Economy*, 99 (1991), 6, 1296–1314.

and spoiling the market again. A monopoly could guarantee a stable market with high but not outrageous prices.

There was, however, another option to achieve this aim, one that was easier and less expensive: to form a cartel with one of the competitors and to agree on how to control the market. Indeed, in 1619, the English and Dutch companies formed such a cartel. The *bewindhebbers* in the Dutch Republic wanted an agreement because they had to resume the war with the Spanish–Portuguese enemy in 1621 when the Twelve-year Truce would end. The 'Accord of 1619' gave one-third of the spice trade of the Moluccas, Banda and Ambon and one-half of the pepper trade of Java to the EIC. But the treaty did not last. Jan Pietersz Coen, the energetic Governor-general in Batavia, who had just defended the new Dutch rendezvous against an attack by the British fleet under Sir Thomas Dale, had to allow the English to set up a factory in Batavia, with the EIC providing ten ships for an Anglo-Dutch 'defence fleet'. Coen was furious when he received notice of this treaty in 1620, fearing that the new allies would take advantage of the agreement and that he had been forced to 'embrace the serpent'. The agreement was an undeserved gift to the British, who 'could not pretend [to own] a single grain of sand of the Moluccas, Ambon or the Banda islands'.[5] And in a letter a year later: 'if you, gentlemen, want great and notable deeds in the honor of God and for the prosperity of our country, so relieve us from the English'.[6] In short: Coen was not prepared to obey his masters.

Thus, soon after the agreement of 1619, Anglo-Dutch relations in the East were disturbed again. The injustice, perfidy, and cruelty shown by Coen and his men on the Banda islands and Ambon has been pictured in such popular books as *Nathaniel's Nutmeg* and *The Scents of Eden: A History of the Spice Trade*.[7] The indignation about the so-called 'Amboyna Murders' of 1623 was widespread in seventeenth-century England, providing the inspiration for pamphleteers time and again to depict the Dutch as treacherous and cruel enemies, and indeed, showing the true face of the Dutch, who intended to expel their main competitors, the British, from the Archipelago by all necessary means.

It is understandable that relations between the Dutch and the servants of the EIC in Batavia were far from cordial. The EIC closed its factory Batavia in 1628, and moved it to the nearby port of Banten. The English presence on Java ended with the intervention of the VOC in Banten in 1682–84. Since the Dutch had conquered Jacatra and founded Batavia in 1619 as their headquarters, there had been an antagonistic relationship between Batavia and Banten. When Sultan Agung developed Banten in the 1660s and 1670s into a thriving port, irritation grew in Batavia. Textiles and opium were distributed from Banten throughout Java and Sumatra, at the expense of the sales in Batavia. European and Asian

---

5 'Meenen sy 't recht en wel, 't sal wel wesen; maer wederomme quaet willende, hebt ghylieden, is het te duchten, 't serpent in de bosom geseth', and: 'Niet een sandeken van 't strandt hadden zy in de Moluccas, Amboyna ende Banda te pretenderen', H.T. Colenbrander, ed., *Jan Pietersz. Coen. Bescheiden omtrent zijn bedrijf in Indië* (The Hague, 1919), pp. 543–4, from Coen to the Heren XVII, 11 May 1620.

merchants, often working closely together, organized shipping from Banten to Manila; European products, like wine or beer, were brought by the English to Banten and were exported from there to the Dutch settlements, including Batavia. The *bewindhebbers* at home and the Government in Batavia hesitated between more liberal or monopolistic trade policies. What, after all, was the use of chasing Asian merchants away from Batavia to Banten? And even if it were possible to stop Asian shipping from using that port by blockading the harbour, then, so warned the *Hoge Regering*, the only result would be that the Europeans in Banten would easily get rid of their competitors. The VOC was unable to regulate Asian trade via a system of issuing passes: European shipping, and indeed all ships under European flags had to be respected, and so the English, the French and the Danish should laugh at 'our imaginary right on the sea'.[8]

While the directors at home deliberated, the Batavian Government came into action and used the opportunity to intervene in the internal struggle in the Sultan's house. The result was predictable. The 1684 treaty with the young Sultan gave the VOC the monopoly in Banten and the Lampongs, the landscape on Sumatra near Strait Sunda that belonged to the sultanate of Bantam. The English, French and Danish factories in Banten were closed and the European competitors were forced to leave the city. The first and nearly panic reaction of the directors on this intervention was more influenced by the fear of repercussions in Europe than by the prospect of eliminating a troublesome competitor in Asia. This was partly due to the lack of adequate information from Batavia. In December 1682, the *bewindhebbers* were informed and alarmed about the intervention by private letters and by protests from London, Paris and Copenhagen. The Gentlemen Seventeen were unable to defend the Company in June 1683 against the accusations from the European rival companies, because they still did not have a complete picture of the events. They advised the *Hoge Regering*, headed by Governor-general Speelman, to withdraw from Bantam, to re-install the older Sultan and to let the European competitors return.[9]

But the pattern had been set since the days of Coen: the Governor-general and Council gave the directors a *fait accompli*, leaving it to them and diplomats of the States General to appease the adversaries in Europe. When Speelman and his councillors in Batavia were asked to comment upon the English claims that had

6 'Begeeren de heeren wat groots ende notabels ter eeren Goodts ende de welstant van dese lande gedaen te hebben, soo ontlast ons van d' Engelsen', *ibid.*, p. 662; from Coen to the Heren XVII, 16 November 1621.

7 Charles Corn, *The Scents of Eden: A History of the Spice Trade* (New York, 1998); Giles Milton, *Nathaniel's Nutmeg Or, the True and Incredible Adventures of the Spice Trader who Changed the Course of History* (London, 1999).

8 See F.S. Gaastra, 'Competition or Collaboration: Relations between the Dutch East India Company and Indian Merchants around 1680', *Merchants, Companies and Trade: Europe and Asia in the Early Modern Era*, eds Sushil Chaudhuri and Michel Morineau (Cambridge, 1999), pp. 189–201.

9 Algemeen Rijks Archief (ARA), The Hague, VOC Archive, inv. n 321, Heren XVII to Governor-General and Councillors, 24 August 1683.

been received at The Hague, their tone was similar to Coen's, and they dismissed demands from London in a high-handed, even offensive way.[10] The requested compensation of £360,000 was ridiculous, the turnover of the EIC in Banten had never amounted to more than 200,000 or perhaps 300,000 guilders per year (that was less than 10 percent of the claim) and, moreover, the English factory had had always been in debt to the old sultan and other merchants. The EIC were fortunate that their creditors did not accept Dutch law and thus could not ask for the assistance of the Dutch courts in Batavia in the recovery of these debts. The High Government argued further that it was actually the British who should pay an indemnity because they had plundered the Dutch factory after the VOC's Resident had left the town before the hostilities began.

The second British demand was for the retreat of the VOC and the reestablishment of the EIC-factory. Batavia replied that there was no reason to do so, for it was completely legitimate for the new sultan to make an exclusive contract with the Dutch. The VOC soldiers were accused of tearing the Royal standard and the Company's flag into pieces. This was denied: there had been only one white piece of cotton with a red cross and the Dutch did not really consider, of course, that it might be a Royal standard and EIC-flag in one – and there had certainly never been any intention to insult this flag. The charge of plundering the EIC factory was equally denied as the man who accused the VOC of this deed was not a reliable witness. This man, Captain Fisher, had not accompanied the other EIC servants when coming from Banten to Batavia, but had stayed in a tavern of doubtful reputation (belonging to a Miss Moray) and had already left Batavia in May 1682 on the EIC vessel *Amoy Merchant*. The *bewindhebbers* showed less confidence and – grudgingly, because of the high costs – hired more soldiers and sent out more ships because they feared an English naval assault. But the English threat did not lead to a naval action. The directors of the EIC insisted on the need for such a course, but Charles II had no wish to enter into a new military conflict with the Dutch.[11]

The directors of the EIC in London interpreted the Dutch intervention in Banten as a step toward the creation of a world monopoly in pepper, seeing that once the Dutch had installed themselves firmly on the Malabar coast, the pepper-producing area of India, they then moved forwards on Java and Sumatra. But the EIC's version of events is not supported by the evidence in the VOC documents. The VOC decided on military action to eliminate competition in intra-Asian trade; it was Banten's position as a distribution centre for Asian products in the Archipelago that had most irritated and worried Batavia. The

---

10 W.Ph. Coolhaas, ed., *Generale Missiven van Gouverneur-general en raden aan Heren XVII der Verenigde Oostindische Compagnie*, Deel IV, 1675–1685 (The Hague, 1971), no 134, 641–4, missive 31 December 1683.

11 J. Israel, 'England, the Dutch and the Mastery of the World Trade in the Age of the Glorious Revolution', *The World of William and Mary: Anglo-Dutch Perspectives on the Revolution of 1688–89*, eds Dale Hoak and Mordechai Feingold (Stanford, 1996), p. 76.

idea of creating a monopoly in the pepper trade played no role in the correspondence between the Dutch directors and Batavia about Banten.

II. 1684–1760: a new balance

If we consider the years after the expulsion of the EIC from Banten as a time of rapid change or even as a caesura in European–Asian trade and relations, what then should the change be? Some historians see, at least for the relationship between the VOC and India, a change during the 1680s from the 'monopolistic' to a 'competitive' phase that lasted from around 1680 to 1748.[12] Seen from the perspective of South-east Asia the situation looked rather different: Anthony Read has argued that South-east Asia witnessed a crisis in its trade in the middle of the seventeenth century, and that the contraction of commerce left room for only one winner. That winner was the VOC. All the others, the European rivals as well as the South-east Asian, Chinese and Indian traders, lost. The success of the Dutch Company was based on the fact that it had used its power selectively to establish monopoly conditions.[13]

But not all historians see the VOC as a winner. On the contrary, it can be argued that, after the 1680s, the position of the VOC was weakening. It was, as is sometimes thought, ironical that the Dutch had directed all their costly efforts to monopolize the traditional products in the European–Asian trade, the spices and pepper, and that these products had lost their commercial relevance at the very moment that the Dutch had achieved their goals. A major shift in European consumption was responsible for a fast-growing demand for cottons and silks and for tea and coffee.[14] Such a view dovetails with the idea that VOC gradually lost its advantage in its intra-Asia trade and that, after 1690, the Asian part of the enterprise was always in the red.

However, such an interpretation of the position of the VOC is difficult to reconcile with the substantial increase of Dutch shipping and trade to Asia after the 1690s. It is hard to believe that the Dutch *bewindhebbers* were so smart as to create an enterprise that could grow enormously in size – sending out more ships, more men, more money then ever before – and which, at the same time, could endure losses year after year. It is equally hard to believe that these *bewindhebbers* had invested their money for 70 or 80 years in a trade that, either through bad luck or a stupid investment policy, finally only brought losses, while at the same time the EIC was able to take over the new profitable trades thanks to

---

[12] George D. Winius and Marcus P.M. Vink, *The Merchant Warrior Pacified: The VOC (Dutch East India Company) and its Changing Political Economy in India* (Delhi, 1991).

[13] Anthony Read, *Southeast Asia in the Age of Commerce, 1450–1680*, vol. 2, *The Age of Expansion and Crisis* (New Haven and London, 1993), p. 290.

[14] K.N. Chaudhuri and Jonathan Israel, 'The English and Dutch East India Companies and the Glorious Revolution of 1688–9', *The Anglo-Dutch Moment: Essays on the Glorious Revolution and its World Impact*, ed. Jonathan Israel (Cambridge, 1991), pp. 407–38.

good luck or to a well-considered and subtle market policy. The problem is that such a view is based upon false premises. There can be no doubt that the position of the VOC relative to its rivals and especially to the EIC, was changing during this period. But it is not accurate to speak of a 'shift' in the European–Asian trade leading to an increase in the demand or consumption of textiles or tea and coffee at the expense of the demand for spices. The volume of the trade in spices and pepper stayed at the same level and these products remained important and profitable trade items until the very end of the existence of the Dutch Company. Enormous investments had been made to acquire the monopoly, but the costs of maintaining it in the eighteenth century were less high, not least because the British and other rival companies acknowledged the hegemony of the Dutch in these parts of Asia.

It is obvious that relations between the Dutch and the English companies after 1688 were changing and becoming more relaxed. The political situation in Europe, where both countries had become allies after the Glorious Revolution and France had become the common enemy, was an important factor. The fear of the Dutch directors that the EIC would seek revenge for the Banten case disappeared. But it was not only the international political situation that was responsible for a change in the local relations. The new conditions in the European–Asian trade resulted in a more 'normal' commercial competition. There can be no doubt that there was a fierce competition in India for the procurement of the most wanted textiles for the European market. This competition had been well underway since the early 1670s. The Dutch directors warned their servants in India time and again not to give in to British pressure, and to do their utmost to get the best quality and most sought-after textiles before the British merchants could lay their hand on them. As the EIC began to have its own financial problems after 1684 through investing too heavily in the textile trade and because of their aggressive policy towards the Mogul Empire, the Dutch might reasonably have thought that they had won the first battle for the Indian textiles. But in the long run they could not, of course, prevent the British from enlarging their trade with India.

Relations, rivalry or cooperation varied from time to time, from place to place or from factory to factory and from product to product. It seems that attitude of the local servants and their personal contacts and understanding were an important factor in the way in which the relations developed. We may take as an example the saltpetre trade in Bengal. Around 1740 it was reported that the Dutch and English residents in Patna, where the saltpetre was procured, were 'seldom or never good friends'. It was hard to keep to the agreements made by the Companies for buying, and Indian merchants were able to profit from the European rivalry. In 1744, Jan Sichterman, director of the Dutch factory in Hugli, a man with an extensive private trade, proposed an alliance between the British, French and Dutch for buying saltpetre, and the agreement held for some years despite irritations and mistrust.

But these small incidents of varying character were not as important as the common effort from both the Dutch and the British to eliminate a successful new competitor on the scene: the Ostend Company. The governments in London and The Hague backed the companies, and, in 1727, European diplomacy led to a suspension of the Charter of the Ostend Company. In 1731, it was abolished. The Emperor Charles VI had sacrificed the Company for the promise of the succession of his daughter, Maria Theresa.

Perhaps one should conclude that the period from 1688 onward was characterized by cooperation as well as by commercial competition, but not by the intense rivalry and conflicts of the earlier period. The fact that the Republic and Great Britain were allies, sometimes even both shoulder-to-shoulder engaged in large wars was, of course, an important reason for the attitude of the Companies overseas. But again, the conditions in European–Asian trade were also an important factor in the rivalry. The enormous growth in demand for textiles, tea and coffee, produced not only competition in these markets, but provided enough space for both companies to take advantage of the new situation. The struggle for spices during the first period could only be won by one of the contesting parties, but the booming trade in textiles, tea and coffee offered opportunities for both.

Moreover, the companies did not, by and large, challenge their positions in Asia any longer. The EIC recognized the dominance of the VOC in the Archipelago, and the Dutch jurisdiction over Sunda Strait was undisputed after the conquest of Banten. The VOC demanded salutes from foreign ships and had the right to hail them and ask for their destinations etc. Two 'post-holders' were stationed there for this purpose. The Dutch did not dispute the British possessions and strongholds in India. The only source of possible conflict seemed to be Sumatra, where Batavia met any British expansion from Bencoolen with great suspicion.

It may well be that the VOC's increase of trade and shipping, and the fact that the Dutch position in the East was not contested, concealed the internal weaknesses of the Dutch Company in the middle of the eighteenth century. This was soon to reverse after the battle of Plassey, where Clive created a new situation for the EIC, not only *vis-à-vis* the Indian authorities, but also *vis-à-vis* its European competitors.

III. 1760–1795: fights and fortunes

Clive's victory at Plassey, however, did not lead immediately to growing antagonism between Dutch and English company servants in Bengal. The director of the Dutch factory in Bengal, Adriaan Bisdom (director from 1755 to 1760) was personally on good terms with Clive, and it is no surprise that Clive and his men turned to the Dutch director for the transfer to Europe of a considerable part of their fortunes acquired with the succession of Mir Jafar. In July 1757, Bisdom and his council discussed the acceptance of around 12 lakh of rupees (or ƒ 1,890,000) for bills on Europe, as was proposed by John Walsh, who had come to Bengal as Clive's secretary. Bisdom argued strongly for the acceptance of this money, because it gave the Dutch company the chance to pay off its debts and to invest money without the need for huge consignments of silver from Europe. The councillors agreed, but since they feared that paying this amount of money in one instalment would not please the directors of the VOC in Amsterdam, they imposed some restrictions on its payment in Europe, deciding to accept the money on the condition that the bills should be paid out in Amsterdam in three instalments between 1758 and 1760. The Company would, of course, have to pay interest on the money that it held back during these years, but Bisdom calculated that even with the payment of interest taken into account, the whole transaction would bring the VOC a handsome profit of around 175,000 rupees.[15]

In August 1757, Jagatseth Fatehchand placed this money in the Dutch hands, 'on the account of several English persons, to be paid to Joshua van Neck in London in 1758, 1759 and 1760 to a total amount of ƒ 2,204,496 guilders'.[16] The VOC in Bengal issued, after deduction of the costs, three bills of respectively ƒ 638,487, ƒ 676,045 and ƒ 713,603, drawn on the Gentlemen Seventeen in Amsterdam. The transaction was completed in the name of Bisdom and Robert Armenault, the bookkeeper and second in the Council at Hugli.[17] However, Bisdom and his councillors had been right to forsee the unwillingness of the directors to cooperate. The *bewindhebbers* were furious. They postponed a decision on the payment, when, in April 1758, a Dutch merchant representing Van Neck asked for the money and did so again in October of the same year. An agreement was reached in March 1759. The *bewindhebbers* adhered to the proposed scheme of payment in three instalments, while at the same reducing the amount of payment, because they thought the interest that Bisdom had promised to the English was far too high.[18] It is not clear from Dutch sources what exactly the part of Clive and of others was in this transaction.

Clive had also transferred a part of his newly acquired fortune via Batavia to Europe – an amount of £50,000.[19] I haven't yet been able to trace all the details of this transfer in Dutch sources, but we can be pretty sure that a large part of the amount of ƒ 546,616 that was paid in Amsterdam to Joshua van Neck in 1760 for 16 bills drawn from Batavia belonged to Clive. This money had been deposited

---

[15] VOC 2894, f. 202, *Over de voordelen van de Engelse negotiatie,* 4 July 1757; VOC 2895, ff. 560–563, *Res. Raad te Hougly,* 4 July 1757. See also Lequin, *Het Personeel,* 177 and 192.

[16] BGB, no. 10780, *Generaal Journaal* 1756/57, f. 378.

[17] Lequin, *Het Personeel,* 189, 192.

[18] VOC 129, *Res. Heren XVII,* 18 April, 10 October 1758, 12 March 1759. VOC 7050, lists with payment against bills of exchange drawn on the Heren XVII, 1755–73. The contract between the VOC and Jan Wijnants, acting for Joshua van Neck in London, was signed on 14 April 1759. The VOC paid in three instalments of ƒ 638,487 each, thus ignoring the 6 percent interest agreed to by Bisdom. The first instalment was paid in cash, the other two in bonds. VOC bonds normally yielded 2½ percent interest in these years. The bonds were payable before 1 December 1759 and 1 December 1760 respectively. In the eighteenth century an English Pound was equivalent to about 11 guilders.

[19] Peter Marshall, *East Indian Fortunes: The British in Bengal in the Eighteenth Century* (Oxford, 1976), p. 225.

in cash with the Company in Batavia by 'private persons' and was later transferred via bills, drawn on the Gentlemen Seventeen by the bookkeeper of the
VOC, Christiaan Lodewijk Senf, to Joshua van Neck in London.[20]

While Clive's fortune, or at least a part of it, was entrusted to the VOC, the
Dutch company tried to intervene in Bengal in a most extraordinary way, one
that demonstrated its complete lack of knowledge or understanding of the new
political situation and growing English power. The complaints and accusations
levelled against the French and the English by the local Dutch servants of the
Indian factories induced the Governor-general and Council in Batavia to
develop a large scheme to intervene with a number of troops somewhere in the
Indian continent. The plans were rather vague: a force of 2,000 European and
6,000 indigenous soldiers should be used wherever it was most necessary to
uphold Dutch prestige and privileges against rival European or Indian forces.
Bringing together such a force was far beyond the capacity of the malaria-ridden
Batavian garrison, but new information from Bisdom and Vernet gave the
Batavian councillors new inspiration. The indigenous population in Bengal had
turned against the *nawab* Mir Jafar, it was said, and his son might take the
opportunity to stand against his father. The Batavia Government thought they
had have found an opportunity to intervene on behalf of the son and to improve
the VOC's position in Bengal. It was only wishful thinking. Interventions of this
type might have worked in the Indonesian Archipelago, where the Batavian
Government was experienced in intriguing in local courts; on the Indian
subcontinent, however, where the British were on their way to becoming the
dominant military force, such schemes went far beyond the power of VOC, even
if Bisdom and Vernet's information had been right.

The plan was unrealistic from the start. It was a blessing in disguise that every
blunder and every fault that could be made, was made, so that it was not long
before the predictable catastrophe arrived at the end of 1759. The director
Bisdom and his *secunde* Vernet were incapable of commanding a military expedition, they were hesitant about employing their military forces against English
or indigenous militia and they were also trying to make each other the scapegoat
for the expected failure. The masters of the ships of the fleet were not ready for
action – but the Dutch were naive enough to gave the EIC a pretext for an attack
when they seized some English ships. The Dutch forces, led by a French soldier
of fortune, Roussel, were insufficient in number and knew little of warfare in the
field. There were two skirmishes and it is perhaps hardly necessary to say the

---

[20] VOC 334, BGB, *Generaal Journaal 1758/59*: 'Wijders wat hier aan ingelegde capitalen der
particulieren alhier bij Comp. Negotie pag . . . [not noted] afgeschreven is om in
conformité de daaronder verleende assignatiën op patria weder uitgekeerd te worden; 16
door de eerste boekhouder Christiaan Lodewijk Senf aan Joshua van Neck, koopman te
Londen: 15 van totaal rsd 225,000 en één van 2340, totaal: rsd 227,340.' (The rijksdaalder
was equal to 48 stuiver, the amount was ƒ 545,616.) The payment is also recorded in VOC
7050, a list of payments by the chambers of the VOC in the Netherlands.

'Battle of Bidara' did not make a significant contribution to the military glory of the Dutch.

The whole episode underlined the fact that Dutch power in the East was much weaker than the figures of trade and shipping suggested. During these years still more East Indiamen sailed from the Netherlands than from any other country, manned with large numbers of sailors and soldiers, and return fleets were as richly loaded as the British. But Dutch military and naval power was weakening and the VOC could certainly not achieve its goals by using military force outside the Archipelago or Ceylon. The blunders and mistakes of the clumsy operations revealed the real weakness of the VOC in India, and that may have been the reason – apart from Clive's money – that the relations between the VOC and EIC were only hurt temporarily. Bisdom was called back and his successors tried to continue the trade, trying to avoid conflict with the British.

Money reconciles

There was a way to induce the English Company servants to take a more lenient attitude towards the Dutch: to present them with an opportunity to transfer their private capital to Europe. George Vernet and his council had asked for the permission from the High Government in Batavia in 1765 to accept some 200,000 rupees from British servants in Bengal for bills on Europe. The argument was that such a measure was urgent, because the VOC in Bengal was in great need of money.[21] Batavia granted this permission, probably because of the permission granted by the directors at home to the factories to accept money on bills in case of local need for money. It might well be, however, that the initiative did not came from the Dutch but from the English company servants, who had acquired substantial fortunes when the *nawab* Mir Jafar died and the young *nawab* Najm-ud-daula succeeded him. According to Marshall, over 1 million rupees had been 'levied' by the EIC servants on the succession of Najm-ud-daula.[22] Robert Clive, just starting his second term as Governor, made an inquiry into this case, which even in his eyes had gone too far. Some of those involved thought it wise to leave the Company's service and return to England, others were dismissed. Several of those involved (John Johnstone, Playdell, Ralph Leycester, George Gray and Ascanius William Senior) chose in 1765 the VOC as the channel for remitting at least a part of their capital safely to England, while in the following year their example was followed by Randolph Marriot and William Sumner. But Clive too turned to the VOC to transfer a large part of the fortune that he acquired during his second term of office. And there were others, such as Robert Gregory, who in 1766 transferred via the Dutch to Europe the substantial sum of 378,000 guilders or 302,000 rupees, and who had earned his fortune (said to be well over 1 million guilders) by trade alone.[23]

---

[21] VOC 3130, f. 39, Directeur and Raad at Hugli to Heren XVII, 7 November 1765.
[22] Marshall, *East Indian Fortunes*, pp. 172–5.
[23] *Ibid.*, p. 240.

The *bewindhebbers* did not agree with this interpretation of their orders, and reacted to this sudden increase of transfers in the same way as they had done in 1760. Confronted with the obligation to pay large amounts of money after the autumn sales in 1766 and 1767, they decided to stop the Bengal factory from accepting British capital for bills on Europe.[24] One of the objectives of the directors may have been the fact that they could not control the amount of money that was transmitted through bills, thus making it difficult for them to determine the amount of silver that had to be shipped to Bengal.

But a new way of acquiring British money in Bengal for financing the Dutch trade solved this problem. The *bewindhebbers* started buying bills in Amsterdam from Anglo-Dutch banking houses. Individuals in London drew these bills on merchants in Calcutta. The VOC sent the bills to its director in Bengal who handed them over to the Calcutta merchant named in the bill for payment. The banker in Amsterdam was paid after the return of the ships and the auctions in Holland in October or November. A merchant called J. Fremeaux proposed such a transaction to the Dutch directors in Amsterdam as early as 1767. In December 1768 the *bewindhebbers* agreed that the VOC should buy four bills of 50,000 *sicca* rupees each in London via the well-known banking house of Clifford & Sons. Ascanius William Senior in London drew these bills on two Calcutta merchants, Joseph Jekyll and James Lister. Should the merchants in Bengal not fulfil their obligations, Clifford & Sons would pay 4 percent on the amount unpaid. The papers were sent in triplicate to Bengal, one set with the 'direct' ship of the chamber of Amsterdam bound for Hugli, one with a Dutch East Indiaman sailing via Batavia, and one via London with an English East Indiaman.[25]

The entire operation, however, ended in failure. Vernet and his council had already warned their superiors in Amsterdam that the unfavourable exchange rate of the rupee (27 *stuiver* for a rupee) disadvantaged the merchants in Bengal. Vernet argued that the French had offered the same unfavourable conditions, and that their correspondents had been unable to meet most of the bills.[26] The first letter from Jekyll and Lister at Calcutta to Vernet and his council was reassuring: 'the money is ready whenever you please to send the proper bills . . .'. But soon a subtle game of evasion and postponement developed. Jekyll finally saw the original bills on 20 February, but as Lister had gone down the river without giving his associate any directions, Jekyll could not pay. Ultimately the bills were

---

24 Van der Chijs, *Realia*, 371 (Res. G.G. en R., 6 June 1768); Marshall, *East Indian Fortunes*, p. 242.

25 VOC 178, *Res. Heren XVII* 14 October 1767 and 31 March 1768; VOC 278, *Res. Kamer Amsterdam* 10 and 24 October, 3 and 7 November, and 29 December 1768. See also F.S. Gaastra, 'British capital for the VOC', *Commerce and Culture in the Bay of Bengal, 1500–1800*, eds Denys Lombard and Om Prakash (New Delhi, 1999), pp. 261–84.

26 These rates are mentioned in the *Missive van Directeur Vernet en Raden aan Heren XVII*, 11 Jan. 1770 (VOC 3257, ff. 785–786). It may well be that Jacques Necker, the director of the French East India Company and later the well-known minister of finance of Louis XVI, had been the first to use this channel for developing French trade; see H. Lüthy, 'Necker et la Compagnie des Indes', *Annales: Economies, Sociétés, Civilisations*, 15 (1960), 869–70.

formally refused. A general shortage of ready money (it was the time of the great famine in Bengal) was the main cause for this failure, according to Vernet.[27]

The directors as well as Clifford & Soonen had good reason for being disappointed about the failure.[28] Nevertheless, the *bewindhebbers* tried once again to tap English capital sources in Bengal and signed a contract in August 1773 with the banking house of Pye Rich & Wilkieson, which delivered four bills of 125,000 guilders each to the VOC, to be paid in Calcutta at a rate of 26 *stuiver* per rupee. The compensation to be paid by Pye Rich & Wilkieson, if the bills were not honoured in Calcutta, was put at 12 percent.[29] But the bills were paid promptly. After 1773 the VOC could finance its trade with Bengal almost entirely with these bills, that were bought not only via Pye Rich & Wilkieson but also via the house of Hope & Co. and Francis Melvill.[30] Each year, when the Gentlemen Seventeen decided on the amount and composition of the precious metals to be sent to Asia, a fair amount of silver was destined for Bengal. Starting in 1773, they included in their resolutions the provision that bills that could be bought in London to replace the amount, and this normally happened.

At the same time, the VOC reopened the door for the remittances of Anglo-Indian capital in the traditional way. In 1775, the directors allowed their factory in Bengal to accept some *f* 500,000 or *f* 600,000 for bills from the British.[31] The 'Engelse Heeren' were offered an exchange rate of 25 *stuiver* or *f* 1.25 for the rupee, receiving 5 percent interest (on a yearly basis) for the time between the depositing of the money and the actual delivery of the bill at the

---

27 VOC 3257, ff. 785–786, *Extract missive Directeur en Raden te Houghly aan Heren XVII,* 11 January 1770; VOC 3823, ff. 1–20, Letters concerning the bills of exchange refused by Joseph Jekyll and James Lister.

28 It is not clear how far the house of Clifford was hurt by this case. Could Clifford have charged Senior for the 4 percent he had to pay? It is possible that Clifford had already paid Senior the entire sum of the bills, in which case his loss would be fairly substantial. But it is not possible to make a direct connection between this event and the fall of the House of Clifford in 1773, which caused a general crisis in the Amsterdam financial market. This crisis is generally ascribed to the failure of Scottish and London banks in 1772, partly caused by the over-extension of credit and speculation in shares of the East India Company.

29 VOC 281, *Res. Kamer Amsterdam,* 8 July and 26 August 1773. The house of Pye Rich & Wilkieson was probably the firm of Henry Pye Rich, who was born in England in 1737 or 1738 and who lived in Amsterdam from 1773 and acted as consul for the British king. When the son of Henry Pye Rich was baptized in 1784, Charles Wilkieson was a witness; see O. Schutte, *Repertorium der buitenlandse vertegenwoordigers, residerende in Nederland, 1584–1810* (The Hague, 1983).

30 VOC 135, *Res. Heren XVII,* 18 October 1774, 4 March and 9 October 1775; VOC 283, *Res. Kamer Amsterdam,* 15 December 1774, 16 January 1775. There is a collection of contracts regarding these bills of exchange, officially made up by the notary Van Beem in Amsterdam, in VOC 7051. Cf. Holden Furber, *John Company at Work: A study of European Expansion in India in the Late Eighteenth Century* (Cambridge, Mass., 1948; reprint New York, 1970), pp. 78–108. For Hope, see M.G. Buist, *'At Spes non Fracta': Hope and Co, 1770–1815* (The Hague, 1974).

31 VOC 135, *Resolutie Heren XVII,* 9 October 1775.

time of the departure of the ships.[32] Bills were also issued for products such as cottons or saltpetre, although no interest was paid on these goods. The time for attracting Anglo-Indian capital was well chosen. Private capital in Bengal accumulated rapidly while the directors of the EIC restricted the issue of bills (in 1768 to £70,000). Moreover, the English Company offered bills on rather disadvantageous terms of 2s per rupee. The VOC became an attractive alternative.

Relations between VOC and EIC also improved on the official level after 1775. Two members of the VOC government in Hugli, Jacob Eilbracht and Wilhelm von Danckelman, made an official visit to Calcutta in April 1775 to plead for the removal of all sorts of restrictions on Dutch trade. A long memorandum of complaints – about restrictions on the textile trade, the small amounts of opium and saltpetre allotted to the VOC, disadvantageous rates at the mint – was read in full in a special meeting of the Supreme Council in Fort William. The Dutch envoys did not fail to notice that the Supreme Council was split into two parties, 'who disagreed about almost everything they have to decide upon'. Indeed, Governor-general Warren Hastings and his secretary, Richard Barwell, were bitterly opposed by Philip Francis and the other two members of the Supreme Council. The VOC servants were at great pains to keep their case out of these internal struggles. They had to explain to Hastings that their complaints should not be interpreted as grievances against him in person, and that it had not been their intention to blame him in front of his adversaries in the Council for the bad relations with the Dutch Company.[33]

Although the Council in Fort William did not give in to all the Dutch complaints, it issued a proclamation in 1775 allowing the Dutch unhindered trade in textiles,[34] although the opium trade was still strictly controlled. Under the directorship of Johan Mathias Ross (1776–81) mutual relations were further improved. Ross was a personal friend of Hastings, and his stepdaughter, Johanna Ribaut, was married to the well-know orientalist and *protégé* of Hastings, Nathaniel Brassey Halhed. Ross maintained good relations with many other British in Bengal, and he used his position to enter into all sorts of private trade operations. He negotiated with Richard Griffith, who was appointed as opium contractor by the EIC, for extra deliveries of opium over and above the VOC's official allocation. A British merchant, Cutberth Thornhill, carried this opium to Batavia. Moreover, he accepted huge amounts of British capital for bills, apparently making profits by lending out the money he thus received between the time that the money was accepted and the bills issued.[35]

---

32 VOC 3451, *Directeur en Raden te Hougly aan Heren XVII,* 23 August 1776. For Dutch bills, the rate of the rupee was 27 *stuiver,* but the VOC paid out with a reduction of 7 9/13 percent.

33 F.S. Gaastra, 'De VOC en de EIC in Bengalen aan de vooravond van de Vierde Engelse oorlog (1780–1784)', in *Tijdschrift voor Zeegeschiedenis,* 19 (2001), 24–35

34 Om Prakash, *European Commercial Enterprise,* p. 285.

35 For the opium deal, see Gaastra, 'De VOC en de EIC in Bengalen', pp. 31–2. For Halhed, see Rosane Rocher, *Orientalism, Poetry and the Millennium: The Checkered Life of Nathaniel Brassey Halhed, 1751–1830* (Delhi, Varansi and Patna, 1983).

Table 1: Payment on Bengal bills by the VOC in the Netherlands, 1773–89 (in guilders)

Year	A	B
1773/74	349,773	429,200
1774/75	315,000	536,995
1775/76	376,212	851,400
1776/77	872,335	1,209,567
1777/78	1,793,861	1,399,987
1778/79	3,301,757	1,227,508
1779/80	1,258,831	1,764,054
1780/81	1,400,074	1,936,675
1781/82	0	
1782/83	0	
1783/84	0	
1784/85	381,930	
1785/86	1,578,857	
1786/87	1,124,470	
1787/88	326,504	
1788/89	0	
1789/90	16,747	
1773–90	13,096,351	9,355,386

A: Bills bought by the British in Bengal.
B: Bills bought by the VOC in Amsterdam and sent to Bengal to be cashed there.

The increase in remitted Anglo-Indian capital via the VOC after 1777 is remarkable. Ross was able to serve as an intermediary for a number of well-placed EIC officials and could facilitate the transfer of a considerable part of their private fortune to Europe. We find well-known EIC servants and nabobs mentioned in the VOC documents, for example William Aldersey, Richard Barwell, Ewan Law and, not surprisingly, Nathaniel Brassey Halhed. Aldersey transferred a total amount f 327,880 in 1777 and 1778. Transfers by Halhed, partly to himself and partly to his father, amounted to f 466,237. But servants in more modest positions also bought bills from the VOC. Sometimes, of course, remittances were made in connection with the return to England. James Wiss, for instance, who had been sent out to India to introduce the new Italian method of winding silk and had become the superintendent of the silk filature at Kumarkhali, returned to Europe in 1776. In the same year, he remitted via the VOC f 47,000 for himself and some smaller amounts of money for several others, namely Thomas Chapman (f 5,091), James Grant (f 12,786), James Lucas (f 5,114), Lewis Pictet (f 37,738) and Jacob Rider (f 19,094). Blastus Godley Wright, who was elected to the office of sheriff in 1776 but had instead chosen to sail home, transferred f 38,297 to himself and f 63,591 to the London merchants Bland & Burnet. Many times, one person acted as an agent taking care of the financial transactions for many others. In 1778, Henry Grant deposited f 237,713 in the treasury of the VOC in Hugli on behalf of 12 persons, against which he received 14 bills. Other important agents in that year were Cutberth Thornhill, who transferred four bills ƒ 112,328 on behalf of Edward Golding, and Joseph Cator, who remitted ƒ 258,043 to Ralph Leycester and James Barwell, and another ƒ 76,914 to several others. But perhaps the most prominent agent was William Paxton, whose name already features in the list of 1777 with seven bills, and in the season 1778/79 when he bought 12 bills worth ƒ 130,521 for nine persons.[36]

Ross also accepted products for bills: textiles as well as saltpetre. These transactions were largely made by William Walker, but the bills were mainly put in the name of the Indian merchant Rammichorn. There were a several beneficiaries of these transactions in Europe, apart from Walker himself, who transferred ƒ 127,000 to himself. Large sums were received by Giles Hibbert (ƒ 102,000 in 1779 and 1780) and Nathaniel Middleton (receiving ƒ 232,000 via the banking house of Rumbold, Charlton & Raikes in London).

It is no surprise that the volume of Dutch trade in Bengal was growing because of the abundance of Anglo-Indian capital. Around 1770, the VOC needed only two East Indiamen for carrying the exports from Bengal to the Netherlands, but since 1777, when Ross started to accept large funds from his British friends, he could despatch three richly loaded ships to Europe. This met the high targets set by his company, but soon the directors found that their servants were sending more than they had asked for. There can be no doubt that the remittances of the English induced Ross and his Council to enlarge the shipments to Europe. But the directors, although aware of the advantages of the resulting cheap finance for their trade, complained about the abundance of textiles that could only be sold for moderate prices in Europe. Ross's plan to expand the trade even further and load four vessels with Bengal commodities for Europe was declined.

The Dutch directors also criticized Ross for accepting bills on less favourable conditions than they had bargained for in their contracts in Europe. The directors reasoned that such advantageous conditions could easily be got if so much capital was available for remittance. And indeed, there was much more capital waiting for remittance than could be accepted for bills: jewellery as well gold and silver was sent to Europe. The directors noted that the VOC ship *Ridderkerk* had carried 256 bars of gold and 42,700 gold and silver rupees to Europe on the account of 'private persons'. It may well be that Ross's son-in-law Nathaniel Halhed was one of these private persons as he and his wife returned to Europe on the *Ridderkerk*. It was not unusual for EIC servants using Dutch ships for their return to take part of their fortunes with them in the form of precious stones or precious metals.[37]

---

36 Gaastra, 'British Capital', pp. 272–5.
37 VOC 338, *Heren IIV aan G.G. en R.*, 7 October 1779, 6 November 1780. For Halhed, see Rocher, *Orientalism, Poetry and the Millennium*, pp. 103, 211. An example of an EIC employee returning on a Dutch vessel is a younger brother of Richard Barwell, Daniel Barwell. He sailed home on *Woestduin* in 1779. This ship was wrecked entering the Scheldt, and Barwell was drowned; there is a sepulchre for him in the Church of Flushing. See Jona

War spoils it

The changing relationship between the British and the Dutch company in Bengal reflected the EIC's growing power in the region. Dutch trade became dependent of British toleration. However, the VOC had something to offer – a safe channel for transfers of private capital, and it seemed that after 1775 a situation had been created that by and large pleased at least three parties: the VOC itself, the VOC servants, and the servants of the EIC. Within the total operations of the VOC, the Bengal trade was less important than it had been at the beginning of the eighteenth century. The VOC was still a large commercial enterprise, sending more than 20 East Indiamen to Europe with Asian products each year, and it had slowly expanded its power and influence in Java as well as in Ceylon. It was confronted with enormous problems too: competition from British country trade in Asian waters, profits being eroded through the high costs of trading in Asia, changing markets and intense commercial rivalry in the European Asian trade, malaria in Batavia that killed soldiers and decimated what was supposed to be the flourishing centre of Dutch power and trade overseas. The VOC was still a giant enterprise but its internal weaknesses made the company vulnerable, as was demonstrated in the Fourth Anglo-Dutch war. On 20 December 1780, Great Britain declared war on the Dutch Republic. The war not only showed that the Dutch Company was incapable of defending its factories, it also ruined the Company financially. The war had, of course, a direct effect on the relations between the two nations in Bengal.

It took some time before the news of the war between the nations reached Fort William and Fort Gustavus. On 2 July 1781, Ross returned home from a friendly visit to Hastings; both men were optimistic that the statesmen in Europe would be wise enough to prevent a war. The next day, Hastings received the news of the outbreak of war and was ordered to take the Dutch fort and factory. When, in the evening of that day, two English soldiers asked for the surrender of the Dutch Fort, Ross refused – if war had broken out, he felt, it should have been requested with more dignity: indeed, Hastings honoured him later by sending a good number of soldiers – and Ross duly surrendered the factory. Books and papers and all the company's commodities were confiscated, but thanks to Ross's intervention, the private property was respected. It might not have been too difficult for Ross to persuade Hastings to do that, because Ross had already accepted large sums of British money for bills on Europe. William Paxton, for instance, had already a deposited a sum of ƒ 785,000 in the Dutch factory for remittance to Europe.[38] Ross was taken to Calcutta, but his imprisonment was not particularly harsh, Hastings offering him a house there. In December 1782, Ross returned to Europe on the Portuguese East Indiaman *Princess of Brazil*. Apparently he thought it wise to avoid a direct contact with his superiors in the

---

Willem te Water, *Bericht nopens het verongelukte Oost-Indische schip Woestduin* (Middelburg, 1780).

[38] W.G.J. Kuiters, 'William Paxton (1744–1824): The History of an East Indian Fortune', *Bengal Past and Present*, 3 (1992), 1–22.

Republic, and he settled in Brussels, where lived a life as a wealthy 'continental nabob' until his death in 1787.

The VOC's financial crisis after 1784 meant that the Company was no longer a safe channel for remittance. One day before the outbreak of the war in December 1780, a number of contracts for bills on Calcutta had been signed in Amsterdam with Pye Rich & Wilkieson, Hope & Co., and with Jan Hoffman. The directors tried to resume this practice of negotiating contracts for bills in Europe in 1784. Only two contracts seem to have been concluded: one with Thomas & Charles Wilkieson in December 1784 for 250,000 rupees, and the other one with the house of the Veuve Juran & Fils for 100,000 rupees in March 1785. It is not clear if these transactions actually went through and that the bills were honoured in Bengal. It proved equally difficult for the new Dutch director in Bengal, Isaac Titsingh, to finance the trade with bills on Europe. However, in 1785 and 1786, a fair amount of money was still transferred via the Dutch factory in Hugli, although the conditions for the VOC were much less favorable than they had been before 1780. Soon afterwards Dutch trade nearly came to a standstill.

Aftermath and conclusion

By the end of the eighteenth century it was clear that the large companies had no future as commercial enterprises. The EIC could make a 'soft landing' by gradually giving up its commercial activities and transforming itself into a colonial government. In the Dutch Republic, this process of transformation was more difficult, one of the main reasons being a general inability to transform the institutions of state. The consequences of the Fourth Anglo-Dutch war, however, made such a transformation unavoidable. The Dutch Company was financially ruined and could only survive with state intervention. The first hesitating steps made by the States General to exert some sort of control over the VOC, when the States General gave its financial support, could have been the start of such a transformation. But the outbreak of the French revolutionary wars, the fall of the Dutch Republic and the founding of a new French satellite state (Bataafse Republiek) in 1795 made greater control an urgent necessity. It was successful in so far as the VOC did not go bankrupt: the Company was taken over by the state. But the remnants of the wreck were plundered by the British who first took the most important strategic possessions – the Cape, Ceylon and, of course, the Dutch factories in India, and, in 1811, Java too.

There is a lot of debate about whether the Fourth Anglo-Dutch war in 1780 was the main cause for the fall of the VOC, or if it was simply one factor among many others. Among the other factors was the competition of the EIC, which should have weakened and undermined the VOC from the 1680s onwards. There can be no doubt that British competition was an important cause for declining profitability of VOC. As I have argued here, the Dutch Company was able to expand its trade enormously after 1700 despite growing competition from the EIC. Moreover, commercial rivalry between the companies was not as bitter as it had been in the first 'monopolistic' phase.

It is also clear that the EIC was by far the most powerful European force in Asia in the second part of the eighteenth century. But again, the character of the rivalry between the companies was changing. At the beginning of the seventeenth century not only the companies but their servants had been bitterly opposed to each other. Now they were working together, doing their best to amass private fortunes and bring them safely home. The unique relationship that grew in Bengal was disturbed from outside. If the war between Britain and the Dutch Republic was not the primary cause of the fall of the VOC, it at least revealed the internal weaknesses of the VOC and drove the Company into the hands of the state that tried to uphold her – the Dutch East India Company finally fell when the Dutch Republic fell.

Frank Submissions:
The Company and the Mughals between
Sir Thomas Roe and Sir William Norris*

SANJAY SUBRAHMANYAM

No man hath proprietye in land nor goods, if hee [the King] please to take it; soe that all are slaves. Witchcraft, sorcery, juggling, yea, all cunning that the Divell can teach, is frequent, eaven in the court, wher is wanting noe arte nor wicked subtility to bee or doe evill; soe that, comparing the vices to some cittyes in Europe, which I once judged the treasuries and sea of synne, I find them sanctuaryes and temples in respect of these.

Sir Thomas Roe to Prince Charles, Ajmer (30 October 1616)

Introduction

In recent decades, historians of ideas (above all, political ideas) have returned to the study of the problem of the Birth of Despotism in the centuries that are also termed those of European expansion. Here, what is meant is not despotism as a political 'system' (in the sense that Karl Wittfogel might have construed it), but rather despotism as a political *topos*, which is usually attributed to another land-scape, on which Europeans projected their fears at the time when their own political systems were under challenge both at the level of ideas, and of internal social and political movements.[1] The task is a delicate one, and the dangers facing the researcher are many, of which we may list a few. In the first place, the danger of a return to a form of perverse Euro-centricism is very real, since the greater part of the analyses in question are attempts at explicating what is a history of European ideas.[2] Armed with what is often a formidable textual erudition, leading back to the medieval Christian tradition (if not the classical

* I am grateful to Peter Marshall, V. Narayana Rao, Victor Stater and Robert Travers for comments, and to Kapil Raj for references. The text has benefited from discussions both at the National Maritime Museum, Greenwich in July 2000, and at my seminar in the EHESS, Paris.

1 Lucette Valensi, *The birth of the despot: Venice and the Sublime Porte*, tr. Arthur Denner (Ithaca, NY, 1993).

2 See, for example, Joan-Pau Rubiés, *Travel and ethnology in the Renaissance: South India through European eyes, 1250–1625* (Cambridge, 2000).

representation of the 'Other' in Herodotus), it is thus possible to forget, at least temporarily, that there were really other societies out there, and that they were constituted politically even outside the European imagination. A second danger emanates directly from the literary turn in these studies, since it is for the most part analysts of literature who have led the charge, in view of their superior skills in the analysis of rhetorical tradition. (The first major work in this line is probably Alain Grosrichard's *Structure du sérail* [1979], published at much the same time as Edward Said's *Orientalism*).[3] One result of the literary turn can be that the historical actors disappear, as it were, into a textual miasma, in which process the most banal procedures of historical discipline also fall by the wayside. To be sure, not all literary scholars are equally susceptible to naive ahistoricism, but a sufficiently large number of instances have now accumulated (including from some of the better-known practitioners such as Stephen Greenblatt or Tzvetan Todorov) for a genuine unease to have set in on this front.

Here we stand then, between the Scylla of overblown literary analysis of texts produced by European expansion, and the ever-present Charybdis of reading these materials at face value, to which their very mass, to say nothing of their congealed power of seduction, draws the archivally oriented scholar. The materials I address in this essay have in some measure been dealt with before, and some of the earlier treatments have suffered from precisely the problems that I have outlined briefly above. If I have decided to analyse them here once more, it is because it seems to me that some blood can still be squeezed, as it were, out of these turnips, but also for reasons of a more directly political nature. Having been involved on an earlier occasion in the celebration of a centenary (the quincentenary of Vasco da Gama's voyage to East Africa and India in 1998), it has become painfully clear to me that such centenary celebrations carry a rather ambiguous political charge.[4] What after all was the English East India Company, the fourth centenary of whose foundation the present volume seeks to commemorate? Was it merely a group of merchants, which strayed, in a fit of absent-mindedness, into building a huge and extremely lucrative empire? Or, as certain conspiracy theorists might have it, was it designed from the very start as an exercise in empire-building, which then bided its time for a century and a half, until the right opportunity offered itself? My preliminary response is simple enough. The English Company, from its very inception, was not merely a commercial but a political actor, both in the politics of England (and Europe), and that of Asia. As a political actor, it also produced a political discourse, which was, however, both somewhat fragmented at any point in time, and one that shifted over time. One of the major objects of this political discourse was the state that controlled much of India at the time, namely the Mughal empire.

---

3   For an English translation, see Alain Grosrichard, *The sultan's court: European fantasies of the East*, tr. Liz Heron (London, 1998).

4   The matter is discussed at some length in Sanjay Subrahmanyam, 'We are the World: The Discourse of Autarky in the Land of Discoveries', in Heinz Werner Wessler, ed., *Europe and Asia: Five Hundred Years* (New Delhi, forthcoming).

Englishmen and elephants

In August 1617, some two years into his extended stay in India, the celebrated English courtier and diplomat Sir Thomas Roe (1580/81–1644) wrote to his counterpart, the English ambassador at Istanbul, concerning the Mughal empire (as well as its ruler): 'Neyther will this overgrowne Eliphant descend to Article or bynde himselfe reciprocally to any Prince vpon terms of Equalety, but only by way of fauour admit our stay so long as it either likes him or those that Gouerne him.'[5] Roe was unhappy with the Mughal state in general, and with its ruler Jahangir in particular, who he felt gave neither his own person, nor the Company and monarch he represented, their entire due. While presenting the Mughal empire as an 'overgrowne Eliphant', he also sought to compare it with other such eastern imperial pachyderms, most notably the Ottomans. In the same letter he thus addresses some choice sneers at apparent Mughal military might, not dissimilar to what his contemporaries might have done with respect to the Grand Turk. So, in the same letter to Constantinople, we hear:

> The King [Jahangir] is at present in what they call an army; but I see no souldiers, though multitudes entertaynd in the qualety. The purpose was the oppression of the united Decan kings, who are perswaded to part with some rotten castles that may pretend a shadowe of yeilding somwhat, for which they are pleasd here to thinck themselves woorthy of the glorious prayses due to an honorable conquest.[6]

What is the historian of cross-cultural encounters to make of such rhetoric? Should we assume that it is no more than a tissue of self-referentiality, produced by autistic Europeans in a landscape that they had no real means of coming to terms with? Or, as recent authors armed with the epistemological might of Renaissance and post-Renaissance studies have begun to insist once more, should we take Roe with the same literal-minded seriousness that Peter Burke has accorded to the French physician François Bernier, who was resident in the Mughal domains a half-century after Roe?[7] Before answering these questions, we might do well to ask a rather more basic one: who was this Sir Thomas Roe? The question is easy enough to answer at one level.[8] Born in Leyton in 1580 or 1581, he was the son of a certain Robert Roe, himself the fourth son of Sir Thomas Roe, Lord Mayor of London in 1568. Our Thomas Roe entered Magdalen

---

5   William Foster, ed., *The Embassy of Sir Thomas Roe to India, 1615–19, as narrated in his Journal and Correspondence* (new and revised edition, London, 1926; 1st edition 1899, 2 vols). The citation is on pp. xxviii–xxix of the 1899 edition, and p. xliii of the 1926 edition (which I will hereafter cite unless otherwise stated).

6   Foster, *The Embassy*, pp. 385–86 fn.

7   Cf. Peter Burke, 'The philosopher as traveller: Bernier's Orient', in *Voyages and visions: Towards a cultural history of travel*, ed. Jás Elsner and Joan-Pau Rubiés (London, 1999), pp. 124–37.

8   For the standard biography, see Michael J. Brown, *Itinerant Ambassador. The Life of Sir Thomas Roe* (Lexington, KY, 1970). At the time of writing this essay, I was unable to

College, Oxford, in the early 1590s, and was admitted as a student to the Middle Temple in 1597, after which he perhaps spent some time in France. His step-family (his mother having re-married) were the Berkeleys, and, possibly through their influence, Thomas Roe was eventually made Esquire of the Body to Queen Elizabeth in the very last years of her reign. At the very outset of the Stuart monarchy, in 1603, he was knighted by James I, and became a close acquaintance of the monarch's children Prince Henry and Princess Elizabeth. Henry was instrumental in arranging an 'adventure' for Roe, in the region of Guiana, where he spent some time in 1610, exploring one of the branches of the Amazon, and also the mouth of the Orinoco. Here he learnt a little broken Spanish, though (as becomes clear when he is in the Mughal court) he knew no Portuguese. Returning to England in July 1611, Roe was left in somewhat poor straits after the death of his patron Prince Henry, in November 1612, while soon afterwards his other patroness, Princess Elizabeth left for the Palatinate.

As he himself put it, Roe was pretty desperate by 1614. Though briefly Member of Parliament for Tamworth that year, his resources were threadbare. He was to write a few years later from India:

> I esteeme it an infinite mercy of God that when I had fully ended and wasted my patrimony and saw no way but scorne (the reward of folly), before I suffred disgrace hee vndertooke mee, and beeing as it were new borne, hee restored mee to a new Inheritance and sett me right, for I doubt not but to equall my wastes.[9]

Besides having run out of money, Roe had also contracted a secret marriage with the daughter of Sir Thomas Cave from Stanford, Northamptonshire, who was also the widow of a certain Sir George Beeston. In these circumstances, the East India Company's request to have him sent as ambassador to the Mughal was a godsend. We may recall that the idea of an ambassador at the Mughal court had been mooted by Thomas Aldworth, writing from Ahmadabad in November 1613, and seconded by another Company factor, William Biddulph. Aldworth claimed this was the only way of getting the Company's affairs to be taken seriously, *vis-à-vis* their rivals, the Dutch and especially the Portuguese: 'Their might be a suffitient man be sent in your first shippes that may bee Resident in Agra withe the Kinge, and sutch a one whose person may breade regarde, for they here looke mutch after great men.' This was no doubt the result of the experience of William Hawkins, who had been at Agra from early 1609 to November 1611, but who had not carried sufficient weight with Jahangir to ensure the stability of the Company's position in Gujarat.[10] In September 1614, Sir Thomas Smythe, Governor of the Company, thus officially proposed sending 'one of

consult Colin Paul Mitchell, *Sir Thomas Roe and the Mughal Empire* (Karachi, 2000). Mitchell's work does not affect my argument significantly, however.

9   Cited in Foster, *The Embassy*, p. xxii.

10 For the voyages immediately preceding the embassy of Roe, see William Foster, ed., *The Voyage of Thomas Best to the East Indies, 1612–1614* (London, 1934).

extraordinarye partes to reside att Agra to prevent any plottes that may be wrought by the Iesuites to circumvent our trade'. The sending of this envoy would be in keeping with the *farman* that Jahangir had granted Thomas Best.

However, in debate, several different positions emerged amongst Company circles. Some were against the expense of the envoy, while others thought that sending a merchant was good enough. Still others feared that James I would impose his own candidate, and thus undermine the autonomy of the Company. Finally on 7 October 1614, it was decided to send 'an Embassadour of extraordinarye Countenance and respect'. The first name proposed was Sir John Brooke, whose health was too poor though. Then the name of a certain 'Master Bailie' was mooted, but the proposal met with little enthusiasm. In third place came Sir Thomas Roe 'yf hee may bee had'. Sir Thomas Smythe himself seems to have proposed this name, and he was described as 'of a pregnant understandinge, well spoken, learned, industrious, and of a comelie personage'. King James approved the choice. Roe had instructions from him to impress on the Mughal the greatness of the English monarch, which 'Maketh us even a Terrour to all other Nations; Concluding all with this happines, that Wee be not onlie absolutelie obeyed but universally beloved and admyred of all our People'.

Roe embarked for India on the *Lion*, on 2 February 1615, and reached Surat in six months. During the voyage, it is clear that he was kept at some distance by the commanders of the fleet, so as to avoid a conflict of authority. The fleet eventually arrived at Swally on 18 September 1615; at this time the merchant William Edwards was already at the Mughal court. Roe himself made his way to Ajmer on 23 December 1615, after briefly visiting the Mughal prince Sultan Parviz at Burhanpur. He was, however, taken ill on his arrival, and was thus able to go to the *darbar* for the first time only on 10 January 1616. A longish stay ensued, to which we shall turn at greater length below. He eventually took leave of Jahangir at Ahmadabad in August 1618, when the monarch was about to move to Agra. Roe claimed about this time that he was convinced 'after almost three yeares experience of the pride and falshood of these people, that [they] attended only advantage and were governed by privat interest and appetite'. After a further four months in Surat, he left for home on the *Anne* on 17 February 1619, and arrived at Plymouth in August that year, eventually returning to London in September.

Thereafter too, Sir Thomas Roe may be said to have had a fairly reasonable career. Not every one of his contemporaries and friends was so fortunate. In 1616, after 13 years in the Tower, Roe's sometime friend Sir Walter Ralegh was released and allowed to make plans to go to Guiana. He set sail in June 1617, but in early January 1618, in a major diplomatic *faux pas*, his subordinates attacked a Spanish settlement. One of those responsible, Keymis, committed suicide on ship rather than return; Ralegh returned to England and was somewhat summarily beheaded in the Palace Yard at Westminster on 29 October 1618.[11]

11 From a vast bibliography on Ralegh, see, for example, Stephen Coote, *A play of passion: The life of Sir Walter Ralegh* (London, 1993).

Roe, on the other hand, became Member of Parliament again on his return, and then in 1621 was sent to Istanbul. Here, he is supposed to have secured good conditions for English trade, and also helped block Habsburg overtures to the 'Sublime Porte' while helping cement a treaty between the Ottomans and Poland.[12] He stayed on in the Ottoman domains until Spring 1628, and in June 1629 was sent to help negotiate the peace between Sweden and Poland. In these years, he is reported to have become close to Gustavus Adolphus, and even helped persuade him to invade Germany in 1630.[13] In 1632, Roe's close friend Sir Dudley Carleton (Viscount Dorchester) died, and he began to harbour hopes that he would succeed him as the King's Secretary. Eventually considered too 'liberal', he was set aside, and retired to the country. In 1637, Roe's star rose once more, as he was made Chancellor of the Order of the Garter. He participated in the peace negotiations at Hamburg, Ratisbon and Vienna, and in June 1640, entered the Privy Council, and also re-entered Parliament as Member for Oxford. In 1641, he was again in Germany as a diplomat. As things worsened for him politically in these last years, Roe eventually decided to pull out from public life, and retired to Bath in July 1643. He died in November 1644.

Roe's account of his embassy to India, already known in an incomplete form to his contemporaries, has been used over the years by a number of historians, both of the East India Company and of the Mughal court. The latter have in particular drawn upon the Englishman's account to examine the nature of Mughal court-ritual, of which some have seen him as a keen observer. His description of the first time he was received by Jahangir, in January 1616, brings out the flavour of his account clearly enough.

> I went to court at four in the evening to the *durbar*, which is the place wher the Mogull sitts out daylie, to entertayne strangers, to receive petitions and presents, to give commands, to see and bee seene. To digresse a little from my reception, and declare the customes of the court, will enlighten the future discourse. The King hath no man but eunuchs that come within the lodgings or retyring roomes of his house: his weomen watch within, and guard him with manly weapons. They doe justice on upon another for offences. He comes every morning to a wyndow, called the *jarruco,* looking into a playne before his gate, and showes him selfe to the common people. At noone he returns thither and sitts some howers to see the fight of eliphants and willd beasts; under him within a rayle attend the men of rancke; from whence hee retiers to sleepe among his woemen. At afternoone, he returns to the *durbar* before mentioned. At eight, after supper, he comes downe to the *guzelcan*, a faire court, wher in the middest is a throune erected of free stone wherein he sitts, but some tymes below in a chayre; to which are none admitted but of great qualetye, and few of those without leave; wher he discourses of all matters with much affabilitye.[14]

---

12 Material on Roe's career in Istanbul may be found in Richard Knolles, *The generall historie of the Turkes* (4th edn, London, 1632).

13 For this phase of his life, see Samuel R. Gardiner, ed., *Letters relating to the mission of Sir Thomas Roe to Gustavus Adolphus, 1629–1630* (London, 1875).

14 Foster, *The Embassy*, pp. 84–6.

The tone of irony is not to be missed. Here is an effeminate court dominated by women, where the king 'hath no man but eunuchs' in his intimate surroundings, while his women 'guard him with manly weapons'. This is a court moreover where the decisions are taken in public, 'propounded, and resolved, and soe registred', but even this is not quite to Roe's taste for it means that royal decisions are 'tossed and censured by every rascall'. Besides, there is the issue of the nature of this kingship itself, for even if the king is complimented for 'never refusing the poorest mans complaynt', we are equally reminded that he 'sees with too much delight in blood the execution done by his eliphants'. Two significant passages may be found in the description of the same meeting, which are of some importance for understanding Roe's view of how royal power functions in a Mughal context. After having detailed Jahangir's daily schedule, Roe assures the reader that

> this course is unchangeable, except sickness or drinck prevent yt; which must be known, for, as all his subjects are slaves, so is he in a kynd of reciprocall bondage, for he is tyed to observe these howres and customes so precisely that, if hee were unseene one day and noe sufficient reason rendred, the people would mutinie; two days noe reason can excuse, but that he must consent to open his doores and bee seene by some to satisfye others.

This is a powerful thesis indeed, one that moves from a critical view of royal power, to one of the contract of rulership itself, seen here as 'reciprocall bondage', where the ruler is as unfree as his slavish subjects.

In a slightly later passage, Roe emphasizes the theatrical quality of the Mughal court, and this is a remark that has attracted the attention of a number of recent analysts. Is this a way for King James's ambassador to suggest that the Mughals are somehow unreal, or a way of suggesting affinities between all sorts of courts, which do after all have rituals, ceremonies and their share of theatre? The passage in question runs: 'This sitting out hath soe much affinitye with a theatre – the manner of the king in his gallery; the great men lifted on a stage as actors; the vulgar below gazing on – that an easy description will informe of the place and fashion.' I would argue, however, that this is not a light view of play-acting, but is intimately linked to the earlier passage. This is a repetitive theatre that must be played out again and again, where no one – not even the king – can change the rules. It is difficult to read in this view of the Mughal court a positive appreciation by an open-minded visiting dignitary, as some scholars have wished to have us believe, the more so since theatre to the early seventeenth-century Englishman most commonly carried with it associations of immorality and tawdriness.

The major aspect of Roe's account is its ability to drive a wedge between the ruler as person, and the Mughal court-system. Jahangir, as he emerges in this account, is not an entirely despicable man, and Roe wishes his readers to believe that at a human level a certain complicity grew between him and the Mughal. We have already noted his claim that the so-called *ghusl khana* is a place 'to which are none admitted but of great qualetye'; it then turns out that Roe is one of those who can claim this degree of consideration. Similarly, after an occasion in early September 1616, when an exchange of sundry presents had taken place, Roe reports that 'hee [Jahangir] made frolique, and sent mee woord hee more esteemed mee than ever any Francke'; and for his part, the English ambassador declares that 'so drincking and commanding others, His Majestie and all his lords became the finest men I ever saw, of a thowsand humors'.[15] It is all-too-easy to misread such passages (including one where we learn that Jahangir is 'of countenance cheerfull, and not proud in nature, but by habitt and custome; for a nights he is veary affable, and full of gentle conversation'), and conclude sententiously that 'their initial deep incomprehension about the other's cognitive world impelled each to seek a language in which to achieve a mutual understanding'.[16] In order to do so, we must deliberately shut our eyes to other passages, written by Roe much later, indeed at a time when – according to a 'learning-by-doing' view of communication – the ambassador and the ruler should have come ever closer cognitively. Yet, here is Roe writing from Ahmadabad to Sir Thomas Smythe, in February 1618:

> These Princes and Customes are so Contrarie to ours that I shall travell much in myne owne eies and performe little in yours. Ther is no treaty wher ther is soe much Prid, nor no assurance wher is no fayth. All I can doe is to serve present turnes. The People are weary of us. The King hath no content, who expectes great Presentes and Jewelles, and reguardes no trade but what feedes his unsatiable appetite after stones, rich and rare Peices of any kind of arte.[17]

Or again, in a letter written to James I from Jahangir's camp at much the same time as the above letter:

> To the monarch with whom I reside your Maiesties minister I delivered your Royall letters and presents, which were received with as much honor as their barbarous pride and Custtoomes affoord to any the like from any Absolute Prince, though far inferior to that respect due unto them. I have stroven, sometimes to displeasure, with their tricks of unmeasured greatness rather than to endure any scorne. I dare not dissemble with Your Majestie, their pride and dull ignorance takes all things done of duty, and this yeare I was enforced to stande out for the honor of your free guifts, which were sceazed uncivilly. I have sought to meyntayne upright Your Majesties greatenes and dignitie, and withall to effect the ends of the merchant; but these two sometyme cross one another, seeing ther is no way to treate with so monstrous overweening that

15 Foster, *The Embassy*, pp. 225–6.
16 William R. Pinch, 'Same Difference in India and Europe', *History and Theory*, 38, no. 3 (1999), 389–407, citation on p. 407.
17 Foster, *The Embassy*, p. 466. A fruitful comparison may be made between Roe's image of the Mughal court and corruption in the court of James I itself, for which see Linda Levy Peck, *Court patronage and corruption in early Stuart England* (London, 1993).

acknowledgeth no equall. He [Jahangir] hath written Your Majestie a lettre full of good woords, but barren of all true effect.[18]

Roe's prejudices, from the time of his arrival in India, were clearly in this direction, and we can see that two years' stay has not fundamentally altered his view of the Mughal empire, even if the details are more nuanced and have gained far more local colour over time. The two letters cited above can be read as a direct continuation of another, written to the George Abbot, Archbishop of Canterbury, as early as January 1616:

A discription of the land, customes, and manners, with other accidents, are fitter for wynter nights. They are eyther ordinary, or mingled with much barbarisme. Lawes they have none written. The Kyngs judgement bynds, who sitts and gives sentence with much patience, once weakly, both in capitall and criminall causes; wher some tymes he sees the execution done by his eliphants, with two much delight in blood. His governors of provinces rule by his firmanes, which is a breefe lettre authorising them. They take life and goods at pleasure.[19]

Here then is a key to understanding Roe's presentation of the Mughal to the English reader, an understanding which I would contend is far less subtle than that of the Portuguese and Spanish Jesuits at the Mughal court, and far more apt to drift towards the *topoi* of Oriental Despotism: absence of laws, arbitrary royal power and a penchant for blood-lust, absence of private property.[20] Like his chaplain, Edward Terry, also the author of an account on Jahangir's court, Roe presents the nature of power in the Mughal domains as unreasonable, even if it must be tolerated by the Company for reasons of *realpolitik*.[21] Where he differs from Terry, whose lampooning of the Mughal is far cruder and often requires him to contradict Roe in details, is in the fact that the ambassador must use the Mughal ruler to advance himself. Thus, the account of Thomas Roe, while denigrating the Mughal state and what it stands for (its 'habitt and custome'), cannot present the embassy itself as a failure. Rather, the ambassador must appear a man of rare ability and understanding, who manages to insinuate himself into the rank of the intimates of the emperor, in sum a diplomat who is better received than all his rivals, be they the envoys of other European powers, or the Safavids and Ottomans. If the eventual results of this embassy fall short of the Company's requirements, it is the fault of the Mughals, and that too not as individuals but as

---

18 Foster, *The Embassy*, pp. 464–5.

19 Foster, *The Embassy*, p. 104.

20 On the Jesuit view of Mughals, see *inter alia*, Muzaffar Alam and Sanjay Subrahmanyam, 'Witnessing Transition: Views on the End of the Akbari Dispensation', in *The Making of History: Essays presented to Irfan Habib*, eds K.N. Panikkar, Terence J. Byres and Utsa Patnaik (New Delhi, 2000), pp. 104–40.

21 Reverend Edward Terry, *A voyage to East-India: Wherein some things are taken notice of in our passage thither, but many more in our abode there, within that rich and most spacious empire of the great Mogol* (London, 1655).

a court-society. This view, that Roe successfully managed to communicate of himself, explains the subsequent success he had in his public career. In order that such an image be the dominant one, Roe also had to suppress or discredit some of his own critics in the Company, men such as the factors John Brown and William Biddulph, the former the author of a trenchant letter of complaint to London, accusing the ambassador of waste, extravagance, vanity and dubious private trade, which only earned the letter-writer a sharp censure from the Company. What triumphed eventually was the account of Roe himself, and of his greatest supporter and admirer, the Rev. Edward Terry.

Recent historians have unfortunately displaced the reading of Roe into quite another sphere. Rather than ask what his views of the Mughal political system were, and how they affected his representation both of that empire and of his own embassy, the recent debate has chosen to focus on the problem of 'translatability' or (as historians and sociologists of science might put it), 'commensurability'. Thus, Bernard Cohn has read Roe's account in order to argue that while 'the British in seventeenth-century India operated on the idea that everything and everyone had a "price"', Indians had quite another view of matters. This opposition is brought out further by him in two lapidary phrases: on the one hand, 'Europeans of the seventeenth century lived in a world of signs and correspondences'; while on the other hand, 'Hindus and Muslims operated with an unbounded substantive theory of objects and persons.'[22] Reproaching the ambassador for not having attended the learned courses of Professors Marriott and Inden at the University of Chicago (where such an unbounded substantive theory might have been explicated), the American scholar thus makes himself an easy target for other writers, eager to establish that Roe in fact comprehended pretty much everything in Mughal India, and spoke in a wholly transparent manner. Thus, William Pinch's recent riposte to Cohn claims the following:

> The Mughal darbar and Elizabethan-Jacobean court were differently conceived in many obvious and subtle ways – certainly in terms of their ritual styles and the objects used to convey political authority and power, not to mention their traditions of statecraft. But these were primarily differences of detail, not of substance. The differences were translatable.[23]

---

[22] Bernard S. Cohn, *Colonialism and its Forms of Knowledge: The British in India* (Princeton, 1996), pp. 18–19 (an essay first published in 1985). Cohn's ideas with respect to Roe were further extended in Kate Teltscher, *India Inscribed: European and British Writing on India, 1600–1800* (Delhi, 1995).

[23] Pinch, 'Same Difference', p. 404. Pinch criticizes both Cohn and Teltscher, at times on grounds that are sound; but, as will become apparent, he is extremely selective in reading Roe as well as in understanding the context. In part, this is because of Pinch's desire to demote Cohn's view, in favour of his own preferred alternative, namely C.A. Bayly, *Empire and Information: Intelligence Gathering and Social Communication in India, 1780–1870* (Cambridge, 1996).

This is manifestly less-than-satisfactory as a formulation. What does it mean to say that Mughal court culture was 'translatable' to an English reader in Stuart England? At first sight, it may appear to mean that it was in fact translated, a claim that is, however, quite easily dismissed. The reader of Roe's account in England emerged with a particular view of the workings of power in the Mughal empire, which cannot be presented as some neutral 'translation'. A second possibility is to state that, notionally, Mughal concepts were translatable; but it then remains to specify the real circumstances under which this theoretical translatability could be put into practice. Here, our problems are certainly not solved by claiming (as Pinch does, in a telling ahistorical formula) that one can appeal to concepts that are 'emblematic of all human relationships'. The argument can be advanced further by contrasting Roe's account to that of another visitor to Jahangir's court.

Excursus on Mutribi

The visitor in question was from Central Asia (Samarqand to be precise), a poet and scholar by the name of Mutribi Samarqandi.[24] Over two months, in 1627 (AH 1036), Mutribi was at the Mughal court in Lahore, in the last years of Jahangir's reign, and his work consists of an account of 24 conversations with the Mughal emperor.[25] These conversations were conducted in Persian, a language that both Mutribi and Jahangir spoke with native fluency (Jahangir also knew some Turkish, Arabic and Braj Bhasha, with perhaps a smattering of Portuguese); Thomas Roe, on the other hand, was obviously constantly obliged to take recourse to interpreters, a fact that he is often discreet about, but which must surely have influenced the very nature of the enterprise of conceptual 'translation' we have spoken of above, when that translation passed literally through language, and was not simply a question of interpreting gestures, visual events or physical signs. The account of Mutribi's dealings with Jahangir, initially through the mediation of a certain Khwaja Fakhr-ud-Din Husain, was penned within a few months after their occurrence, when the recollections were still fresh in the author's mind. The text is of course court-literature, and meant to be read by even the Mughals themselves; this had a double significance, for if on the one hand Mutribi (unlike Roe) could not be critical of Jahangir even if he wished

---

24 On Mutribi, see Surinder Singh, 'The Indian Memoirs of Mutribi Samarqandi', in *Proceedings of the Indian History Congress, 55th Session, Aligarh, 1994* (Delhi, 1995), 345–54, and Richard Foltz, 'Two Seventeenth-Century Central Asian Travellers to Mughal India', *Journal of the Royal Asiatic Society of Great Britain and Ireland*, series 3, 6/3 (1996), 367–77.

25 For the text, see *Khatirat-i-Mutribi Samarqandi (being the Memoirs of Mutribi's sessions with Emperor Jahangir)*, ed. Abdul Ghani Mirzoyef (Karachi, 1977). A recent translation, somewhat unsatisfactory, is by Richard C. Foltz, *Conversations with Emperor Jahangir by 'Mutribi' ul-Asamm of Samarqand* (Costa Mesa, 1998). I am grateful to Muzaffar Alam, with whom I have extensively discussed this text.

to be, on the other hand, everything he wrote was subject to evaluation (and ver-
ification) by the other courtiers. Herein lies one of the greatest problems with
Roe's account, one which has been systematically down-played: we simply do not
know how to evaluate the truth-value of his narrative. Save in those instances
when the Reverend Terry was present, no other account exists of Roe's dealings,
for the Mughal sources more or less entirely ignore him. As for Terry, it is unclear
whether his own text can be regarded as an independent one from that of Roe;
the two were clearly in close contact and depended on the same interpreters,
with Terry sometimes adding his own gloss in view of his greater hostility to the
Mughals.

The meetings between Mutribi and Jahangir are described using the term
waqi'a – 'happenings' – and as noted above they are 24 in number. We shall
focus on a few of them in order to present their flavour. In the first meeting,
Jahangir asks Mutribi why, after spending a month in Lahore, he had only now
come to the court. Mutribi answers that he was finishing a text in honour of
Jahangir (the *Nuskha-yi Ziba-yi Jahangiri*), and had only now found a
chronogram to close it. On being presented the text, Jahangir is pleased, and asks
Mutribi whether he would rather stay in the Mughal court, go back to his home-
land, or whether he wanted to make the *hajj* to Mecca and Medina. Mutribi, as
an etiquette-bound courtier, says that he is at the ruler's disposal. Jahangir then
tells him he has four gifts for him, but that he would give them one after the
other. They were, money for his expenses, a *khil'at* (ceremonial and honorific
robe) to wear, a horse and saddle, and a slave to serve him. Which of these did he
want first? Mutribi replies in poetry on the importance of money (*zar*), and is at
once given a platter full of money, amounting to 1,000 rupees. Besides, he is
given 500 rupees on the part of Nur Jahan. Though the visitor is from Central
Asia and not from India, no cognitive dissonance is reported, nor is any 'noise' to
be discerned in the account thus far. True, it may be argued, Mutribi does not
have the critical distance of Roe. He is not likely to say, when a dance has been
arranged in his honour, 'some whoores did sing and dance'.

The stage has now been set for the subsequent meetings and conversations
between Mutribi and Jahangir, which will have a more explicitly comparative
and reflective nature for the most part. In the second meeting, the ruler's
brother-in-law Asaf Khan (who plays a major and somewhat sinister role in
Roe's account), and several other *amirs* are present. Jahangir now enquires on
the state of the burial-place of his illustrious ancestor, Timur, in Samarqand, and
Mutribi replies that details were to be found in his text, the *Nuskha-yi Ziba*. A
discussion ensues, at the end of which Mutribi is given a *khil'at*, a Kashmiri
shawl, a turban and other gifts; his son Muhammad 'Ali too is given expensive
brocade clothes. The horse and the saddle were saved up for the next day. We
have now understood that Mutribi represents a window into Central Asia for
Jahangir, as a sort of authentic eyewitness (*bayan*) to affairs in Transoxania; but,
like the Europeans at the court, he also has a certain potential in the matter of
'wonders'. The next day, some European merchants (*tujjar-i firang*) who are
present at the court, give what are termed 'tributes' (*peshkash-ha*) to Jahangir. A

small booklet (*kitabcha*), four fingers long, fits in the emperor's hand; it has 12 folios, and the paper has a brownish colour. The book is in a small locked box, and calling Mutribi, Jahangir asks him to guess which book it is. The former confesses ignorance, and the emperor opens the box and gives it to him with a stick, and explains that one could write on the paper with it, but also rub the writing off. Mutribi is astonished, and by way of demonstration, Jahangir writes a verse in the book, shows it to him, and then rubs it off. Jokingly, he even offers to sell the book and pencil to Mutribi for a rupee. The latter superstitiously refuses, saying that it is magical (*tilism*), and might harm him; besides he does not have any money on him. Jahangir laughingly gives it to him as a gift, assuring him it is harmless. Mutribi reports his intention to carry it back to Turan, and give it to the ruler there, Imam Quli Khan, as a valuable gift from Hindustan.

In the fourth meeting, the intimacy between ruler and visitor has begun to grow. Matters take a literary turn, as Jahangir has by now read Mutribi's book, and even comments on a verse in it. Once more we see, that as with visitors and envoys from the Ottoman domains (Seyyidi ʿAli Reʾis at Humayun's court) or Iran, the Mughal ruler has a common set of cultural resources with Mutribi on which to fall back, points of mutual reference that mean nothing to Roe.[26] Again, it is conceivable that this might not have been so. Let us imagine that instead of Roe, the English Company had sent George Strachan, the Scottish polyglot and sometime resident of Baghdad and Isfahan in the 1610s and 1620s.[27] Strachan could doubtless have conversed with Jahangir on far more familiar ground, in view of his knowledge of Persian, Turkish and Arabic, in a spirit rather closer to that of the Jesuits at the Mughal court. Yet, would the Company have sent such a man, in view of their own search for 'one of extraordinarye partes', of high social standing?

A few further aspects of Mutribi's account sharpen the contrast further, demonstrating the distinction between 'insiders' and 'outsiders', a distinction which recent protagonists of the cultural-translation thesis continue to obfuscate. Consider the following anecdote relating to Mughal painting. On a certain occasion, Mutribi reports, Jahangir wishes to test him. A freshly made set of portraits from the Mughal ateliers is brought before Mutribi, who sees that they depict the former ruler of Turan, ʿAbdullah Khan Uzbek and his son ʿAbdul-Momin Khan. As someone who has known these individuals, Mutribi is meant to give his seal of approval to the portraits. However, he tells Jahangir that there are defects in the representation of ʿAbdullah Khan's chin, and his son's headgear. At this, the painter is at once summoned, and asked to correct the paintings, which he does by the next day. Another courtier from Transoxania expresses a

---

26 On Seyyidi ʿAli at Humayun's court, see Seyyidi ʿAli Reʾis, *Le miroir des pays. Une anabase ottomane à travers l'Inde et l'Asie centrale*, trans. Jean-Louis Bacqué-Grammont (Paris, 1999); and for a modern Turkish text, Seydi Ali Reis, *Mirʾâtü'l-Memâlik*, ed. Mehmet Kiremit (Ankara, 1999).

27 G.L. Dellavida, *George Strachan: Memorials of a wandering Scottish scholar of the seventeenth century* (Aberdeen, 1956).

contrary opinion on 'Abdul-Momin Khan's headgear, but finally Mutribi's view is upheld. This may be contrasted to a celebrated episode in Roe's account, again on the subject of Mughal painting. Here, Jahangir reportedly boasts to Roe that the painters of his atelier can reproduce any European portrait; the challenge is taken up, and though Roe notes that the copies were well done, 'yet I showed myne owne and the differences, which were in arte apparant, but not to be judged by a common eye'.[28] The text has been much commented on, amongst others by historians of Mughal art: for our purposes, the significance of the incident lies in the fact that while Mutribi is concerned to show the meticulous nature of Mughal portraiture and the confidence that was vested in him as a judge of its quality, Roe's is a grudging acceptance of the painter's skills, framed in a story in which the skills that are brought to the fore are his own, for he tells the reader that he does not have a 'common eye'.

The tensions between Jahangir and Roe are most manifest in matters of gifts and money, where the English ambassador shows periodic uncertainty with how to deal with payments as well as how to receive gifts. This may again be contrasted with Mutribi, who negotiates such matters with consummate skill. We see this on the occasion of a celebration, when Mutribi receives two platters of coins, worth two thousand rupees, and other valuables. As a poet, he then recites verses in the court in praise of the emperor, and pleased in turn at the verses, Jahangir for his part gives him more gifts. Yet, the play between gifts, their value and prices is not entirely avoided; rather it is very playfully dealt with. Thus, Jahangir asks Mutribi what sort of horse and saddle he wants, and the latter asks rather directly for the most expensive sort. A discussion then ensues on the relative quality of different sorts, and Mutribi finally receives an Iraqi horse (rather than a less valuable Turkish one), but a saddle of velvet (rather than a more expensive but less durable one in scarlet). Similarly, in the 16th meeting, Jahangir auctions three slaves in the court, while proclaiming (in a semi-serious fashion) that of all the professions only trade is respectable in the eyes of Islam, an inversion of the usual clichés concerning the culture of the Mughal court.

Yet, these meetings are not entirely devoid of cut and thrust, or repartee between emperor and poet. Thus, in another meeting, Jahangir quite bluntly asks Mutribi whether he thinks white skin is better than black, obviously wishing to test our Central Asian's colour prejudices in respect of Indians. Mutribi replies evasively, saying that it was all a matter of opinion; but Jahangir insists that he wants to know his opinion. Mutribi for his part says that he could only judge by seeing (*binam wa guyam*), and so Jahangir advises him to look right and left and decide. On the right, Mutribi finds a dark young Indian princeling (*rajabacha*), who was extremely handsome, but equally, on the left, a fair and handsome boy is standing, who dazzles Mutribi's eyes. How can he now decide? Looking twice at each, he says to Jahangir that it is not a matter of dark and fair but of the pleas-

[28] Foster, *The Embassy*, pp. 189–90, 199.

antness of the countenance. Jahangir is pleased at the tact of the response, and recites a verse in the same sense, to which Mutribi responds with a supporting *hadith*, in which the Prophet says that his brother Yusuf was fair, but it was he whose countenance had a more agreeable (literally 'salty') quality (*malahat*).[29]

There are hence two travellers within Mutribi's text, the author himself and Jahangir. If Mutribi makes comparisons between Central Asia and Hindustan, based on what he sees (and the insistent emphasis is on the eye, and its superiority to hearsay), Jahangir transforms himself through Mutribi (and, undoubtedly, scores of others like him) into an armchair traveller. If the wonders and the superiority of Hindustan are brought out, it is by constant contrast to Transoxania, and in effect Mutribi becomes the vehicle for the expression of Jahangir's opinions and prejudices. Yet, the account has a vastly different tone and texture to Roe's account, not only because of the ambassador's preoccupation with humiliation (real or imagined), and his inability to participate in the court as he might have done in France or Sweden; the key difference is that Roe's account is caught in a matrix of comparing two political systems and two civilities, whereas this represents a non-issue for Mutribi. We cannot entirely neglect another aspect either (which Cohn also stresses correctly), namely the distance imposed by layers of interpreters and translators on Roe's dealing with Jahangir. A flagrant instance is that of 13 March 1616, when Roe appears in the *ghusl khana* with an Italian interpreter, who is kept out; he then pleads that 'I could speak no Portugall, and soe wanted means to satisfie His Majestie.' The interpreter is hence admitted, and Roe communicates to him in what he himself admits is 'broken Spanish'. Jahangir for his part throws a few Portuguese words into his own conversation, and at a later stage in the proceedings, when an altercation arises with Prince Khurram, further interposes a Safavid prince called Mir Miran into the chain of translation. Thus, we eventually have Roe speaking broken Spanish to an Italian interpreter, who translates into Turkish; the Safavid prince then translates this Turkish into Persian.[30] To imagine then, as Roe does, that his arguments carried all before them ('the Jesuite and all the Portugalls side fell in; in soe much that I explaynd my selfe fully concerning them'), requires a certain optimism. It is not inconceivable that Roe failed to make much of an impression on the Mughals, which would explain why Jahangir, who – on the accumulated evidence of the period, including Mutribi's account – showed considerable geographical curiosity, as well as curiosity concerning flora and fauna, as well as ethnographic difference, found so little of interest in Roe.

---

29 The translation by Foltz, *Conversations*, pp. 48–50, misunderstands much of the text, confounding the expression for adolescent peach-fuzz on the youths' cheeks for their 'candy green colour'.

30 Foster, *The Embassy*, pp. 128–31.

From Oxford to Cambridge

After Thomas Roe, the English Company desisted from sending further ambassadors to the Mughal court for the greater part of the seventeenth century. We know of Dutch and even French representatives at the court of Shahjahan and Aurangzeb, and Englishmen who were sent for example to Golkonda, but it was not until the very end of the seventeenth century that another English ambassador sought to follow in Sir Thomas's footsteps.[31] This is Sir William Norris, a rather more obscure character than his predecessor, and in some sense symmetrically located: if Thomas Roe was a rough contemporary of Thomas Hobbes at Oxford, William Norris was at Trinity College, Cambridge at the same time as Sir Isaac Newton. This section will be concerned with Norris's failed embassy to the court of Aurangzeb, an embassy which in certain respects is in marked contrast both to that of his predecessor, Roe, who turned diplomatic failure into rhetorical success, and later embassies of the eighteenth century (such as that of John Surman), which actually gained the English far greater advantages than in the previous century.

The circumstances surrounding Norris's embassy were already substantially different from those attending the despatch of Roe. From the middle decades of the seventeenth century, English trade to India, which had earlier been on a rather precarious footing, assumed more substantial proportions. Besides Gujarat, which had been the mainstay of their early operations, and Roe's own main concern, the English Company had established factories in Bengal, and also on the Coromandel coast of south-eastern India, where Fort St George in Madras was established in 1639. In the mid-1660s, the Crown acquired territories in Bombay as part of a negotiation with the Portuguese monarchy, and by this means the Company's implantation both within Mughal territories and outside them had been strengthened. The only serious rival operation that had been mounted, namely Courteen's Association in the 1630s and 1640s, did not prove to have staying power.[32] It was only in the last quarter of the century that other English merchants, taking advantage of the fluid political situation in England, were able periodically to penetrate into Asian waters. The increasingly threadbare character of the Company's monopoly allowed their rivals to engage in trade on the Cape Route, but also to combine commerce with filibustering. But even here, the nuisance value of the 'interlopers' was probably greater than their real economic clout. In any event, by 1686 it seemed the Old Company had won its battle. Sir Josia Child, its head, was close to the reigning monarch James

---

[31] For some examples of Dutch and French envoys, see François de La Boullaye-Le Gouz, *Les voyages et observations du sieur de La Boullaye-Le Gouz*, ed. Jacques de Maussion de Favières (Paris, 1994), and A.J. Bernet Kempers, ed., *Journaal van Dircq van Adrichem's hofreis naar den Groot-Mogol Aurangzeb, 1662* (The Hague, 1941).

[32] No full-length study of Courteen's Association exists to date; but see, for an excellent ringside view of its operations, *The travels of Peter Mundy in Europe and Asia, 1608–1667*, eds Richard Carnac Temple and L.M. Anstey, 5 vols (London, 1907–36), especially III and IV.

II, and the 'interlopers' seemed to be in difficulty. But the Glorious Revolution of 1688 changed the politico-commercial map considerably, and a different set of cards was now dealt out to the rival groups. Kirti Chaudhuri and Jonathan Israel have written recently of these changes:

> It is not generally appreciated by historians of early modern Europe that 1688 marked not only a 'revolution' in Britain but also one in the Indian Ocean. During 1687–8 the English East India Company, under the leadership of Sir Josia Child, decided to wage a war on the Mughal emperor and demonstrate to the VOC [Dutch Company] that its naval power was more than a match for the Dutch organization. Tactically, the war went badly for the Company but in the long run its strategic aims were fully realized.[33]

In the short run, the news of the defeat that came back to England in 1689 could not have come at a worse time for the Company. A parliamentary committee was set up to look into the Company's affairs, for it was seen as a Jacobite and Tory organization, whose detractors had every reason to want an alternative structure in place of the old merchant oligarchy that held sway. Thus, ten years after the Glorious Revolution, in 1698, the Old Company was told to wind up its affairs, with its charter ending on 29 September 1701. A New Company was formed, with its merchant members promising much aid to William III. But since the Old Company still dominated in India, where it was well-entrenched, it was thought wiser to send an ambassador to sort things out between the rivals, and also explain matters to the Mughal ruler.

The man chosen was Sir William Norris, an MP from Liverpool, who like Roe had no previous experience of India before being sent out. In this, the English strategy was quite different (in both cases) from that of the Dutch, who always sent out experienced hands – men like Adrichem, Bacherus or Ketelaar – rather than innocents, whose main asset would be their social standing and political connections in Europe. Norris eventually set sail from Plymouth on 21 January 1699, and in September that year, his ship anchored off Fort St George (Madras), where he was given a churlish reception by the governor, Thomas Pitt. His idea was to go to the Mughal port of Masulipatnam, to accede from there to Aurangzeb's camp, in view of the fact that the Mughal emperor found himself in the Deccan, still fighting his interminable campaigns of southward expansion. But Norris could not make much headway. In 1700, after nearly a year at Bandar Masulipatnam, he eventually decided to try access to the Mughal royal camp by a westerly route, and set sail for Surat. Eventually, in January 1701, two years after his departure from England, Norris began to make his way overland from Surat to the Deccan, notably to the obscure town of Panhala, where the emperor was. However, while on his way, Norris received destabilizing news from home. It

---

33 K.N. Chaudhuri and Jonathan I. Israel, 'The English and Dutch East India Companies and the Glorious Revolution of 1688–89', in *The Anglo-Dutch Moment: Essays on the Glorious Revolution and its world impact*, ed. Jonathan I. Israel (Cambridge, 1991), pp. 407–38, citation on p. 407.

turned out that in his absence, the Old Company has managed to regain ground in London, and even obtained a new Act of Parliament, renewing its existence, and eventually paving for the way for the merger of the two into the United East India Company (a process that was completed only in 1709). Norris was thus in a bad way, with his own legitimacy (as ambassador of the New Company) severely compromised. Eventually, after obtaining little of note, he left the imperial camp in November 1701 and painfully reached Surat overland in March 1702. By now, however, he had also lost credit with the New Company, which considered him a waste of money, since he had by then spent the astronomical sum of some eighty thousand pounds. He thus obtained a vessel, the *Scipio*, with difficulty for his return voyage, sailed to Mauritius, and then while on his way to the Cape, died of dysentery on board ship on 10 October 1702.[34]

It would appear that Norris had left behind six volumes of materials dealing with the embassy, entitled 'Journalls of transactions and observations from the time of His Excellency's leaving England to the 14th of September [1702]'. However, only four of the six volumes are extant, two in the Bodleian Library at Oxford, in the Rawlinson Collection, and two others at the Public Record Office, in London. The first of these volumes runs from Norris's arrival at Porto Novo in September 1699 to early May 1700; and the second runs from 10 December 1700, the date of his arrival at Surat, to 23 April 1701, while at Panhala. The other two volumes in the Public Record Office, are in fact the fifth and sixth of the series; one runs from 26 September 1701 to 12 March 1702, when Norris eventually returns to Surat, while the last tome continues the chronology to 14 September 1702. Finally, there is a fragment of his journal, concerned with the outward voyage, and dated from the departure from England to 5 January 1699, while at Cape Verde.[35]

These quite extensive papers have, however, been the object of little attention, and certainly Norris did not enjoy the contemporary notoriety of Sir Thomas Roe.[36] We are, however, quite well informed on the subject of Norris himself. Originally from a Lancashire family, William Norris came from the branch which resided at Speke Hall on the north bank of the Mersey. His father was Thomas Norris, who fought on the royalist side in the civil war; while his mother Katherine, was the daughter of Sir Henry Garraway. Of the couple's seven sons and four daughters, the eldest son, also Thomas Norris, inherited the property in 1686, while William Norris, the second son (born at Speke Hall in 1657) was first

---

[34] Entry for Sir William Norris by Stanley Lane-Poole, *The Dictionary of National Biography*, eds Sir Leslie Stephen and Sir Sidney Lee, XIV, 589–91.

[35] Bodleian Library, Oxford, Rawlinson Collection, C. 912 and C. 913; the other two volumes are in the Public Record Office, Kew, as CO 77/50 and CO 77/51. The fragment of his journal is to be found in the British Library, Oriental and India Office Collections, Original Correspondence No. 54, dated from the departure from England to 5/1/1699 at Cape Verde.

[36] The best account to date is H.H. Das, *The Norris Embassy to Aurangzib (1699–1702)*, condensed and arranged by S.C. Sarkar (Calcutta, 1959).

sent to Westminster School in 1672 as King's Scholar, entering Trinity College, Cambridge in June 1675, where he distinguished himself as a poet and a scholar of Greek. Norris eventually graduated in 1678 and was made minor Fellow of Trinity in October 1681, receiving an MA in 1682 and being raised to the rank of major Fellow during the same year, in which capacity he continued until Christmas 1690. A political profile also begins to emerge in these years. In 1686–87, Norris was delegate for the University and involved in a dispute with James II in which the Vice-Chancellor, Dr John Peachell, was deprived of his office in May 1687. His sympathies were clear enough by 1688, and it comes as no surprise that in 1689 Norris writes a Latin poem praising William and Mary and their accession to the throne. In December 1689, he marries Elizabeth Poxfellen (d.1713), widow of Nicholas Poxfellen; his wife too was closely connected to anti-Tory politics, in part through Lord Ranelagh. By the early 1690s, William Norris's position as a Whig was clear, and his political career was clearly in the ascendant. In 1694, he helped negotiate the Charter granted to Liverpool by the Crown, and the next year, succeeded his brother Thomas, as MP from Liverpool. He was also made Baronet in December 1698, with the express purpose of elevating his rank for his mission to India.

Norris's account, which has yet to be published for the most part, can never-theless be quite easily contrasted with that of Roe in terms of its tone and preoc-cupations. Where Roe is almost exclusively concerned with Mughal political society, notably the court and its intrigues but also the doings of princes of the blood, governors and the like, Norris is far more of a naturalist and an observer of society at large, stopping to examine exotic trees and lizards, commenting on the monsoon winds, on marriage-processions and popular festivals. The familiar tension between political observation and ethnography thus surfaces when we contrast these two figures, and it is further strengthened perhaps by their differing circumstances. Roe's political activity was more or less incessant in India, whereas Norris had a long, more-or-less forced, stay in Masulipatnam, where he was able to accumulate a rather large number of observations on Indian society, which we will have occasion to comment on below.[37] We must also take into account the fact of a significant gap in Norris's papers at the time when his courtly political activity is most intense; this is for the period from 23 April 1701, while at Panhala, to 26 September of the same year. On the other hand, the parallels between the two men are also striking at times, not least their penchant for private trade (Norris's brother Edward, who accompanied him on the embassy, carried back a cargo worth some 87,000 rupees on his account). Neither ambassador really succeeded in obtaining what he wanted from the Mughal court, and both embassies ended on rather sour notes. However, this did not place the basic functioning of English trade in India under a cloud: embassy

---

[37] On Masulipatnam in this period, and the English Company's troubles concerning this port-town, see Sanjay Subrahmanyam, 'Masulipatnam Revisited, 1550–1750: A Survey and Some Speculations', *Gateways to Asia: Port Cities of Asia in the 13th–20th Centuries*, ed. Frank Broeze (London and New York, 1997), pp. 33–65.

or not, the Company continued to conduct business (and more) pretty much as usual after the ambassador had returned, and in the early 1700s even went from strength to strength, with the gradual decline of its main competitor, the Dutch East India Company.

Norris was aware in his own way of the possible comparisons with Roe, who obviously enjoyed a rather good reputation as a diplomat at the end of the seventeenth century. He remarks for example, on arriving in India: 'It was a little remarkable yt I should land ye same day of ye month on ye Coast of India as Sr Tho: Roe did who was ye only Ambassadour ever sent from England to these parts before Ano 1615 25ᵗʰ 7ber att Suratt he landed.'[38] On landing at Surat, Roe claimed to have been rather badly treated by the local authorities, but Norris did not immediately have much to complain about on his arrival. Rather, the initial impression he gives us of society in Masulipatnam is rather favourable, it being only the local climate that did not agree with him, especially when 'ye Raines begin to be dryd up & ye Morasses wch almost encompass ye Town begin to be swampy'. He was given a house that he describes as 'ye K[ing] of Golcundas pallace when he fled into these parts pursud by ye Mogull (. . .) & is not only a very hansome stately & pleasant but a convenient house large enough to Reeceive me & all my Retinue with greate ease to every Body. It stands high & comands & over lookes ye whole Town.' Even the local entertainment made a more favourable impression on him than on his Oxonian predecessor: he appreciated 'a Company of Dancinge women who are much prized & admird by everybody & indeed are very nimble & active', as he would later greatly admire a company of jugglers and acrobats.

But over the next few months, his observations on the society itself begin to sharpen as he begins to enumerate the different groups there: 'Moors' and 'Gentoos' to be sure, but also amongst them 'Bramines', and other 'casts' and 'sects' on whom he attempts to gather information, apparently through the Company's Indian brokers and agents. On the Brahmins, for example, he has this comment to offer:

> Ye Generality of people Greate & small are soe ignorant & foolish as to beleive whatever ye Bramines tell them & depend upon it for certainty (. . .). [The Bramines] themselves are none of ye wisest sort but cunninge enough however in this particular to leade ye Rest of ye people by ye noses & soe their pretended knowledge is very advantageous & bringes ym in greate profitt.[39]

Further, he also has a general theory concerning the historical evolution of the Hindu (or 'Gentoo') religion, for which he has rather more sympathy all in all than for Islam, which he also has occasion to observe at close quarters while at Masulipatnam. Thus:

---

[38] Das, *The Norris Embassy*, p. 115.
[39] *Ibid.*, p. 152.

The account I have been yett able to gett in discoursinge wth their Learned Bramines about their Religion convinces me beyond all contradiction that Christianity was formerly planted here & you may most clearly Trace ye ffootstepps & very foundations of it in ye Traditions they give you of Their Religion, Length of Time havinge worn out both ye Truth & practise of it ye Gentoos beinge now universally given up to Idolatry though some of ye most understanding who have livd amongst ye English seeme to deny it & not to practise it. I shall take another occasion to Treate more largely on this Subject. But already I find it very evident yt In ye Gentoo Religion Christianity is to be Tracd & ye Jewish Religion in ye Moores Practise still retaining severall of their solemnitys particularly ye new moons & sabbaths.[40]

The religion of the Brahmins and other Hindus is thus taken to be a degenerate version of Christianity that the passage of time has 'worn out'; this hypothesis bears a certain resemblance to the claims of earlier Portuguese observers, though these were often based on the legend of St Thomas's apostolate in India.

Norris is understandably anxious to dispel any ideas that he might have any sympathy for the Papists, as we see in his rather odd discussion of the celebration of Muharram in Masulipatnam. Having initially informed the reader that the festival takes place when Muslims commemorate 'ye Death or funerall of Mahomett ye Grand Impostor', he goes on to describe the processions and concludes on this rather interesting and complex note:

I thinke it harde to judge whether ye Moores or Rashbootes are more Ridiculous in their ceremoneys ye Moores favour more of ye papistes & this Ceremony is Like their exposinge ye Relicks off some saint. This I thinke is observable yt there is not ye least clashinge or fallinge out amongst soe many different sects & Casts as there are in this Town. They live quietly & contented amongst one another, each sect & cast enjoyinge his superstition & performinge their Idolatrous worship without any disputes or molestation, & I see no liklyhood of their fallinge out unlesse ye Gentoos & Moores should chance to have a greate feast fall out ye same day & then they must fight it out as boys doe when different parishes meet in walkinge bounds. I heartily pity ym for their Ignorance & mistaken Devotion, but really they might teach Christians this one Lesson who are of different opinions in some points To live quietly & peacably amongst themselves & not Teare one another in pieces.[41]

Here then is an interesting use of the exotic as a mirror, something which Norris is capable of on more than one occasion. Though a classic device, where the traveller turns his distant lens on his own society, Norris's remark, while less than Swiftian in its mordancy, yet represents far more than we find in Roe's account. The experience of the Civil War, in which his own father fought (on the losing side) may have left this trace on Norris. Another instance shows this again with some clarity. This is a passage where Norris describes the discriminatory poll-tax

40 Das, *The Norris Embassy*, p. 163.
41 *Ibid.*, pp. 165–6.

that Aurangzeb has re-introduced, and what he himself thinks of as its deleterious effects on society.

> If Aurengzebe live 3 or 4 yeares longer by severitys usd in fininge & Taxinge ye gentoos above wht they are able to pay, will oblige most of ym to come over to his own Religion wch he uses all possible meanes to propogate. Though ye Gentoos to give ym their due livd strictly sober lives & not soe much given to frequent ye Whores cast as ye moores, yet doe not approve these methods calling ym Inovations, but ye Mogull who is wholly devoted to Religion uses all methods to plant it, & have all under him strict observers of it. In these 3 monthes yt I have been here I have neither seen nor heard of any Drunkenesse disorder Riott or quarellinge in ye Town. It would be well if European City's would take example.[42]

Like the earlier characterization of Indian sects and castes that live 'without any disputes or molestation', this one too can hardly be defended on empirical grounds. The history of Masulipatnam and the records that we dispose, both from the European factories and in Persian, do not authorize this idyllic vision, where no 'Drunkenesse disorder Riott or quarellinge' may be found; but it is nonetheless interesting that Norris is willing to go so far as to hold out these observed aspects of the Indian society as a veritable model for their European counterparts. But matters stop there. For, if Norris's vision of late seventeenth-century Indian society admits of a number of positive aspects (despite the unfortunate religious beliefs and practices of the inhabitants), this approbation cannot be extended by him to the state. For the Mughal state to him is the very epitome of despotism and tyranny, where 'the higher authority squeezes ye Lower and ye Mogull squeezes all'.[43] Not only are these taxes heavy, they are collected moreover by a corrupt state, rotten through and through, with a military system that can hardly be taken seriously either. Here, Norris, like Bernier and Manuzzi, indulges in a characteristic fantasy of how few European soldiers it would take to put paid to Mughal might. In a passage on the fighting style of different groups, such as the Rajputs ('Rashboote'), he concludes:

> [They carry] a sword & buckler for shew & are nimble & expert in shewinge tricks of activity & divertion, but I make no complement to my country att all when I attest yt 20000 English men well armed would beate all ye Mogulls army both Moores & Gentoos (for they are warlick much alike). Their discipline not much exceedinge their Courage & neither to be mentioned ye same day wth what England produces of both. They have one Art of Warr here as in other places, to protracte it for advantage of ye Cheife Comanders, for they say ye Mogulls Army might in much a shorter time have conquered this country but then they should have been layd aside as uselesse, having little more to doe but keepinge a Rajah or two in good order.[44]

---

[42] Das, *The Norris Embassy*, p. 149.
[43] *Ibid.*, p. 149.
[44] *Ibid.*, pp. 124–5.

The overall impression is moreover one where the Gentoos are if anything even weaker and less suited to making war than the Moors. Norris's view of the Mughal state as a Muslim incubus, draining the resources of a predominantly Hindu society, is of course a classic one, nuanced no doubt by his view that within society itself, Hindus and Muslims can normally co-exist without a great deal of tension. The onus is thus clearly on the state and state-power, and Norris, as Christian and Englishman, does leave some rather broad hints in the air on the nature of tyranny and resistance to it. Thus, still commenting on the *jizya*, or differential poll-tax:

> It is said to be ye Mogull's order yt those yt Refuse or are not able to pay this tax shall be obligd to Turn Moores, wch I dare say if they were put to ye Extremity severall of these poore ignorant people are soe well satisfyd in ye sort of worship they are born & bred in yt they would suffer death rather than Embrace Mahoumenatism [*sic*], how much more ought wee who by God's good providence are brought up in ye light of ye Gospell & ye knowledge of Jesus Christ, how much more ought wee to be steadfast in our faith if it ever please God to bring us to ye Tryall.[45]

The 'tryall' in question can of course be read in two ways, first as referring to a situation when the Englishmen resident in India become subject to Mughal taxation, and second – and in my view, far more plausibly – as referring to a hypothetical situation in Europe itself, where the people of one religion becomes subject to a ruler from another. There may be some point to suggesting therefore that Norris identifies Aurangzeb as it were with the Jacobite threat, made all the worse by the nature of the state he rules and the fact that he is a Muslim to boot. But one also senses that the contrast is between peoples who will brook such subjection, and others that will not. Still on the same subject, Norris has this to offer:

> These poore Gentoos are miserably harrassed by ye Moorish Govermt ever Scince ye Mogull conquerd Golcunda & tooke their Kinge prisoner who was one of their cast and used ym kindly, but ye Mogull, who is a great bigott in his own Religion & an Abhorror of their superstition and Idolatry, has already destroyd most of their pagods only for quicknesse sake permitts Jugrenaut wch is ye Cheife & most gainful & will in time bringe ym over to his own Religion though I believe ye Gentoos are 50 for one of ye moores, but an Effeminate people.[46]

Once more, one could point to the flagrant errors of fact and interpretation (the idea that Abu'l Hasan Qutb Shah of Golkonda was to the Gentoos 'one of their cast'), which reflects the cognitive dissonance that runs through the account. But what is of far greater interest is the combination in the portrayal of a tyrannical state run by a 'great bigott' and an 'effeminate people' subject to him, which

---

[45] Das, *The Norris Embassy*, pp. 156–7.
[46] *Ibid.*, p. 157, entry dated November 1699.

rehearses a portrayal that would take deeper root in the years to come. It must take an incurable Panglossian to see this sort of situation as one of 'mutual understanding [that] was the outgrowth of proximity, fueled by basic human curiosity, and achieved by means of fortuitous cultural convergences'.[47]

At the purely human level, it is of course the case that Norris – like Roe – finds some Indians, and even some Mughal courtiers more to his taste than others. A particular target for his annoyance is the *wazir* Asad Khan, described by him as 'ye Greatest & Richest man in ye Empire next ye Mogull & most say Richer then He having amassd vast sums of money by very large Incomes & never paying any body wch makes him generally hated'. The usual accusations of lechery and debauchery follow inevitably: 'They tell us he has 30 wives and 800 other women wth him & has change of 3 or 4 every night wch I thinke might be spard considering his age wch is 90 yeares Old.' Norris then concludes, explaining at the same time his own incapacity to make much diplomatic progress: 'It is impossible to believe how dissolute & luxurious ye lives of these greate men are. The vizier spending his whole time with his women, his eunuchs & pandars, who have liberty of accesse at all times & his secretarys in Relation to business but rarely & yt as ye eunuch pleases.' Even if he were to meet him, it would do the ambassador no good, since the *wazir* allegedly consumes great quantities of 'Hott spiritts wth wch they make themselves drunke every day if they can gett it'.[48] But to Asad Khan is contrasted another figure, namely a certain Yar 'Ali Beg, a high official of the *diwani*, to whom Norris pays the most fulsome compliments:

> [In the] midst of ye most base vitious & corrupt court in ye Universe this minister alone is virtuous. The sole businesse of all other ministers is to gripe squeeze all ye money they can from all people by ye basest & Indirect meanes Imaginable openly & barefaced. This man alone despises riches & is above ye Temptation of any bribe can be offerd. Just to ye greatest nicety & firme to ye Intrest he espouses & not to be disobligd, but by suspectinge his Integrity or offering bribery to debauch it, He is courted by everybody & dreaded by all ye corrupt ministers of the court who stand in aw of his virtue & rigid maners. The virtue of ye antient Romans eminently appears in him & seemes a compound of Ffabritius [and] Cato ye Censer.[49]

We would be mistaken however if we believed that this was seen as a redeeming feature of the Mughal system. Rather, notes Norris, 'it is Impossible for one man to stem ye current of vice & corruption or else this good man's example might be very prevalent'. This then is the very uneven struggle between a system, which

---

[47] Pinch, 'Same Difference', p. 407.
[48] Das, *The Norris Embassy*, pp. 267–8.
[49] *Ibid.*, p. 303. The classical references are to the Roman Republican statesman Marcus Porcius Cato (234–149 BC), known for his austere scrutiny of Senate officials; and to the Roman general and statesman Caius Fabricius Luscinus (d.250 BC), famed for his simplicity and probity.

can only be condemned, and some individuals within it, whose honesty and modestly puritan lifestyle can still be held up, if only to heighten the contrast.

Norris's view of the Mughals assumes a rather ironic dimension in view of the immense luxury and pomp with which the ambassador surrounds himself. We have already noted that the costs of the embassy were eventually judged crippling by the Company itself; Norris himself notes unabashedly that it was his custom to have '14 or 16 good dishes every day' for dinner, and another '6 dishes' for supper. The Italian Niccolò Manuzzi, who had briefly been deputed to aid the embassy, but begged off using the excuse of 'age, blindness and other infirmities', claimed in his *Storia del Mogol*, that Norris 'made a great show, and his expenses were extraordinary', to the point that he was given the nickname of the 'King of England'.[50] The 'pomp and ostentation' to which Manuzzi refers is clear enough when we see how the ambassador presented himself at the Mughal *darbar*, where he was received for the first time on 28 April 1701. Accompanied by carts with brass cannon, much glassware, two Arabian horses, a state palankeen, several crests and flags, musicians on horseback in livery, troopers and pages, and Norris himself in a 'rich palanquin, with Indian embroidered furniture', the embassy may have impressed observers but it also rendered them suspicious by the largesse that was indiscriminately distributed by way of bribes (with the agents of the Old Company competing to out-bribe those of the New). Norris's sour view of the Mughals can only be seen then as a case of the pot calling the kettle black.

A number of the statements made by Norris at various times to Mughal officials can only have increased their sense of suspicion. Besides declaring that his ruler, William III was 'King of England, Scotland, France and Ireland, the richest and most victorious of all Europe', Norris also made strenuous efforts to separate himself from the Old Company, again a tactic that must have seemed less than credible. We may consider a petition directed by him to Aurangzeb, for example, in which he declared:

> This New company is distinct from the old one. This New company has no re-lation whatsoever with the Old company. The Old company is responsible for its obligations, and has no connection with the New company. If the New Company does anything against (the law) or shows any unfairness in its deal-ings and trade then it is the obligation of our King to answer for that.[51]

In view of the accumulated complaints against English freebooters and pirates in the western Indian Ocean, as well as the assurances already given by Sir Nicholas Waite, the Company representative at Surat, on this matter, the position of Norris must have appeared contradictory to his interlocutors in the Mughal

---

[50] William Irvine, trans., *Storia do Mogor; or, Mogul India, 1653–1708, by Niccolao Manucci, Venetian*, 4 vols (London, 1907–1908), III, 300.

[51] OIOC, Mss. Eur. D. 1075, Type Copy of Correspondence dated 1701, translated from the Persian between Sir William Norris, Ambassador of the New English East India Company, and the Mughal Emperor, from OC 57–I, 7572.

court. Who spoke for the New Company, Norris or Waite? Further, what precisely was the status of the Old Company with respect to the King of England?
How did William III claim to be King of France at certain moments, while the
English Company also admitted (in a list submitted to Ruhullah Khan), that
Louis XIV was in fact the King of France? We may well wonder what the Mughal
court would have made of an explanation from Norris's embassy, where it was
stated that European diplomacy functioned in such a way that 'if by the going of
the ambassador, no purpose is reached, and no work is done, and between the
Kings no concord is arrived at, then the ambassador is allowed to depart with
honour and respect; but afterwards they declare war'.[52]

Conclusion

A comparison of the two embassies sent out by the East India Company to the
Mughal court in the seventeenth century should ideally be completed by a
framing of these in a still larger context, where one would be able to compare the
reception and comportment of these embassies with others in Mughal India,
whether Dutch, French, Portuguese or indeed Safavid or Ottoman. This larger
task must await another occasion, but even on the basis of our limited examination of materials certain conclusions seem to impose themselves. It is clear that
what has come to be known as the 'Todorov model' of the cross-cultural encounter cannot hold in this case, any more than it does in the initial context in which
it was mooted, namely that of the meeting of Cortés and Moctezuma in
Mexico.[53] That is, one cannot simply assume an opacity or incapacity to communicate on *a priori* grounds stemming from semiotic incompatibility; few would
dare to declare today, with Todorov, that 'Moctezuma is located at a first level of
semiotic incapacity: he misunderstands the signals of the other and interprets
them badly; his own messages do not attain their goal, for he is incapable of perceiving that the Spaniards are at the same time similar (humans) and different.'[54]
But to demolish this model is all-too-easy, and does not address the complex
problem of how the Company's ambassadors communicated in a Mughal
context, and how they perceived and represented the Mughals. To my mind, the
counter-proposition which argues that everything was translatable, or at least as
translatable here as in 'all social relations', cannot be acceptable to the historian.
To accept such a position is to deny the specificity of the problem at hand,

---

52 OIOC, Mss. Eur. D. 1075, from OC 57–I, 7561. 'The answer of the King of England, the
    Wearer of Hats, concerning what was demanded of the Ambassador'. The document also
    contains a brief description of the political structure of Europe that is not without interest.
53 Tzvetan Todorov, *The conquest of America: Perceiving the other*, tr. Richard Howard (1st
    edn, New York, 1984).
54 Tsvetan Todorov, 'Cortés et Moctezuma. De la communication', *L'Ethnographie*, 81, nos.
    1–2 (1980), 69–83, quotation on p. 83. Compare the account to that in Carmen Bernand
    and Serge Gruzinski, *Histoire du nouveau monde*, 2 vols (Paris, 1991–93); vol. 1, *De la
    découverte à la conquête, une expérience européenne, 1492–1550.*

namely one in which England, a medium-sized power from the western end of Eurasia, was seeking to impose its terms on a diplomatic relationship with a far larger power, the Mughals, who also belonged to a religious category that was seen as fundamentally antagonistic to Christianity.

To sum the matter up schematically, we might say that the problem we are dealing with here is not one where knowledge is shaped by actual power (for the English had very little power in India, whether at the time of Roe or that of Norris); rather it is one of a will to power where a form of political ethnography, in which various political systems are compared and ranked, has become the standard framework for the ambassadorial account. This was not inevitable, nor had it always been the case, as a comparison of the accounts of Roe or Francisco Pelsaert (the Dutch factor at Agra in the 1620s) with those of the Jesuits at the courts of Akbar and Jahangir shows. The latter's evaluation of Akbar does not, in the final analysis, seem to differ very much from the manner in which they might have judged a Christian monarch in Europe, whereas by the time of Roe, the tone and the nature of the judgement has shifted. This shift seems to crystallize and become standardized over the course of the seventeenth century, whether with Bernier, Norris or even the thoroughly marginal Manuzzi, who both despised and modelled himself on Bernier. Seen through this prism, exceptional and sympathetic individuals might exist even in the Mughal court, but the framework was one in which Mughal rule itself was political anathema, a form of government so constitutionally corrupt and despotic that it could only be compared with that of the Ottomans.

This still leaves us with an unanswered question. What if the roles were reversed? Would Mughal ambassadors to England have seen the Stuart court in an analogous way to that in which the Mughals were perceived by Roe or Norris? We cannot answer with any certitude, because the first Mughal (or Indo-Persian accounts) of England date to a period after the seizure of Bengal by the Company, and are very much shaped by those events.[55] The closest comparison we can find is with the Ottomans, for we know of Ottoman accounts of France in the eighteenth century that can be read against European accounts of the Ottoman empire. Amongst these, we can count the embassy-account of Yirmisekiz Çelebi Mehmed Efendi to the court of the young Louis XV in 1720–21;[56] and in the same line of narratives, one may equally number the reports from Revolutionary and Napoleonic France of Morali Seyyid Ali Efendi and Seyyid Abdürrahim Muhibb Efendi, the first dating from the years 1797 to

---

55 I have addressed a related question in an earlier essay, Sanjay Subrahmanyam, ' "Through the looking glass": Some comments on Asian views of the Portuguese in Asia, 1500–1700', in *As Relações entre a Índia Portuguesa, a Ásia do Sueste e o Extremo Oriente: Actas do VI Seminário Internacional de História Indo-Portuguesa*, eds Artur Teodoro de Matos and Luís Filipe F. Reis Thomaz (Macau and Lisbon, 1993), pp. 377–403.

56 For this account, see Julien-Claude Galland, *Le Paradis des infidèles. Un ambassadeur ottoman en France sous la Régence*, ed. Gilles Veinstein (Paris, 1981).

1802, and the second from 1806 to 1811.[57] These accounts do not seem to me to confirm the view that when the roles were reversed, the proto-Orientalism of one was simply replaced by the Occidentalism of the other. The reasons for this are surely at least twofold: the asymmetry of the relationship between the two parties, even in purely commercial terms; and the differing traditions of xenology within which the Ottoman ambassadors and, say, the Venetian or French consuls in the Levant, located themselves.

To return then to the point of departure, our problem in dealing with the East India Company's relations with Mughal India in the seventeenth century lies in our very characterization of the period. Clearly, this is not an epoch when we can assume any direct European domination over South Asia, and so it is naturally tempting to assume that the history of representations too is characterized either by symmetry or by its relatively 'innocent' character. Yet, without wishing to impose a crude teleology on the Company's dealings in India, or assuming that the conquest of the Mughal empire was already written on the wall by 1615, it is important to understand that a form of conflict did exist already by the time of Roe, and even more so by that of Norris. If at times this conflict between Mughals and Europeans expressed itself as open war, as with the Mughal capture of Portuguese Hughli in 1632, or Sir Josia Child's Mughal war of the 1680s, at other times the conflict was far more in the nature of a 'war of images', to borrow – and slightly displace – a phrase.[58] It is with this 'contained conflict' that we must come to terms in understanding the world of our ambassadors, rather than return once more to the time-honoured cliché of the period as a supposed 'Age of Partnership'.

---

[57] Morali Seyyid Ali Efendi and Seyyid Abdürrahim Muhibb Efendi, *Deux Ottomans à Paris sous le Directoire et l'Empire. Relations d'ambassade*, tr. Stéphane Yerasimos (Paris, 1998).

[58] Cf. Serge Gruzinski, *La guerre des images. De Christophe Colomb à 'Blade Runner' (1492–2019)* (Paris, 1990).

The East India Company and the Trade in Non-Metallic Precious Materials from Sir Thomas Roe to Diamond Pitt

BRUCE P. LENMAN

'Precious materials' is a term of art. It implies high value with decorative function. Obviously cocaine or even saffron is, ounce for ounce, just as valuable, if not more so, than some gem stones. The definition and relative value of precious materials may vary between contemporary cultures, thus stimulating long-distance trade. Crystalline precious stones constitute much of this trade, but it has always included non-crystalline organic materials, and pearls are as central to the trade of the jeweller as diamonds or rubies. A renaissance nautilus-shell loving cup gifted by James VI & I's Scots jeweller, George Heriot, is still used on high table at the annual trustees' dinner of the Edinburgh school named after him. *Nautilus pompilus* is a gregarious bottom-feeding warm-water octopus, caught for food. The Chinese probably pioneered the decorative carving of its shell, but 'By 1609 Amboyna, where many nautili were caught, had become one of the corner-stones of the Dutch East Indian Trading Company.'[1] Today, Amboyna is remembered as the place where ten Englishmen, ten Japanese, and a Portuguese were brutally tortured and murdered by the agents of that Dutch company (its Dutch acronym is the VOC). Though their small bulk and high value made precious materials some of the earliest materials traded globally, the nautilus demonstrates the tendency towards dominant producer areas and markets, even for organic materials.

Large pearls are another example. There was a European freshwater small pearl industry, and pearls from Scottish rivers were known to the Romans and went on being used in specialist jewellery into the twentieth century, notably by the firm of Cairncross in Perth. On his third voyage Columbus collected some Caribbean pearls, and his Spanish successors established a lucrative pearl fishery in the sixteenth century that was based on Margarita Island and contiguous waters off the coast of present-day Venezuela;[2] this fishery used slave divers, but at an early stage experimented with diving machines. Some of these Caribbean

---

1 'Nautilus Shell', *The Oxford Companion to the Decorative Arts*, ed. Harold Osborne (Oxford, 1975), pp. 584–6.
2 Manuel Luengo Munoz, 'Inventos para acrecentar la obtenacion de perlas en America, durante el siglo XVI', *Anuario de Estudios Americanos*, 9 (1952), 51–72.

pearls were large: the most famous, which came from the waters of the Gulf of
Panama in the sixteenth century, was *La Pelegrina*, which, after being owned by
European royalty, was bought by Richard Burton in 1969 as a St Valentine's Day
present for Elizabeth Taylor.[3] Yet the most valuable pearls in the early-modern
era were large 'orient pearls', from the fisheries of the Persian Gulf and the Coromandel Coast of India, between India and Ceylon (Japanese natural pearls came
on the market later). Orient pearls were on average vastly superior in size and
lustre. Within the looser usage of the word pearl there are far rarer categories
such as the orange pearls of Vietnam, which come from a marine gastropod.
Only one major piece made from these – a 23-pearl necklace, almost certainly
once the property of the Vietnamese imperial family – survives.[4] Even organic
jewellery can have a narrow geographical provenance.

Nowadays precious stones come from a bewildering variety of sources.
Diamonds are exported in quantity from Russia. The diamonds being smuggled
out of Africa in 2000 to fund insurgent warfare there have been described as
'blood' diamonds. This does not describe their colouring. They could come from
innumerable sites in Liberia, Sierra Leone, Gambia, Guinea, Gabon, the Congo,
Angola, Namibia, Botswana, or South Africa.[5] Yet before the third quarter of the
eighteenth century, when the Brazilian diamond mines opened up, most
diamonds came from India, from the Deccan. There was a small flow of stones
from Borneo. The only other exception was a handful of coloured fancies that
the Spaniards obtained from the Guiana Shield. When Queen Elizabeth chartered the English East India Company (EIC) on the last day of 1600, the already
global trade in precious materials was marked by the dominance of a limited
number of primary markets and source areas, often in Asia. That was why travelling jewellers, from the late medieval Venetians to the Englishman Ralph Fitch,
who set out from London accompanied by the jeweller William Leedes in 1583,
reaching Malacca before he turned back, made such a contribution to European
geographical knowledge.[6] Mostly, precious materials moved westwards from
Asia towards Europe in exchange for the flow of Mexican and Peruvian bullion,
mainly silver, which underwrote Europe's heavy negative balance of payments
with the Orient. However, precious materials, both crystalline and organic,
could move eastwards as well as westward. Baltic amber and Mediterranean red
coral are examples. The coral fisheries and coral processing industries of seven-
teenth- and eighteenth-century Marseilles, Genoa, and Leghorn were largely

---

[3] Nigel Sitwell, 'The "queen of gems" ', *Smithsonian* (January 1985), 48.

[4] Derek Content, ed., *The Pearl and the Dragon: A study of Vietnamese pearls and a history of
     the oriental pearl trade* (Maine, 1999).

[5] See the report on 'Diamonds with ultimate price tag' in *The Scotsman*, Saturday, 1 July
     2000, p. 7.

[6] Bruce P. Lenman, 'England, the International Gem Trade and the Growth of Geographical
     Knowledge from Columbus to James I', in *Renaissance Culture in Context: Theory and Prac-
     tice*, eds Jean R. Brink and William F. Gentrup (Aldershot, 1993), 86–99. For Finch and
     Leedes, see Michael Edwardes, *Ralph Fitch, Elizabethan in the Indies* (London, 1972).

geared to the Indian market. This Mediterranean coral industry became a major object of interest to the Sephardic Jewish merchant dynasties (mostly of Portuguese extraction), who, by the eighteenth century, were very prominent in EIC trade as bullion brokers. They were also prominent in diamond dealing and cutting. As early as 1613 the EIC knew there was a large Indian market for both coral beads and for the rough coral which was burned on funeral pyres as a mark of respect to the dead in western India.[7]

Many emeralds were transported to Asia after the Spaniards had discovered the Chibcha Indian workings for emeralds in 1537 at Somondoco, renamed Chivor. By 1567 the Spaniards were exploiting that other major site for hydro-thermal gem deposits in present-day Colombia, Muzo. In the Orient, emeralds had always been highly esteemed, and Hindu ancient Sanskrit epics mention emeralds as the fifth most precious gem in rank after diamonds, pearls, rubies and sapphires. Those emeralds almost certainly came from the same Egyptian mines that supplied the needs of the Romans, for emerald sources in Asia were much rarer then than they are today as a result of modern geological exploration. Islamic rulers were attracted by the religious significance, to them, of the emerald's fathomless green colour. Venetian gem merchants, active in Asian gem markets from the medieval period, seem to have moved great Colombian emeralds (identifiable from their inclusions), into the hands of rulers such as the Mughal emperors Shah Jahan and Jahangir. The emperors valued them the more because they could be sliced to produce the large flat areas that could then be carved with dynastic or religious inscriptions or floral patterns. The collections of the Ottoman sultans of Turkey, preserved in the Topkapi Palace in Istanbul, are likewise rich in Colombian emeralds. Surpassing both Ottoman and Mughal collections of Colombian emeralds were the holdings of the Safavid dynasty of Iran, developed especially in the reign of Shah Abbas (1587–1629).[8]

So when the EIC was chartered in 1600, its direct entry into the Asian gem markets was a major development, for English goldsmith jewellers had had to access Asian sources indirectly before 1600. An anonymous manuscript called 'The gouldesmythes Storehowse', which survives in two versions and five copies, gives us a fair notion of how they did this. The initials H.G. are associated with the copies in Goldsmiths' Hall, the British Museum and the Folger Shakespeare Library, and the work is usually thought to be the joint product of a father and son, both named Hannibal Gamon, of whom the elder was a City goldsmith. The work is dated 1604 and is in two books. The first is concerned with weights and measures, the assaying of gold and silver, and the coinage of England, including the testing of its quality through the traditional Trial of the Pyx. It is difficult to see why the Gamons should produce these handsome illustrated books, which were clearly being circulated to the influential in a type of MS publication common in the Jacobean era. There are indications of involvement by Sir

---

7 Gedalia Yogev, *Diamonds and Coral* (Leicester, 1978), pp. 102–3.
8 John Sinkankas, *Emerald and Other Beryls* (Arizona, 1989), pp. 120–4.

Richard Martin, a much more political animal. He had been a controversial Master of the Mint under Queen Elizabeth, Prime Warden of the Goldsmiths and Lord Mayor of London. Before his death in 1617 he desperately needed favours from James VI & I, especially back payments for services rendered, to avert ruin.[9] The second book is a lapidary. Each of the 79 short chapters includes discussion of the curative and magical properties of a stone, including ones that are natural secretions in animals' intestines.

Nevertheless, the work also contains hard information about the London gem market. The first book makes the point that the carat weight, which was used exclusively for precious stones and pearls was 'a weight broughte from the Venetians and derived from a weight of the Indians or Moores called a Mangiar or fanan which is a weight not much different from this weight called a carott'.[10] Venice had been the main European gem market, but by 1600 Lisbon was more important, and behind Lisbon stood Goa, the capital of the Portuguese Estado da India. The fourth chapter of the second book deals with diamonds, which the author says 'grow' in India. He knew the main sources were in the Deccan, naming some of the more important producing areas, usually by a Portuguese version of their name. He even knows the name of one of the country 'fairs' situated equidistant from Portuguese Goa and from Gujerat, where the gem merchants from both centres bought their stocks. He explained that a rough guide to value is obtained by taking the square of the carat weight of a diamond and multiplying that figure by the market value of a one-carat diamond. He specifically said that his figures were for 'Dyamons bought in the Indies'.[11] He distinguished these primary prices from costs elsewhere, as when he discussed the weight 'and prices of Brute or Ruff Dyamons bought here by my selfe in London from the Portingale Marchauntes, before the coming in of the greate Carrick which brought great store of Dyamons into Darteworth in the west Countrie in Anno Dei 1592'. This was the huge Portuguese carrack the *Madre de Dios* captured in 1592 by the privateering fleet of the Earl of Cumberland, commanded by Captain Norton, who brought his 1600-ton prize into Dartmouth on 7 September 1592, but failed to stop his crews from stealing the pearls, diamonds, rubies and sapphires, not to mention most of the gold and silver, on the ship. The jewels were resold at low prices to the London goldsmiths, including H.G., who descended on Dartmouth. The Queen was furious, having

---

9   Janellie Auriol Jenstad, ' "The Gouldesmythes Storehowse": Early Evidence for Specialisation', *The Silver Society Journal,* 10 (Autumn 1998), 40–43. For Sir Richard Martin see *DNB* entry and J.S. Forbes, *Hallmark: A History of the London Assay Office* (Goldsmiths' Company, Unicorn Press, London, 1999), 73–8, 82–3, 86–92.

10 'Goldsmith's Storehouse' (hereinafter GSH), Bk 1, f. 3v. I have studied both the Folger Shakespeare Library's MS of the 'Goldsmith's Storehouse' and the MS version in Goldsmiths' Hall in the City of London. The versions are not identical, but the differences are not significant. My quotations are drawn from the Folger MS.

11 GSH, Bk 2, ff. 61v–66r.

hoped to take the entire cargo by royal prerogative.[12] Prices per carat of precious stones plummeted, though they soon picked up again.

H.G. next recorded the prices he paid for a parcel of 'brute dyamons bought by me from the Portugall Marchant in anno 1594'. Writing less than a decade later, he said that the current price per carat was now much higher than the 1594 figures.[13] This is extraordinary. England had been at war with Philip II of Spain since 1585. Future leaders of the EIC like James Lancaster, General of its first fleet sent out in 1601, had been fighting Philip II since 1580. As Englishmen resident in Portugal, they had fought alongside the Portuguese to resist the army with which Philip enforced his claim to the Portuguese throne. Yet in 1594 H.G. could buy a parcel of rough diamonds from Goa. Early-modern governments were incapable of controlling their subjects' dealings in materials as easily concealed and smuggled as gemstones. When talking about balas rubies, which are really spinels and not carborundum gems like rubies and sapphires, H.G. explained that though from central Asia, they were marketed mainly by Islamic merchants in the port of Calicut on the Malabar Coast of India south of Goa. He remarked that by trafficking them in Turkey and North Africa, where demand was high, English dealers had secured much better prices per carat for them than had previously been the case. So the Calicut market for spinels was available to Elizabethan gem dealers.[14]

In 1604, an Anglo-Spanish peace came with the signature of the Treaty of London. The elaborate tables of weights and prices for precious stones at the end of H.G.'s manuscript simply assume that the jewellers of England and the Low Countries buy their gemstones uncut (or 'brute'), along with pearls, 'as they come from Lisbone in Portugal',[15] behind which was Goa. This accounts for the detailed knowledge of the Goan market displayed by the author in his remarks on chrysolite. This he reports as being 'of small estimation in the Indies at Goa, where they are sould and bought because they use them but for beades, seales, seal rings and sutche like' just like inferior amethyst or beryl.[16] English jewellers had always maintained indirect access to the dominant Indian gem market at Goa. The EIC aimed at taking over some of the middleman profit going to the Portuguese. It secured market share by lowering prices for precious materials in London and in re-export markets like the Islamic societies in the Maghreb and Ottoman Turkey with which England had established a civilised trading relationship under Queen Elizabeth.

The early EIC voyages were directed towards the spice islands of what is now Indonesia, and especially the Moluccas. It was natural for the Company to become involved in the diamond trade of Borneo (now Kalimantan). The

12 Richard T. Spence, *The Privateering Earl: George Clifford, 3rd Earl of Cumberland, 1558–1605* (Stroud, 1995), chapter 6.
13 GSH, Bk 2, f. 66v.
14 GSH, Bk 2, ch. 15, f. 72r, 72v.
15 GSH, Bk 2, f. 101v.
16 GSH, Bk 2, f. 75v.

diamond mines there may be the oldest of all. They fall into two groups: the Sundai Landak placer deposits in western Kalimantan, and the placer swamp deposits just west of Martapura in south-eastern Kalimantan.[17] EIC commanders were advised that on the outward voyage precious stones were among the most advantageous goods that could be purchased with a view to exchanging them for spices in the Moluccas. India was merely a point where ships touched and traded for goods in demand further east. At Malabar, it was noted that pearls, sapphires and diamonds could be obtained as well as rice, and that they could be obtained in exchange for English lead and iron, weapons, and the universal currency of silver pieces of eight. At Cochin, diamonds, rubies, pearls and bezoar stones (concretions from the alimentary tracts of ruminants, believed to have magical curative powers) could be had, though they were 'brought from Goa'. The 'gem island' of Ceylon offered above all pearls and sapphires. When the EIC started trading in the Gujerati commercial metropolis of Surat, which involved permanent factors and warehousing, it was told in 1609 that it should lay out 100,000 rupees (at roughly 2/-3d the rupee) on balases which would 'sell to a very good profit' if of red colour, and 'besides the King will the more esteem both us and our country'. Since the King of Cambay or Gujerat was the Moghul emperor, dealing in precious materials in demand in imperial court circles would enhance the humble status of English traders. Diamonds were purchased primarily for direct importation into England. Though the bulk of diamonds came from the Deccan in India, the EIC was advised that Borneo offered great potential.

John Saris wrote to the EIC in December 1608 from Bantam, that 'the Flemings', i.e. the VOC, were driving a profitable trade in western Borneo in Sukadana, 'which place yieldeth great store of diamonds'. The VOC was buying diamonds there with gold and with valuable Chinese blue beads, which Saris hoped could be copied more cheaply in England.[18] The EIC did establish a factory at Sukadana, but it then ran into two problems. One was the difficulty of controlling the actions of its own servants. In 1618 George Cockayne wrote from Sukadana to George Ball in Bantam that the EIC servants there were running a 'disordered and shameful business'. They were throwing away Company money 'in fustical and lewd fashion – to our shame and the Flemminges' glory'. Cockayne denounced them as 'besotted with drunknes, hores and careles liveinge'. In the purchase of large diamonds the EIC did not have the capital to compete with the VOC. Cockayne explained that the local 'Queene' had sold him a diamond of '8 & 1/8 carrets' at a stiff price but under that being offered by VOC representatives 'beecause the English hath had no great stones this long tyme'. He paid 488 rupees for that stone, which was about 54 pounds and 18 shillings sterling. There were three large stones (16, 12½, and 10¾ carats respectively) coming in from Landak, but they were out of the EIC's league. Even the

---

[17] Peter C. Keller, *Gemstones and their Origins* (New York, 1990), p. 6.
[18] John Saris to EIC, 4 Dec. 1608, in, *Letters Received by the East India Company from its Servants in the East*, Vol. I, 1602–1613 (London, 1896), pp. 20–3.

VOC had to send for more bullion to make bids for them.[19] The EIC could, however, play the market for smaller diamonds. In early 1614 the *Globe* had sailed from Bantam carrying what a previous ship, the *James*, could not carry away from the Company warehouse. The bulkiest item was '25 chests of China Silks', but the cargo also included '337 diamonds great and small containing carats 119&5/8 and costing, 1,002 rials of 8'.[20] Since the exchange rate of the rial of 8 at Sukadana in 1614 was 4 shillings,[21] the cost of that bulse of diamonds was roughly 250 pounds and 10 shillings. Given the cost of the diamond a little over eight carats, the bulk of the stones in the bulse were clearly small.

Profitability depended on the going rate in the fluctuating London diamond market. John Jourdain in Bantam forwarded in vain four letters asking about this. One of them was 'by William George the Scotchman': EIC Court Minutes in 1614 record the receipt of information from one of their servants who was accompanied by a Scot who had served the Portuguese for 32 years in the East Indies. Jourdain, still complained that when buying diamonds, 'I am forced to buy them here at haphazard, not knowing whether I overrated them or not'.[22] Despite Dutch attacks, the EIC traded in Nusantara – the mighty archipelago – into the eighteenth century, and beyond. The EIC was squeezed out of key trades like the spice trade of the Moluccas and the diamonds of Borneo, and it began to pay much more attention to the Indian subcontinent, funding the sending of Sir Thomas Roe as ambassador of James I to the Emperor Jahangir between 1615 and 1619. A huge pear-shaped pearl of 29½ carats arrived with the 1617 EIC fleet as part of a collection of presents for the emperor by which Roe set much store. To secure it from predatory Mughal officials on the journey from Surat to the court in the Delhi, Agra region, Roe suggested that it should be concealed in the bored stock of a musket.[23] Roe was an experienced and active gem dealer. From 1621 to 1625, when ambassador to the Sublime Porte, he was paid by and acted as agent for the Levant Company in Constantinople, still a very important gem market. Towards the end of his spell in India, early in 1618 he wrote advice for the EIC about commodities that were appropriate for the Surat trade. That city, since its conquest by the Emperor Akbar, had been the Mughals' window on the Indian Ocean. Roe said that ropes of pearls, worn by Indian dignitaries, would command a ready market, especially if they were of large size. In 1622 the EIC was to ally with the Shah of Persia and the VOC to drive the Portuguese out of Ormuz, the fortress – city commanding the exit from the Persian gulf. Ormuz

---

19   George Cockayne at Sukadana to George Ball at Bantam, 16 June 1618, OIOC, E/3/6, 662. I am grateful to Tony Farrington for this reference.

20   John Jourdain to EIC, 10 Feb. 1614, in *Letters Received by the EIC*, Vol. II, 1613–1615 (London, 1897), p. 316.

21   Figure given in Robert Larkin at Sukadana to EIC ('12 rials or 48s'), in *ibid.*, p. 61.

22   John Jourdain to EIC, Bantam, 30 September 1615, *ibid.*, p. 257. For the Scot who had been in Portuguese service, see Court Minutes of EIC, 8–9 June 1614, in Noel Sainsbury, ed., *Calendar of State Papers, Colonial Series, East Indies, China and Japan, 1513–1616* (London, 1862), p. 296.

23   Michael Strachan, *Sir Thomas Roe 1581–1644* (Wilton, 1989), pp. 107–8.

was the market for the products of the famed pearl fishery of Bahrein. Indians preferred highly coloured gems, so Roe reckoned good rubies would be the most profitable import of all, the market for emeralds was promising, and that big balas 'rubies' would be in demand, partly as a substitute for rubies proper. Well-cut agates Roe considered sellable. He said certain kinds of jewellery work would sell in India, especially armlets or bracelets if 'mede to lock onne with one Joint, sett with stones, diamonds Rubies good worke, will give you proffit'. Roe believed the Company needed a steady supply of the highest calibre of gemstones and large pearls, to persuade the connoisseur Emperor Jahangir and his courtiers to take it seriously. Naively, he even thought King James, might open his heart and the Jewel House in the Tower of London to the Company because 'The Tower I ame persuaded could furnish you with manie great old stones that are useless.'[24]

The EIC was anxious to expand its activities in Persia. There its servants came into friendly contact with an Englishman, William Robbins, who was on good terms with Shah Abbas I, the Great, and the principal nobles. Robbins bought jewels, sending them for sale in Aleppo and Constantinople.[25] He must have been selling gems, and probably also western-style jewellery. Gems could have been bought by the EIC from the Venetians in Constantinople, for the first two Governors of the Company, Sir Thomas Smythe and Sir Morris Abbot, were, like many other EIC men, also prominent members of the Levant Company. More often, gem material must have come from Portuguese Goa. In 1635, William Methwold, President of the EIC council in Surat, signed the Convention of Goa that established an Anglo-Portuguese alliance in Asia, opening Portuguese ports and markets to Englishmen. By then, the EIC was approaching 'what may be regarded as the nadir of its eastern commerce'.[26] Before the disasters of the 1630s and the virtual eclipse of the 1640s, the EIC had followed Roe's advice. The 1624 Court minutes talk of selling no less than 156 chests of coral at Surat for £34,000, 'which produced great benefit to the Company'.[27] Letters from the EIC establishment in Surat in 1624 spoke of selling very valuable gems. It was reported that 'the £1000 Jewell sold for 5280 Rupees', and that a pair of pendant pearls, which must have been of exceptional size and lustre sold for 2,300 rupees. There is reference to the sale of balases, and a reference to two packets of emeralds sold, by permission of the Company, for the private account of Sir Morris Abbot. Three emeralds had been sold for 3,000 rupees. Deducting a 4 percent duty and 1 percent brokerage, Abbot's final payment was 'ruppees 2850', which was paid to his cash account as £398 11s 3d sterling. By Captain Weddell's fleet, Abbot had

---

[24] Sir Thomas Roe to EIC, enclosure of 1618, probably March, OIOC, E/3/5, f. 376.

[25] Edward Pettus to EIC, Isfahan, 2 June 1617, OIOC, E/3/5, f. 68r.

[26] John Keay, *The Honourable Company: A history of the English East India Company* (London, 1991), p. 108.

[27] EIC Court Minutes, 6 Aug. 1624, in *Calendar of State Papers* [hereinafter *CSP*], *Colonial Series, East Indies, China and Japan, 1622–1624*, ed. W. Noel Sainsbury (London, 1878), p. 349.

sent out '5 fair Emerauldes' to be sold for his own account; two of them, of 117 and 136 carats, sent set in gold with a couple of small rubies, were reported already 'sould for 2910 rupees net of dyutie and brokeredge and that according to his orders have delivered into his worship's cash'.[28] The EIC dreaded thievish servants. Their servants in Batavia in 1623 complained that 'The Company seem to be very jealous that there should not be faithful dealing in the buying of diamonds.'[29] Fraud started with keeping and reselling privately the best stones, sending the EIC inferior ones. However, senior members of the Company were also greedy for private profit. After 1619 Roe embarrassed the Court of the EIC, by overvaluing items he sent east for sale on commission. He would then ask for an advance on the strength of his highly optimistic figures. One Tyon, a jeweller, offered to sell the EIC for £10,000 a crystal looking glass set in £500 worth of gold, the frame set with balases and other stones. His workmanship was valued at £1000. Tyon threatened to send it out independently if the EIC did not buy it, refusing the EIC's offer to send it out and take a third of the profit. Sir Thomas Roe was sure the Great Mughal would jump at it.[30] Roe had seen Jahangir leave Ajmer in state in November 1616, wearing ropes of superb pearls, his clothes and accoutrements dripping with diamonds and rubies.[31] Nevertheless, Roe inclined to fantasise retrospectively about the Mughal court. This syndrome produced a masterwork of the European baroque: the jewelled fantasy diorama of 'The Court at Delhi on the Birthday of the Great Moghul Aurangzeb', made for Augustus the Strong of Saxony by his court jeweller Johann Melchior Dinglinger in 1708.[32]

Though Goa had been the prime gem market, the natural outlet for the diamond mines of the Sultanate of Golconda was its eastern port of Masulipatnam. The EIC tried to enter the Masulipatnam diamond market, but had had problems with the Portuguese and Dutch, especially during fighting between them after the lapse of a Luso–Dutch truce in 1652. The Portuguese lost out heavily in the 1670s and then Golconda fell to the Mughals in 1687.[33] The EIC had been out of the game for a couple of decades before 1660. An EIC ruling of 1609 theoretically forbade private trade in diamonds. De facto, the EIC allowed its servants and naval officers on its shipping to trade privately in

28 These details are drawn from the summaries of letters to the EIC from Surat of dates 22 December 1622, 9 February 1623, and 14 and 15 February 1624, in Original Correspondence OIOC, E/3/9, f. 155.

29 Thomas Brockedon, Henry Hawley, and John Goninge to EIC, Batavia, 14 December 1623, in Sainsbury, ed., CSP, 1622–1624, p. 199.

30 Both the Tyon and Roe episodes can be found in Sainsbury, ed., CSP, 1622–1624, pp. 8 and 14; and 432, 450, 452, and 457 respectively.

31 Sir William Foster, The Embassy of Sir William Roe to India 1615–19 (Delhi, 1990), pp. 283–84.

32 Joachim Menzhausen, At the Court of the Great Mogul (Leipzig, 1965).

33 Sanjay Subrahmanyam, The Portuguese Empire in Asia, 1500–1700 (London, 1993), pp. 202–6.

diamonds after 1625. A ruling of 1650 making this legal was irrelevant, for by then the EIC was moribund.

The Company was virtually reestablished after 1658. In 1659, the EIC directorate was told that their servants in Asia knew 'but to buy amber-greece, pearls, cuff [bort or imperfectly crystallised diamonds used as abrasive] and diamonds'. It was a start. By the early 1660s the EIC had opened the trade in precious stones to anyone. Sephardic Jewish businessmen of Portuguese extraction settled in London after the readmission of the Jews by Cromwell in 1655. They made London the main European market for uncut diamonds. Into coral and bullion as well as diamonds, these Jewish merchants had contacts in the Amsterdam Jewish community, with its diamond-cutting skills, as well as in Lisbon and Goa. The latter city remained so major a source of imported diamonds that in 1684 the EIC ruled that persons importing diamonds from Goa should pay 5 percent duty if they had not already paid duty on silver or goods exported to pay for the diamonds. A brief attempt by the EIC to take the diamond trade into its own hands in 1679 had collapsed by 1681, when free trade was restored. Interestingly, the Company allocated £60,000 in 1681 for the purchase of diamonds in Madras, which it vowed to make the main Indian diamond mart. The Company had made £1,765 on diamond freight charges in 1680, at 2 percent, *ad valorem* for freemen of the Company and 4 percent from Portuguese Jews and others. The trade was peaking, much of it generated by EIC servants repatriating their fortunes. After 1689, wartime financial stringency destroyed the French Court as a diamond market. Low European diamond prices and high ones in Golconda depressed profits to the point where the EIC quit. After the confused situation of the 1690s, which saw two antipathetic East India Companies and a restriction on the export of silver to pay for diamonds, the situation stabilised by 1713 on a liberal basis. Smuggling of diamonds and of silver had been rampant, so it was sensible to lift restrictions and charge only very modest dues. It was taken for granted that Madras was India's new diamond emporium.[34]

Madras offered security. Local factors had breached the usual EIC rule against fortification, starting to build Fort St George there in 1640. Streynsham Master, Governor of Madras visited the diamond fields in Golconda in 1679, where the EIC already had an agent, Master's associate, Nathaniel Cholmley – who made a fortune buying on commission for individuals in England, before returning home in 1681.[35] Master found that the 'mines', were really pits and tunnels which men bought a licence to drive into the gravels associated with the River Kistna. He conferred with a delegation of Madras merchants at a ford on the Kistna before returning to Madras.[36] Indian businessmen were attracted to that rapidly

[34] Gedalia Yogev, *Diamonds and Coral: Anglo-Dutch Jews and eighteenth-century trade* (Leicester, 1978), chapters 5 and 6.

[35] Edgar R. Samuel, 'Nathaniel Cholmley: An English Diamond Merchant in India, 1663–1682', *North Yorkshire Record Office Publication No. 54: Miscellany 1993*, pp. 14–20.

[36] Sir Richard Carnac Temple, ed., *Indian Records Series: The Diaries of Streynsham Master 1675–1680, Vol. I: The Diary, 1675–1677* (London, 1911), pp. 81–93.

growing city, with its easy access to the diamond-producing area through Masulipatnam. It was also the obvious base for EIC dealings with Burma.

In 1650, the Madras factors opened a general trade with Burma, the principal world source of rubies. Indian buyers seem initially to have preferred the colouring of the much smaller supply of rubies from the gem gravels of Ceylon, besides which Burmese rubies were expensive, for local Burmese officials demanded bribes. The Company set up a factory in Burma at Syriam, but abandoned it about 1657. Nevertheless, the 1680s saw Madras replace Masulipatnam as the main port for Burmese trade, including gems. When in 1680 the EIC reopened negotiations with the Burmese court, through a resident Portuguese merchant, Joao Perera de Faria, it tried to attract 'Pegu ruby merchants' to Madras by means of a cowle or letter of intent. This promised kindness, low customs, no breaking bulk packages for inspection on entry, and payment only on sales made – none on goods returned unsold. Total brokerage charges were only 2 percent. Perera came back to Madras with several ruby merchants promising to trade and settle.[37] They were not to be a unique minority.

The London Jewish community became involved with Madras. Leading Jewish dealers like Manuel Levy Duarte (1631–1714), were in the first generation often Amsterdam-based. They saw opportunities in London where Duarte commissioned a market survey from David Gabay. Dealing in gems, though potentially lucrative, was much riskier than the normal goldsmith jeweller's trade. Sephardic Jews accepted the higher risk especially in diamonds. In London, Levy bought diamonds from three sources. One was Lisbon, in effect Goa. He also bought from captains and crews of homecoming east-indiamen, and he joined syndicates sending out money to buy from Golconda. After 1684, when the EIC Madras Council formally permitted Jews to reside, Jews seized the opportunity.[38] Sir Josiah Child, who dominated the EIC, admired Dutch tolerance of industrious minorities. Child's disastrous war with the Mughal Empire in 1688 was a brief aberration opposed by the Madras Council.[39]

The Portuguese Jewish network was only one of many that interconnected in Madras. Some were inter-Asian, others European, like the Huguenots. Charles II encouraged persecuted French Huguenot refugees to come to England after 1681, and the Revocation of the Edict of Nantes in 1685 saw mass emigration, with Huguenot goldsmiths settling in London and Dublin. Over 120 were goldsmiths in London between 1688 and 1710.[40] French goldsmith gem dealers were

[37] D.G.E. Hall, *Early English Intercourse with Burma* (London, 1928), pp. 80–118.
[38] I am very grateful for personal help from Mr Edgar R. Samuel. See also his articles: 'Manuel Levy Duarte (1631–1714): An Amsterdam Merchant Jeweller and his Trade with London', *Transactions of the Jewish Historical Society of England*, 27 (1978–80), 11–31; 'David Gabay's 1660 Letter from London', *ibid.*, 25 (1973–75), 38–9; and 'Sir Francis Child's Jewellery Business', *Three Banks Review* (March 1977), pp. 43–55.
[39] Bruce P. Lenman, 'The East India Company and the Emperor Aurangzeb', *History Today*, 37 (February 1987), 23–9.
[40] Joan Evans, 'Huguenot Goldsmiths in England and Ireland', *Proceedings of the Huguenot Society of London* [hereinafter *PHSL*], XIV (1929–33), 496–555.

great travellers, as the memoirs of Tavernier in Mughal India demonstrate. Jean Chardin (later Sir John, Jeweller to the King) settled in England in 1681 after years of travelling in India and Persia. Persian court ladies showed him their spectacular native pearls, and told him how much their imported rubies and diamonds had cost in Constantinople.[41] He bought sold and smuggled gems, as well as dealing in fine jewellery, for European jewellery was highly esteemed in Persia; Chardin would also accept and execute commissions, sometimes to designs by Shah Abbass II himself.[42] In London, in the Royal Society, Chardin renewed acquaintance with Huguenot friends like Paul Rycaut, English consul at Smyrna in Turkey in the period 1667–78.[43] Chardin's brother Daniel, a partner from 1686, settled in Madras. Sir John believed Anglo-Indian trade the most lucrative of all trades, especially diamonds.[44]

The Chardin brothers dealt, with local Portuguese and Governor Elihu Yale,[45] within a complex business web. Sir Josiah Child wanted to attract the ubiquitous Armenian traders into the EIC orbit. He consulted an Armenian Coja Panous Calendar, and the agent of the Armenian nation in England, one Sir John Chardin. A contract was negotiated giving Armenians religious toleration, equal rights of office, permission to trade within EIC charter limits, and to travel in Company ships. They acquired the legal rights of Englishmen in EIC presidencies.[46] Sir John remained Jean Chardin. As late as 1708 he was providing loans to enable servants of the French Compagnie des Indes at Pondicherry near Madras to purchase diamonds.[47] It is nonsense to suggest that the EIC was in any way dominant in some sort of global 'system' in the early eighteenth century. It was, however, very much part of an Atlantic English (by 1707 British) world that East of the Cape of Good Hope extended its trading connections to truly global proportions, often by interacting with other Europeans, and always by working closely with Asian commercial and financial groups.

Elihu Yale, born in Boston of Welsh extraction, is an interesting example of this. He became a humble EIC writer; began to make a great deal of money as a gemstone dealer and rose to be Governor of Madras but was superseded in 1692, after allegations about the way he and his brother Thomas had accumulated

41 *Sir John Chardin's Travels in Persia* (London, 1927), p. 111.
42 Ronald W. Ferrier, *A Journey to Persia: Jean Chardin's Portrait of a Seventeenth-Century Empire* (London, 1996), pp. 11–12 and 165–6.
43 Sonia P. Anderson, *An English Consul in Turkey* (Oxford, 1989), p. 262.
44 Letter from Jean to Daniel Chardin of 1700 cited in Laleh Labib-Rahman, 'Sir Jean Chardin, the Great Traveller (1643–1712/3)', *PHSL*, 23 (1977–82), 316, footnote 18.
45 Based on a preview of an unpublished paper delivered to the Huguenot Society of London by Mr Edgar Samuel.
46 A.L. Crowe, 'Sir Josiah Child and the East India Company', unpublished PhD, University of London, 1956, pp. 164–5. I am profoundly grateful to Dr Julian Crowe for making a copy of his late father's thesis available to me.
47 Contemporary duplicate of a letter to Jean Chardin, dated Pondicherry, 3 August 1708, with endorsement mentioning purchases of 'Diamants Cruttes', dated 5 August. Probably forwarded to his brother Thomas in Madras, *penes autoris*.

their huge private fortunes. Retiring to England and Wales, he continued to deal in diamonds, corresponding with his friend Governor Thomas Pitt of Madras, and endowing Yale University. He was not just a 'Welsh-American', as a certain kind of anachronistic and self-obsessed historiography in the United States is wont to try to make him. He was a cosmopolitan American Englishman, who had made his career before the Anglo–Scottish Act of Union of 1707 made the EIC a British rather than an English company.[48] His crony Thomas 'Diamond' Pitt, father of the politician William Pitt the Elder, was another. His Madras career took off in 1698 with an EIC commission making him 'President for their affairs on this Coast and Governor of Fort St. George and Fort St. David'.[49] Like Yale he made a great private fortune trading in diamonds. There were rows, but that was normal. The Chardin brothers fell out. Yale reached England exchanging abuse with the EIC, thinly disguised as petitions to 'The king's Most Excellent Majesty' and counter petitions.[50] They operated in a gem market more important than Goa, because more cosmopolitan, more tolerant and more dynamic. It was a gemmological *translatio imperii*.

[48] For Yale, see *DNB* and the *Dictionary of American Biography*.
[49] Council at Madras to William Hatsell, Deputy governor of Fort St David, 8 July 1698, OIOC, G/19/24.
[50] Preserved in the London Public Record Office, PRO, CO/77/16.

I. *Bomanjee Jamsetjee*, anon.,
nineteenth-century British
School, *National Maritime
Museum* (neg. BHC2803)

II. Model of HMS *Cornwallis*,
National Maritime Museum
(neg. D628).

III. *Lascar seamen manning the yards*, William Wyllie, *National Maritime Museum* (PV3062)

SERANG, or Cockswain of a Bombay Pilot Boat.

IV. *A Serang*, from a collection of visiting-card size watercolours, Robert Temple, 1810–1813. By permission of the British Library (WD315)

V. *Lascars celebrating the Muslim Festival of Hirah on* Mary Anne, John Thomas James, 1827. By permission of the British Library (WD11)

VI. *The East Indiaman* Princess Royal, John Cleveley the Elder, 1770, National Maritime Museum (neg. BHC3564)

VII. *Dutch Shipping off the Coast in a Fresh Breeze*, Ludolf Bakhuizen, 1665,
National Maritime Museum (neg. BHC0916)

VIII. *Society at Sea*, Robert Dodd. National Maritime Museum (neg. PV8429)

Bengkulu: An Anglo-Chinese Partnership

ANTHONY FARRINGTON

This paper focusses on a relative backwater in the East India Company's concerns, which nevertheless was the setting for a first great experiment. At Bengkulu on the west coast of Sumatra the English attempted to reach an accommodation with the overseas Chinese – the sojourners and settlers of the South China junk trade, characterised by Anthony Reid as the 'unthreatening alternative' to the Europeans in South-east Asia.[1]

Banten on the north-west corner of Java was the site of the Company's oldest factory in Asia, and was the largest single source of its pepper imports into London. Early in 1682 Abu'l Fatah, the 'old' Sultan of Banten, who had resigned his throne under pressure from his son Sultan Abdul Kahar two years before, resumed the government by force. Abdul Kahar, under siege in the fort at Banten, appealed to the Dutch at Batavia and on 28 March 1682 the city fell to VOC Governor-General Cornelis Speelman's forces. Fulfilling one of the conditions for Dutch assistance, the English factory was ordered out and its personnel evacuated Banten on 11 April.[2]

News of their expulsion reached London in mid-March 1683. Preparations to meet force with force began but were soon abandoned; Sir John Chardin, Charles II's French jeweller and intrepid traveller to Persia, was sent to open negotiations at The Hague; and the price of pepper rose by $2d$ a pound.

Pepper had been the most important single commodity in the Company's portfolio at mid-century, and even as late as 1682 it came third (after Coromandel-Bengal and Surat textiles) in terms of cash receipts at the half-yearly sales in London. Pepper was vital to the mechanics of shipping. The Company's charterparties with shipowners called for at least one-third of each return cargo from Banten to be in pepper, which was shot loose into the hold to

---

[1] Anthony Reid, ed., *Sojourners and Settlers: Histories of Southeast Asia and the Chinese* (St Leonards, NSW, 1996); Anthony Reid, 'The Unthreatening Alternative: Chinese Shipping to Southeast Asia, 1567–1842', in *Pho Hien. The centre of international commerce in the XVIIth–XVIIIth centuries* (Hanoi, 1994).

[2] See the narrative of the final days in David Kenneth Bassett, 'The factory of the English East India Company at Bantam, 1602–1682' (unpublished PhD dissertation, University of London, 1955), 415–19. The factory staff of 16 Englishmen with 2 wives and some 40 servants, including 17 slaves, went first to Batavia and then left for Surat in August 1683, carrying with them the factory library of 165 books, overwhelmingly theological (BL, OIOC: E/3/43 nos 4961 and 5089).

provide ballast for the return voyage. On arrival in London it was bagged up and sold in lots of 100 bags of 2 cwt each at pre-determined starting prices per pound. Europe's appetite for it was enormous – the VOC was regularly bringing in double the EIC tonnage – and most of what was sold in London was re-exported to markets as far away as Poland, Russia and the Ottoman Empire. Although profit margins were small, the sheer volume of the trade coupled with its historic, even sentimental associations as a 'foundation commodity' made the Company determined to keep market share as a matter of national pride and a sign of resistance to Dutch monopolistic ambitions not only in Indonesia, where the VOC had successfully debarred its rival from the fine spices of the eastern islands, but also on the Malabar coast of India, another major source of pepper.[3]

Most of the pepper shipped from Banten originated in Sumatra. English efforts to find an alternative regular supply were now concentrated there, beginning at Aceh in 1684.[4] Aceh was fiercely anti-Dutch and was a long-established entrepôt for the Indian Ocean trade; a disadvantage was that it lay far to the north of the pepper producing areas. Separate initiatives by the Madras Council and the Directors in London both foundered over Aceh's refusal to permit a fortified settlement; but during negotiations a group of *orangkaya* from Pariaman invited the English to settle in their territory and sent representatives to Madras.

The subsequent expedition from Madras, intended for Pariaman, instead accepted another invitation, from the rulers of Bengkulu, which was much further south and adjacent to the important pepper-collecting point of Silebar.[5] The expedition reached Bengkulu in June 1685. A settlement was agreed and preparations began for building York Fort on a small hill to the south of the Bengkulu river mouth. Two infantry companies recruited in London became the first garrison.[6] In spite of Dutch attempts to intimidate the local Rajas under cover of suzerainty claims by their client Sultan of Banten, pepper began to come

---

3   This is based on Chapter 13 in Kirti Narayan Chaudhuri, *The Trading World of Asia and the English East India Company, 1660–1760* (Cambridge, 1978). For pepper import statistics, see his Chapters 11–14. The sale receipts for the period Sept. 1681–Mar. 1682 are: Coromandel and Bengal textiles £323,939; Surat textiles £177,580; Pepper £117,983 (4,715,135 lbs).

4   See Anthony Farrington, 'Negotiations at Aceh in 1684: an unpublished English document', in *Indonesia and the Malay world*, 27/77 (London, 1999), 19–33.

5   See John Bastin, *The British in West Sumatra, 1685–1825* (Kuala Lumpur, 1965), for details of the west-coast pepper-collecting ports. The pepper was grown in the foothills of the great ranges of mountains which parallel the west coast and was brought down dozens of small rivers. Chronic warfare between the 'Hill Rajas' frequently interrupted supplies, as the pepper plantations of the rival were usually targeted.

6   See Alan Harfield, *Bencoolen: A history of the Honourable East India Company's garrison on the west coast of Sumatra, 1685–1825* (Barton-on-Sea, 1995). Mortality rates were high, and before the arrival of Madras Sepoy Companies in the mid-eighteenth century numbers were sustained by enrolling Bugis mercenaries and, remarkably, some of the Madagascar slaves.

in – for instance, the *Williamson* in October 1689 loaded 900 Bengkulu bahars, or 504,000 lbs (225 tons).[7]

Fort building and a permanent garrison were serious intiatives for the EIC. In 1685 it only had fortifications at St Helena, Bombay and Madras, compared to the massive Dutch castle at Batavia[8] and numerous VOC forts scattered throughout the eastern islands. York Fort and its successor, Fort Marlborough, begun on a new site in 1714, should be seen as symbols of the Company's determination to remain in Sumatran pepper and to offer protection to their network of suppliers. The English had an 80-year history of broken promises to local rulers in Indonesia. Now they had come to stay. The model was Dutch, but unlike the VOC at Batavia the Bengkulu settlement always had a severe shortage of manpower.

While relying on slaves brought in from Madagascar for manual labour,[9] the English were in no doubt that the magic ingredient guaranteeing success would be a substantial Chinese population. First Banten and then Batavia were the main destinations for Chinese junk traffic to the south, which saw an explosion of voyages after the Manchu conquest of Taiwan in 1683 and the lifting of restrictions on the ports of the Fujian and Guangdong coastline. As well as commodities, the junks brought economic migrants, often earning more from passage money arrangements than from selling their cargoes. In 1686 eight junks from Amoy and three from other ports brought more than 800 migrants to Batavia. The incoming 'rabble from China' grew so large that in 1690 the VOC imposed a total ban, with fines of 10 dollars per person payable to the city's Chinese poor relief funds, quite impossible to enforce. By 1699 the Chinese, at 39 percent, were the largest group, excluding slaves, within Batavia, and were also settling uncultivated land around the city.[10]

Benjamin Bloom, the first Governor of Bengkulu, wrote to Madras in May 1686 'this place may in time prove as famous as Bantam, but untill that the Chinesses, who are the only tradeing men and the upholders of Batavia, are assured that wee are able to defend ourselves against an ennemy we must not expect there here, and without them never must wee expect any considerable trade'.[11] The credibility gap he identified lingered well into the eighteenth

---

7 OIOC: E/3/48 no. 5682, Bengkulu to London 26 Oct. 1689.

8 The equally impressive VOC Fort Zeelandia on Taiwan, begun in the late 1620s, had been captured by Cheng Ch'en-kung (Coxinga) in 1662.

9 Robert J. Young, 'Slaves, coolies and bondsmen: a study of assisted migration in response to emerging English shipping networks in the Indian Ocean 1685–1765', in Klaus Friedland, ed., *Maritime Aspects of Migration* (Köln, 1989), pp. 391–402. Young does not cover the Chinese.

10 See Leonard Blussé, *Strange Company: Chinese settlers, Mestizo women and the Dutch in VOC Batavia* (Dordrecht, 1988), and Leonard Blussé, 'Chinese century: the eighteenth century in the China Sea region', in *Archipel*, 58 (1999), 107–29. The 1699 population figures (*Strange Company*, p. 84) are: Chinese 3,679, Mardijkers [Christian, non-Indonesian freed slaves] 2,407, Europeans 1,783, Mestizos 670, others 867 – total 9,406.

11 OIOC: G/35/1(3) p. 72, Bengkulu to Madras 6 May 1686.

century and was not helped by a temporary evacuation in 1719 occasioned by panic over a local disturbance.

Bengkulu never became a place of 'considerable trade' though it did fulfil its function as a pepper source and permitted the settlers to experiment with other cash crops. As far as the dream of a Chinese-driven inter-Asian entrepôt was concerned, its location was wrong. Throughout the seventeenth century, Chinese based in Banten and Batavia had participated as intermediaries and brokers in the pepper-collecting process on the west coast, in south Sumatra and in the important east coast centres of Palembang, Jambi and Indragiri, either as agents for the Europeans or on their own account. This activity was not a function of the junk trade; it was carried on in local *prahus*, many of them Chinese-owned or Chinese-captained. Bengkulu, lying about 180 miles up the coast from the Straits of Sunda, had no attractions for the South China junks.

The desire for Chinese participation as partners and co-residents proved remarkably powerful. The *nokhodas* of Chinese *prahus* passing Bengkulu were enticed ashore with lavish promises and messages were sent through them to 'Captain Conco', the head of the Chinese residents at Batavia, inviting him to begin the surreptitious transportation of migrants from Java.[12] It was pointed out that Conco would not send 'men of great dealeings, but poore, and onely come to seeke their bread' and that the English would be expected to refund Conco's expenses. Another Chinese *prahu* master was told that 'if any industrious people such as his countrymen and trading men would come, no doubt but in a short time [this place] would, because of the mild government of the English, become more famous than Batavia'.[13]

A Chinese community slowly grew up at Bengkulu. Its members always arrived via Batavia and never directly from the Fujianese, Hakka and Chaozhou emigrant heartlands. The first settlers were five men from a passing *prahu* in September 1689, who were given a small house and a loan of 440 dollars.[14] *Nokhoda* 'Quaquo' acted as fixer in these early years and was flattered with regular salutes of seven guns from the Fort. It was reported to London in February 1693 that Conco had sent Chinese 'as carpinters, smiths and bricklayers to inhabitt with us, and hope he will send Chineese to make sugar'.[15] In March the Madras Council ordered that the Chinese should be granted 'ground to build on, and that their buildings range the more regularly and all stand at a convenient distance from the fort, lay out the streets and divisions by lines, and gratify them in all their reasonable requests'.[16]

The Bengkulu archive presents a picture of an immigrant heaven. 'Miserable poor' men were assured of land, work and cash advances. The Chinese were

---

12 OIOC: G/35/2(7) pp. 16–18, consultation 19 Aug. 1689, has a lengthy report of an interview with *nokhoda* Quaquo.
13 OIOC: G/35/2(7) pp. 22–3, consultation 12 Sept. 1689.
14 OIOC: G/35/2(7) pp. 24 and 36, consultations 15 Sept. and 2 Dec. 1689.
15 OIOC: E/3/49 no. 5856, Bengkulu to London 1 Feb. 1693.
16 OIOC: E/3/49 no. 5869, Madras to Bengkulu 1 Mar. 1693.

constantly praised as peaceable and industrious, in other words, useful. The downside was a growing prejudice against the local Malays, as in 'one Chinese will do the work of four Malays'.[17] The number of settlers cannot be quantified; the documents merely give occasional hints. Forty Chinese came in 1713. In September 1716 London was informed that 'above 100 are arrived' and that 500 more were expected.[18] I would estimate an eventual community of about 1,000 including wives and children, which hardly compares with the 15,000 at Batavia by the 1730s.[19]

Entrepreneurs soon emerged. Small retailers occupied a 'China bazaar', tea shops were opened,[20] market gardening flourished,[21] and brickmaking for the incessant building and repair of the fortifications became a Chinese preserve. In 1699 there are references to 'Kenco' the goldsmith.[22] In 1702 'Yoanco' the brick-maker, 'a diligent and industrious young man', also took on the monopoly licence for selling arrak and other spirits, let to farm at 46 dollars per month.[23] Sugar and arrak came to be the main products of Chinese enterprise, offering a useful addition to the Company's return cargoes.

As in the port cities throughout South-east Asia the community was repre-sented by a China Captain. The first 'head of the Chinese' recorded was 'Booko or Booker' who died in 1695 and who then had a share in the Madras country ship *Satisfaction*. His estate was sold, to pay his debts to the Company, 'att publick outcry by the riverside, all the Chinamen being first called to see the same fairly and honestly carryed on'.[24] In 1717 the Chinese community came in a body to the Fort to demand the removal of Captain 'Ponko' – 'we thought it but reasonable, since they desired it, that they should choose one themselves, upon which they chose See Gibb, who we confirmed their Captain by delivering him a kitasol and firing five guns, *as usual*.' Clearly there were established public accla-mation procedures for taking office.[25]

'See Gibb' emerges as a substantial figure in the sugar and arrak business. The Company advanced his start-up capital and guaranteed yearly purchases of some 23,000 gallons of arrak and 40,000 lbs of fine sugar. Between November 1715

17 OIOC: G/35/7 p. 90, Bengkulu to London 6 Feb. 1712.

18 OIOC: G/35/7 pp. 109 and 158, Bengkulu to London 10 Sept. 1713 and 29 Sept. 1716.

19 T'ien Ju-K'ang, 'The Chinese junk trade: merchants, entrepreneurs and coolies, 1600–1850', in *Maritime Aspects of Migration*, Friedland, ed., p. 383.

20 OIOC: G/35/4(3) p. 7, diary entry 19 Nov. 1699, refers to two *orangkaya* who 'accidentally met at a Chinese house whither they went to drink tea'.

21 So much so that a supply of 'salad oil' was requested from London. OIOC: G/35/7 p. 165, Bengkulu to London 29 Sept. 1716.

22 OIOC: G/35/4(3) p. 7, diary entry 19 Aug. 1699.

23 OIOC: G/35/4(6) p. 56, consultation 12 Feb. 1702. He is also referred to as 'Jury Tullis', i.e. Malay *juru tulis*, a scribe/clerk/purser of a ship, which may indicate conversion to Islam or merely his occupational origin.

24 OIOC: G/35/3 p. 27, consultation 8 July 1695.

25 OIOC: G/35/58(1) p. 47, consultation 19 Jan. 1717.

and July 1716 he had built a small village a mile above Bengkulu, cleared a great deal of ground, planted sugar canes and sent for more Chinese and equipment from Java.[26] Production was flowing by 1718 and See Gibb was employing a variety of craftsmen and labourers at wage rates which, for the skilled men, compared favourably with the nominal salaries of the Company's officials;[27] he was also branching out as a pepper broker. The business must have been hit badly by the panic evacuation of 1719.[28] In 1729 he was declared bankrupt, with a debt of about 17,000 dollars to the Company, his estate was seized and he was confined in the Fort on a monthly subsistence allowance of 2 dollars. The inventory of assets taken by the Company on 24 March 1729[29] reveals the scale of the enterprise – 23 slaves, an estimated 600,000 sugar canes, 400 coconut trees, 32 buffaloes, a large timber dwelling house, 2 rows of buildings containing 5 apartments, 15 outhouses for slaves, 2 large timber buildings for the sugar works and a large room for distilling arrak. Unsurprisingly the details of his house furnishings point to a modest personal lifestyle.

In 1750 the leader of the Chinese community was 'Quasey'. Together with 23 others 'long standerd on the west coast of Sumatra and inhabitance in Bencoolen for about these forty years' he addressed a petition to the Directors in London requesting an extension of commission for Governor Joseph Hurlock.[30] This remarkable document, if not quite a Rosetta Stone, throws some light on the families and individuals lying behind the attempts at romanisation of unfamiliar sounds with which the Chinese are saddled in the Company's archives. All 24 subscribers to the petition also have their names written in Chinese characters, making it clear that the English were romanising elements of the personal name only, and that the Chinese themselves were customarily adding the final character *guan/kuan*, meaning 'official', which in its pronounciation *qua* is so common in the records of the Company's trade at Canton. Lying behind these 'known-by

---

[26] OIOC: G/35/7 pp. 142 and 151, Bengkulu to London 21 Nov. 1715 and 17 July 1716.

[27] For example, 14 dollars a month for arrak distillers, 10 for sugar boilers, compared to 18 and 15 for Company factors and writers. In January 1719 he brought in nearly 30,000 lb. of pepper against a cash advance of 500 dollars: OIOC: G/35/7 p. 179, Bengkulu to London 10 Jan. 1719.

[28] According to Alexander Hamilton: 'Some Chinese merchants who had settled at Bencolon, being also frightened, embarked on their vessels and dispersed themselves in places where they thought they might be most secure. The chief merchant of the Chinese, who is generally called the China Captain in the places where the Chinese have trade, went to Batavia to some relations he had there, but the Dutch, according to their wonted hospitality in India, punished him as a criminal and taught him to make lime and carry stones the remnant of his days for daring to settle among the English. Some of the Chinese I saw the same year at Trangano in Johore, who gave me this account': William Foster, ed., *A New Account of the East Indies*, 2 vols (London, 1930), II, 62. Whoever this was, it was not See Gibb.

[29] OIOC: G/35/8 no. 409.

[30] OIOC: E/1/35 no. 271, Quasey and others to the Court of Directors, Bengkulu 31 Dec. 1750.

names' are South China families and clans like the Chen, Chang, Ye, Li and Wu. The petition awaits detailed investigation by South China dialect specialists.[31]

Bengkulu never became 'another Batavia' but it was the first EIC experiment in creating and governing a Chinese community, allowing free rein to Chinese entrepreneurs with a minimum of administrative interference. A second attempt was made at Penang after 1786,[32] with similar promises aimed at luring north the Chinese of Melaka. In 1825 Bengkulu was handed over to Dutch control in exchange for Melaka. Meanwhile Raffles, late Governor of Bengkulu, had launched the settlement at Singapore. The partnership finally became a reality – 'when the British flag was first hoisted there were not perhaps a hundred Chinese on the island, in three months the number did not fall short of five thousand'.[33]

[31] I am indebted to my British Library colleagues Dr Frances Wood, Beth McKillop and Graham Hutt for their preliminary examination of this unique document. Weng Eang Chong, *The Hong Merchants of Canton: Chinese merchants in Sino-Western trade* (London, 1997), has a useful list of 'qua' trade names at Canton.

[32] Leonard Blussé in 'Chinese century', p. 127, describes Penang as the *first* British attempt to link up to the networks of Chinese traders in the archipelago.

[33] Raffles to the Government of India, 20 Dec. 1819, OIOC: Mss Eur F.33 p. 342.

Establishing the Sea Routes to India and China: Stages in the Development of Hydrographical Knowledge

ANDREW S. COOK

This paper seeks to identify phases in the development of the body of knowledge, increasingly shared among ships' captains, of the safe routes to sail from Europe to India and China, and of the dangers to be avoided; the manuscript charts and accounts used and developed on board the ships venturing out from Europe in the seventeenth century; the problems and uncertainties in establishing a pre-dictable navigation to meet the trading expectations of an increasingly institu-tionalised East India Company in the eighteenth century; the proposals made by the hydrographer Alexander Dalrymple in the later eighteenth century for col-lecting and codifying knowledge of the seas, and the extent to which he was able to implement them; and the culmination in series of comprehensive charts and nautical directories published by James Horsburgh and his successor John Walker for the East India Company at almost exactly the time the Company was relinquishing its monopoly of shipping in the 1830s.[1]

Early East India Company voyages were as much voyages of exploration as were any of the sixteenth-century voyages of Cabot or Drake. Each was an indi-vidual speculative venture, with its own investors. The only difference was that they were going into an ocean where they believed other Europeans, specifically Portuguese, had gone before. The sixteenth-century creation of the Portuguese maritime empire; the incursions of the Dutch; the claims made by some of French infiltration: all these produced manuscript mapping in the sixteenth century of a type known to us for other reasons, as in the Rotz Atlas of the Dieppe School, and the early Portuguese charts of the coasts of Africa. Manu-script charts for use at sea, portolans as well as coastal and island charts, had been in common use since the late thirteenth century, but chiefly in the enclosed Mediterranean, where it was unusual to spend more than a few days out of sight of land, and where the winds and currents to set the bearings for the standard traverses were well known.[2]

---

[1]   This paper is derived from notes of the conference presentation, which was intended to indicate in broad terms lines of possible future research.

[2]   The history of the development of the portolan chart has been comprehensively treated by Tony Campbell, 'Portolan Charts from the Late Thirteenth Century to 1500', in J.B. Harley

The sea chart differs from the land map not only in its form but in the way it is used. A land map shows the positions of places to which the observer can relate, at will, by processes of measurement. At sea, particularly out of sight of land, he places himself beyond any observable relationship with known points, in an inherently hostile medium in which he is carried at rates and in directions which he can estimate but cannot accurately measure. Assuming the sea-worthiness of his vessel, and fair weather, the 'safest' part of any voyage is the period when the mariner is headed away from land to open ocean, and, with the problems in measuring his progress at sea, the most hazardous time is when he tries to approach land again (or arrives unexpectedly at unforeseen land). The sea chart allows the recording of progress or movement only by a series of esti-mates of daily position, not in relation to known topography, but by astronom-ical observations for latitude, and by compass bearing, modified by informed guesses for distance covered, and the effects of wind and current. Aboard ship the chart, as a means of recording progress of the voyage, was just another instrument, like the compass, the sextant (or backstaff), the sailing directions, the log and line, and the log-book (or account).

Blank paper, with graticule, could (sometimes did) suffice to keep such a voyage record: geographical information, coastlines, rocks, shoals, and dangers, and offshore islands, cumulated from previous voyages, could be present sepa-rately either in textual directions or in cartographic form on charts. The nautical or oceanic chart to suggest long courses to shape in open ocean to avoid landfall; the coastal approach chart to navigate straits or archipelagos, to approach coasts, or (less desirably in a sailing ship) to proceed along coasts; the harbour plan to identify entry paths (with leading and clearing lines and marks) and anchorages. With the coastal approach chart went coastal profiles or land recognition views, on the chart or separately, and with the harbour plan (usually on the plan itself) was commonly found the profile of leading or clearing marks to be brought into alignment for safe entry or anchorage. Each book of charts, manuscript or printed, contained, often with text, charts of all three types (with their associated profiles) for use at sea.

As the navigational interests of European countries spread from the Mediterranean to Northern European, North Atlantic, and African waters, portolan-type charts, including those of the 'Thames school' in London, and text 'rutters' covered wider and increasingly disparate areas. But their manuscript dissemination was slow, and the mariner, with few charts to hand, and no basis for the objective assessment of those he had, continued to be reliant, in Halley's terms, on 'latitude, lead and lookout'. The mariners who had most need of aids to oceanic navigation, and of coastal approach charts, were those of the trading companies primarily of England, France and the Netherlands, particularly the East India Companies. The most complex navigation was that from Europe to

and David Woodward, eds, *The History of Cartography*, vol. I: *Cartography in Prehistoric, Ancient, and Medieval Europe and the Mediterranean* (Chicago, 1987), pp. 371–463.

the East Indies: it required first a passage of the Atlantic currents in both hemispheres, an eastward turn at the Cape of Good Hope, and either a passage through the Mozambique Channel and archipelagos to Bombay and Madras, or dead reckoning runs in southerly latitudes before turning northward to India or to the straits between the Indonesian islands to Batavia, China or Bantam.

The character of investment in the East India Company changed in the mid-seventeenth century, from individual voyage investment and accounting to a permanent rolling joint stock paying dividends on the whole of the Company's current operations. This reinforced the need to maintain a yearly pattern of voyages visiting the same eastern ports, such as the Malabar Coast of India and Macassar, where permanent agents or factors were increasingly established to maintain the inflow to the factory of local goods for export. The need to repeat voyage patterns year after year, and to make predictable visits to a series of ports, necessitated a formal knowledge of currents, coastlines and directions for sailing to them. In England, France and the Netherlands, formal organisation of chart provision for ships' captains in the East Indies trade generally preceded and overshadowed the establishment of government hydrographic departments.

Unlike the French and Dutch East India Companies, the English Company had never established a hydrographic office. The Dutch Company had traditionally organised chart production as a secret central function, until the eventual publication of the sixth part of Van Keulen's *De Nieuwe Groote Lichtende Zee-Fakkel* in 1753, furnishing ships until then with charts only in manuscript. The chart workshops, in Amsterdam and later in Batavia, produced coastal pilotage charts of the East Indies in large quantities, for issue to captains and officers, who accounted for each item on inventories after each voyage, with money penalties for losses.[3] The French Company's hydrographic materials were in the hands of D'Après de Mannevillette, a retired Captain, at Lorient in Brittany. As the Company's hydrographer he maintained at Lorient an office sanctioned by the Dépôt des Cartes et Plans de la Marine (founded in 1720) in Paris, until his death in 1780, when his collections reverted by agreement to the French Crown.[4]

The East India Company in London had no formal mechanism for official chart publication, and generally exercised looser control over shipping and routes. Typically in the eighteenth century the Company controlled the provision of shipping by regulating the activities of consortia of private shipowners. A ship's equipment, including navigation instruments and charts, though

---

3   The Dutch practice is summarised by Kees Zandvliet, *Mapping for Money: Maps, Plans and Topographic Paintings and Their Role in Dutch Overseas Expansion during the 16th and 17th Centuries* (Amsterdam, 1998), particularly pp. 86–117.

4   Andrew S. Cook, 'An exchange of letters between two hydrographers: Alexander Dalrymple and Jean-Baptiste d'Après de Mannevillette', in Philippe Haudrère, ed., *Les Flottes des Compagnies des Indes, 1600–1857* (Vincennes, 1996), pp. 173–82. D'Après de Mannevillette is currently the subject of more detailed study by Manonmani Filliozat: see, for example, her '*Le Neptune Oriental.* une somme de la cartographie de la Compagnie des Indes', *Cahiers de la Compagnie des Indes,* 3 (1998), 21–30.

inspected by Company surveyors, was the responsibility of the captain as employee of the owners. The captain's qualifications and experience were subject to ratification by the Company. His responsibility extended to chart supply: the Company did not, at first, prescribe what charts were to be carried, only that a fair copy of the journal (embodying the daily log) was to be deposited at East India House at the conclusion of each voyage.[5] The accumulation of these journals, each with daily observations for position, hourly observations of conditions at sea, notes of land dangers observed, often hand-drawn coastal profiles, and sometimes sketch plans of harbours, was a potential resource for the analysis of voyages, but, despite their wealth of information, no system of chart compilation, either through examination of these journals or independently, had developed in the Company in London. Though they were open to inspection by Company captains, the information they contained was not exploited fully in the seventeenth and early eighteenth centuries. Instead information was provided by returning captains to the commercial chartmakers of London, the masters and apprentices of the Thames School, producing manuscript vellum charts and atlases in establishments in Rotherhithe and Wapping.[6] One of these practitioners, John Thornton, converted into print in 1703 the corpus of knowledge of the navigation to the East Indies, revising and expanding John Seller's *The English Pilot for the Oriental Navigation* of 1675.[7] *The English Pilot, The Third Book* was continued in print by the chartsellers Mount and Page for most of the eighteenth century, to be used alongside Cornwall's 1720 pilot book *Observations on Several Voyages to India*.[8] The 1745 edition of D'Après de Mannevillette's *Le Neptune Oriental* also served the East India Company captains in the Thames, particularly in the successive editions of the English translation by William Herbert from 1758.[9] Each was a compendium of textual directions, oceanic charts, coastal charts, harbour plans, and views of land. Captains who had made

5   The British Library, India Office Records [hereafter IOR], L/MAR/A–B. See Anthony Farrington, *Catalogue of East India Company Ships' Journals and Logs, 1600–1834* (London, 1999). On the equipping of East India Company ships, see also Jean Sutton, *Lords of the East: The East India Company and its Ships (1600–1874)* (London, 1981; revised edition 2000).

6   T.R. Smith, 'Manuscript and Printed Sea Charts in Seventeenth-Century London: The Case of the Thames School', in N.J.W. Thrower, ed., *The Compleat Plattmaker* (Berkeley, 1978), pp. 45–100; Tony Campbell, 'The Drapers' Company and its School of Seventeenth-Century Chart-Makers', in H.M. Wallis and S.J. Tyacke, eds, *My Head is a Map: Essays and Memoirs in honour of R.V. Tooley* (London, 1973), pp. 81–106.

7   Andrew S. Cook, 'More Manuscript Charts by John Thornton for the Oriental Navigation', in C.C. Marzoli, ed., *Imago et Mensura Mundi: Atti del X Congresso Internazionale di Storia della Cartografia* (Florence, 1985), pp. 61–9.

8   See the introduction to Coolie Verner and R. A. Skelton, eds, *John Thornton, 'The English Pilot, The Third Book', London, 1703*, facsimile edition (Amsterdam, 1973). H. Cornwall, *Observations upon Several Voyages to India* (London, 1720).

9   J.B.N.-D. D'Après de Mannevillette, *Le Neptune Oriental ou routier general des cotes des Indes Orientales et de la Chine . . .* (Paris, 1745). William Herbert, *A New Directory for the East Indies* (London, 1758; 2nd edition, 1759; 3rd edition, 1767; 4th edition, 1776).

harbour plans or amended coastal charts were free to sell their work to these and other publishers, and the resulting publications owed more to commercial opportunism than to systematic analysis.

But by the 1750s much of the information available to commanders was severely out of date, and seen as such. Charles Noble, in a 1755 pamphlet comparing French and English shipboard conditions, gave his opinion of the relative quality of charting from the two countries:

> The French have been at pains, to improve their Navigation and their Charts; Those of the Indian Seas, by Monsieur D'Apres de Mannevillette, a Captain in their Service, exceed every thing of the kind in Europe. It is a pity they are not translated into English, for the benefit of our Navigators. Those who understand the language, and have seen them, must have a despicable opinion, of our Indian Pilot, with which Messrs. Mount and Page have long imposed on, and picked the pockets of our Countrymen, and which are only fit for the Grocers and Chandlers Shops, or posterior uses.[10]

Company captains, particularly those experienced in navigation eastwards from India, could see for themselves the deficiencies and inaccuracies of the European product in areas they themselves knew well. To be of general utility sea charts had to command general respect, and to command respect they had to be compiled to satisfactory standards.

The Atlantic Ocean, the routine passage from Europe for all fleets to the East Indies, offered many problems to navigation, few of which were recorded in charts. The Dutch and English East India Companies each sent out four or five fleets each season to India, China and Java, the departure date being dictated by the need to catch the south-west monsoon in the China Sea. For the English Company alone this amounted to between 25 and 30 ships a year. Ships would try to keep company, but inevitably separations would occur, and it was always a relief to complete the Atlantic passage on the outward voyage, either by safe arrival at Table Bay or False Bay, or by sighting the Cape to take a new departure for the Indian Ocean. The Atlantic passage might well take four or more of the seven or eight months voyage to India or China. A letter written from the Cape in September 1775 by the hydrographer Alexander Dalrymple when a passenger in the ship *Grenville* well illustrates the nature of the passage:

> I paid my respects to you from Madeira on the 15th May. We arrived at False Bay on the 21st August after a very tedious and uncomfortable passage. We had light winds after we passed the Cape de Verde Islands, none of which we saw sight of, leaving them to the westward. We had frequent soundings off the Coast of Guinea to the southward of Cape Verde, and saw the land to the westward of Cape Palmas, and again at that Cape, as we supposed. Notwithstanding which we met such violent currents, setting us for several days together above 70 miles a day to the westward, that we had sight of Trinidada,

---

[10] C.F. Noble, *The French, and English, Marine Regulations Compared* (reprinted [London, 1793]).

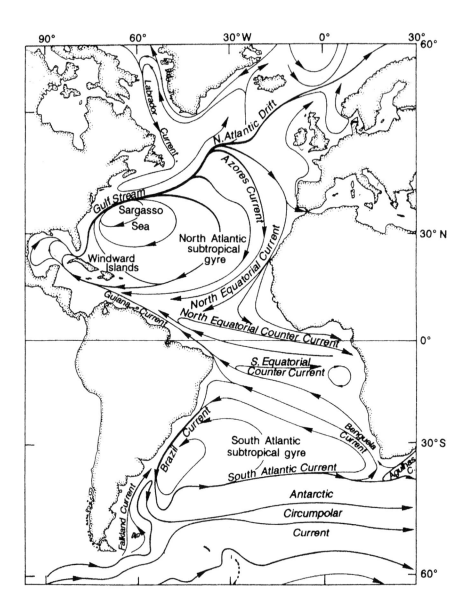

1 Schematic representation of the Atlantic Ocean current system. Reprinted
from John Gould, 'James Rennell's View of the Atlantic Circulation:
A comparison with our present knowledge', *Ocean Challenge*, 4, nos. 1and 2
(1993), pp. 26–33, by kind permission of the Challenger Society for Marine
Science.

which we could not go to windward of. After passing the line, instead of meeting with a regular trade wind and smooth water, we had squally blowing weather and a great sea. And after we had passed Trinidada we had a violent gale of wind from the south-west.

We found the Marine Barometer of great use to us as we got to the south-ward, and is a great favourite of all the seamen, who never wish to go to sea without it.

Some days after we had got into Table Bay the Gatton, which sailed two days after us from Madeira came into Table Bay. They passed to the westward of the Cape de Verde Islands, and fell in with the Easternmost part of Brazil. He was in 12 fathoms within a few miles of the land when the wind came round to south, with which they stood off ESE, and had soundings till out of sight of land. This wind continued a whole day, and came round again to the south-ward: they stood of ENE next day and then put about, and saw no more of the land as they stood to the southward.

The Coventry has not been here: I think it is very probable she has not weathered the coast of Brazil, as it not likely she would pass the Cape without touching here.

Our timekeeper has stopt three times, but Mudge's watch going very well, and, a regular register have been kept of all the watches, it was set a-going, and an account kept of the Times it had stopd. The Timekeeper gave us the land a little more than 1° to the westward of its true situation, which is very near considering the length of our passage from England. Our lunar observations were about ½ a degree too far East, but we had no sights for some days before we made the land.[11]

Such an account gives insights into the techniques of navigation in the Atlantic. Even for an experienced navigator there were many uncertainties. The importance of sighting land in passing is clear, but nowhere is a chart or pilot book mentioned. The winds are observed with considerable care, as is the force of the not unexpected current. The intention after leaving the Cape Verde Islands was to sight Trindade, off Brazil, as a new point of departure, but *Grenville* was forced to the lee of the island. *Coventry* was less lucky, and got into soundings on a lee shore, before the wind changed to allow her to stand off. Each ship stood southward, or south-eastward, to the latitude of the Cape of Good Hope, running that latitude to within sight of the Cape. In the case of *Grenville*, a combination of lunar observation and chronometer brought her home, at least to within 60 miles. With the exception of the chronometer observations, this was navigation by latitude, lead and lookout. Charts, if any, provided only a sense of the limits of the ocean, and approximate locations of islands.

The major problem of the outbound Atlantic navigation was not recorded on charts – the ocean circulation pattern, the currents known to mariners only by experience. A modern diagram of current patterns gives the clues.[12] The

---

11 Alexander Dalrymple to Robert Orme, 8 September 1775 (Orme Collection [IOR: MSS Eur Orme O.V.171(1)]).
12 John Gould, 'James Rennell's View of the Atlantic Circulation: A comparison with our

prevailing currents in both north and south Atlantic drive towards the Caribbean and the Gulf of Mexico, the North Equatorial Current from the Azores and
the West African coast, and the Benguela Current and the South Equatorial
Current from the west coast of southern Africa. A ship sailing south-west from
Europe encountered first the southward currents spinning off the Gulf Stream,
and would try to sight the Canary Islands to take advantage of the Azores
Current. Next sighting would be Cape Verde Islands, the sign to turn southwards
out of the main current as it swung towards the West Indies. A commander had
to estimate how far to allow his ship to be carried towards the Gulf of Guinea by
the counter-current, before striking southwards across the South Equatorial
Current. Too far east and he would be in dead water in the Gulf of Guinea, not
far enough and he could find himself on the Brazil coast without having turned
Cape Recife. The relative strengths of the counter-currents varied, and were
accentuated or mitigated by seasonal winds. The assessment of the westward set
of the South Equatorial Current was one of the most important decisions a
commander had to make, on very little information. Determined to avoid a West
African lee shore, his dead reckoning from the Cape Verde Islands was the chief
input. His aim was for Trindade or Martin Vaz, off the Brazil coast, as his next
point of departure, to steer southwards or south-eastwards, benefiting from the
Brazil Current, to reach the latitude of the Cape of Good Hope, either to make
Table Bay, or to take a more southerly path, avoiding the Lagullus Bank, into the
Indian Ocean.

The navigation of the Indian Ocean offered different problems, but the critical part of any outward voyage was spent in the Atlantic. A ship which failed to
make Cape Recife could easily lose a further four or six weeks in making a
second attempt, and would then need to water on the Brazil coast before continuing. It was simply impossible to sail direct for the Cape. Decisions at the
three turning points all had to be taken in open ocean by dead reckoning and
without reference longitudes. Mariners preferred open ocean to lee shores:
isolated islands, such as Trindade or Cape Verde Islands were ideal sighting
points: they had a known relationship to the mainland, but were far enough out
to allow ships to pass to either side before continuing. Latitude, lead and lookout
were the guides, as well as the measurement of daily distance by log, bearing, and
the constant assessment of floating vegetation and of bird life. Before the capacity to make longitude observations these were the only guides a commander
had. At any point he knew his daily latitude, he knew what land he had last seen
(if he recognised it), he knew his bearing, he thought he knew how far he had
sailed along that bearing, and he could estimate what lateral effect the wind had
had. But he had to guess the effect of current.

Popular historians of the chronometer relate that John Harrison's invention

present knowledge', *Ocean Challenge: The Magazine of the Challenger Society for Marine
Science,* 4, nos. 1/2 (1993), pp. 26–32, figure 4 (p. 29): 'Schematic representation of the
Atlantic current system' [illustrated here as figure 1 on page 124].

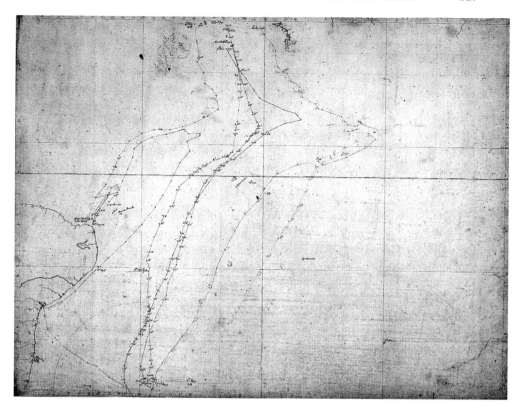

2　Blank engraved chart for East India Company captains to enter their tracks from the latitude of Cape Verde Islands to 21°S, by Alexander Dalrymple (Admiralty Library Collection [Vf 1/13]). This example has been completed by Dalrymple himself, with coastal outlines and tracks both 'by account' and by a combination of latitude observations and chronometer, including the track of Dalrymple's own voyage in *Grenville* in 1775.

solved navigation problems by enabling mariners to tell their longitude position with accuracy. A timekeeper was only a machine for carrying local time through a voyage: it was only as good as its maker, and it could stop. Pocket watches served on board ship from local noon to local noon, but a timekeeper had to be reliable over months – and consequently had to be checked by lunar observations. The reputation of the timekeeper had not yet been established: for reliability reasons three or more were later carried, but it was accepted that too firm a reliance 'relaxed the vigilance which the known uncertainty of dead reckoning kept perpetually alive'. As important, in order to use knowledge of the longitude of one's position effectively in navigation, is the need to know the longitudes of the land one sights (and of the dangers to avoid) with the same accuracy. Anson's problem in clearing Cape Horn and running a latitude to Juan Fernandez would not have been solved by knowing his longitude, unless he had known the longitudes of Cape Horn and Juan Fernandez with equal precision. Knowledge of absolute longitude is useful, then, only in relative terms. Without accurate longitude charting of the coasts and islands of the Atlantic, knowledge of longitude was only another aid to navigation for the commander of the *Grenville*. And even with knowledge of longitude, ships were still subject to winds and current.

To this system of experience, observation and intuition the East India Company entrusted 30 ships a year, the generation of its wealth, and the safety of its employees. The oceanic navigation pattern of later years was not recorded on charts: only in the 1720s were a few limiting suggestions marked on the Atlantic Ocean chart in *The English Pilot*.[13] Though a wealth of track information was building up in East India House, there was no machinery for examining it and for connecting it with commercial chart production. Perhaps it was for this reason Noble was scathing about English charts.

In *Grenville* Dalrymple had access to one of John Arnold's new chronometers, which he used daily, and later published his journal of observations. This voyage introduced Dalrymple to the uncertainties of oceanic navigation, particularly outbound from England, to the possibilities of the increased accuracy which chronometer longitudes could allow, and to the lack of precision with which longitudes of coasts and islands were marked on charts. Back in London in April 1777 Dalrymple soon developed a scheme to assemble data from the deposited journals of oceanic voyages by East India Company ships, to predict the safest and quickest courses to follow, and to explain the effects of the currents, particularly in the Atlantic:

> A comparison of the several tracks of the Company's ships would, in a few years, determine with great precision what is, at every season, the most eligible course to pursue out and home. The improvement made lately in the art and practice of navigation, by the lunar observations for determining the longitude, and by the use of timekeepers, will be very conducive towards explaining the currents, that most curious and important phenomenon in nautical history.[14]

He issued special journal forms to allow parallel recording, in detail, of positions by account, and by chronometer or lunar observation, and distributed with them blank charts calibrated at 5 degrees to 1 inch for marking tracks. The East India Company subscribed for 100 sets, for the ships of the new season. The following year Dalrymple added an equatorial chart specifically for the Atlantic:

> As in low latitudes between Brazil and Africa the winds are generally faint and variable, and the daily runs consequently short and irregular, so as not to be easily expressed in so small a Scale as the general chart, I have thought it will be

---

13 From the 1723 edition onwards, the equatorial part of the Atlantic Ocean chart in *The English Pilot, The Third Book* (see note 8 above) was marked with a diagram of lines suggesting east and west longitude limits for a favourable passage.

14 Alexander Dalrymple, untitled pamphlet 'A comparison of the several tracks . . .' ([London,] 1778), example at IOR: Mss Eur Orme O.V.88(8), pp. 101–8.

proper to give a plain Chart on a Scale of half an inch to 1°, from the Cape de Verde Islands to 21°S.[15]

One example of this chart has recently been identified among manuscript charts in the Admiralty Library collection in the Hydrographic Office. As issued, it had engraved frame and graticule, but the remainder empty. This example has been completed by Dalrymple himself, with coastal outlines and tracks both 'by account' (i.e. dead reckoning) and by a combination of latitude observations and chronometer, including that of the Grenville in 1775.[16]

For greatest accuracy the tracks had to show longitudes by chronometer based on established points of departure of known longitude. Dalrymple issued a list of useful places whose longitudes had been adequately observed, i.e. where a land observer had been stationed, or longitudes had been established by short-run timekeeper voyages.[17] To achieve a useable series of chronometer tracks, Dalrymple needed to get commanders to buy chronometers, make series of observations, and complete not only track charts but extra journal forms. He had no authority to order the use of his system, and results did not materialise. But he had taken the first step towards the systematic collection and analysis of East India Company navigational information.

He proposed himself for a new position 'for examining the Ships' Journals from the earliest times that Notice may be given of every danger which has hitherto been discovered, and for publishing from time to time such Charts and Nautical Directions as a comparison of the various Journals and other Materials may enable him to do'. On 1 April 1779 the East India Company appointed him to this new responsibility. The immediate occasion on which the success of Dalrymple's proposal turned was the loss of the East India ship *Colebrooke* on the Anvil Rock, in False Bay, Cape of Good Hope, in August 1778. He argued that the danger had been known since the *Caesar* struck in 1745, and was confirmed by the French ship *Mergé* striking subsequently. D'Après de Mannevillette had published the *Mergé*'s account in 1765, and Dalrymple was already corresponding with him privately in 1767 about the *Caesar*'s journal. A visual search for the Anvil was one of Dalrymple's self-appointed tasks during his short stay in False Bay in 1775.[18]

---

[15] Alexander Dalrymple, untitled pamphlet 'The East India Company having thought proper to employ me . . .' ([London,] 1779), examples at Washington, Library of Congress: G1059.D23 Text 4(5–6), Paris, Archives Nationales: Marine 3JJ 1(29), and Stockholm, Universitetsbibliotek: Rf.142.

[16] Taunton, United Kingdom Hydrographic Office (Admiralty Library collection): Vf.1/13 [illustrated here as figure 2, page 127].

[17] Appended to his 1778 and 1779 pamphlets (see notes 14 and 15 above).

[18] 'Angles for determining the reciprocal Positions of the Lands around False Bay at the Cape of Good Hope, and especially intended to assist in compleating a Survey of Simon's Bay. Taken in August and September 1775 by AD . . .', in Alexander Dalrymple, ed., *Collection of Views of Land and of Plans of Ports in the East Indies* (London, 1781), pp. 1–24, particularly p. 18: 'In 1775 when I was at Simon's Bay I intended to have gone upon the Hills, towards

Dalrymple's argument in his Memorial to the Company was that the proper co-ordination and publication of hydrographical information from the fair copies of the journals routinely deposited in East India House by the commanders of returning ships would alert officers on subsequent voyages to particular dangers. He was supported by the Chairman, Sir George Wombwell, whom he reported as remarking that 'I had timed it very well', and that 'the loss of the *Colebrooke* was more than the expence of such an Office to all eternity'. It clearly did not work to leave to commercial chart publishers the job of publicising promptly new dangers at sea.

Though Dalrymple later called himself 'Hydrographer to the East India Company', his position never appeared in establishment lists or salary books: he was paid a quarterly fee, always 'For examining the Ships' Journals, &ca.'[19] The provision for chart publication was that Dalrymple's expenses in engraving and printing 100 copies of any chart he chose to compile would be met by the Company, after which the plate became his property, and further impressions to use or sell as he pleased were at his own expense of paper and presswork. The editorial control was entirely in his hands, as was planning for publication. Market forces were conspicuously absent.

Dalrymple issued a notice on 20 April 1779, based on his Memorial, chiefly for East India Company ships' commanders and officers, explaining his appointment, and proposing to compile a new set of charts for the navigation to the East Indies, improving on D'Après de Mannevillette's *Le Neptune Oriental* by including the sightings of rocks and shoals from East India House ships' journals. His first task was to examine all the journals, and his second to produce charts:

> The Plan I propose to pursue is, with the utmost Expedition to get an Index made to all the Journals, containing the day of seeing every Land or shoal, or having soundings, so that as soon as possible the Company's Ships may have notice of every danger which has been discovered form the earliest times: and thus knowing every Ship which has seen any particular danger, the comparison of the different Journals will facilitate the laying down thereof.[20]

If such an Index was ever completed it has not survived. Dalrymple had no research assistant, nor was there any Company provision for an office for him, and at his death almost 20 years later his executors had to ask the Company to

the Cape Good Hope, to have endeavoured to have got sight of the Anvil from thence, but unluckily I was prevented by the weather.'

19   East India Company, Court Minutes, 1781–1808, s.n. Dalrymple (IOR: B/97–146); East India Company, Cash Journals, 1779–1811, passim (IOR: L/AG/1/5/21–27).

20   Alexander Dalrymple, untitled pamphlet 'Notwithstanding the many years that the Europeans have navigated to India . . .' ([London,] 1779), examples at The British Library: G.2198(13.), Paris, Archives Nationales: Marine 3JJ 341(19), and Stockholm, Universitets-bibliotek: Rf.142.

take back over 700 ships' journals and other manuscript books found in his house.[21]

As his first year's output Dalrymple proposed to compile and publish a small-scale chart (60 nautical miles to 1 inch) of the Mozambique Channel and Madagascar, and larger-scale charts of the Strait of Bangka, the Strait of Singapore, and the Parcelar Banks in the Strait of Malacca. The longer-term plan was for a series of 27 coastal charts at a common scale of 20 nautical miles to 1 inch covering the most frequented coasts of the Indian Ocean and the Eastern Archipelago. The areas chosen included the passages most frequently used by Company ships: many chose to water at Anjouan in the Mozambique Channel on the outward journey, then to proceed through known latitude channels in the Maldives to India. At the request of the East India Company Secret Committee, he compiled in June 1782 a 'Memoir concerning the Passages to and from China'.[22] This analysis of the wide range of routes in the Eastern Archipelago for ships from England or India to avoid French or Spanish interception was the first synthesis of the results of his ongoing examination of the ships' journals, but it detracted from his aim of producing charts.

But incoming information, often lacking a chronometer basis, was too disorganised to be used effectively, while at the same time conflicting with the topography in the older printed mapping. And Dalrymple had no authority to order surveys to resolve these points. In 1784 he proposed a survey of the Coromandel Coast, but only as an academic exercise.[23] Only once, in 1786, was he asked to advise on a proposed survey, in this case the Bombay Government on a chronometer survey of the coast of Western India, which he said would provide data for the Malabar Coast charts of his series, and he sent instructions to Bombay for the use of Arnold chronometers.[24] John McCluer, of the Bombay Marine, was chosen for the survey on his reputation for similar surveys in the Persian Gulf in the early 1780s:

---

[21] Charles Wilkins, East India Company Librarian, reported complying with the executors' request (East India Company, Court Minutes, 28 June 1809 [IOR: B/149, p. 449]).

[22] Alexander Dalrymple, *Memoir Concerning the Passages to and from China* ([London,] 1782). The first 'edition' was printed in restricted numbers for issue by the East India Company Secret Committee in 1782 to China ships: it is now known only from the copy sent to the Governor-General in Bengal in January 1783, now in the National Archives of India, and published in C.H. Philips and B.B. Misra, eds, *Fort William–India House Correspondence, vol. XV: Foreign and Secret, 1782–1786* (Delhi, 1963), pp. 20 and 24–40. The second (1785) and third (1788) editions enjoyed a more open peacetime circulation.

[23] Alexander Dalrymple, *Proposition for a Survey of the Coast of Choromandel* (London, 1784), example at The British Library: G.2197(22). Later re-issued in the preliminary pages of Alexander Dalrymple, ed., *An Hydrographical Journal of a Cursory Survey of the Coasts and Islands of the Bay of Bengal by Capt. John Ritchie 1770 and 1771* (London, 1784), itself re-issued in Alexander Dalrymple, *Collection of Nautical Papers concerning the Bay of Bengal* (London, 1785).

[24] [Alexander Dalrymple,] *Instructions concerning the Chronometers, or Time-Keepers, sent to Bombay, 1786* ([London, 1786]), only known example in a private collection.

We would have the vessel proceed along the coast, from Bombay to Surat, determining carefully the Latitudes and Longitudes of the various points, as well as of the Peaks of Hills inland, with explanatory views of the Lands, taking altitudes for determining the time by Chronometer every hour; & taking the bearings and altitudes of the Lands &ca., by the Hadley at such time.[25]

Dalrymple's association with Arnold continued a close one, and he continued to recommend Arnold as supplier of chronometers for East India Company ships' captains who wished to take observations on their voyages.[26] The Company took a passing interest in the work Dalrymple was encouraging captains to do, but all knew that the first concern of the captain had to be his ship, cargo and orders. There was rarely time for surveying on the side, and the scheme for systematic coastal chart compilation faltered. Dalrymple's table of sufficiently accurate longitudes was not comprehensive enough, the firm longitudes not at close enough intervals, to allow charts to be compiled by filling in the intervening detail, at least not at his chosen scale. As a step towards remedying this deficiency, he consistently advocated the collection of views of land, as an aid to coastal navigation and, in island groups, to aid recognition and position fixing.

The problems with using dead-reckoning longitudes irreconcilable with others, are exemplified in his correspondence with D'Après over the non-existent islands Ady and Candy, thought to lie to the east of the Chagos Archipelago in the same latitude.[27] Circumstantial evidence from journals had encouraged mapmakers to place them on the chart, but their relationship to the Chagos could not be confirmed. They had to remain on Dalrymple's charts, even in the 1780s as a warning to shipping, despite the increasing likelihood that they were false. The same caution appears in the reciprocal longitude charts Dalrymple was preparing in the 1780s. On one, showing part of Madagascar with the Indian Ocean islands, he could enter very little with certainty.[28] The published pilot books all showed different versions of the Mozambique Channel, and he had no basis for preferring one over the others.

25 Alexander Dalrymple, ed., *An Account of the Navigation between India and the Gulph of Persia, at all Seasons, with Nautical Instructions for that Gulph, by Lieutenant John McCluer* (London, 1786).
26 Andrew S. Cook, 'Alexander Dalrymple and John Arnold: Chronometers and the Representation of Longitude on East India Company Charts', *Vistas in Astronomy*, 28 (1985), 189–95.
27 Cook, 'An Exchange of Letters' [see note 4 above]. [Alexander Dalrymple,] untitled pamphlet 'Some Notes of the Islands to the Northward of Madagascar, extracted from a letter of M. D'Après de Mannevillette . . .' ([London,] 1772), example in Canterbury Cathedral Library: H/U–13–19(1).
28 Untitled chart, showing part of Madagascar and islands to the northward (Taunton: United Kingdom Hydrographic Office: A13 in folio A). This is a impression made for archive purposes when the plate, which the Hydrographic Office acquired with others after Dalrymple's death, was cancelled and destroyed as part of normal working practices.

Whoever knows anything of making Charts from a variety of materials, must know that it is impossible to reconcile those materials perfectly. Indeed it often happens that they are totally contradictory: where I find disagreement in particular charts, I have thought the best way was to engrave both, when I had nothing to enable me to decide on the merits of either.

In consequence he sent out five charts on which the Mozambique Channel appeared, each from a different source, and six representations of the Malabar Coast appeared on another plate.[29] Dalrymple tried to collect and reconcile conflicting longitudes on the peninsula of India for a small-scale chart from Karachi to Sumatra. Five small areas only are shown: Gujarat and Sind from a 1783 chart, the Maldive Islands, Ceylon, the Madras coast, and the head of the Bay of Bengal, each area based on known longitudes. Another chart of the wider Indian Ocean has more detail, but also remained unpublished.[30] These small-scale essays are known in no more than two or three proof copies. Dalrymple's practice of publishing conflicting representations together, without critical evaluation, and declining to issue compilation charts until he was sure of the longitudes, did not provide the standard set of charts he had promised. There were no market pressures on Dalrymple the researcher.

But by the early 1790s Dalrymple had systematised the production and issue of the harbour plans and single-source coastal and archipelago charts which formed the bulk of his output. By 1789 he had produced 28 charts, 40 plates of views, and over 450 harbour plans and large-scale coastal charts, but by no stretch of the imagination could Dalrymple's charts be called a pilot book.[31] Samuel Dunn, who took over William Herbert's *New Directory for the East Indies* in the 1770s, incorporated impressions of Dalrymple's plates loaned to him, but only to supplement the coherent Herbert coastal chart series which still formed the basis of the book. Laurie and Whittle's *East India Pilot* flourished after 1781,

---

[29] 'Chart of the Mozambique Channel and Island Madagascar by N. Bellin, 1767', published by Dalrymple 7 May 1791; 'Chart of the Mozambique Channel and of Madagascar by John Thornton 1703', published 7 May 1791; 'Chart of the Coasts of Suffalo and Moçambique with the Island Madagascar by John Van Keulen', published 20 May 1791; 'Chart of the Mozambique Channel with the Island Madgascar and the opposite Coast of Africa by M. D'Après de Mannevillette, 1753', published 27 May 1791; 'Chart of the Moçambique Channel with Madgascar and the opposite Coast of Africa from the New Edition of the Neptune Oriental by M. D'Après de Mannevillette 1775', published 29 May 1791. 'Charts of the Malabar Coast comparing the various published and MS. Charts from Mangalore to Bombay', published by Dalrymple 4 January 1789, with the parallel sources given as 'M. D'Après 1775', 'M. D'Après 1745', 'Van Keulen', 'a Dutch MS.', 'an Old English MS. by Augustus Fitzhugh', and 'John Thornton 1705'.

[30] 'Chart of the Indian Ocean with the Coasts, Islands, Rocks and Shoals from Madagascar to India, Sumatra and Java composed from various Materials explained in a Memoir by A Dalrymple 1787', with 'publication' date 24 January 1793, examples in Washington, D.C., Library of Congress: G1059.D23 Maps 3a/49r and G1059.D24 Maps 5/7. Alexander Dalrymple, *Memoir of a Chart of the Indian Ocean* . . . (London, 1787).

[31] *List of Charts, Plans of Ports, &c. published by A Dalrymple, before 1st of June 1789* (London, 1789).

and when James Horsburgh, Dalrymple's eventual successor in the East India Company, proposed to publish privately his China Sea charts in 1805, Dalrymple encouraged him and recommended his own plan engraver, John Walker, to him.[32]

Dalrymple had had, in 1779, a clear vision of the needs of the maritime community in the East Indies for a system of standard charts for navigation - and for reliable harbour plans – but the resources allowed only for him to examine the ships' journals and to publish single-source charts and plans. Many East India captains supplied him with their track charts, or with harbour plans, but, with responsibilities to their owners, none could go out of their way to conduct the coastal surveys he needed. Only the Bombay Marine had men and ships, and then only for locally authorised survey work in the Laccadives and Andamans.[33]

Almost Dalrymple's only success in persuading the Company to direct a ship off-course to conduct a survey, the *Vansittart* in 1790, ended in disaster. The Court appointed Lestock Wilson, commander of the *Vansittart*, to spend some days surveying in the Gaspar Strait, east of Bangka, on the journey to China. Wilson wrecked his ship on the very bank he had been ordered to locate, though he brought journal, observations and charts home.[34] Francis Beaufort, later Hydrographer to the Admiralty, was captain's boy on that voyage.

With the changes in the patterns of East India Company trade in the late eighteenth century the initiative in developing knowledge of tracks and coast-lines passed, through the medium of the surveys of the Bombay Marine, to the commanders of country trade ships, chiefly those based in Bombay. The economic imperative to import tea from China to Britain resulted in more cargoes being shipped from India to Canton, supplementing (and later overtaking) direct British exports to China, all to provide the liquidity in the Company's treasury in Macao to buy tea each season at Canton. The commodity chiefly desired from India in China, and most easily sold, was opium, a carrying trade in which the Company in India did not wish to be publicly involved, even though the continued flow of tea from Canton to Britain depended on it. Private commercial houses in Bombay, Madras and Calcutta developed into shipping firms to fill the need: the commanders of their ships, the ships of the 'country trade' which sailed from India ports through the Malacca Strait and the China Sea to Canton at all seasons, became, through constant experience, the reposito-ries of knowledge of how to sail among the islands of south-east Asia *en route* from India to China.

---

[32] Alexander Dalrymple to James Horsburgh, Cheltenham, 3 October 1805 (Letter-book of James Horsburgh (IOR: Mss Eur F305(II), p. 147).

[33] For the hydrographic surveying activities of Bombay Marine officers and vessels, see C.R. Low, *History of the Indian Navy*, 2 vols (London, 1873), passim.

[34] Alexander Dalrymple, ed., *Memoir of a Chart of the Passage to the Eastward of Banka, with the Relative Positions of Batavia, and the several Places from the Strait of Sunda, to Canton, by Capt. Lestock Wilson, 1789* (London, 1806).

James Horsburgh was most prominent among these, a sailor from Fife who had joined the country trade in the 1780s, and who had been stranded on Diego Garcia in 1786 in the wreck of *Atlas* on her journey from Batavia to Ceylon. The crew of *Atlas* were rescued by Archibald Blair's surveying party, sent out from Bombay shortly before to assess Diego Garcia for a settlement.[35] Horsburgh later attributed the origin of his interest in nautical survey to this coincidence. When Horsburgh, as first mate of *Carron*, taken up in Canton as an 'extra ship' for Europe, met Dalrymple in London in 1796, Dalrymple undertook to publish charts and sailing directions which Horsburgh had compiled.[36] Horsburgh was encouraged, on his visits to London (latterly as commander of *Anna*, also taken up in Canton for Europe), by introductions to Cavendish, Banks and Maskelyne, and in subsequent years sought to promote surveys in the China Seas. Disappointed in 1804 when the commercial imperative ruled out his proposal for a boat survey of the Paracels shoals, Horsburgh conceived the idea to bring to Europe on retirement a set of charts and sailing directions, chiefly of the Malacca Strait and the China Sea, for publication, with Dalrymple's encouragement, in 1805.[37] With the assistance of Peter Heywood, also returning to Europe from Canton in *Cirencester* in 1804, Horsburgh had drawn up a set of charts for the whole navigation to China, both Atlantic Ocean and Indian Ocean, and published these later as his *East India Pilot*.[38] In doing so he accomplished the set of small-scale charts which Dalrymple's caution had prevented him from completing. The East India Company had continued to use commercial publishers' charts to augment Dalrymple's harbour plans.

Horsburgh used both these publications and his work on a comprehensive two-volume *Directory for Sailing to the East Indies* in support of his request in 1808 to continue, after Dalrymple's death, the hydrographic work in East India House for which Dalrymple had sought to appoint Horsburgh as his assistant.[39] Horsburgh was himself appointed as Company Hydrographer by resolution of the Court of Directors on 2 November 1810.[40] His stated responsibility was to

35   R.H. Phillimore, *Historical Records of the Survey of India*, vol. I: *18th Century* (Dehra Dun: Survey of India, 1945), pp. 123–4 and 313.

36   Alexander Dalrymple, ed., *Observations on the Navigation of the Eastern Seas, by Mr. James Horsburgh* (London, 1797).

37   [James Horsburgh,] *Memoirs: Comprising the Navigation to and from China, by the China Sea, and through the various straits and channels in the Indian Archipelago; also, the Navigation of Bombay Harbour* (London, 1805).

38   The charts were issued at various dates from 1805 onwards, and combined by publishers Black, Penny & Co., as an atlas of fifteen charts in *Horsburgh's East India Pilot* (London, 1815).

39   James Horsburgh to the Chairman and Deputy Chairman, 27 June 1808 (James Horsburgh Letter-book [IOR: MSS Eur F305(I), p. 180]). The two volumes of the first edition of *Directions for Sailing to and from the East Indies, China, New Holland, Cape of Good Hope, and the Interjacent Ports; compiled chiefly from Original Journals at the East India House* were published in 1809 and 1811 respectively.

40   W. Ramsay, Secretary, East India Company, to James Horsburgh, 2 November 1810; James Horsburgh to Committee of Shipping, East India Company, 8 November 1810 (IOR: MSS Eur F305(I), pp. 196–7).

compile charts from an examination of the ships' journals in East India House, and to run a chart office for the supply of charts to ships, but Horsburgh soon found himself more a publisher of the works of others, as the incoming manuscript surveys of Ross and Maughan in the China Sea, and Brucks and Haines in the Persian Gulf, were passed to him to oversee the printing.[41] Oceanic charts of his own compilation, and supported by the comprehensive accounts and directions in successive editions of the *East India Directory*, were gradually overshadowed by the charts from regular surveys by Bombay Marine officers in the 1820s and 1830s. At the same time the East India Company's monopoly of British commercial shipping to India and China, the safety of which had been the first reason for hydrographic activity, had steadily eroded from the 1780s, and, with the termination of the China to Europe shipping monopoly in 1834, the Company Hydrographer's work became a service industry to commercial shipping in general.

On Horsburgh's death in 1836, he was succeeded as Geographer (also with responsibility for compiling and engraving *The Indian Atlas*) by his engraver John Walker. Chart publication and issue continued in East India House until the East India Company's functions were taken over by Government in 1858. New surveys by Indian Navy officers were published by the Admiralty Hydrographic Office from the 1850s, and the plates and chart stocks were taken into the numbered Admiralty Charts series in 1860. Horsburgh's *India Directory* continued to be revised, as a 'leisure' activity, by Edward Dunsterville in the Hydrographic Office, until its eighth (and last) edition in 1864.[42] Thus a 'knowledge' activity which had begun quietly with notes made by commanders in their journals to help them retrace their paths, ended with the seamless absorption into the Admiralty Hydrographic Office of almost a hundred years of charts and sailing directions. The need to establish the sea routes to India and China, for others safely to follow in the interests of commerce, had caused those difficult waters to be the most comprehensively charted in the world.

[41] In his return of 'salary, perquisites and duties' in 1813 to the Special Committee of the East India Company gathering information for the Parliamentary enquiry into the Company's affairs, Horsburgh reported one of his duties as 'Selecting the best of the Charts and Plans published by the late Mr. Dalrymple, which are bound up together with my late publications, and a Copy delivered to each of the Company's Ships when they sail from England, and returned into the Chart Office at their arrival in this Country' (IOR: MSS Eur F305(I), p. 215). One such bound 'atlas' survives in the India Office Records from use by the ship *Castle Huntly* (IOR: X/3628); another, from *Berwickshire*, is now in the National Maritime Museum's collections. The range of miscellaneous tasks Horsburgh was called on to perform can be gleaned from a study of the book in which he noted the matters referred to his attention (IOR: L/MAR/1/24).

[42] Editions subsequent to the first bore the title *India Directory, or Directions for Sailing . . .*: the second edition appeared in 1816–17, the third in 1826–7, the fourth in 1836, the fifth in 1841, the sixth in 1852, and the seventh in 1855.

Strategy, Policy and Shipbuilding: the Bombay Dockyard, the Indian Navy and Imperial Security in Eastern Seas, 1784–1869

ANDREW LAMBERT

It is curious that the naval history of British India should have received relatively little attention, when the strategic world of the East India Company was bounded by the sea, and dominated by British control of the Atlantic and Indian Ocean routes. If the Company relied on sea power for the security of its isolated trading stations, and the safety of the shipping that linked London and India, it had to pay a heavy price to secure the support of the Royal Navy. Because the Company could only flourish under Britannia's *aegis*, the British Government was able to take an increasing degree of control over its external and military policy from 1784. The home government directed the development of the Company, and began to break down its commercial monopoly. In the middle of this process lay the Company's direct support of the Royal Navy, and although the long-term relationship between the Company and the Navy was mutually beneficial it can also be seen as part of the wider debate on the nature of the Company. As the British government transformed the Company from trade to rule, from commercial concern to an imperial agency, it made ever greater demands on Company resources to support state interests.

In the mid-eighteenth century the Company had funded Royal Navy warships (which received suitably 'Indian' names),[1] loaned seamen, provided military transports, and above all paid taxes that helped to maintain the Royal Navy. In India the Company provided a local naval force, secure bases, local finances, stores and store houses for Royal Navy equipment. After the American War of Independence, when British rule was threatened by French fleets, and the Company became more closely connected with the British Government, two new elements entered into this relationship. It is necessary to distinguish between two roles the Company fulfilled: the core strategic need for secure docking accommodation and supporting dockyard facilities, and the subordinate capability to build warships for the Imperial fleet. The creation of a fully integrated dockyard at Bombay provided the Royal Navy with the infrastructure needed to sustain operations in Indian waters, especially so the dry-docks. When

---

[1] D. Lyon, *The Sailing Navy List* (London, 1993), pp. 70–1, for the *Bombay Castle* and *Carnatic* 74s ordered in 1780.

they were not required for fleet maintenance dockyard artificers could be employed on other tasks – most obviously naval shipbuilding, which used the same combination of skills although in different proportions. The development of this relationship between 1784 and 1869 provides a fresh perspective on the relationship between India, the Company and the British Government.[2]

The wars of the mid-eighteenth century demonstrated that the external defence of India against European rivals, like other overseas territories of the British Empire, was the responsibility of the British Government.[3] As the last, and the most successful of the European maritime invaders of India, the British were well aware that trade and dominion were the products of naval superiority. The strategy of imperial defence was based on controlling the Western Approaches, thereby limiting the opportunity for rival fleets to reach the Indian Ocean. However, in the American war the strategy had been applied too late. As a result the French were able to mount a serious threat to India, but Suffren's impressive effort was defeated by his inability to repair battle damage and refit his ships with the same facility as Admiral Sir Edward Hughes's squadron. Hughes relied on Bombay dockyard, the Company's main contribution to external maritime security.

Alarmed by the loss of America the British government adopted an imperial perspective, in which India would be closely integrated with the home islands, transforming the Company into a government agency.[4] In January 1784 Pitt told the House of Commons that India should be 'the source of infinite benefit to the empire at large', and framed his India Bill accordingly.[5] His concept was obviously at odds with the commercial priorities of the Court of Directors, and implied national access to resources that were owned by the Company. This dichotomy took 50 years to resolve, the Company ultimately assuming a purely politico-military role. Having set the broad lines of policy Pitt left implementation to Henry Dundas, later President of the Board of Control.[6]

A strong Royal Navy squadron was essential to the naval defence of India, so long as any European rival retained local facilities. Because the base at Bombay enabled the Royal Navy to remain on station, it was the key to sustained British dominance in Eastern Seas. Bombay remained the key to British strategy in the East because it combined a secure island location, a strategic position commanding the communications of the Indian Ocean and Persian Gulf, a Company dockyard with the only dry-docks in the region, a burgeoning shipbuilding industry and access to skilled labour and materials. A fleet at Bombay would keep the French out of India, and deny the Indian powers of Mysore and

---

2   A.D. Lambert, 'Empire and Seapower: Shipbuilding by the East India Company at Bombay for the Royal Navy, 1805–1850', in P. Haudrère, with R.E. and G. Bouédec, eds, *Les Flottes Des Compagnies Des Indes, 1600–1857* (Vincennes, 1996), pp. 149–71.

3   C.H. Phillips, *The East India Company, 1784–1834* (Manchester, 1961), pp. 57–9.

4   J. Gascoigne, *Science in the Service of the Empire* (Cambridge, 1998), for this movement.

5   A.J. Frost, *Convicts and Empire: A Naval Question, 1776–1811* (Oxford, 1980), pp. 81–3.

6   *Ibid.*, p. 83.

the Maratha confederacy access to French support. However, the small, and economically weak Bombay Presidency seemed to have little future, and Governor-General Earl Cornwallis proposed to abolish it in 1788. Dundas stressed the strategic importance of the position, calling for locally built 64–gun ships to carry the China trade in peace time, and secure command of the Eastern seas in war.[7] Teak and pepper dominated his perception of western India, and the collapse of the market for the latter only increased the importance of the former.[8] Ultimately increased sea-borne trade would save Bombay,[9] under the protection of locally based naval forces.

Dundas recognised that the key to shipbuilding at Bombay would be a secure timber supply. Like so much else at Bombay this had been far from certain in 1784, with the Mysore ruler Tipu Sultan excluding the British from the market. After the first defeat of Tipu in 1792 the Company secured the forest areas of Malabar and Coorg, which produced the best teak, and with the final defeat and death of Tipu at Seringapatam in 1799 the timber problem seemed to be resolved. Yet Governor-General Wellesley still favoured reducing Bombay to a military outpost of Madras, replacing the costly political government with a military commander, and keeping up the marine.[10]

Bombay also had its own navy, the Bombay Marine. Essentially a local police service, the Marine was not intended to meet the fleets of European rivals; it patrolled the sealanes and escorted merchant shipping against pirates. It operated small cruisers and light warships manned by locally raised seamen, European petty officers and officers. Anyone with the stamina to read Low's 1,000-page testimonial will see a pattern emerging.[11] The service was never large enough to meet all the demands that were placed on it; it lacked the prestige of the Royal Navy, and the large-scale war-fighting role of the Company armies, for the Indian states did not construct European naval forces. It served British interests best by allowing the Royal Navy squadron to focus on the enemy fleet, without the need to detach units for trade protection.[12] The weakness of the Marine led Governor-General Wellesley to press for control over Royal Navy forces stationed in the Indian Ocean, and the Cape.[13] However, the Bombay dockyard more than compensated for any inadequacy of the Marine.

As an island with a sheltered anchorage, Bombay fulfilled the basic requirements of a British naval base. It was relatively easy to defend, so long as the Company had a working naval superiority, and therefore was economical of troops, yet it commanded the trade of the coast. From the beginning of English

7   P. Nightingale, *Trade and Empire in Western India, 1784–1806* (Cambridge, 1970), p. 5.
8   *Ibid.*, pp. 47 and 65.
9   *Ibid.*, pp. 12–13.
10 E. Ingram, ed., *Two Views of British India: the Private Correspondence of Mr Dundas and Lord Wellesley: 1798–1801* (London, 1969), pp. 167, 183 and 251.
11 C.R. Low, *History of the Indian Navy: 1613–1863*, 2 vols (London, 1877).
12 H. Richmond, *The Navy in India: 1763–1783* (London, 1931), p. 382
13 Ingram: Royal Navy, at pp. 143 and 173; Cape, at p. 305.

rule at Bombay the value of a dry dock had been obvious, not just for Company shipping, but as a national object.[14] Consequently it should not be seen as coincidental that the first dry-dock was built after the War of the Austrian Succession, when control of the Indian Ocean had been in doubt.[15] The dock was specifically configured to take a 50-gun battleship.[16] A second dock was built outside the first and completed in 1762, doubtless inspired by the demands of the next major war. This and the third dock, of 1773, were large enough for 74-gun ships.[17] These docks proved to be the key to maintaining British naval supremacy in the American War. After the war, as Admiral Sir Edward Hughes stressed, the security of the Company's possessions depended:

> in a very great degree, if not entirely, in time of war on the superiority or exertions of His Majesty's squadron . . . then is the safety of Bombay of the utmost importance to the safety of the whole, for at no other port or place in our possession could the ships of the squadron be even properly refitted, much less repaired. At Bombay, as the only place of refit, are deposited all the masts and other stores for ships, and it not only furnishes a great number of expert native artificers, but its docks are of the utmost importance. In short, without Bombay, or some other as convenient in our possession, no squadron or force could be kept up in this country.[18]

During the war Hughes had stressed the need to deepen the existing docks, to allow them to be used more easily by 74-gun ships, to build two more docks and enlarge the dockyard to meet the greater demands that were being placed on it by the sudden arrival of his squadron.[19] Bombay was the key to the entire eastern arc of empire, a role it would retain until the end of the sailing-ship era.

When Pitt and Dundas decided that Bombay would build a fleet for the eastern seas, the construction of Hughes' two additional docks became necessary.[20] However, nothing was done for over a decade. In 1801, Jonathan Duncan, Governor of Bombay (1796–1811) sent a proposal to the Board of Control to improve the drainage of the existing docks, but this was rejected, 'being attended with a very considerable expense, and unnecessary, the more so for the return of peace'.[21] Within three months another project, already in hand, to enlarge the

---

[14] R.A. Wadia, *The Bombay Dockyard and the Wadia Master Builders* (Bombay, 1955), pp. 25 and 32.

[15] Richmond, p. 15.

[16] Wadia, pp. 38–9.

[17] *Ibid.*, pp. 42–3.

[18] Hughes – Admiralty 27.1.1784: Wadia, pp. 47–8, from ADM 7/759. Hughes – Governor and Select Committee of Bombay 13.5.1784: Richmond, p. 424. Richmond's analysis reflects both his own term as C-in-C in the East Indies in the early 1920s, when he conducted the research for the book, and the importance of the Singapore Dockyard, then under construction to contemporary British strategy.

[19] Hughes – Governor and Select Committee of Bombay 24.4.1781: Wadia, pp. 44–6.

[20] Frost, p. 146.

[21] Board of Control – Governor in Council 31.12.1801: OIOC, E/4/1017 f. 113.

Upper or building dock to take a large frigate was approved. Even though the work was being conducted on a reduced scale and the Board admitted its utility, they insisted that no further improvements should be made without their sanction.[22]

When the Admiralty raised the prospect of building large warships at Bombay, on a commercial basis, the Board of Control became more enthusiastic. The shipbuilding project developed, painfully slowly, over the next four years. The Upper Dock, otherwise of little use was deepened at a cost of 5,990 rupees and a wall was built round the yard. Critically the favourable report of Master Builder Jamsetjee Bomanjee had been received, and a silver rule had been sent for him.[23] (The rule can be seen tucked in his waist band in the famous portrait.)

Until new, larger docks were built, Bombay could not build battleships, so the first ship built for the Royal Navy was the frigate *Salsette*, laid down in 1803 in the Upper Old Dock.[24] By 1806 enough timber had been collected to build the first battleship, and despite the weakness of the Company's finances the new docks were begun. The spark came with a new Commander in Chief and the letter he brought from Dundas to Wellesley, stressing the need for ships. Admiral Sir Edward Pellew, a dynamic and forceful man soon persuaded Governor Duncan to act. Although an honest servant of the Company, Duncan lacked the leadership and willpower for such a responsible position, and was unable to control corruption in the Presidency. Ever anxious for the approbation of his masters he was better at justifying failure than ensuring success.[25] The Board of Control, with a notable lack of enthusiasm, concurred in Duncan's decision to construct a new dock, parallel to the existing docks. While lamenting the expense, the Board was, 'much pleased to find that many advantages are likely to accrue to us by this measure, as well as in the future accommodation of His Majesty's Squadron'.[26] Evidently Pellew had been more concerned to dock his squadron than to build ships.

The double docks were conceived as a unit, with the innermost being used for construction, the outer for repair. The building dock was completed in November 1807, just in time to receive the keel of the first Bombay 74, the *Minden*. The two new docks were 63ft wide, over 240ft long and 23ft deep, more than enough for the largest two-decker battleships. A steam engine was sent from England to pump out the excavation,[27] but the engineer needed to run the engine was only sent in 1809.[28]

Although out of office after 1805, Dundas retained his interest in India.

22 Board of Control – Governor in Council 23.3.1802: OIOC, E/4/1017 f. 258.
23 Board of Control – Governor in Council 28.8.1804 and 31.8.1804: OIOC, E/4/1019 ff. 574, 737–8, 857.
24 R. Gardiner, *The Frigates of the Napoleonic Wars* (London, 2000), pp. 11–12.
25 Nightingale, pp. 94–6 and 100.
26 Board of Control – Governor in Council 2.5.1806: OIOC, E/4/1021 f. 570.
27 Wadia, pp. 53–5. Board of Control – Governor in Council 7.1.1807 10.2.1807: OIOC, E/4/1022 ff. 17, 35.
28 Board of Control – Governor in Council 11.1.1809: OIOC, E/4/1024 f. 199.

Duncan informed him of the progress of the New Docks, and the 74 that was being built in them. In 1808 Duncan estimated the timber supply equal to two 74s a year, with one or two frigates. This proved over sanguine, while problems with the bed rock delayed the dock, and although a magnificent construction they cost far more than the original 'estimate'. When the cost overrun became apparent, Duncan, nervous that he might be held responsible, claimed that Pellew had over-persuaded him of the importance of the docks for naval service.[29] In fact the new docks had been begun without sense of science, in haste, with only a sketchy, utterly unrealistic cost estimate. Although the Board did not censure Bombay, their displeasure was clear. As the shipbuilding project was still experimental, they saw no need for the Outer Dock, and would have suspended it, had not the bulk of the money been expended already. They now hoped that by completing the dock they might recover part of the cost.[30] After this lecture Governor Duncan understandably tried to squeeze every rupee of dock hire he could out of the Navy.

The completion of the Duncan docks in 1810 coincided with important strategic developments. The final defeat of the French naval threat, through the capture of Mauritius and the Dutch colonies, was now inevitable. This would secure Company shipping in the Indian Ocean, reducing the Royal Navy's need for the docking and maintenance facilities at Bombay. This shifted the focus of naval attention to the other, subordinate arm of Dundas's policy, using the resources of the yard and the Malabar forests to build large warships.

The construction of warships at Bombay was an imperial task which the home government considered itself perfectly entitled to impose on the Company as their agent. The Government took control of the external relations of the Company in 1784, and began to break down the link between territorial rule and commercial activity. Over the next three decades the struggle between Whitehall and the City for the soul of the company witnessed a strong, if doomed, rear-guard by the commercial concern.[31] Little wonder that the development and implementation of the shipbuilding process proved strained.

The growth of locally built 'country' shipping for trade with China, largely by and for Parsi interests, proved vital to the commercial survival of the Presidency, and the development of its strategic role. The Parsi community had been lured from Surat by the security of the Island, and the protection afforded by the Marine and the Royal Navy. The Parsi traders and shipbuilders, often members of the same families, invested in large ships that carried trade to China. This process, in full spate by the mid-1780s, also led to an increase in the size of the Marine.[32] Local construction was sufficiently advanced by the late 1790s for the

---

[29] Duncan to Dundas 14.10.1808 and 16.4.1809: Scottish Record Office (SRO) GD 51/3/158 1 and 2.

[30] Board of Control – Governor in Council 11.1.1809: OIOC, E/4/1024 ff. 54–100.

[31] See Phillips for this development.

[32] Nightingale, pp. 17–22. H. Furber, *John Company at Work: A Study of European Expansion*

ships to be considered for carrying the trade with England, as way of reducing the demands for construction at home.[33] Wellesley allowed Indian-built shipping to enter the home trade in 1798.[34]

Teak (*tectona grandis*) has long been recognised as among the finest shipbuilding timber. It is very durable, the highest grade of timber, and unusually resistant to marine borers such as the dread mollusc (*teredo navalis*) that rapidly ate through oak hulls.[35] Teak requires only a brief period of seasoning, while the natural oils, in sharp contrast to the tannic acid of oak sap, preserves ferrous metals, allowing Indian shipbuilders to fasten their vessels with iron spikes. The ability to deliver fully seasoned ships in little more than a year from laying the keel was a major attraction of the Bombay yard. Furthermore, because teak does not expand when heated like European timbers, these ships could be used in hot climates when new, something that was considered undesirable for European oak-built ships.

The advantages of teak-built ships were obvious, while the talent of the local builders was well known to those officers who had been to Bombay, notably Edward Hughes, and one of his midshipmen, Thomas Troubridge, who would be St Vincent's right-hand man when he pushed the Indian shipbuilding project to completion.[36] The industry had developed rapidly after the Company hired Parsi shipwrights of the Wadia clan from Surat in 1736 to build small craft. They controlled a large locally recruited workforce of skilled labourers, applying regional methods to the replication of British designs (see Plate I).

As with the rest of the Bombay project the original impetus for shipbuilding came from Dundas, a great enthusiast for developing the resources of India *in situ*.[37] Dundas's wide network of Hiberno-Indian connections, built up through his long tenure as political master of the Indian Administration, provided him with numerous reports on the shipbuilding resources of the region over a period of 20 years. This work finally bore fruit after Earl St Vincent became First Lord of the Admiralty in 1801.[38] With the apparent failure of the native oak supply, St Vincent threatened to limit Company shipbuilding on the Thames to 800-ton ships, in place of the preferred 1,200-ton class. At the same time he expressed a desire for the Company to build one ship of the line and one frigate at Bombay every year. These, he concluded, 'would be of great importance to the support of

---

in India in the Late Eighteenth Century (Cambridge, 1951), pp. 186–90. A. Bulley, *The Bombay Country Ships, 1790–1833* (London, 2000), pp. 11–33.

33 Phillips, p. 96.

34 *Ibid.*, pp. 108–13.

35 R.H. Farmer, *The Handbook of Hardwoods* (2nd edn, London, 1972), pp. 201–3.

36 Troubridge – Bomanjee 30.5.1802: Wadia, pp. 189–90.

37 H. Furber, *Henry Dundas* (Oxford, 1931), pp. 126–41.

38 East India Company to Navy Board 3.4.1805 encl. Deptford Dockyard to Navy Board 22.1.1805 ADM 8//1. St Vincent to Dundas 14.7.1801, in D.B. Smith, ed., *The Letters of Lord St. Vincent 1801–4*, 2 vols (London, 1921 and 1926), I, 301.

the naval strength of the Empire'.[39] Aware that key tools and components could not be easily obtained in India, St Vincent recommended that they be sent out.[40] The initial order for a 74 and a frigate were given in 1803. The Company would build the ships at Bombay, under the supervision of a Navy Board Shipwright Officer: in return they would be paid for the hire of the dock while the ship was being built, their costs and 20 percent profit.

This arrangement, entered into in time of war and emergency, not to mention strife between the Company and the Ministry, proved to be a charter for the Company to exploit naval funds. The Board now declared it would be:

> highly beneficial to the service of the Public if the Company would undertake to build a ship of the line and a frigate annually at Bombay of teak timber – and being desirous of ascertaining, by actual experiment, how far it may be practical to carry into execution their wishes, thus communicated to us, plans and models proper for directing the execution of the measure have been sent to you by the *Sir Edward Hughes.*

While the Bombay authorities awaited this auspiciously named ship they were to collect timber and ensure that no 'perquisite or emolument, of any description or kind whatever' should be allowed on this project. Strict accounts were to be kept of all expenses incurred, while local experts were to be consulted on the stores and supplies that would have to be sent from England. At the same time the Company was interested in building ships of 1,200–1,400 tons at Bombay.[41]

In 1804 Dundas, as First Lord of the Admiralty, attempted to widen the approach. Impressed by the Bombay ships seen on the Thames, and short of warship timber at home, he believed it was essential to act. He hoped to build at a variety of locations; Bombay, Cochin, Rangoon, Pegu and Penang, exploiting the apparently limitless resources of the regional forests.[42] Predictably the shipyard set up at Penang built one frigate, HMS *Malacca*, but she was late, way over budget, did not follow the intended design and was not even built of teak.[43] The yard collapsed before the first 74 could be launched, forcing the Navy to rely on Bombay.[44] As Bombay was the only place with the infrastructure, skilled labour force, and local financial power to carry out such large-scale work this development pleased the Navy Board, which preferred to deal with large, well-organised concerns. To avoid becoming completely dependent on the Company the Navy planned to build a naval arsenal at Trincomalee, located in the British colony of

---

[39] Navy Board to Admiralty 5.5.1802: ADM106/2229. Earl St Vincent to the deputy Chairman of the EIC 31.3.1802 and 17.4.1802, Smith, II, 238 and 241–3.

[40] Admiralty to Navy Board 12.5.1802 and Navy Board to Woolwich and Bombay Officers 13.5. and 21.6.1802: ADM 106/3123 f. 1 (a case of relevant documents apparently assembled in 1822, when the decision was taken to cancel construction).

[41] Board of Control – Governor in Council 5.5.1802: OIOC, E/4/1017 f. 465.

[42] Dundas to Wellesley 4.7.1804 Add. 37, 275 ff. 260–387.

[43] Gardiner, pp. 22–7, 69–71 and 142. This ship cost more than twice the average for her domestic contemporaries, and was broken up in 1816, after only six years service.

[44] R.G. Albion, *Forests and Seapower* (Cambridge, Mass., 1926), pp. 366–9.

Ceylon rather than the Company Presidency of Bombay. This impressive harbour was ideally placed for sailing operations on the Indian coast, but these factors could not outweigh the advantages of an existing facility, and the high costs of replicating the docks. Trincomalee remained a support facility, rather than a base.[45]

Under pressure from the Government, the Court of Directors ordered a survey of the timber resources of India. The initial inspection of the major forests caused a sharp downward revision of the earlier estimates. Malabar teak was no longer seen as an inexhaustible resource, and the supply of large curved timber remained a major problem for Bombay.[46] The results of the surveys varied, not least because the surveyors had an unfortunate habit of dying on the job.[47] Finally Bombay reported that the shipbuilding project 'appears . . . practicable' estimating costs at 306,000 rupees for a battleship, and 170,700 for a frigate. This information arrived in mid-1803, encouraging the Admiralty to forward the necessary stores.[48] By contrast the Board of Control viewed naval construction as an opportunity to liquidate some of Bombay's debts.[49]

> The great importance of these Forests, as a means for supplying requisite timber for the Dock Yard at your Presidency and ultimately to the construction of ships of war for His Majesty's Service has frequently engaged our earnest attention, and . . . we have certainly had a fair claim to expect some revenue from them.

Even so there was still a need for a full survey at Malabar, without which any projects would remain 'visionary speculation'.[50]

Although the forest survey was far from complete, there was enough timber in the yard for a second frigate and a 74 to be laid down. As naval construction was still experimental, one of the ships would be sent home for inspection, and no further contracts were to be entered into until the Admiralty had reached a decision. That the linked decision to proceed with the new dock was also taken at this time demonstrates the degree to which docking capacity was the dominant concern.[51] It was indicative of the financial problems then facing the Company and the Presidency that the largest ships in the marine were either transferred to the Navy or laid up,[52] while a 1,200-ton Indiaman under construction was sold.[53]

By 1809 financial pressures were closing in on the Company. The second frigate had been delivered to Pellew in March 1807, but the statement of

---

45 G.S. Graham, *Great Britain and the Indian Ocean: 1810–1850* (Oxford, 1967), pp. 305–28.
46 E.P. Stebbings, *The Forests of India*, 4 vols (London, 1922), vol. I, 63–5.
47 Board of Control – Governor in Council 28.3.1800, 31.8.1804: OIOC, E/4/1017 f. 755, 1019 ff. 836, 857.
48 Admiralty – Navy Board 5.6.1803: ADM 106/3123 f. 2.
49 Board of Control – Governor in Council 3.7.1805: OIOC, E/4/1020 ff. 478–82.
50 Board of Control – Governor in Council 2.5.1806: OIOC, E/4/1021 ff. 485–502.
51 Board of Control – Governor in Council 8.4.1807: OIOC, E/4/1022 ff. 208–18, 273.
52 *Ibid.*, f. 299.
53 *Ibid.*, f. 136.

expenses had not been sent home, 'in consequence of which we are unable to submit our claim upon His Majesty's Government'. In future, Bills drawn on the Navy Board in London '(including Indian Interest)' were to be taken prior to delivery.[54]

The problem of controlling a shipbuilding enterprise in India under four distinct boards in London was becoming increasingly obvious. Company instructions sent in 1807 to enter into no new contracts had effectively suspended work in India. The Board still hoped to make the resources of India 'available for the aid and advancement of the Navy of Great Britain', and although the frigates had been a success, the Admiralty still wanted to see the first battleship. The key to the future remained the new docks, and here Bombay had signally failed to control costs.

In early 1810 the Navy Board Commissioner at Bombay, George Dundas, had reported good progress on the first battleship, HMS *Minden*, although construction of the dock in which she was building was interfering, as was the shortage of structural ironwork. However, the delay had been exploited to prepare almost all the timber for the next ship, the *Cornwallis*.[55] Within a year Dundas had to report that Governor Duncan was intent on a little sharp practice, if nothing worse, at the Admiralty's expense. Not only was he charging the Navy for the use of a dock in which a merchant ship was being built, but he appeared to be deliberately delaying work on the timbers for *Cornwallis*, particularly trimming the frames. Dundas was convinced the object was to ensure more work had to be done after the keel was laid, from which point dock hire was chargeable: 'by which means the ship will be so many months longer in docks, and he will receive so many more thousands of rupees for these additional months'. Furthermore Duncan refused point blank to provide any information on the cost of timber; having his assistant secretary respond to Dundas's enquiries with a mean, obstructive and legalistic letter that simply ignored the request (see Plate II).[56]

While the *Minden* was completed and delivered to the Royal Navy ready for sea in late 1810[57] (she would carry Vice Admiral Sir Samuel Hood's flag on the East Indies station in 1813), construction costs at the yard were rising, with the increased demand for materials, and the Board was still rejecting any major dockyard infrastructure projects, until the Navy made the construction project permanent.[58] The accounts for the *Salsette* were deemed so unsatisfactory that the Dockyard would have to prepare a fresh set. For the future the Board introduced a new accounting regime. Bombay was to fix a fair market price for the timber, including profit, as the Company could not be expected to incur all the risks without some compensation. In future, starting with the current 74, all

54 Board of Control – Governor in Council 11.4.1808: OIOC, E/4/1023 f. 137.
55 Geo. Dundas to Navy Board 26.1.1810 rec. 20.7.1810: ADM 106/2008.
56 Dundas to Navy Board 14.3.1811 and 9.8.1811 rec. 28.4.1812: ADM 106/2009.
57 Board of Control – Governor in Council 5.1.1810: OIOC, E/4/1025 f. 9.
58 Board of Control – Governor in Council 27.6.1810: OIOC, E/4/1026 f. 69, 94.

stores supplied to build or equip the ship, were to be charged a commission of 30 percent, '(to cover interest, risk etc), and you will observe that these directions are equally to apply to the repair of HM Ships, concerning which you will keep and forward to us the most particular details'. The Governor was left in no doubt that the driving force behind the new methods was the pressure being applied to the Company by the Government. Unable to borrow enough money in London, the Company had insisted that the Commissioner at Bombay paid for all work with Bills drawn on the Navy in London.[59] The question of cost and prices would remain central to the relationship between the Navy and the Company, exposing a fundamental clash of cultures. The Navy wanted to build ships to meet a need; the Company needed to build them to run the dockyard at a profit.

Communications remained a problem. In 1810 the Admiralty ordered the Resident Commissioner at Bombay to begin another 74, but omitted to tell the Board which only discovered the oversight when Bombay wrote home for instructions! Bombay had not been told that the shipbuilding project was now going ahead, and having been rapped over the knuckles often enough over ships, docks and timber, was loath to act. Having ascertained the truth, the Board considered it 'very desirable that no further time should be lost'. The work was to go ahead as fast as possible, but the new accounting rules of 1810 were to be rigorously applied.

> And when we consider the heavy expense we have incurred by the survey of the forests on your coasts, as well as the construction of the Docks at your Presidency, which were undertaken upon National Grounds, We think it but justice due to the Company that they should be reimbursed the heavy outlay they have sustained on these accounts; but when it is moreover considered, that the former sovereigns of the Territories from when we procure our timber enjoyed an ample Revenue from the forests, we may, after the blood, and treasure expended by us in obtaining them, fairly look for some benefit from them.
>
> We therefore rely upon your vigilance, that upon this and upon every other occasion, an equitable remuneration should be found for the exertions which we shall ever be ready to make for the purpose of aiding as much as it may be in our power to do, the interests of the public.[60]

The unfortunate, oft misled Governor Duncan did not live to receive this calm but firm demolition of his administration. The instructions of 1810 were repeated for his successor's benefit in 1812, with the same stress on accounting and interest charges.[61] The Board of Control read the forest reports of 1808–9 as promising 'a permanent and valuable supply of large ship timber', which they wanted to exploit to repay the cost of the surveys and rather more significantly of

59 Board of Control – Governor in Council 27.6.1810: OIOC, E/4/1026 ff. 154–64, 131.
60 Board of Control – Governor in Council 13.11.1811: OIOC, E/4/1028 ff. 55–62.
61 Board of Control – Governor in Council 21.10.1812: OIOC, E/4/1028 ff. 675–9.

the new docks. To this end they hoped to build two 74s per year.[62] Negotiations with the Admiralty indicated that both parties were anxious to contract for a second 74, and despite the Company's high charges the Admiralty continued to order ships as soon as the dock was vacant while the war continued.

At the end of the war the Admiralty took stock of the arrangements for building in India. By this stage the Surveyors of the Navy were impressed by the teak ships that had arrived, and recommended procuring as many teak ships as possible. They ordered the *Malabar* to follow the *Melville* and also to bring home two duplicate frames. The additional duplicate frame would improve the bargain. Their decision reflected the poor condition of the existing fleet, the high opinion already formed of the Indian ships, in particular their immediate availability for use in hot climates, and the value of the duplicate frame. In 1816, once it was determined that the docks could hold a ship of the 84-gun *Canopus* class, the order was given to build the *Ganges*.[63] The yard also produced 46-gun frigates. It was no accident the 84-gun *Asia* was the first of the new *Canopus* derivatives to see action. None of her British-built sisters had been completed by the time she fought at Navarino in 1827.

One of the ships built in this period has survived, the frigate HMS *Trincomalee*, ordered in 1812 and launched in 1817. After an interesting naval career she managed to avoid the ship-breakers by fulfilling a variety of harbour-service roles. Her survival was a tribute to the quality of her timbers, and the workmanship of the men who built her, under the great Jamsetjee Bomanjee. Restored at Hartlepool she is the largest surviving product of the East India Company.

While the Admiralty questioned the utility of continuing the effort at Bombay, the Company recognised that only a sustained construction programme would provide any return on the capital laid out in the expensive new docks, offering to build in both of the Duncan docks if the programme continued.[64] At the same time small frigates were built at Cochin[65] and enquiries were made at Calcutta to obtain comparative costs.[66] While some of the increase was due to the rising price of timber, about which the Master Shipwright remonstrated,[67] it was obvious that other costs were also rising faster than they should. The dockyard remained ill organised, overcrowded and inefficient. Anxious to keep up the dockyard labour force at home, as a strategic reserve, and dissatisfied by the rising cost of work at Bombay, the Navy Board secured the cancellation of construction for the Royal Navy in 1822.[68]

---

[62] Board of Control to Bombay 27.6.1810 and 18.12.1812 F/4/429.

[63] A.D. Lambert, *The Last Sailing Battlefleet: Maintaining Naval Mastery 1815–1850* (London, 1991), pp. 178–88 for post-war battleship building.

[64] Admiralty – Navy Board 28.4.1819: ADM 106/3123 f. 41.

[65] *Ibid.*, ff. 43–4.

[66] Admiralty – Navy Board 1.1.1820: *ibid.*, f. 46.

[67] Navy Board to Master Shipwright at Bombay 11.2.1820: *ibid.*, f. 46.

[68] Captain Sir Charles Malcolm (Superintendent of the Bombay Marine) to Hugh Lindsay 21.9.1828 and Malcolm to Byam Martin 24.9.1828: MAL/3 NMM.

By this time the docks had lost their immediate strategic purpose. Since the end of the Napoleonic wars Britain had complete command of the Indian Ocean, and its approaches, secured through the conquests of 1793–1815. In preparing for the peace settlement that followed the defeat of Napoleon in April 1814, Foreign Secretary Lord Castlereagh advised the Prime Minister to consider 'Malta, the Cape, Mauritius, and Tobago as *sine qua non;* also the regulations restricting the French to a commercial occupation of their factories in the East Indies'.[69] As the British now held all the worthwhile naval bases in the Indian Ocean, their local squadron was greatly reduced. This carefully planned development had little effect on the Marine, the usual local security and navigational requirements of western India and the Gulf Region kept it busy.

However, with complete control of the Indian Ocean, and the sharp decline in European threat in the east generally, the Royal Navy lost interest in Bombay, while the cost of a establishing a new dockyard at Trincomalee were prohibitive. The construction of a dry dock, the key element of any serious base, was never raised, and the other facilities withered away after 1822.[70] Dry docks were, and remained, the basis of an Imperial strategy that required global mobility for the fleet. Their construction, almost invariably at local expense, was the precursor of a new stationed force.

The Indian Ocean was now a strategic backwater, the future of British maritime power lay further afield. Rather than develop Trincomalee or remain at Bombay, British interest shifted to meet the new strategic needs at Aden, and support commercial development at Singapore and Hong Kong. By the mid-1840s Hong Kong was the most active Royal Navy base in the eastern arc of empire. In the absence of a serious naval challenge, the Bombay Marine, renamed the Indian Navy by order of King William IV, was reconfigured as a steam cruiser force, with the primary mission of conveying the mails and important passengers from Suez to Bombay.[71] The new paddle-wheel warships were also ideally suited to act as fast troop transports, one even carried a cavalry regiment to Suez for service in the Crimean War.[72] Improved communications were intended by the Earl of Ellenborough, as President of the Board of Control in 1828, to reduce the delay on Indian Correspondence. His object was to exert direct control from London over the policy followed in India.[73]

By reducing the isolation of India Ellenborough restricted the freedom of action of the Governors-General, as he would discover for himself in the 1840s. In this respect the new policy, although considered demeaning and non-naval by

69 Castlereagh – Lord Liverpool 19.4.1814, in C. Webster, ed., *British Diplomacy 1813–1815* (London, 1921), pp. 177–8.

70 G.S. Graham, *Great Britain and the Indian Ocean* (Oxford, 1967), p. 319.

71 G.S. Graham, *The Politics of Naval Supremacy* (Cambridge, 1967). Chapter 3 concerns communications with India.

72 The 10th Hussars, carried in the *Punjaub* of 1854, a large paddle-wheel frigate: Wadia, p. 282.

73 Phillips, pp. 264–71.

Marine officers, actually turned a local police force into a vital imperial asset. The Indian Navy was more important to Britain between 1830 and 1860 than it had ever been before. Steam packets imposed a timetable on Imperial activity, reducing the effective size of the Empire, making it possible for London to rule India. They also provided a vital force multiplier in every campaign east of Suez between 1820 and 1860, including two Burmese wars, the First Opium war and the Persian campaign of 1855–56. In China the Indian steamships transformed the strategy of the theatre. Critically they provided the power to tow Royal Navy battleships into action, landed troops, carried vital reinforcements, and over-awed the opposition.[74] It would not be an exaggeration to say that the Indian steamships, many built at Bombay with British engines, were the key instrument of Imperial power east of Suez. To service these paddle-wheel warships the Duncan docks were widened between 1839 and 1844. At the same time three big slips were laid down to build further battleships for the Royal Navy,[75] but the construction of HMS *Meeanee*, dogged by poor management and greatly over budget, was the last new work for the Royal Navy.

When the Company was wound up it still had a Navy, with a new flagship being built at Bombay, the 50-gun screw frigate *Dalhousie*. Delayed by the Mutiny, *Dalhousie* was eventually dismantled, shipped to Woolwich, and completed in 1869 as HMS *Thalia*, a corvette/troopship for service in eastern seas.[76]

Conclusion

Bombay became the centre of British Empire in the east because it provided a secure defensible anchorage, a Company dockyard, with dry-docks and a locally raised cruiser fleet to complement the battlefleet. These resources, especially the docks, enabled the Royal Navy to operate in the Indian Ocean more effectively than any rival fleet before 1810, and after the last vestiges of the Franco-Dutch threat were removed, the yard concentrated on the secondary task of shipbuild-ing to support the wider Imperial war. Ultimately Bombay produced a fleet of truly Imperial battleships. In all the Royal Navy obtained 15 'Indian' battleships. They comprised one-fifth of the serviceable fleet, and saw active service in every major naval campaign between 1815 and 1860. While the eight frigates and ten smaller ships might have been statistically less important, their imperial policing and exploring work was highly significant.

However, the needs of the Empire, and above all those of the Home islands remained paramount, and when the use of Indian shipbuilding came into

[74] G.S. Graham, *The China Station: War and Diplomacy, 1830–1860* (Oxford, 1978) pp. 85–229.

[75] Wadia, pp. 61–3.

[76] A.D. Lambert, '*Dalhousie*: the Last Flagship of the Indian Navy and the question of Impe-rial Defence', in R. Gardiner, ed., *Warship 1993* (London, 1993), pp. 9–18.

conflict with a domestic shipbuilding slump, India was always going to lose. The very real superiority of teak was counter-balanced by the commercial imperatives driving Company policy, and the inadequate management of the yard, a problem that only worsened after 1820, allowing costs to spiral. The practice of building at Bombay made sense while everything worked in its favour: the wartime shortage of ships, the availability of enough timber to permit at least one duplicate frame to be sent with each ship, a buoyant domestic shipbuilding industry and a relatively high level of naval estimates. When those elements began to falter British policy-makers lost faith, although for differing reasons. Teak remained a major attraction, but it could not compensate for the poor management and hostile attitude of the Company. By contrast the forces operating out of Bombay, together and the docks with support facilities on the Island retained their Imperial role to the end of the Empire.

'An Undiscovered Ocean of Commerce Laid Open': India, Wine and the Emerging Atlantic Economy, 1703–1813

DAVID HANCOCK

In historical circles around the Atlantic today, a lot of fuss is being made over what has been dubbed 'Atlantic History'. Published studies of commercial exchanges, migration flows, labour systems and intellectual influences have uncovered a hitherto neglected early-modern Atlantic World. What was earlier dubbed Anglo- or British-, Dutch-, French-, Spanish- or Portuguese-America is now as often described as part of Atlantic-America – a community that exchanged commodities, services, settlers and labourers, waged war on itself, and shared political ideas and institutions, even while its constituent states also exhibited distinctive cultures. For earlier Atlanticists, it was enough that the Atlantic be a space or community in which certain uniform ideas and precepts were expressed or certain goods were traded. More recent scholars posit a much more vigorous interdependent construction. They find a community that was 'the scene of a vast interaction' among two old worlds and one new one; it was 'a sudden and harsh encounter' that transformed all involved.[1]

Now, it may not be the most obvious way to approach the subject of the East

---

1   Jacques Godechot and Robert Palmer, 'Le Problème de l'Atlantique du XVIIIème Siècle', *Relazioni del X Congresso Internazionale di Scienze Storiche,* Storia Contemporanea, 5 (Florence, 1955); Pierre Chaunu, *Séville et l'Atlantique,* 8/1 (Paris, 1959); D.A. Farnie, 'The Commercial Empire of the Atlantic, 1607–1783', *Economic History Review,* 2nd ser., 15 (1962), 205–18; Donald Meinig, *The Shaping of America: A Geographical Perspective on 500 Years of History* (New Haven, 1986), I, 65; Bernard Bailyn, 'The Idea of Atlantic History', *Itinerario,* 20 (1996), 12–14, 33. See also John Thornton, *Africa and Africans in the Making of the Atlantic World, 1400–1800* (2nd edn, Cambridge, 1998), p. 1 ('interactions on an intercontinental scale'). Cultural and literary historians have not been shy about extending the definition and broadening the subject, at least in theory. Beginning in the 1970s, John Pocock began to call for the study of a pan-Atlantic culture, but, oddly, what distinguished that culture were English language and institutions. Gordon J. Schochet, ed., *Empire and Revolutions* (Washington, D.C., 1993). In *Cities of the Dead: Circum-Atlantic Performance* (New York, 1996), Joseph Roach (heavily influenced by Paul Gilroy's *The Black Atlantic*) struggles to recreate the flow of information around the Atlantic in his analysis of the relationship of memory, performance and substitution and to locate 'the peoples of the Caribbean rim at the heart of an oceanic interculture embodied through performance'; in the end, though, he succeeds merely in comparing theatrical performance only in London and New Orleans. Laura Brown, in *Ends of Empire* (Ithaca, 1993), is more successful in writing a history of one aspect of 'oceanic interculture' – the way the image of the female shaped capitalist

India Company with thoughts on the Atlantic, but I don't think it is odd. I would argue – and in the pages that follow I will offer a detailed example to show – that both analytically and conceptually, India and the Company in the eighteenth century were *in the Atlantic*, that they were very much part of that interactive community as much as they were in Britain or India. What is important about so-called 'Atlantic History' in the early-modern period is not the particular body of water, but instead its emphasis on contexts, on linkages among peoples, places and activities, on boundary crossing and interpenetration. Partially, this inter-pretation of Atlantic History is a response to recent criticism that Atlantic History separates 'Northwest Europe too sharply both from other parts of Europe and from Eurasia as a whole' and misrepresents 'through overstatement the place of Europe in the order of things'.[2] But it is also an attempt to emphasize the progression we're making as scholars from domestic history and local history to imperial history to Atlantic History and to the realization that the early-modern era was the very first time in the history of our planet that we had a true world exchange.

So, what was the relationship between India and the Atlantic commercial and social world (as distinct from the British world) that leads me to be so bold? This is a question of immense proportion. In partial answer, this essay will proceed by example, looking at the relationships between India and Portuguese Madeira and its British- and American-dominated wine trade. Madeira wine was an important trading commodity in the eighteenth-century maritime community. Grown and produced on the mid-Atlantic island of Madeira in particular, it was one of the principal drinks of British colonists in both the new American world and on the subcontinent of India.

One of the signal features of the Madeira wine trade in the Atlantic was its lack of central direction or organization. The trade developed and ramified around the Atlantic as individual producers, shippers, wholesalers, retailers and consumers responded, frequently creatively, to their own particular business and social situations, with little direction or intervention by the state. The Madeira wine trade developed opportunistically, but not haphazardly: over the century a rather common table wine was transformed into a modern luxury product that has been fortified, aged, heated, agitated and differentiated. Its producers were

---

commodification in early eighteenth-century English literature; her world, though, is only a community of the mind. Unfortunately, few scholars have picked up the gauntlet thrown down by the geographer Donald Meinig. The exception may be the work of slave-trade scholars, whose new work highlights the 'interactivity' of peripheral regions. See Robin Law and Kristin Mann, 'West Africa in the Atlantic Community: The Case of the Slave Coast', *The William and Mary Quarterly*, 3rd ser., 66 (1999), 307–34; and Paul Lovejoy and David Richardson, 'Trust, Pawnship, and Atlantic History: The Institutional Foundations of the Old Calabar Slave Trade', *The American Historical Review*, 104 (1999), 333–55.

2   Peter A. Coclanis, '*Drang Nach Osten*: Bernard Bailyn, The World-Island, and the Idea of Atlantic History' (Unpublished Comments, Omohundro Institute Annual Conference, Toronto, 2000).

3   E 3/98/280v, 281r, 322, and E 3/99/81, 193–4, 194, 221, 254, 329, OIOC; Henry Love, *Ves-*

active pre-industrial innovators; it was an important component of the infrastructure that traders and distributors were forging to the backcountry of Ohio and the interior of Bengal; and consumers everywhere used it in everyday ways and in sophisticated class and status display rituals.

By contrast, the India Company's trades were generally not left to the vagaries of the market. Indeed, the Company looms large in any understanding of Indian–Atlantic commerce because of its attempts to manage the trade. As the Company loosened its hold on the imported wine sector (as with other trades) in the last half of the eighteenth century, the Atlantic commercial world reached out to incorporate India into its networks and institutions. And in this way the Madeira wine traders brought India into the Atlantic.

In the rest of this essay, I will outline the development of the India market for Madeira over the eighteenth century, and then examine how Madeira's traders integrated India into their production and marketing institutions. These results come from my research into the Madeira wine trade as an example of the organization and development of the eighteenth-century Atlantic economy. Madeira wine, of course, may not be the most important example of India's relationship with that economy; India surely had even more connection, say, with the Atlantic cloth trade, a woefully understudied subject of reciprocal trans-oceanic exchange. But the tie is revealing nonetheless.

First, consider the broad historical trajectory of Madeira's trade. The American market dominated the Madeira wine trade through most of the eighteenth century. Merchant letters for 1702–13 identify almost 75 percent of ships leaving Madeira as heading for the western hemisphere – principally Britain's mainland and Caribbean colonies and Portuguese Brazil. At the turn of the next century, during the French Revolutionary wars, exports to the Americas still constituted almost 60 percent of Madeira wine exports.

However, these gross numbers disguise the changing direction of the trade. India's share of that trade started small, almost accidentally. As early as 1703, Madeiran merchants were expecting some English East India Company ships to anchor, although it is not clear whether they did so. One Indiaman called in 1707 and loaded 100 pipes for wine for India; two years later, another Indiaman did the same. Only 3 percent of ships in 1702–13 left for the East. This probably understates the size of the India trade, since wine could be purchased from other ships on the high seas, as when Company ships purchased Azorean wine from English vessels anchored off the Cape Verde Islands. Still, to Madeirans, India was an afterthought around 1700.

After three experimental trials with the wine, an official Company trade began in 1718 when the Directors appointed Joseph Hayward's firm their agent for supplying their forts in India with 100 pipes of wine per year.[3] The agency

---

tiges of Old Madras, 2 vols (London, 1913), II, 135, nos. 2–3, *Records of Fort St. George: Diary and Consultation Book of 1714* (Madras, 1929), pp. 89–90. At first, the agent was

had little effect on the rest of the island's commerce, however, because the volume was small, and the agency stayed with the Hayward firm. Only in the 1760s was Thomas Cheap granted a second supply contract. The two firms maintained a lock on official Company orders until 1785, when the Madeira agency system was discontinued. The 'first houses' thereafter engrossed 'the whole Company business' and the rest did not think it worth their while to fuss about the loss of such a customer.[4]

The influx of servants and the buildup of the military after the Battle of Plassey and the grant of the *diwan* spurred greater wine imports. Military men were the largest single source of new consumers and potential customers. In 1763, the Presidency of Bengal had 'fresh experience' of the demand, 'for, altho the quantity sent' them in 1762 'was more than usual', the excess had been 'put up at public sale' and they had nothing with which to satisfy current uses and annual dividends. Again, in 1764, the quantity was 'very inadequate to the wants of . . . servants alone, exclusive of the inhabitants of the settlement'. The 'number of servants both on . . . civil and military lists' was 'so much increased that' there was needed at least 300 pipes just to satisfy demand from the army. 'Enlarge the export of this article as far as you possibly can', they begged. In response, from an average of 100 pipes per year, average orders placed by the Company rose to 300 pipes.

The Company tried to augment its wine offerings with Vidonia from the Canaries; but the report came back from all settlements of a 'general dislike'; it was 'much inferior to the Madeira' which had 'more body' and was 'esteemed' as 'a more healthy and pure wine'.[5] Other wines like Vidonia were available to

Joseph Hayward, who in 1715 previously supplied a Company ship needing 25 pipes of wine for the Company's settlement at St Helena and 15 pipes for its operation at Bencoolen; through the 1760s, the agency remained in the hands of the successor of Hayward's partnership: Hayward & Rider (1721–23); Hayward, Miles & Rider (1725–30); Hayward, Rider & Co. (1731); Hayward, Rider & Chambers (1732–34); Rider, Chambers & Baker (1734–41); Chambers & Baker (1742–47); Chambers, Baker & Hiccox (1748–51); Chambers, Hiccox & Chambers (1751–63), Chambers, Hiccox & Denyer (1764–70), Chambers, Hiccox, Smart, Macky & Co. (1770–75), Chambers, Hiccox, Macky & Co. (1775–77), Chambers, Hiccox & Denyer (1777–85). The agency was doubled in the 1760s when Scott, Pringle & Co. (1766–77) were also named Company agents on the island; in 1777, they were replaced as agents by Fergusson, Murdoch & Co. (1777–80). Agent houses always possessed London partners who were present or past Directors of the Company's Court of Directors (William Rider in 1754, Charles Chambers in 1756–57 and 1764–67, Robert Scott, Thomas Cheap in 1785 and Samuel Smith in 1785), or a substantial Proprietor (Charles Fergusson, whose brother-in-law George Dempster sat on the Direction in 1769). Court of Directors' Minutes, January 8, 1766, B 81/315; James G. Parker, 'The Directors of the East India Company, 1754–1790' (University of Edinburgh, unpublished PhD thesis, 1977).

4   James Gordon to James and Alexander Gordon, 15 December 1765, Gordons of Letterfourie, Presholme, Bannffshire, Scotland [hereafter 'Gordon of Letterfourie'].

5   National Archives of India, *Fort William–India House Correspondence* (Delhi, 1969), III, 543 (19 December 1763), IV (1962) 270 (26 November 1764), V (1962) 287 (16 February

consumers in India: Claret, four other types of French wine, four types of Cape wine, White, Red, Rhenish, Moselle, Spanish, Sack, Malaga, Canary, Muscatel, Palm, and Persia. But, it was felt, Madeira gave 'the best Tast'.[6] One cellar held up as a model in the 1740s contained 100 bottles of Madeira, 12 bottles of Claret and 4 bottles of beer.[7] Fifty years later, John Barrow noted that Madeira and, to a lesser extent, Claret were 'the only wines in general consumption at both the Presidencies and in the army', and that the former was more 'freely used during dinners'. The taste for Madeira even spread among Asians: Maria Graham, in describing the area around Bombay, observed that the Parsees 'often give dinners to the English gentlemen, and drink a great deal of wine, particularly Madeira'.[8] Only after a full opening of India's trade in 1814 did Madeira's popularity and share decline among the British and well-to-do Indian drinkers.[9]

In addition to the official Company trade in wine, the Company always allowed some private trade. Combined orders, one discovers, rose dramatically in the 1760s, with private orders outstripping official orders. In January 1764, for instance, island merchants were told by their London partners to expect six ships to take 2,000 pipes, considerably more than the four ships and 209 pipes ordered by the Directors.[10] Similar demand was noticed two years later when, after two months of the season, some 2,000 pipes had been dispatched on the outbound India fleet.[11]

The private trade was divided between Privilege Traders and Allowance Traders. The Privilege Traders were the captains, officers and crew working aboard Indiamen. By custom, they were allowed to buy and carry *in toto* 20 pipes of wine to the subcontinent freight-free, individual amounts varying with rank. The ship itself was allowed to carry an additional five pipes, for the captain to

1767), 525 (2 February 1769), 259 (7 December 1769), and VI (1960) 178 (25 January 1770). See also E 4/863/193–95/No. 27, 307–9/No. 3, 431–2, 443–6, 674.

6   *Ibid.* The Europeans stationed in Madras appear to have drunk their Madeira with water – three-quarters water, and one-quarter wine – that was found to be 'very savoury to quench the Thirst', Love, *Vestiges*, II, 234. Cf. later advertisements of Calcutta newspapers of the 1780s for a similar availability range; non-Madeira wines were always present in shorter stocks.

7   *Madras Dialogues* (1740–45), reprinted in Love, *Vestiges*, II, 330.

8   John Barrow, *A Voyage to Cochinchina, in the Years 1792 and 1793* (London, 1806), p. 21; Maria Graham, *Journal of a Residence in India* (Edinburgh, 1812), p. 42.

9   In Bengal, for instance, only 590 pipes of Madeira wine were imported each year in 1824–29, and that number fell to 161 pipes by 1829–34. 'As Madeira has been neglected' by the consumers in Calcutta, 'preference has been given to Sherry'. Port declined in popularity, and Claret deteriorated and thus lost its usefulness. John Bell, *A Comparative View of the External Commerce of Bengal* (Calcutta, 1834), pp. 14–15.

10 Newton & Gordon to Johnston & Jolly, 27 March 1764, III, f. 288, Newton & Gordon Letterbooks, Private Collection, Suffolk, England.

11 Robert Bisset to Henry Hill, 20 January 1764, f. 106, VI, John Jay Smith Family Papers A, Hill Papers, 8 February 1766, Thomas Lamar to Henry Hill, 8 February 1766, Sarah A.G. Smith Family Papers, Box 1, Folder 3, Hill Papers, Historical Society of Pennsylvania [hereafter HSP], Philadelphia. See also Newton & Gordon to Francis & Tilghman, 12 March 1773, Newton & Gordon Letterbooks.

dispense or sell as the need arose. Allowance Traders were passengers granted permission by the Captain to stow, for a fee, any number of pipes the space would allow. According to Company tradition, Privilege space comprised roughly 5 percent of all cargo space. Allowance space depended on the passengers and the voyage.

The War for America and its aftermath represented a crisis for the Madeira distributors and introduced real change to India's supply. The early years of the war witnessed a drastic decline in all wine exports to British North America, as the Americans boycotted Madeira and the Portuguese closed ports. As early as 1775, merchants began complaining that, at what should have been the busiest time of the year for filling correspondents' requests, 'the Americans coming in & going away *without*' taking wines made 'matters very quiet'. By the next year, combined with an especially good harvest, the lack of American demand caused wine prices to tumble. To compensate for the loss of North American markets, distributors turned to India more vigorously. Island traders began cultivating markets in India, South East Asia and China.[12] Conservative firms previously reluctant to enter these markets, even during the 1760s when these markets grew by leaps and bounds, were now – out of necessity – forced to accept India contracts and develop consumer bases in that part of the world or to face bankruptcy.

Imports into British India rose during the war and soared thereafter. Company exports averaged 600 pipes per year in 1786–90 and 670 pipes per year in 1803–8 – a fivefold increase over pre-1740 levels.[13] Private trade again augmented the volume. In the late 1780s and early 1790s, total export to India was 'near 4,000 pipes'. In 1799, one firm wrote, Calcutta regularly demanded 4,000 pipes, while Madras took another 2,000, and, the following year, the settlements had taken 6,435 pipes.[14] The share of Madeira's wine taken by India, China and Asia rose to 40 percent of total exports between 1783 and 1793, and continued strong at 28 percent of exports through 1815.

Three Company policy changes fuelled this explosion. In 1785, the Directors discontinued the agency system, and established an auction system, whereby would-be Madeira suppliers placed formal written bids before the Directors. In the first year of its operation the American John Searle won with the lowest bid of 536 pipes at £20 per pipe. Two years later, six different firms were awarded contracts for 510 pipes at £25 per pipe. London auctions for the supply quickly

---

[12] 3 November 1767. *Fort William–India House Correspondence*, V (Delhi, 1962), *sub* 17 March 1769, VIII (1981), *sub* 25 October 1776, and IX (1959), *sub* 22 December 1785, and XI (1974), 27.

[13] William Milburn, *Oriental Commerce* (London, 1813), I, 6.

[14] Newton & Gordon to Francis Newton, 7 June 1793, XV, f. 151, to James Sheafe, 4 October 1794, XVI, f. 128, to Thomas Gordon, 13 June 1795, XVI, f. 289, to Colt, Baker, Day & Co., 10 October 1798, vol. XIX, f. 105, and to Thomas Gordon, 25 October 1799, XX, f. 81, Newton & Gordon Letterbooks; John Leacock, Jr, to William Leacock, 18 October 1799, f. 80, 8 December 1800, f. 215, Leacock Letterbook 1799–1802, Leacock Papers, Funchal, Madeira.

injected a new, more heated spirit of competition into the body of Madeira merchants for Company orders. Secondly, the 1793 Charter Act required the Company to allow for up to 3,000 tons of 'private' cargo each year. Now, non-Company business seized their imagination.[15] Finally, in 1799, Governor-General Lord Mornington opened the gates of trade even further by granting leave 'to individuals unconnected with the East India Company to take up & load ships directly for London upon their private account'. It had become possible to use India profitably as a route back to Europe. Opening the Company's custom to all, allowing greater individual initiative in importing, and giving the previously denied opportunity to ship Madeira wine back to Europe constituted 'a totally new turn' for 'the Commerce'.[16]

What then were the consequences of that 'turn'? When India's demand for Madeira rose substantially after 1765, and especially later in the century as the English East India Company liberalized trade, the Madeira wine merchants reached out to integrate India into their networks and institutions. Nearly every large firm on the island attempted a move on the subcontinent, as did many firms in London, Lisbon and Philadelphia. Two manifestations of the integration are noteworthy. The Madeirans responded to India by producing more wine and more grades of wine, and developing new production techniques. Furthermore, competition among merchants increased sharply, leading them to deploy their marketing techniques more aggressively, as well as developing some new ones. The remainder of this essay examines these responses; taken together, they show Madeirans modifying their business processes to meet India's needs and, as a consequence, bringing India into the emerging Atlantic sphere.

First of all, Madeirans increased the volume of wine produced for export to satisfy Indian tastes. Madeirans had long divided their island horticulturally into the south side of the island, where the best grapes were grown for export-quality wines, and the north side, where poorer soil and harsher climates produced grapes that customarily were marked for local consumption or brandy distillation. After the Seven Years' War, the Madeirans began to channel wines made from north-side grapes into the export trade. If they did not export this must, they blended it with south-side must. This was one of the few ways they could expand the exports of a small, fully cultivated island.

At roughly that time (the 1760s), the houses began to market these north-side or blended concoctions specifically to India consumers. From the 1710s through

---

15 Similarly, Madeira's exports to all Indian and Asian settlements, British and non-British alike, rose: from 1,589 pipes on average in 1779–83 to 3,734 pipes on average in 1805–7. Overall, wine exports averaged 4,130 pipes per year in 1785–1807.

16 Newton, Gordon & Murdoch to Robert Lenox, 16 September 1799, XIX, f. 414, Newton & Gordon Letterbooks. On the Leacock scheme, see John Leacock to Cleland, White & Co., 31 January 1798, Leacock & Sons Letterbook 1794–1801, f. 193; John Leacock to William Leacock, 31 January, 6 April, 29 May, 18 October, 1 December, 1799, 18 January, 12 May, 8 July, 1800, 27 March, 1802, Leacock Letters 1799–1802, ff. 10, 17, 35, 80, 104, 107, 142, 178, 215, 219, 310, Leacock Papers.

the 1780s, the Agents who supplied the Company typically shipped 'fine' London Market wine, although they sometimes added better 'high colored' wines (bearing a deep red hue) which were hard to sell to British and Americans, who preferred pale wines.[17] Yet during the heady competitive days of the 1760s, they began to develop a new intermediate grade of north-side or blended wine they called 'India wine'.[18] They gave this grade its own price for the first time in 1770, when the association of British and British-American distributors known as 'the Factory' set a rate of £24 10s per pipe. The India market, like other major markets, deserved its own pricing. The Factory priced 'India wine' as a 'third quality' wine – not as good as the wine sent to 'Particular' knowing customers and to the London market, but better than the wine sent to America.[19]

In addition, over time, responses from Indian customers helped the Madeirans identify ways to improve the lower grades of wine. Chief among their suggestions was enhanced heating. The first heating experiments occurred about 1775, although successful techniques were not fully devised and implemented until the 1790s. Heating was not an entirely new process for the wine. Some heating arose naturally on the island: from the time of the first Madeira exports, the wine received a natural heat treatment from direct exposure to the sun while sitting outside in vats during the harvest, and indirect exposure while sitting in attics awaiting shipment. Additional heating occurred in the holds of ships: Madeira was by the logic of geography and weather the favoured outbound stop for British, northern European and American ships en route to India, Africa, the Caribbean and North America; wine loaded in Madeira followed either the long, indirect southern route to America or the even longer route around the Cape to India; on these trips it was subjected to temperatures as high as 120° Fahrenheit.[20] After buyers in America *and* India began reporting they liked wines that had made the voyage, distributors began sending the wine on long circuits even when quicker, more direct routes were available. The first note of sending it the long way via the Caribbean intentionally was in 1749 and India in 1772. Through

---

[17] Scott, Pringle & Co. to East India Company, 23 July 1786, E 1/79/No. 47, OIOC.

[18] John Gilliam & Co., 14 January 1768, IV, f. 164, Newton & Gordon Letterbooks.

[19] Newton & Gordon to John Frazer, 15 January 1770, IV, f. 432, Newton & Gordon Letterbooks. On a vote for a separate price, which some merchants vehemently opposed, see 6 May 1776, Gordon of Letterfourie Papers.

[20] Present-day knowledge about the influence of the ocean currents and the trade winds was not fully acquired until after 1850, even though the currents and winds, and the place of Madeira in them, had been studied for centuries. David W. Waters, *The Art of Navigation in England in Elizabethan and Early Stuart Times* (London, 1958), pp. 20–1, 147–8, 201–6, 261–8, 284–7, 311–12. The winds were examined by Edmond Halley, who delivered what became the *locus classicus* on the subject to the Royal Society of London in 1686. 'An historical account of the trade winds, and monsoons, observable in the seas between and near the Tropicks, with an attempt to assign the phisical cause of the said winds', *Philosophical Transactions of the Royal Society* (London, 1686–87), XVI, 153–68. For later accounts, see Benjamin Franklin's explication of the Gulf Stream, in Albert Smyth, ed., *The Writings of Benjamin Franklin*, 10 vols (New York, 1906), IX, 372–413; Thomas Pownall's *Hydraulic and Nautical Observations on the Currents in the Atlantic Ocean* (London, 1787).

numerous trials, a circuit of 'floating ovens' was established by 1775.[21] Then, during the American Revolution, distributors shifted heating processes to land. About 1775, one begins to find vague references to ovens, stoves and hothouses being used for warming pipes and cellars on the island, allusions which become explicit in 1794 when special rooms were built and warmed to 100° Fahrenheit by fire, and into which were placed wine casks set on trestles.[22]

By 1813, warming rooms had won over all merchants; 'all the Houses' were using them. Considerable savings in time and money accrued from shortening production periods and avoiding long-distance cargo fees: a wine that would only be palatable after five years in England, three years in Madeira, or one year in India could be readied in an *estufa* (oven) in three months. Through mellowing, the distributors also mitigated undesirable characteristics and increased the quantity of their low-grade export wines – both necessary if they were to meet the simultaneously rising demand from India and America.

21 Hans Sloane, *A Voyage to the Islands Madeira, Barbados, Nieves, S. Christophers and Jamaica*, 13 vols (London, 1707), I, 10; Warren Johnson Journal, *sub* 12 January 1761, in *The Papers of Sir William Johnson* (Albany, 1962), XIII, 198; Francis White to Richard Derby, 7 May 1766, Richard Derby Papers, Box 10, Folder 5, Philips Library, Essex Institute, Salem.

22 *Livro do Saida*, no. 22, f. 24, Arquivo Nacional, Lisbon. Experiments are recounted in Thomas Gordon to Francis Newton, 24 October, 17 November 1783, VIII, f. 124, 14 April 1785, VIII, f. 139, Thomas Murdoch to Thomas Gordon, November 20, 1789, XII, f. 177, and Thomas Murdoch to Francis Newton, 1 September 1792, XIV, f. 322, Newton & Gordon Letterbooks. On earlier uses of stoves, see Edward Barry, *Observations, Historical, Critical and Medical, on the Wines of the Ancients* (London, 1775), pp. 1–10, 48–58, 67–84, 442–3; and Daniel Henry Smith to James and Alexander Gordon, December 1775, Gordon of Letterfourie Papers. As early as 1727, wine producers along the Moselle appear to have been building iron stoves in their cellars and using them to meliorate wines. But the practice was not widely known, and no Madeiran mentioned German practice. Barry's influence is a far more likely one on the Anglo-centred Portuguese. On Fernandes and the first *estufas*, see History of *Estufa* Heating, 8 February 1803, Arquivo Marino Ultramarino, no. 1431, Arquivo Historico Ultramarino; Newton & Gordon to Henry Heskith, 15 October 1799, and to Edmund Middleton, 20 April 1801, XX, f. 67, XXII, f. 367, Newton & Gordon Letterbooks. The love of experiment should not be overlooked, for it played an important part. Visitors to the island remarked on it, especially among the foreign merchant community. On later *estufas*, see Thomas Murdoch to John Campbell, 14 April 1798, XVIII, f. 316, Thomas Murdoch to Thomas Gordon, 27 June, 15, 25 October, 1799, XIX, f. 337, XX, ff. 52, 81, Thomas Murdoch to Robert Lenox, 2 February 1802, vol. XXIII, f. 81, Newton & Gordon Letterbooks; John Leacock, Sr. to William Leacock, 18 January, 29 April, 27 June 1799, 18 January, 28 August, 28 October 1800, 23 January 1801, Leacock & Sons Letterbook 1799–1802, ff. 6–9, 27, 52–8, 107, 192–4, 223, Leacock Papers; Arquivo Marino Ultramarino, no. 1431; Anonymous, *Account of the Island of Madeira* (London, 1801); Nicholas Pitta, *Account of the Island of Madeira* (London, 1812). Throughout the period, however, firms remained reticent about placing their best wines in an *estufa*. Newton, Gordon & Murdoch to Robert Lenox, XXV, f. 173, 30 September 1803, Newton & Gordon Letterbooks. On early trials with dung heating, see Daniel Henry Smith to James & Alexander Gordon, December 1775, Gordon of Letterfourie Papers.

*

Thus, Madeira's traders integrated Indian consumers into the process of production. But there is another part to the integration story: marketing. There was an increase in entrepreneurial competition that can be tracked directly to changes in the supply institutions of the Company. In 1768, the Company hired two agents (two houses). In 1785, the Directors switched from an agency system to an auction system of choosing official suppliers. By 1789, island firms were approaching individual firms and customers in India on a hitherto unprecedented scale. After the Company's monopoly was breached in 1793, individual allowances rose further and consistently dwarfed official orders. Then, when the monopoly officially ended in 1813, the sluice gates were fully opened.[23]

Madeira merchants had competed for years to sell wine to the servants of the Company and, to a lesser extent, to passengers. From the 1710s, each Indiaman bought some wine as part of her store, and the captains had discretion over which sellers to patronize. In 1756, a merchant in London, the uncle of one Madeiran, acted on his nephew's behalf and 'secured all the officers' of one ship ordered to stop at the island for wine. His nephew was not sanguine about gaining the custom of the men of other ships in the fleet, for he was 'afraid the Interest of' the Company's official Agents would 'prevail with a great many of them'. Further, despite the privilege in principle, it was his experience that 'the captain seldom or never allows the officers to ship above a hogshead or quarter cask for their own drinking', in the interest of maintaining order or of making room for more of his own privilege wine.[24]

Competition among merchants for the private trade became much more intense in the closing years of the Seven Years' War and remained so for the rest of the century. Each house, through contacts in the metropolis, began to approach individual captains, officers, crewmen and passengers.[25] The struggle for their custom became so heated that most firms in Madeira felt it desirable to

[23] See Agreement of 1756 (East India Company to Fort St George, 29 December 1756, E 4/861/663–65, OIOC, and *Fort William–India House Correspondence*, I, 178–9), 1786 Regulations (B 103–104/567 and 868, OIOC), 1793 Charter, and 1803 Regulations (B 137/249–51, 316 [8 June 1803] and E 4/891/73–5 [6 July 1803]), and 1813 (*Oriental Commerce*, p. 6). For reference to the 'usual indulgence' of 20 pipes allowed to 'the Captain and Ship's Company', see *Fort William–India House Correspondence*, I (Delhi, 1958), 2 (1753, Letters from Company). 'If any more is landed in India', however, the extra was considered 'unlicensed' and 'confiscated to the use of the Company', probably put up for sale at public auction. On the sale of unnecessary wines at public auction and the discounts given to military officers, see *ibid.*, I, 238 (10 January 1748), 465 (4 February 1751). Under the 1803 regulations, the commanders were allowed to take 2 pipes of wine freight free on the Company's extra ships; individual passengers travelling on these ships had to pay freight charges (*Oriental Commerce*, p. 6). On the ship's own allowance of five pipes, see *Fort William–India House Correspondence*, VI, 158 (25 March 1772).

[24] Francis Newton to George Spence, 15 January 1756, I, f. 189, Newton & Gordon Letterbooks.

[25] Alexander Gordon to James Gordon, 12 April 1761, Gordon of Letterfourie.

station a partner in London on a permanent basis, as well as to direct their partners to invest more heavily in Company stocks and bonds.[26] With each passing year another house sent representatives to lobby the service. The Gordons, who never seemed to win an order, were livid. As to Captains' business, wrote James Gordon,

> it is reduced to such a pass that I will not attempt it. You may guess who will have the cream if any of it is worth while, which in my opinion is but little. There are now here so many new impudent Madeira adventurers from the Island, as well as people in the City connected with new Houses they have erected there of late which you can have no idea of, that have made the India business so different from your time & mine that I think it not worth looking for nor desirable. I wish you would seriously think of settling your matters abroad & let one of the younger folks come & busk about for their own support.[27]

Much the same attention showered on the servants in London was lavished on them when they anchored off Funchal. With characteristic understatement, Alexander Gordon of Madeira wrote his brother James Gordon in London that if 'the East India Man you mention puts in here, I shall be as early as any in my application to him and make use of the arguments you have put in my mouth'.[28] The established houses engrossed the captain trade, and often the smaller houses could 'stand no chance', unless they adopted unscrupulous tactics – which many were willing to do. In the context of a relatively gentlemanly trade carried out by a fairly small, insular, mostly expatriate community, unscrupulous tactics meant each firm working to outdo the other, each house attempting to shave the price on the margin by foregoing traditional profits or traditional aspects of quality, manufacture or package. Sometimes they effected this by sending cargo to the Cape Verdes where captains could buy without scrutiny. Reduced prices in particular – considerably short of shipping prices agreed upon the Factory – were the usual means of currying favour with captains and officers.[29] James Duff detailed some of these practices in 1778 for his partners in London. The new merchant firm of Phelps & Co:

> stepped in & offered the wine at £13.0 payable in 20 months. This is all very fine & dirty work, of which some of our best houses have been also guilty of. Chisholm takes the greatest quantity; he does business with Smyth & Scott's house. This man is at the bottom of all this work. The general price for India wine is £15 with all charges on board; it is impossible to ship for this price any

26 James Gordon to Alexander Gordon & Co., 29 August 1772, James Gordon's London Letterbook, 1765–75, f. 352; Thomas Lamar to Henry Hill, 26 July 1773, VIII, f. 146, John Jay Smith Family Papers A, Hill Papers, HSP.
27 James Gordon to Alexander Gordon, 24 September 1778, Gordon of Letterfourie Papers.
28 Alexander Gordon to James Gordon, 12 April 1763, Gordon of Letterfourie Papers.
29 Daniel Henry Smith to Gordon Brothers, 9 November 1775, Gordon of Letterfourie Papers.

that are of a good quality. The lowness of the North wine & of the Tinta gives
them a gain of 10 to 12$ per pipe. . . . [By the shipping of south wines, we
cannot get a farthing.] Our business is come to a fine pass . . . Ahmuty of
London offered Capt Morris wine at £13.0.0 & to advance him £2,000 stg in
money. He told him that he would guarantee the wines & ship them as good as
any house here.[30]

Longer terms of credit, low prices, forswearing of freight and related charges,
offers of full insurance, substantial advances, new arrangements for pay involving half bill and half bond: such became the stock in trade for merchants eager to
acquire a piece of the growing India traffic, and was in line with what was being
done in London.[31]

Madeira traders also cultivated the shippers, traders and monopoly companies of other Western European powers, achieving an unusual inter-imperialism
in the trade. Portuguese ships out of Lisbon and trading to India always figured
heavily in Madeira's India trade, but they became more prominent after 1750.[32]
Their heyday was during and after the War for America, when, one Madeira resident noted, 'the natives have lately got much into the spirit of trading, no less
than 4,000 pipes having been sent annually to India, for these years past, all in
Portuguese ships, & shipped by Portuguese'.[33]

Other Europeans also rose in importance to Madeira's burgeoning India
trade. The first reference we have to the servicing of non-English and
non-Portuguese Indiamen appears in 1753, when Charles Chambers (the Directors' Agent) sold 160 pipes to an English captain who in turn transported them
to Port L'Orient for the French India Company. Three years later, Richard Baker
(a partner and brother-in-law of Chambers, and a brother of the influential
London merchant Sir William Baker) supplied a Dutch ship with 300 pipes for
the French Company.[34]

Other countries' India shippers would take double and sometimes triple the
number of pipes traditionally taken by British vessels. Thomas Murdoch's

---

[30] James Gordon to Alexander Gordon, 5 December 1765, 1765–75 Letterbook, Gordon of
Letterfourie Papers.

[31] Newton & Gordon to Wilkinson & Gordon, 22 April; to Francis Newton, 1 June 1778, VI,
ff. 378, 388, Newton & Gordon Letterbooks.

[32] Since the Portuguese Indiamen departed from their home base of Lisbon, there was less
need for reprovisioning in Madeira. As a result, they often hugged the Portuguese and
African coasts and reprovisioned along the African coast. Those which did stop are difficult
to track with any rigour, however, since Portuguese Indiamen were not required to be
entered into the official books of *entradas* and *saidas* kept by the *Alfandega*. In the second
half of the century, that custom seems to have lapsed, and they appear with greater frequency.

[33] Joseph Gillis to Henry Hill, 4 April–6 May 1783, John Jay Smith Family Papers A, vol. 9, f. 2,
Hill Papers, HSP.

[34] Francis Newton to George Spence, 27 October 1753, 19 July 1756, I, ff. 77, 218, Newton &
Gordon Letterbooks. See also Newton & Gordon to Francis Newton, 4 May 1768 ('a French
Indiaman now in port who carries about 400 pipes'), IV, f. 211, *ibid.*

Madeira firm commonly shipped off 400 pipes or more in a sloop owned by the French Company.[35] The size of French orders amazed those who had laboured in the trade for decades. In 1778, over 800 pipes lay at Port L'Orient on one Madeira house's account,

> & 1000 to 1200 pipes are to go from Donaldson's house in one French ship for the India market directly. I never heard, nor did anybody else, of such a qty going in one bottom. But whether in one or more, it is said with certainty that such a parcel is going, & that it is an adventure chiefly if not wholly on the house's account, . . . [It is, in a word,] incredible.[36]

It was not just the Portuguese and French who took such large volumes. By the middle of the 1770s, just as the Madeirans were coping with the closing of Portugal's ports to American vessels, Danes started pouring in, largely as truckers. In one month in 1783, after three Lisbon ships had carried off several thousand pipes, the Danes took away a thousand more. One of the wealthiest of Portuguese landowners and traders loaded 400 pipes on board a Lisbon India-bound ship and, 'not satisfied with that' dispatch, she offered 50,000 cruzados for a Danish ship now in port, with the view of loading more wine on her own account; the captain demanded 70,000, however, and she demurred. The Briton James Ayres felt no such reticence, for he was in the habit of making 'astonishing shipments for every sort of trash which . . . Danes . . . offered him in exchange', and he accepted. To many looking on, it seemed, traders were 'all possesst with downright infatuation and galloping on to ruin, without a ten pence' in their coffers.[37]

The point of all this foreign trade was not lost on contemporaries. Foreign competition changed the nature of the trade with the English East India Company.[38] Larger sales and higher prices became the order of the day. The connection was plain to the Directors in London, who with each passing year were ever 'more desirous of increasing our Consignments of Wine' to India. Why? Because 'the Portuguese and other European nations' derived 'great benefit by what they sent there'.[39]

In addition to more aggressive cultivation of ships' crews and passengers and of non-English Indiamen during the last quarter of the century, the Madeirans reached out to individual consumers in India. This became especially widespread

---

35 Newton & Gordon to Thomas Gordon, 28 November 1774, V, f. 409, to Francis Newton, 7 January 1775, ff. 426, 436, Newton & Gordon Letterbooks.

36 James Gordon to Alexander Gordon, 20–23 February 1778, Gordon of Letterfourie Papers.

37 Daniel Henry Smith to Gordon Brothers, 17 February 1776, Gordon of Letterfourie Papers.

38 Newton & Gordon to Francis Newton, 24 May, VIII. f. 67, 7 June, to Thomas Gordon, VIII, f. 73, 10 July 1783, to Montgomery, Sealy & Co., VIII, f. 93, Newton & Gordon Letterbooks. On more Danish Indiamen, see Newton & Gordon to Francis Newton, 24 January 1784, VIII, f. 178, *ibid.*

39 Newton & Gordon to Donaldson & Stotts, 8 June 1785, Newton & Gordon Letterbooks, IX, f. 30, Newton & Gordon Letterbooks.

40 James Duff to James Gordon, 27 June 1778, enclosing a proposal from Patrick Duff,

when the 1793 Charter Act opened up cargo space to non-Company traders. To do this, the Madeirans replicated the institutions that had worked to such good effect in the Americas: they called on their relations, school-friends, county neighbours, and passing acquaintances – usually in that order – to fill orders. For instance, the Gordons leaned heavily on their nephew General Patrick Duff in Bengal, and he responded with a proposal for 'introducing good wine into' the region 'and giving the people here a taste for such'. If the firm would get the captains to take 30 pipes of London Market wine every year to Calcutta, paying prime cost 'as usual', Duff pledged to 'take the wines off their hands', without

> any farther trouble to them, and [to] pay them a price in proportion to what other wines sell for in this country, . . . which I should think would be a great advantage to them, [for] . . . any person who brings goods for sale here ought to be very glad to have the certainty of an immediate sale at the market price, as some have of late been obliged to leave effects unsold in the country, at great loss and risque.

Plans hinged on personal ties such as Duff's abounded in the 1770s, 1780s and 1790s.[40]

Personal linkages were the key to making the India market as profitable as the American arena. Consider the work of the large Newton & Gordon firm. Before the end of the American Revolution, one finds no mention of a private customer or correspondent in India. But by 1784, the firm established relations with four there. Messrs. Newton & Gordon advised John Scott in Calcutta that if his 'friends in Bengal adopt the method of importing wines for your own use, we fancy the difference of the quality of what is so introduced would be very distinguishable'. By 1787, they had added four more to their list of customers, all of them relatives, friends or relatives of friends. In 1789, they established contractual relations with a Calcutta firm to handle their orders. Ten years later, their customers numbered 30, mainly in Bengal. By 1807, Newton & Gordon had 110 customers in India, dispersed from Dacca to Madras.[41]

Gordon of Letterfourie Papers. On the developing tastes of men in India, see T.G.P. Spear, *The Nabobs: A Study of the Social Life of the English in Eighteenth-Century India* (London, 1932), and Cyril N. Parkinson, *Trade in the Eastern Seas, 1793–1815* (Cambridge, 1937). An American, James Searle, won the Company's contract in 1786. John Marsden Pintard to Elias Boudinot, 29 December 1786, Folder 41, Boudinot Papers, American Bible Society, New York. On the arrival of the American Indiaman *Washington* in 1788, see Extracts of Letters from Robert Duff's Journal at Madeira, 1 February 1788, Gordon of Letterfourie Papers; Brown & Benson to John Searle & Co., 20 December 1787, Box 10, Folder 10, as well as Sundry Extracts, 1788, Box 546, Folder 8, Box 547, Folder 2, William Megee's Log Book, 27 December 1787–8 March 1788, Box 737, Folder 3, Remarks, 1788, Samuel Ward to Brown & Benson, V–G35, V 150, John Searle & Co. to Brown & Benson, 22 March, 10 May 1788, PE–9, John Marsden Pintard to Brown & Benson, 26 August 1788, PE–9, Brown Papers, John Carter Brown Library, Providence, R.I.

41 Newton & Gordon to John Scott, 30 April 1784, VIII, f. 230, Newton & Gordon Letterbooks. See also IX and XI, passim, Lists, 1807, XXIX, ff. 269, 803.

*

At the outset of this essay, I asserted that India was in the Atlantic. That claim, I admit, may beggar geographical reality. But let me expand slightly upon this peculiar construction. As an American historian who studies trans-oceanic affairs in the colonial period, I spend much of my time thinking about how Atlantic economic and social institutions were invented and evolved. When I look at India and the East India Company, what is remarkable is how quickly the unorganized and decentralized Atlantic traders reached out and embraced the organized and centralized India market as an important corner of the trade polygon. This hitherto untold story highlights three salient characteristics – or, some like Douglass North would say, 'institutions' – of the Atlantic system that the Atlantic traders imported to India:

1   The decentralized organization of its emerging trade and the opportunistic mode of competition among participants.
2   The powerful reliance on face-to-face contacts and personal links – for making acquaintances, for gaining customers, for conducting business, and for solving problems. The importance of personal links was so strong that they were still dominant in 1813 when they had to span three oceans, and when impersonal ties were increasingly viable.
3   The highly interactive nature of commercial relationships among producers, distributors and consumers. The discovery of the value of heating Madeira is an example of what those interactions produced, through continuous, reciprocal conversations.

Over the century, the Company came to rely on island growers and traders over whose entrepreneurial egos they had no direct control. Those uncontrolled entrepreneurs on their own deployed their relatives and partners in London, Bengal, Madras, Bombay, Bencoolen and Canton to extend their markets. And they began a vigorous set of conversations with their distributors and customers in India that effectively refined the produce and increased the custom and that worked both within and without the official Company system, and took advantage as well of the possibility of contraband. In doing so, they brought India into their self-organizing Atlantic system. And – they, too, were changed by it, for the India wine trade affected the way Atlantic merchants viewed the world, causing them to look east as well as west.

The East India Company conference at the National Maritime Museum in July 2000 had a major panel on the Company in India and Asia, and one on the Company in London and Britain. As far as I can tell, the presentation on Dutch companies was the only one to place British India in a wider comparative context, although an allusion to Brazil was made in another. Previously, historians like Huw Bowen have linked America to the story, but little of that was heard at the conference in Greenwich. In that spirit, I've tried to push even further: to sketch some of India's relationship with emerging Atlantic commercial institutions, and vice versa. By the end of the eighteenth century, for all it was still primarily a British institution, the Company had to adapt its actions and gauge its successes in an inter-imperial, multi-oceanic context that embraced more than just Britain and just India and its Presidencies. These categories are convenient but certainly not accurate; the more we as historians interested in India and the Company factor in non-British European, Atlantic and American commodities, financing, entrepreneurs and consumption, the more accurate an understanding of both the Company and the early modern world we achieve.

Contested Relations: the East India Company and Lascars in London

SHOMPA LAHIRI

Introduction

'Britannia rules the waves – not by her own sons only, but those from India's coral strand too.'[1] The missionary who wrote these words was describing the important, but neglected role of Indian seamen or 'lascars' in enabling the East India Company to control trade in the East. Indian seamen remain marginal figures in the maritime historiography of the late eighteenth and early nineteenth centuries, provoking one writer to label them the 'forgotten seamen'[2] As with other groups of subaltern actors, historical records are frustratingly silent. The few scholars, who have written on the subject, have focused on issues of lascar nationality, mendicancy and survival strategies, relating specifically to London. However, relatively little attention has been given to the dynamics of lascar–East India Company relations. Company records that have survived emphasise dispute and conflict, with evidence of good relations remaining hidden. Greater understanding of lascars provides a glimpse of the way the Company functioned as an employer, in addition to valuable evidence of early Indo-British encounters in the period before direct rule, not just in India, but in Britain too. Sources uncovered suggest that Company policy was characterised by neglect and the dominance of commercial considerations, in stark contrast to the Company's public pronouncements, stressing moral duty and benevolent concern for the welfare of its employees.[3] Tensions manifested themselves in several ways. Protectionist navigation legislation ran counter to increasing demand for maritime labour, complicated further by issues of lascar nationality. The East India Company's attempts to defend itself against allegations of neglect raised questions about its responsibility for Indian maritime employees, as well as wider concern about the extent to which lascar behaviour and actions should be subject to regulation and intervention.

From its earliest trading days in Asia, the East India Company employed

---

[1] *Sailors Magazine*, 50 (1843), 36.
[2] C. Dixon, 'Lascars: The Forgotten Seamen', *Working Men who got Wet*, ed. R. Ommer and G. Panting (Newfoundland, 1980), p. 270.
[3] British Library, Oriental and India Office Collections (OIOC): L/MAR/C/902, 23 February 1815.

lascars to navigate its ships. In 1667 the English Council at Surat recorded payment to lascars for services rendered.[4] Initially lascars were involved in the coastal trade between East Africa, India, the Eastern Archipelago and China, which operated from the end of the seventeenth century until the introduction of steam power to the middle of the nineteenth century. Goods made in India, particularly opium and cotton piece goods, were shipped to Canton via Calcutta on 'country' ships officered by Europeans and manned by lascars. In this way the resources of India were used to finance the Company's China tea investments. The confinement of Indian seamen to the Indian Ocean had been promulgated by navigation legislation, dating back to 1660, enacted to ensure that 75 percent of British ships crews were ethnically British. The act prevented the employment of lascars in ships sailing to and from Britain and protected British sailors from foreign competition. However, despite the existence of prohibitive laws, the East India Company flouted legislation and recruited Indian seamen to replace Europeans, who had fallen prey to disease and impressment on the journey out to India. But it was not until the beginning of the Napoleonic wars in 1793 that demand for Indian maritime labour, on journeys to and from Britain, expanded rapidly. Between 1804 and 1813 the number of lascars rose from 471 to 1,336.[5] Press-gangs robbed the Merchant fleet of their best seamen creating large gaps in personnel on homeward-bound ships to Britain. Forcible enlistment of civilians into the navy was not confined to Europeans; Indians with no experience of sailoring were also taken, against their will and put on ships in India.[6] Crimping houses were established in seaports to which Indians, kidnapped both by their countrymen and Europeans, were taken.[7] Thus adherence to the 1660 Navigation Act became increasingly problematic, both at the beginning and the end of voyages. The 1794 Act declared that after the end of hostilities lascars would revert back to their previous nationality and only be classified as British in the area east of the Cape of Good Hope. As late as 1840 the East India Company petitioned parliament requesting that the Navigation Acts be amended to allow British subjects from India to be treated as such, when navigating vessels. It was suggested that lascars were acutely aware of the discriminatory nature of the navigation legislation. They had questioned why it had been applied exclusively to Indians and not to other groups of colonial subjects.

---

4   J. Walsh, 'The Empire's Obligation to the Lascar', *The Imperial and Asiatic Quarterly Review*, 30, 59–60 (1910), 341–2. In 1699 East India Company officials in Bengal employed a number of lascars to alleviate the shortage of sailors in India and were commended for their foresightedness. They and other lascars on the ship *Duke of Gloucester* were well fed and clothed. The *serang* was contracted to furnish more lascars should the necessity arise. OIOC, E/3/93, President in Council in Bengal, 20/12/1699, p. 128.

5   OIOC, L/MAR/C/902, Table of Expenses for Lascars, p. 120.

6   C.N. Parkinson, *The Trade Winds: The Study of British Overseas Trade during the French Wars, 1793–1815* (London, 1948), p. 148.

7   *The Times*, 9/12/1814.

Conflicting interests

From the start acrimony dogged Company dealings with lascars, particularly over wages. As early as 1713 disagreement arose over payment on the return voyages back to India. The *serang* Sultan Golam Mahmud and his crew had complained bitterly to the Company about the conduct of Captain Goodman of the ship *Saint George*, who, they claimed, had taken advantage of the fact they did not understand English to impose a constraint whereby there was no provision for wages on the return journey to India. The Company was sufficiently concerned about the case to pay out four months' pay, taking on what should have been the responsibility of ship owners in order to silence lascar disaffection. The Company was evidently keen to avoid a similar situation arising again, as a despatch from the Court of Directors reveals: 'The *serang* is an impudent fellow, never let him or Tandell come on any of our ships to England and if you can help it, none of the rest of them neither.'[8] In 1731 the Company were presented with similar grievances. As before the lascars insisted that their contracts of employment, written exclusively in English, were unintelligible to them. The Company, concerned to limit additional expenses, decreed that in future contracts would be drawn up in local vernaculars as well as English.

Unlike other European, Chinese and black sailors, who were recruited by the Company, lascars were unable to enjoy a direct relationship with their employers. Instead the supply and recruitment of lascars was controlled by Indian intermediaries known as 'ghat serangs' at the ports of Bombay and Calcutta. The *ghat serang* was a combination of 'moneylender, labour recruiter and lodging-house keeper'. Another *serang* was employed on board ship to supervise and pay the men. This system of indirect recruitment was introduced by Warren Hastings, Governor General of Bengal, in 1783 and remained unchanged until the 1940s. Limited knowledge of the English language meant that lascars were unable to receive instructions from British officers; instead they were communicated via a *serang*. The *ghat serang* was contracted by the East India Company to furnish a crew for a voyage at a given sum per head, of which he was given a proportion in advance. He made individual agreements with lascars.[9] The *serang* on board the ship was responsible for paying wages and disciplining the lascars. However, the prevalence of bribery and corrupt practices resulted in lascars receiving considerably less in wages than they would have expected to receive had direct recruitment been introduced. Not only were *serangs* accused of defrauding lascars of their wages, shipowners also complained to the Court of Directors that *serangs* were demanding four months' advance for lascars, even in cases of voyages under four months, which created labour shortages and delays in finding full crews of men to man ships. In order to tighten up the recruitment system, *serangs* were fined if the number of men promised failed

---

8   OIOC, E/3/97, Proceedings of the Court of Bengal, 2/2/1712, p. 175.
9   BPP, 1814–15 (471), 111, 1.

to materialise.[10] Despite the many accusations levied against *serangs* from all quarters, the East India Company showed marked resistance to reforming the recruitment system. This partially reflects the increasing power of the *serang*, which continued to grow after the demise of the East India Company. It also reflects the Company's reluctance to engage with their employees. Language and race barriers meant that a direct relationship between British officers and Indian crews was not regarded as possible or desirable. *Serangs* were seen as indispensable to exercising control and discipline over Indian crews. Consequently the East India Company was prepared to turn a blind eye to corruption, as long as it did not jeopardise their commercial interests.

Although the use of intermediaries was intended to produce more harmonious and disciplined relations on board ship, the numerous examples of deaths on vessels with lascar crews illustrate the potential for violent discord at sea. In 1802 the East India Company's Committee of Shipping investigated allegations of maltreatment on the ship *Union*. Of a crew of 74 lascars, who had boarded from Calcutta, 28 died on the passage to England. The *serang* claimed the chief mate had flogged and beaten the men in a most cruel manner 'till he could see their backs and bones'.[11] The *serang*, who was also threatened with violence, believed several had died at the hands of the chief mate. The Boatswain, John Moore, gave evidence of the Captain's brutality to white officers as well as lascars. Additional supportive medical evidence was provided by the Royal London Hospital, which stated that 'within a very short period several [lascars] in the most deplorable situation have been admitted from Indian ships belonging to the Company'.[12] Damage to the feet and shoes were particularly apparent, resulting from attempts to escape violence. Yet curiously despite the abundance of evidence against the Captain, the Company judged the charges to be unfounded, originating from the 'mutinous and disaffected disposition of John Moore, Boatswain of the *Union*'.[13] Even in those cases where the Company felt that 'very great and unnecessary severity had been exercised by British officers', as in the treatment of crews on board the *Fort Wilhelm* and the *Java*, the Company's solicitor viewed the complaints as frivolous and argued against a prosecution on the grounds that lascar evidence was contradictory and would increase the likelihood of acquittal.[14] The evidence available suggests that the East India Company and the English legal system were unreceptive to lascar censure. Very few disputes seem to have been settled in a way which satisfied lascars. For example, in 1815 the crew of the *Winchelsea* complained of ill treat-

---

[10] OIOC, H/MISC/190, p. 94.

[11] OIOC, H/MISC/501, Committee of Shipping, 26 May 1802, p. 7. A contemporary writer concluded: 'It is possible that there were ships in which the native seamen had come to fear their officers more than they feared the elements or the enemy', Parkinson, *The Trade Winds*, p. 216.

[12] *Ibid.*

[13] *Ibid.*, p. 45.

[14] OIOC, L/MAR/1/3, 30/7/1813, Committee of Shipping, pp. 105–6.

ment, but their accusations were dismissed when the case was tried at Thames Police Court.[15] Increasingly Indian seamen decided to take matters into their own hands, by deserting when grievances about overcrowding and lack of adequate provisions remained unheeded. On 6 October 1819, 20 lascars deserted the ship *Victory*, giving the cause as want of proper accommodation and provisions.[16]

Negative images of lascars promoted during the period also marred Company–lascar relations. Unfaltering depictions proved exceptionally persistent.[17] Nevertheless concerns about apparent shortcomings appear to have faded in light of the considerable savings which were accrued from employment of Indian seamen. It cost only one shilling a day to feed a lascar, and up to double that amount to maintain a European sailor. This disparity stemmed less from any physical differences between South Asian and European sailors than the perception of difference and deep-seated prejudices that surrounded lascars. In 1812 the political economist David Macpherson wrote in his book *History of European Commerce with India*

> Lascars who from their feeble habits of body and being accustomed only to short voyages during the fine weather season upon the tranquil seas of India are unable to bear the cold and utterly incapable of vigorous exertion and rapid movements, necessary in the boisterous seas of Europe and not to be depended upon for defending a ship against an enemy, to say nothing of their ignorance of the language in which the preservation of life and property frequently depends, nor of the frequent conflagrations of ships manned by lascars.[18]

Macpherson's account failed to acknowledge that the lascar's inability to withstand cold stemmed from the inadequate provision of warm clothing, rather than physical weakness. While there is evidence of lascars and Chinese seamen showing a distinct reluctance or indifference to defend a ship from attack, equally accounts of lascar courage are also available.[19] The apparent indifference and cowardice of lascars and Chinese can also be interpreted as defiance of cruel masters, who failed to earn the respect of their Asian crews. Indian seamen were

---

15 OIOC, L/MAR/1/5, 14/7/1815, p. 178.

16 OIOC, L/MAR/1/8, p. 385.

17 'They lived in filthy, overcrowded conditions, whoring and gambling away their miserable existences, until there was room on a ship, herded together below deck, probably already infected by typhus contracted in their crude accommodation ashore, they died off in scores . . . Lascars were notoriously useless: cowardly and prone to cold, they were incapable of going into the tops in a gale and were the first to die off when illness spread on board.' J. Sutton, *Lords of the East: The East India Company and its Ships* (London, 1981), p. 931.

18 D. Macpherson, *History of European Commerce with India* (London, 1812), pp. 235–6.

19 In 1810 the *Bombay Courier* reported that Peerboy Semjee, *Serang* of Gogo, was to win a gold medal from the Governor for 'brave defence of a treasure boat' and permitted to retire on full pay. Any family who survived him was also to be financially provided for. Also see A. Bulley, *Free Mariner: John Adolphus Pope in the East Indies, 1785–1821* (London, 1992), p. 14.

able to contest power relations on board ship by withdrawing their assistance at the time of most need, when the vessel was under attack. Thus Macpherson's observations reveal something of the nature of lascar resistance, as well as the myopia of imperial perceptions.

Outcry in London

Relations between lascars and the East India Company reached their lowest depths in 1814 when the Society for the Protection of Asiatic Sailors (formed in the same year) sent a highly critical letter to *The Times* castigating the East India Company for dereliction of duty towards lascars, under its protection in London. Specific areas of criticism included, pay, accommodation, health and nutrition. Conflict over wages had long been a source of contention. After all deductions had been extracted, lascars were left with a severely depleted wage packet. The Society concluded that the amount actually received by lascars was a 'mere pittance'.[20] Moreover there was no guarantee that even the smallest remuneration would be forthcoming. The Society reported that in 1814 Captains and shipowners had withheld wages amounting to £1,457. Lascars were obliged to employ navy agents to obtain the remainder of their wages, but the commission charged by the agents ate into the amount retrieved. Adherence to the navigation laws meant that lascars who manned ships to Britain were required by law to be returned back to India as passengers. This in itself was, according to the Society, 'a grievous evil', as paid employment on ships returning to India would have been welcomed by lascars to support their families and supplement income derived from agriculture. The Company's critics claimed that once ships were no longer visible from the shore, lascars were coerced into navigating vessels, without payment. While it was possible for the Company to blame individual shipowners for the treatment of lascars on board ship, criticism of its management of the Company barracks in the London docks was much harder to deflect. The Society accused it of excluding deserving cases from its barracks in Ratcliff Highway. Even those who had been able to obtain admittance orders, after initially being expelled from the barracks, complained that their documentation was not accepted, leaving them homeless once more. Other lascars found themselves passed between Captain, shipowner and barracks, only to find that none were willing to house them. Exclusion from the barracks resulted in lascars taking up residence with so-called 'criminal elements' of the dock community and selling their meagre possessions in order to subsist. The Society responded to the crisis by providing shelter for 19 lascars who had been refused accommodation at the barracks. Many more had been turned away by the Society due to lack of sufficient funds.

---

[20] *The Times*, 9/12/1814. In addition, lascars paid one shilling per month at the Merchant Shipping Office.

The Company also came under attack for its neglect of lascar health and nutrition. Attention was focused on the alleged shortfall between the food and provisions that the Company was contractually obliged to provide and the actual goods received by the lascars. The Society noted that it was usual for Indian seamen to be given meat or fish when they first boarded ships. However, once they had set sail their diet deteriorated rapidly, consisting of only rice and *ghee* (clarified butter). The need for medical care, both on board ship and within the Company barracks, as well as the provision of suitable warm clothing to protect against the inclement British weather was also highlighted. Among European sailors, sickness and mortality declined drastically over the course of the Napoleonic Wars. In 1778, one in 2.4 became sick, with 1 in 42 dying of their complaints. By 1815, 1 in 10.7 fell ill, with only 1 in 143 fatalities.[21] Although equivalent statistics do not exist for lascars, fragmented evidence from ship surgeons suggests that sickness and mortality rates among lascars were higher. Surgeon reports for the year 1798/9 show that on the ship *Cabrel* over one-third of lascars died en route to England, with similar statistics for other ships. The *Lucy Maria*, a 'country ship' which sailed for England in 1801 with a crew of 86 lascars, had 22 fatalities during the voyage, with a further 20 ill when the ship arrived in England. On the *Surat Castle* 36 died and 45 were ill in a crew of 123 men.[22] Beriberi and scorbutic diseases were particularly common among Indian seamen. However, where figures have survived they must be treated with caution. In the case of one lascar crew of 71 men, 16 arrived in London sick and 4 died. But as the ship's surgeon reported, if the ship had been delayed by bad weather over half the crew would have been effected by disease.[23] It was noted that when ships stopped off to collect fresh provisions in France, disease was much rarer.

Company fights back

Although scathing criticism was directed at the East India Company as a whole, the Society's unnamed target was the superintendent of the Company barracks, Hilton Docker. Docker was incensed by the memorial published in *The Times* and set out to systematically refute the Society's numerous allegations of neglect and defend the reputation of his employers. As superintendent of clothing, Docker described his job as 'arduous and unpleasant to perform',[24] alleging that his attempts to prevent the sale of clothes had exposed him to abuse and in some instances threats of violence. He also claimed that the sale of clothes resulted in

[21] C. Lloyd, 'Victualling of the fleet in the eighteenth and nineteenth century' in *Starving sailors: The influence of nutrition upon Naval and Maritime History*, eds J. Watt, E.J. Freeman and W.F. Bynum (London, 1981), p. 18.
[22] C.N. Parkinson, *The Trade Winds*, p. 216.
[23] BPP, 1816 (279), X, Committee of Shipping Medical Report: Condition of Lascars on Homebound Ships. 11/12/1814.
[24] OIOC, L/MAR/C/902, July 1810, p. 4.

exposure to the adverse effects of a cold and damp climate. In this way it was argued that lascars had needlessly made themselves vulnerable to diseases of the lungs, leading to premature death.[25]

Both lascars and the Company attempted to elicit the public's sympathy by appropriating the role of injured party. Just as lascars argued they were the victims of negligent employers, who had cast them adrift, friendless and home-less in a foreign country; equally the Company, in the person of Hilton Docker, claimed to be the target of lascar machinations and duplicity. Docker's paranoia can be illustrated by the fact that even when lascars were able to prove that they were in need of additional clothing from the company stores and extensive searches had failed to reveal hidden sources of clothing, Docker still refused to sanction the release of supplies, on the grounds that fraud was intended. Suspi-cion of fraud and black-marketing was also used to withhold bedding and hammocks. Docker argued that not only would the provision of beds and hammocks be an 'immense expense', but no advantage would be gleaned, as lascars preferred to sleep on the floor and had refused bedsteads and hammocks when offered. He claimed that the fact lascars were able to put aside fish for the return journey to India and sell tea, sugar and tobacco was evidence of the abun-dance of the Company's allowance. The barracks's superintendent refuted accu-sations concerning lack of medical care and special accommodation for the sick. Attempts had been made to establish sick wards, but they had proved impractical as patients had exhibited reluctance to be separated from their messmates. Docker was keen to show that no expense had been spared when implementing a supplementary diet for the sick, which included milk, barley, lemons, port, sugar, wine and broth made with meat. Not only did Docker defend himself and the Company against allegations of neglect, he felt vindicated in arguing that contrary to claims of negligence, lascars received superior accommodation, clothing and diet than the same class of English sailors were able to provide for themselves and their dependants. Ultimately he believed lascar social habits, namely lack of hygiene and in his words the propensity to 'plunge into every excess of drinking and debauchery',[26] was at the root of the problem. The Company and its critics hotly contested lascar death statistics. It was estimated 130 lascars died in the six months ending 1814. Little had improved by 1830 when the annual death rate remained constant.[27] However, the Company main-tained that on average only one lascar died per week, with figures rising during the winter. Five died on a particularly cold day in 1813. This conflicted with the Society's statistics of 6–10 lascars found dead per night.

The only point on which Docker did not attempt to disclaim the Society's allegations was the use of punishment, which he felt, was completely justified in order to prevent 'assaults actually committed or to check those threatened on

---

[25] Hilton Docker's brother, William, the previous incumbent of the post of Superintendent, had died from an illness contracted from lascars.

[26] OIOC, L/MAR/C/902, July 1810, p. 9.

[27] M.D. George, *London Life in the Eighteenth Century* (London, 1992), p. 143.

themselves'.[28] Docker claimed that while floggings were rare, those that did take place were implemented by *serangs*, not British officers. He praised the discipline exerted by *serangs* and warned that any attempts to erode the *serang's* authority would result in further lawlessness both in the barracks and among the local community. Not content merely to defend the Company from what he viewed as malicious falsehoods, Docker went on the offensive and accused the Society of Gentlemen of pursuing a hidden agenda calculated 'to mislead the public and to effect a premature judgement injurious to every person concerned in the management of Asiatic seamen'.[29] According to Docker, sinister and malevolent forces were guiding the Society's work, namely 'lascars of profligate, discontented character, who had deserted ship' and had collected information on the running of the barracks, which formed the basis of the Society's case against the Company. He questioned why the investigators had not examined '*serangs* and other natives of respectable classes'.[30] Docker concluded that criticism of the barracks was unfounded and exaggerated. The Society had been duped by discontented and criminal lascars, who were able to take advantage of the gentlemen's ignorance and impose upon them.

Consumption, control and intervention

The discussions provoked by the Company's treatment of lascars in London were strikingly adversarial in nature. But who exactly was exploiting whom? The answer is not as clear as has been suggested. The Company, through its representative Hilton Docker, claimed that it had fulfilled its contractual and moral obligation to lascars, by providing suitable welfare and aid for those in its care, but rather than be thankful to the Company for its largesse, the lascars had instead chosen to sell their provisions and appear naked and destitute in the streets of London. To support his argument Docker drew attention to the behaviour of Chinese sailors. He argued that the Company's care was sufficient, 'when bestowed on objects not entirely destitute of moral capacity, evinced in the healthy, well-clothed appearance of the Chinese, who are much superior in their habits to the natives of India'.[31] However he failed to mention that, unlike Indian sailors, Chinese wages were higher and not subject to the same level of corruption and non-payment as seen among Indian seamen. Consequently, Chinese seamen were not forced to resort to desperate measures, such as selling basic provisions. Docker's conclusions that the selling of bedding, clothing and food demonstrated an over-abundance of provisions, enabling surplus items to be sold for profit, ignores the actual levels of impoverishment facing lascars. However, the subversive satisfaction of capitalising on Company rations cannot

28 OIOC, L/MAR/C/902, p. 9.
29 OIOC, H/MISC/501, p. 16.
30 OIOC, L/MAR/C/902, p. 2.
31 *Ibid.*, p. 14.

be ruled out as a significant factor in lascar deliberations, and it is typical of the opportunism exhibited by other sections of the plebeian dock community in London.[32]

At the heart of the dispute was the issue of consumption. The extent to which the Company had any jurisdiction over what lascars chose to do with their rations is questionable. The Navigation Acts made no reference to how provisions should be consumed. Thus Docker's attempts to police the consumption of clothes, food and bedding was not part of his official duties. However, as a loyal and zealous employee, he was keen to protect the Company's reputation. Not only was the sight of poorly clothed destitute Indian sailors on the streets of London an embarrassment to the Company, the lascars' ability to conduct private economies, through goods intended for personal consumption, was also seen as an attack on the Company's authority. Commerce was the Company's raison d'être, and while lascars were clearly not viewed as a serious economic challenge, nevertheless the audacity of lascars trading, not in the distant periphery but right under the noses of their employers, in London, the Company's headquarters, besmirching its reputation and provoking adverse publicity, caused great consternation. The Company's irritation when confronted by lascar entrepreneurship contrasts with the laxity shown to British Company employees in India, who also supplemented their official salary by conducting private trade.[33]

Lascars' ability to act independently of the Company and defy its control was an issue that also concerned parliament, resulting in a Parliamentary Committee of Inquiry to investigate whether the 1814, East India Trade Act was in need of amendment. The Committee's main complaint against the East India Company was its 'total want of all regular authority either to prevent them [lascars] wandering from the barracks by day or night or maintaining order amongst them while within'.[34] For parliament, issues of control and discipline were of principal importance. Several proposals were put forward. Firstly the establishment of a commission or body empowered to enforce obedience and secondly the employment of an individual, representing the Company, who could run the hostel with the authority to address grievances, prevent the sale of clothing and bedding, return seamen to India and generally police lascars. Committee members believed that in order to enforce discipline it was necessary to relocate the barracks to a less populous part of the city, near the East India Docks. The

---

[32] See I. Duffield, ' "I asked how the vessel would go": the contradictory experiences of African and African Diaspora Marine and port workers in Britain, 1750–1850', *Language, Labour and Migration*, ed. A.J. Kershen (Aldershot, 2000), p. 131, and P. Linebaugh, *The London Hanged: Crime and Civil Society in Eighteenth Century London* (London, 1991), p. 418, for discussions on the prevalence of theft and pilfering of goods in the London docks.

[33] P. Lawson, *The East India Company: A History* (New York, 1993), pp. 72–3.

[34] *Ibid.*, p. 6.

emphasis on separating lascars from the indigenous community was an extension of imperial policy in India, where presidency cities such as Madras and Calcutta were divided into 'white' and 'black' towns.[35] Two years after the committee published its report in 1816, the issue of segregating the lascar population had not subsided. The East India Dock Company suggested that hulks, traditionally associated with the housing of convicted felons, be used for the reception of lascars.

Following the publication of the Parliamentary Committee of Inquiry in 1814, the East India Company was approached and requested to take responsibility for the running of the hostel outlined in the report's recommendation. However, the Company declined the invitation, although it recognised the need for a publicly run and funded establishment. Why was the East India Company reluctant to take responsibility for lascars? In a letter defending its stance the Company denied its decision was based on a desire to avoid expense. However, despite the Company protestations, cost was clearly a significant, if not central consideration, in all its dealings with lascars. The Company's attitude to expense must be viewed within the wider backdrop of the Napoleonic Wars, which contributed to the erosion of its trade monopoly on all routes, barring the China trade. The Company's poor economic performance at the beginning of the nineteenth century put additional pressure on administrators in London to cut costs and maximise efficiency. The expense involved in lascar maintenance and repatriation had long troubled the Company directors. In 1782 complaints were voiced when lascars brought to London, on Danish ships, applied to the Company offices for relief.[36] The Company was adamant that it was not prepared to bear the burden of maintaining lascars brought to Europe. Prior to 1795 shipowners had been responsible for the care and return of lascars to India. But neglect had led to increasing levels of destitution among Indian seamen in London, and numerous complaints from the public had caused the Company to intervene directly in the welfare of lascars and to establish a barracks, firstly in Shoreditch and then in Shadwell. Sympathy for the plight of destitute lascars was voiced in the press, and a Society (known as the Committee of Gentlemen, which later became the Committee for the Relief of Black Poor) was established in 1786 to organise relief for lascars. Although the 1814 Act enabled the Company to recoup the expense of lascar maintenance from shipowners, lascars still cost the Company £13,000.[37]

The Company viewed lascar residence in Britain as a temporary necessity, provoked by labour shortages during wartime. Thus, once the war ended, the Company believed it would no longer have to resort to employing lascars on

---

35 T.R. Metcalf, 'Imperial Towns and Cities', in P.J. Marshall, ed., *Cambridge Illustrated History of the British Empire* (Cambridge, 1996), pp. 224–7.

36 OIOC, H/MISC/163, pp. 182–3.

37 Between 1803 and 1813 the Company spent on average £370,486 per annum on lascars, which included maintenance, medication, clothing and repatriation.

ships sailing to Britain. But while it was envisaged that East India Company involvement and responsibility for lascars would end, private shipowners would
still be required to provide suitable accommodation for Indian seamen. However
the lascar acts of the 1820s suggests the Company was not able to shirk its
responsibilities for maritime Indian labour quite so easily in peacetime. The
1814 Act had put emphasis on the responsibility of shipowners and masters to
feed, clothe and house lascars, with the East India Company taking responsibility
for vagrant lascars who had slipped through the welfare net. Legislation in 1823
ended bonding, but the Company was still held liable for repatriating stranded
lascars, with any expenses incurred to be charged back to shipowners. Consequently, although the Company was in theory able to recover expenses, it was
still responsible for returning lascars to India up until its demise in 1833.

Conclusion

The increasing employment of Indian seamen during wartime, on routes previously designated exclusively for European sailors, heralded an era of growing
dispute between the Company and its employees. The prevailing orthodoxy of
protectionism, embodied in the Navigation Acts, conflicted with escalating
demand for maritime labour, during a period of prolonged war. Elastic notions
of nationality expanded and contracted both to include and exclude Indians in
response to the Company's fluctuating labour requirements. Despite negative
representations of lascars, based on powerful, but erroneous climatic and racial
discourse, increased labour demands and the savings accrued from employing
lascars proved irresistible. Disagreement between Company officers and lascars,
was not just confined to land, as complaints of maltreatment by Indian seamen
on board ships reveals. However, the Company remained unresponsive to lascar
grievances and refused to amend the corrupt recruitment system. But it was in
London, heart of the Company's trading empire, that tensions between the
Company, lascars and their supporters came to greatest prominence in *The
Times* newspaper, leading to parliamentary intervention. All aspects of Company
management of lascars including accommodation, welfare, health and discipline
came under scrutiny. The Company, in turn, countered damming allegations of
neglect with counter-claims of lascar fraud, deceit and conspiracy to misrepre-
sent the Company. Central to the dispute were unresolved issues of control, consumption and responsibility. Although the Company recognised the need for
control over lascars, it refused to take on greater responsibility, pleading that
peace obviated the need for further intervention.[38] While there is little doubt
that when the war ended Company officials were keen to dispense with what it

---

[38] OIOC, L/MAR/C/902, 22/2/1816. James Cobb, Secretary to East India Company to J.P.
Courtnay, Secretary to Board of Commisioners for Affairs of India.

viewed as a 'troublesome' stopgap labour force, the desire to disengage from the financial and social burden of lascar care had also been affected by wartime experience in London; when the Company's reputation had taken a battering at the hands of Indian seamen and their influential allies.*

Further reading

Bulley, A. *The Bombay Country Ships, 1790–1833* (Richmond, 2000).

Greenberg, M. *British Trade and the Opening of China, 1800–1842* (London, 1969).

Lahiri, S. 'Patterns of Resistance: Indian Seamen in Imperial Britain', in A.J. Kershen, ed., *Language, Labour and Migration* (Aldershot, 2000), pp. 155–78.

Myers, N. 'The Black Poor of London: Initiatives of Eastern Seamen in the Eighteen and Nineteenth Centuries', in D. Frost, ed., *Ethnic Labour and British Imperial Trade: A History of Ethnic Seafarers in the UK* (London, 1995), pp. 7–21.

Sherwood, M. 'Race, Nationality and Employment among Lascar Seamen, 1660 to 1945', *New Community*, 2, 17 (1991), 229–44.

*   Research for this paper was funded by the Lord Ashdown Charitable Foundation.

Signs of Commerce: the East India Company and the Patronage of Eighteenth-Century British Art

GEOFF QUILLEY

As the leading mercantile company of eighteenth-century Britain, the East India Company was routinely regarded as the pulse of the commercial life of the nation as a whole. In substantial part, of course, this attitude was based on the enormous wealth and potential for wealth vested in the Company, and its uniquely privileged status after 1765 as the governing authority in the British colonies in India. Yet, the Company's authority rested not only on financial and political power, but also on a deeper association of its commercial function and character with the perceived identity of the nation at large.

British national identity during this period was increasingly articulated as being essentially maritime and commercial. On the one hand, the special character of the Anglican Church together with an insular geographical position giving on to the open expanse of the Atlantic demarcated Britain from the rest of Europe in an apparently divinely sanctioned manner. On the other hand, its political constitution was taken to encourage an entrepreneurial and individualistic society, where individual interests were inhered to the larger collective good through the mutually beneficial bonds of commerce.[1] Commentators from Defoe to Adam Smith broadly subscribed to the view expressed somewhat mystically by Jonas Hanway in 1753:

> Commerce is the link by which men are united in love . . . so long as commerce is conducted with integrity, it must produce a connexion and harmony, such as constitutes an universal commonwealth, among the whole of mankind.[2]

In addition, commercial society produced individuals able and motivated to exploit Britain's geographical advantages for global maritime development, with the result that, from at least the War of the Austrian Succession, the national identity was regarded as naturally imperial and colonial, with a prosperity that relied upon navigation. Four years after Hanway's statement, John Entick's *New Naval History* assured its readers

[1] See especially Linda Colley, *Britons: Forging the Nation, 1707–1837* (New Haven and London, 1992).

[2] Jonas Hanway, *A Review of the Proposed Naturalization of the Jews* (London, 1753, 3rd edn), pp. 97–8.

By Navigation the whole World is connected, and the most distant Parts of it correspond with each other. And it is this Correspondence which introduces new Commodities, and propagates the most advantageous Manufactures. . . . It is Navigation that has realized and secured us to these Advantages, which Nature has invested us with by our Situation in the Midst of the Ocean. . . . And from hence we must perceive of how great Importance it is, that it should be free and undisturbed: That whatever clogs or obstructs it, must be an universal Detriment; and that whatever promotes Navigation must be allowed to promote the general Interest of the Nation: For thereon depends our Trade; and upon our Trade depends the Value of our Houses, Lands and Produce.[3]

As Huw Bowen makes clear in his essay in this volume, by the second half of the eighteenth century the East India Company was also an imperial agency.[4] Against such a cultural and ideological backdrop, it is perhaps not difficult to see how the fortunes of the Company, with its emphatic reliance upon navigation, and a financial structure designed to enable the maximization of individual profit through mutual association and investment in colonial trade, could stand for the fortunes of the nation in a way that similar mercantile companies, such as the Russia Company, or a similarly lucrative exercise of colonial commerce, such as that of the West India trade, could not.

This is not to say that the Company was not perceived negatively: its special concern with the east automatically involved it in the discourse on luxury, and it was always open to accusations of immorality and corruption.[5] I shall return to this theme later in this essay. Yet, its positive image was that of a beneficent orga-nization extending the '*Commerce* and *Dominion* of *this Kingdom*' by being 'founded on *principles* of *justice* and *benevolence*, [which] will equally conduce to the *welfare* of *mankind*'.[6]

In no small measure the promotion of the East India Company was achieved through visual culture: paintings, prints, architecture, sculpture, illustrated books and scholarly works, maps, medals, and virtually every other type of visual artefact produced during the eighteenth century. Indeed, the impact of the Company on British art, just in terms of the quantity and variety of artwork produced in connection with it, was astonishing. And it is clear that, from the rebuilding and pictorial decoration of the Leadenhall Street offices in the 1720s, the directors were aware of the value of the visual in presenting the Company as

3   John Entick, *A New Naval History: Or, Compleat View of the* British *Marine* (London, 1757), p. i.
4   Huw Bowen, 'No longer mere traders': continuities and change in the metropolitan devel-opment of the East India Company, 1600–1834', in *The Worlds of the East India Company*, eds Huw Bowen, Margarette Lincoln and Nigel Rigby (Woodbridge, 2002), pp. 19–32.
5   See, especially, P. Lawson and J. Phillips, ' "Our execrable banditti": perceptions of nabobs in mid-eighteenth-century Britain', *Albion*, 16 (1984), 225–41.
6   Alexander Dalrymple, *Plan for Extending the Commerce of this Kingdom, and of the East-India-Company* (London, 1769), Preface.

the product of a Shaftesburian civilized politeness rather than that of a Mandevillean rapacity.[7]

It is perhaps not surprising that the Company should have provoked so much artistic production. For if commercial society was the apogee of human social development – and the Company could therefore present itself as material evidence of this – the index of a nation's attainment of politeness and civilization was taken to be its artistic culture, with its attendant values of judgment, sensibility and taste. In 1752 David Hume contested the orthodox civic humanist stance on luxury as being necessarily detrimental to the public good:

> where luxury nourishes commerce and industry, the peasants, by a proper cultivation of the land, become rich and independent; while the tradesmen and merchants acquire a share of the property, and draw authority and consideration to that middling rank of men, who are the best and firmest base of public liberty . . . . The lower house is the support of our popular government; and all the world acknowledges, that it owed its chief influence and consideration to the increase of commerce . . . How inconsistent, then, is it to blame so violently a refinement in the arts, and to represent it as the bane of liberty and public spirit![8]

In the rest of this paper, therefore, I want to explore some of the connections between eighteenth-century art and commerce by considering some aspects of the artistic patronage of the East India Company. Specifically, I shall concentrate on an aspect almost completely disregarded in the study of the Company's influence on art, but which, in view of the value of East India shipping to the identity of the commercial nation, ought to be of considerable significance: that is, the visual representation of the maritime aspect of the East India Company.[9] This is a remarkable omission: the prolific amount of material produced treating of East India shipping and voyages bears witness to the fundamental role of shipping in the Company's operations, for it was not solely, or even primarily, a colonial administrator, but a maritime trading organization. It is curious also in view of the central ideological place of navigation generally in the conceptualization of British national identity.

Perhaps this substantial visual imagery has been overlooked because of its seemingly mundane and prosaic character; its indirect relation to Company patronage; and because of the more general marginalization of marine art as a

---

7   On the opposition between Anthony Ashley Cooper, Third Earl of Shaftesbury's aesthetics and those of Bernard Mandeville, see David H. Solkin, *Painting for Money: the Visual Arts and the Public Sphere in Eighteenth-Century England* (New Haven and London, 1992), pp. 1–26.

8   'Of Refinement in the Arts', in David Hume, *Selected Essays*, eds Stephen Copley and Andrew Edgar (Oxford and New York, 1993), pp. 174–5.

9   Something of an exception here is Jean Sutton, *Lords of the East: the East India Company and its Ships* (London, 1981).

subject for serious art history.[10] Yet a considerable number of marine paintings and prints of the eighteenth and nineteenth centuries depict East Indiamen. A further issue here may be that these works were produced overwhelmingly by academically untrained artists, attached not to the metropolitan artistic community but to the maritime communities of Limehouse, Wapping and Blackwall, who had usually had direct experience of working on board ship, thus fostering contacts with the shipboard communities who worked on the ships in the East India Company's service.[11] Still, the body of work produced by such artists as Thomas Luny, Francis Holman, John Cleveley the elder (Plate VI), Robert Dodd (Plates VIII and 5) or Thomas Whitcombe constitutes a distinctive image for the Company in terms of its impact upon shipping and shipbuilding, and their representation; one which invites serious consideration. Moreover, despite the various and numerous artists involved, this is a remarkably consistent image.

The paintings (very often reproduced as prints) tend to follow a clear compositional formula, deriving from Dutch seventeenth-century prototypes, but greatly simplified in the treatment of space and light: a profile view of the ship, usually getting under way, and a second three-quarter profile stern view of the ship sailing towards the horizon. Sometimes included is a third view showing the bow of the vessel. The ubiquitous low horizon, large expanse of sky and high-lighted strip of water in the middle distance all attest to the Dutch derivation. Yet these images, produced in great number from the 1750s on, show a stylistic uniformity which, in its reductive lack of ostentation and its documentary character, is far removed from the work of Ludolf Bakhuizen (Plate VII) or Willem van de Velde the elder and younger, and instead shows a closer resemblance to the shipboard practice of coastal profiling, a practice in which officers were routinely trained.

The practice of coastal profiling offers a clue to the provenance and purpose of paintings such as these. For they were not commissioned by the Company, which did not build or own the ships employed in its service; even though the owners of East Indiamen were frequently Company members, and the Shipping Committee was, conversely, substantially made up of ex-commanders and ship-husbands of Company vessels.[12] The Company's direct patronage of artists, in any case, was not of specialists rooted in the maritime community, but of professional artisans such as Samuel Scott and George Lambert, who jointly produced the six views of Company factories decorating the Court Room of the newly built Leadenhall Street offices in the 1730s; or the obscure Greek-born artist Spiridione Roma, commissioned to paint the allegorical ceiling roundel

[10] On this, see Geoff Quilley, 'Missing the boat: the place of the maritime in the history of British visual culture', *Visual Culture in Britain*, 1/2 (December, 2000), 79–92.

[11] Geoff Quilley, 'The imagery of travel in British art, *c.*1740–*c.*1800: with particular regard to nautical and maritime imagery' (unpublished PhD dissertation, University of Warwick, 1998), Chapter 5.

[12] Sutton, pp. 31–6.

Britannia Receiving the Riches of the East for East India House in 1778.[13] It is also unlikely that these ship 'portraits' were commissioned by the owners, since vessels were multiply owned through the buying of shares in them. Rather, the direct involvement of the artists in the maritime community suggests that it was the commander or other officer, also part of that social sphere, who acted as patron. One of Thomas Buttersworth's several depictions of *The Action off Palo Aor, 15 February, 1804*, celebrating the successful escape from French warships by a fleet of merchantmen, was completed in 1804 after 'a sketch made by an officer at the time'; while another version was presented to Christ's Hospital by Captain Charles Shea, who had commanded one of the ships involved.[14] Presentations were made in the opposite direction as well: for his commanding role in this action, the Company's Patriotic Fund resolved at its meeting of 14 August 1804, to present Captain Nathaniel Dance with 'a sword of 100L. value, and a vase of silver of 100L. value . . . with an appropriate inscription'. The Court of Directors also resolved to award Dance '2000 guineas and a piece of plate to the value of 200 guineas'.[15]

Similarly, a series of five paintings of 1790–92 by Thomas Luny of the *Hindustan* East Indiaman (in the collections of the National Maritime Museum) show the vessel against the backdrop of various coasts and ports, in what is clearly a reference to Lambert and Scott's paintings of the Company's factories hanging in East India House. But they beg the question of how the London-based artist produced images of the ship off the coasts of India and China unless by reference to available published prints, or to drawings made by an officer on board, or both.

These paintings are also overwhelmingly celebratory and commemorative. To consider briefly works in the collection of the National Maritime Museum, Greenwich: Luny's series of the *Hindustan*, a ship launched in 1789, is a record of its maiden voyage to Madras and China between 1789 and 1791. John Cleveley's 1770 picture of the *Princess Royal* (Plate VI) is of a vessel launched just the previous year. The *Royal George*, painted by Holman in 1779 was launched in 1777; and the East Indiaman *William Pitt*, the subject of a 1786 painting by Dominic Serres, was launched in 1785. Moreover, these were all conspicuously large vessels at the time of their respective launches. The *Princess Royal*, of 878 tons, was by some way the largest ship of its time, when most East Indiamen were still below 500 tons. The *Royal George* and *William Pitt* were 758 and 798 tons respec-

13 On these, see Brian Allen, 'The East India Company's settlement pictures: George Lambert and Samuel Scott', in *Under the Indian Sun: British Landscape Artists*, eds Pauline Rohatji and Pheroza Godrej (Bombay, 1995), pp. 1–16; and 'From Plassey to Seringapatam: India and British history painting', in *The Raj: India and the British 1600–1947*, eds C.J. Bayly (London, 1990), pp. 26–37.

14 Oriental and India Office Library collection, catalogue number F60.

15 Charles Hardy, revised by Horatio Charles Hardy, *A Register of Ships, Employed in the Service of the Honourable the United East India Company, from the Year 1760 to 1810: with an Appendix, Containing a Variety of Particulars, and Useful Information, Interesting to those concerned with East India Commerce* (London, 1811), Appendix, p. 122.

3   *The Capture of the* La Venus, *French Privateer, after a close engagement with the* Union *Extra East Indiaman, 22 August 1804.* Anon., National Maritime Museum (neg. B9275).

tively; while the *Hindustan* was an enormous 1,248 tons, again the largest tonnage to that date, built to service the rapidly developing China trade.[16]

The collective image, therefore, offered by such paintings and prints is of a unanimous and stylistically homogenous expression of celebration and affiliation towards a company represented as characterized by inexorable growth and ever greater efficiency and productivity: an image of that apparently seamless continuity of development, by appeal to which the Company was representing itself in the second half of the century.[17] The question remains to what uses such works might have been put: whether simply for private commemoration, or whether, for example, for presentation by ship's officers or commanders to members of the Board in pursuit of advancement and patronage within the Company's shipping business. This would be consistent with similar usages of visual imagery by naval officers seeking position or promotion.[18] It was also, surely, one of the concerns of Captain William Stokoe in the dedication of his print *The Capture of the La Venus French Privateer after a close Engagement with the Union Extra East India-man* (Plate 3) 'most humbly . . . to the Honble Court of Directors of the United East India Company, by their Obed.^t humble ser.^t Wm Stokoe'. The crudity of the drawing and the lack of any other signature suggest that it was engraved from Stokoe's own drawing, to supplement his written account, as captain of the *Union*, in the ship's journal and log submitted to the Directors. Certainly, the picture aims to give prominence to the *Union's* seemingly single-handed role in the capture of the French vessel: although the caption states that the *Union* was in company with the *Sir William Pulteney* and *Eliza Ann*, these vessels are relegated inconspicuously to the background and forced to the right-hand margin of the composition. The caption also gives details of the relative strength of the vessels, 'the Privateer mounting 16 Guns 12 large Swivells & 73 men, the Union 18 Guns 80 men Lascars'. The latter are prominently visible on the *Union's* quarterdeck, offering a highly positive image of a ship in harmony with its subaltern crew members, thus addressing and mollifying an issue – that of the treatment of Lascar seamen in the Company's ships – to which the Company was at this time very sensitive.[19] There is no pretension to art here; rather, the image is of a documentary character, simultaneously celebratory of military success against France, and self-promotional of Stokoe in the eyes of the Court of Directors.

A similarly commemorative motive, conjoined with self-promotion on the part of the artist, was presumably behind Robert Dodd's pair of coloured

[16] Anthony Farrington, *Catalogue of East India Company Ships' Journals and Logs, 1600–1834* (London, 1999).

[17] Bowen, 'No longer mere traders', *op. cit.*

[18] Sarah Monks, 'Our man in Havana: representation and reputation in Lieutenant Philip Orsbridge's *Britannia's Triumph*, 1765', in *Conflicting Visions: European culture and war, 1700–1830*, eds Geoff Quilley and John Bonehill (London, forthcoming).

[19] See Shompa Lahiri's essay, 'Contested relations: the East India Company and Lascars in London', *The Worlds of the East India Company*, pp. 169–81.

4 *Portrait of an East Indiaman Coming to an Anchor at Spithead*, Robert Dodd.
By permission of the British Library.

engravings produced in 1797 after his own paintings of East Indiamen. One, *Portrait of an East Indiaman coming to an Anchor at Spithead* (Plate 4), the caption informs us, was done 'from an Original drawing in the Possession of William Fraser, Esq.', to whom the plate is dedicated. Likewise, the second, *Portrait of an East Indiaman sailing from Madras* (Plate 5), is dedicated to Robert Preston MP, Master of Trinity House, and was executed after 'the Original Picture in his Possession'. Both Fraser and Preston, like Stokoe, had worked their way up the ranks, by the late 1780s becoming sufficiently senior and wealthy to retire from the sea service and continue as important shipowners in their own right.[20] Both, at the date of these prints, were Principal Managing Owners of recently launched prestigious 1,200-ton vessels built for the China trade.[21] As a complementary pair, Dodd's images depict a fully transparent, open and successful East India commerce, conducted with modern, efficient ships; and, by implication, represent their owners or commanders as honest servants of the Company and the state, deflecting the common accusation levelled against the 'shipping interest' among the Company's Directors and their associates, of putting their personal profit and interests before the Company's.

For what such positive images of East Indiamen disguise is the fiercely contentious debate over the Company's policy on shipping between the 1770s and 1790s, as well as the much-publicized corruption among the Company's 'shipping interest' and the commanders of vessels in its employ. In 1770 William Hickey witnessed a deal between Captain Waddell, commander of the *Plassey*, and a Cornish smuggler. The latter purchased a large quantity of tea, for which he casually wrote out a cheque for 'twelve hundred and twenty-four pounds'.[22] Numerous other cases were reported in the early 1770s.[23] It was estimated that in the decade to 1773 the Company had lost over £1.6 million to corruption and inefficiency in the costs of freight and demurrage:

> This waste of money arose in several manners. . . . The dimensions of the ships
> . . . were too small; so that they not only carried less in proportion than larger

---

[20] Fraser began his East India Company career as fourth mate on the *Prince Edward* in 1759/60. By 1772, at the age of 35, he had gained his first full captaincy, of the *Lord Mansfield*. His final voyage was as commander of the *Earl of Mansfield* in the 1783/84 season. Preston began as fifth mate on the *Streatham* in 1757/58, and worked his way to captaincy by 1767, first of the *Asia*, then the *Hillsborough*, and finally of the *General Elliott*, which he commanded on his final voyage in 1786/7: Anthony Farrington, *A Biographical Index of East India Company Maritime Service Officers, 1600–1834* (London, 1999).

[21] Fraser was Principal Managing Owner of the *Neptune*, which embarked on its maiden voyage from Portsmouth on 18 March 1797. Preston's most recently launched ship, the *Cirencester*, sailed from Portsmouth on its maiden voyage on 9 July 1795: Farrington, *Catalogue*. I am not suggesting that these are the vessels represented in Dodd's prints, which are unable to be identified securely.

[22] William Hickey, *Memoirs of William Hickey*, ed. Alfred Spencer, 4 vols (London, 1913), I, 250

[23] Summarized in Keane Fitzgerald, *A Letter to the Directors of the East India Company* (London, 1777).

5 *Portrait of an East Indiaman Sailing from Madras*, Robert Dodd. By permission of the British Library.

ships, but called for more officers and men, and consequently for more provisions, &c. than was necessary. The freight likewise was calculated in a complex manner, under the name of freight, half-freight, &c. and this complication, as usual, served to cover fraudulent bargains. The officers serving in these ships moreover possessed privileges favourable to smuggling, and other incroachments.[24]

Corruption among commanders and their mates was further thought to be enabled by their family or business contacts with ship-owners and Company Directors; a problem exacerbated by the Board of Directors being increasingly composed of ex-commanders who had bought their way to the top by the fraudulent methods of which Fiott complained, an ironic development of the Company's expansion of shipping. In 1777 Keane Fitzgerald observed that, whereas in the past only one or two ex-commanders had served on the Board, the increase in the number of ships contracted to the Company, from around 20 to over 80, had resulted in an increase of the Board's 'shipping interest' to nine or ten members.[25] Worse, the Committee of Shipping, before which was laid 'all business relative to the Shipping, or the officers belonging to them', was substantially made up of former commanders, creating a potential for nepotism and self-interest in the commissioning and contracting of ships, their builders and officers. At the heart of this was the practice of selling the command of a vessel,

> the price of which has been advanced from one, to seven thousand guineas; which is such an extravagant price, as could not possibly be given for fair or honest purposes. – Yet it is well known that the commanders sell their ships before they retire into the Direction, for such prices, and generally to their chief mates, who have been their chief assistants in carrying on their private trade, and to whom they give a proper credit for the payment.[26]

The route that William Fraser and Robert Preston had taken, in advancing from ship's officer to captain to ship owner, with potential access to the Court of Directors, and which they commemorated in Dodd's paintings and prints, was a notoriously suspect one, and necessarily involved the accumulation of wealth properly beyond the grasp of a ship's mate.

The depiction, therefore, of recently launched and unprecedentedly large vessels in the Company's service, painted in a consistently plain, unornamented and transparent style, may be seen not just as celebrations of the Company's growth and continuing modernization, but also as a response to such outraged anti-corruption rhetoric as Fiott's and Fitzgerald's: an affirmation that the represented vessels are engaged in open, honest plain dealing, on behalf of the

---

[24] John Fiott, *An Address to the Proprietors of East-India Stock, and to the Public* (London, 1790), pp. 65–6.

[25] Fitzgerald, *A Letter*, pp. 26–7.

[26] *Ibid.*, pp. 27–8.

company alone, and thus by extension serving the larger commercial interests of the nation.

Many vessels and their captains were named in official documents on the problems of smuggling and other types of corruption presented to the Board in the 1770s, including the *Hawke, Ceres, Prime* and most conspicuously the *York,* whose captain, George Hayter, appealed in print to the Directors against the accusation levelled at him by the ship-husband Sir Richard Hotham, that he had caused the ship to be 'lumbered in the stowage' before taking on board the Company's outward cargo, thus maximizing his own potential profit margin from his private trade, in order to pay off his debt to the previous captain from whom he had bought the command of the vessel.[27] Not surprisingly perhaps, none of these was the subject of a ship portrait at the time, the earliest representation of the *York* being a 1788 painting by Luny commemorating its sixth and final voyage under a newly appointed commander, William Huddart.[28]

Certainly, there were negative visualizations of East Indiamen. It is very noticeable that, in the iconography of shipwreck of this period, wrecks of East Indiamen figure very prominently. But these images were produced within a much wider frame of reference than the narrow maritime sphere of ship portraits. Anthony Brough extended the issue of corruption among ships' officers to a more complex discourse of luxury, rooted in a classical moral framework, by associating the luxurious shipboard life of the corrupt East India captain rather 'with an idea of Cleopatra sailing down the Cydnus to meet Mark Anthony, than of a rough Captain venturing across immense oceans, and defying their storms and hidden rocks, to import the merchandise of India'.[29]

Similarly, the visual imagery of wrecks of East Indiamen formed part of a more general moralized category of maritime disaster, which offered a speculative ground for artists from both marine and academic backgrounds to produce works that could more closely conform to Sir Joshua Reynolds' demand for history painting, that the subject should be 'generally interesting', and thus appeal to a universal spectatorship.[30] Thus, highly celebrated wrecks such as that of the *Grosvenor* (1782), the *Halsewell* (1786) or the *Earl of Abergavenny* (1805) were each represented in number by various artists, increasingly from a non-maritime background, seeking to exploit the ready market attached to such disasters.[31] Furthermore, these images, following the increasing tendency

[27] *Ibid.,* p. 32. See also Sir Richard Hotham, *A Candid State of Affairs relative to the East India Shipping for the Year 1773, addressed to the Proprietors* (London, 1774) and *Reflections upon East India Shipping* (2nd edn, London, c.1773), which accounts are rebutted in George Hayter, *The Case of Captain George Hayter, Commander of the Ship York* (London, c.1775).
[28] In the collection of the National Maritime Museum, Greenwich, BHC3735.
[29] Anthony Brough, *Considerations on the Necessity of lowering the exorbitant Freight of Ships employed in the Service of the East-India Company* (London, 1786), quoted in Fiott, *An Address,* p. 72.
[30] Sir Joshua Reynolds, *Discourses on Art,* ed. Robert R. Wark (New Haven and London, 1975), p. 57.
[31] For commentary on some of these works, see Barry Venning, 'A macabre connoisseurship:

towards melodrama in the published narratives of the events, placed decreasing emphasis on the material loss of the ship and its cargo, in favour of privileging the human element from a perspective of empathetic, emotive sensibility.[32]

The loss of the *Halsewell* offers a striking example. Wrecked off Purbeck in January 1786, the narratives of the disaster, as well as other literary accounts in the form of poetic laments, all emphasize the virtuous conduct and generally model citizenship of its commander, Richard Pierce.[33] This exemplary Christian family man had on board with him his two daughters. When it was clear at the last that the women would not be able to be saved from the wreck, rather than attempting to save himself, he chose to tie his fate to theirs and remained on board, to be lost without trace. Such emphasis ensures that the event of the loss of an East India Company ship is extrapolated into much wider discourses of heroic self-sacrifice, the virtues of family unity, and the precariousness of commercial endeavour.

Robert Smirke's 'The *Halsewell* East Indiaman' (Plate 6) treats the vessel as the arena for human responses to the sublime events of the storm, and emphasizes that it is already lost: half-submerged, the mast cut away, and the wheel conspicuously abandoned, the family group turn their faces heavenward, in a compact figure grouping which would later be employed to great effect in the highly sentimental views of Louis XVI's final interview with his family.[34]

Similiarly, the poet of the lengthy *Monody on the Death of Captain Pierce* (1790) uses the event as a vehicle not just to eulogize the virtues of Pierce's Christian fortitude, but in a sub-narrative to meditate on oriental slavery, and more generally to remind readers of the fatal effects of excessive commercial ambition, particularly through contact with the luxurious east. So, at the outset of the voyage all is well and the wind set fair, as Dodd's print depicts (Plate VIII). Yet, Dodd's image invites the viewer to reflect with the knowledge of hindsight upon the deceptiveness of such a scene, appearing to be a visual equivalent to the moral message of the sermon preached at Pierce's memorial service:

Turner, Byron and the apprehension of shipwreck subjects in early nineteenth-century England', *Art History*, 8/3 (1985), pp. 303–19, and T.S.R. Boase, 'Shipwrecks in English Romantic painting', *Warburg and Courtauld Institute Journal*, 22 (1959), 332–46.

32 On the development of the cult of sensibility at this period, see G.J. Barker-Benfield, *The Culture of Sensibility: Sex and Society in Eighteenth-Century Britain* (Chicago and London, 1992).

33 The official account is [Henry Meriton and John Rogers], *A Circumstantial Account of the Loss of the Halsewell* (London, 1786), which ran to 21 editions in its first year of publication, and was pirated by *An Interesting and Authentic Account of the Loss of the Halsewell, East-India-Man, with all its Dreadful Circumstances* (London, 1786). Verse accounts are *Monody on the Death of Captain Pierce, and those Unfortunate Young Ladies who perished with him, in the Halsewell East Indiaman* (London, 1790); E. Thomas, *The Shipwreck of the Halsewell East-Indiaman; a Poem* (Shrewsbury, n.d.).

34 Cf. P.W. Tomkins's engraving of Mather Brown's *The Final Interview of Louis the Sixteenth*, 1795.

6 *The Halsewell East Indiaman, 6 January 1786*, Robert Smirke, National Maritime Museum (neg. B4619).

Let us conceive for a while, instead of one individual, or one family, a number of persons, on whom many families are dependent for support, employed together in extending the commercial intercourse, and promoting the commercial prosperity of their country. . . . They set sail under the kind auspices of the winds; and every thing around them seems to encourage confidence, and insure success. But mark the sudden change of the scene – Scarcely does the shore, which they have left, retire from their sight, when the face of the sky is darkened, the stormy winds arise, and all the fury of the tempest rages upon the bosom of the deep. . . . Where is now, alas! the joy that sparkled in the eye of hope? Where are now the schemes of happiness that agitated the bosom of affection? *They are gone even as the vapour that appeareth for a little time, and then vanisheth away*.[35]

Dodd's print depicts a scene also featured in the *Monody on the Death of Captain Pierce*, that of the party prior to sailing, but transposed from Pierce's house to the stern gallery of the ship, which would later afford the means of escape from the wreck to the second mate, John Rogers.[36] This transposition reinforces the sense of the scene in terms of Raine's sermon, as an episode redolent with the potential for moral, religious and philosophical speculation.

At the centre of both the pictorial and verbal accounts is the evocation of the family, the naturalized bonds of which are shown to be, or about to be, sundered. By association, it is to be supposed that it is also the extended 'family' of the Company itself, its members connected by the ties of sympathy engendered by commerce, which is being broken up along with the ship. Thus Pierce was eulogized as 'one of the brightest ornaments of society; who . . . united elegance of manners, refinement of sentiment, and a taste for the polite arts'.[37] As a captain, Meriton and Rogers praise him as 'the friend of his officers, the protector of youth . . . a father to the crew'.[38] So, in the final analysis, his decision to resist 'the almost resistless impulse of . . . self-preservation', by staying with his helpless daughters and going down with his ship, rendered him, with respect both to his immediate family and also to the 'family' of the Company, 'a Glorious Sacrifice to Parental Tenderness'.[39] It is not insignificant, therefore, that Smirke's composition most closely resembles, and sits chronologically between two of the century's most influential and sentimental images representing family destruction: Richard Wilson's *Destruction of Niobe's Children* (1760) and Mather Brown's *The Final Interview of Louis the Sixteenth* (1795), both of which tie a presumptuous ambition and immodest claims to social status to a consequent disruption of the fundamental bonds of family life, a point made by one writer

---

35 Matthew Raine, *A Sermon, preached at Kingston upon Thames, on Sunday, February 19, 1786, upon the Death of Captain Richard Peirce* [*sic*] (London, 1786), pp. 15–16.

36 *Monody*, p. 10 and note; *A Circumstantial Narrative*, pp. 35–6.

37 *Monody*, p. 6, note.

38 *A Circumstantial Narrative*, p. 64.

39 *Monody*, p. 7, note.

in questioning Pierce's motives for taking his daughters as passengers at all: 'Possessed of fortune sufficient . . . to make happy some worthy men, natives of their own climate, . . . why should they be trusted to the precarious elements to seek for *nabob husbands* in Asia?'[40] Similarly elsewhere, the fate of the *Halsewell* is seen as a consequence of the beguilement of the passengers and crew by the prospect of India and its temptations of luxury and commercial fortune:

> Already to Imagination's eyes
> The glowing scenes of India's coast arise:
> Bright gems that glow beneath a warmer sun;
> And duteous slaves in countless numbers run;
> Rich palanquins, adorn'd with fragrant flow'rs;
> And charms of wealth, and gay luxuriant bow'rs.
> But ah, ye fair! beware the glitt'ring bait;
> In fairest meads oft dang'rous adders wait;
> Delusive pleasures fatal arts employ,
> And, Siren-like, sing sweetest to destroy.[41]

If, for Fitzgerald, Fiott and others, the 'family' connections enabled by the commercial structures and practices of the East India Company entailed an undesirable potential for nepotism, patronage and corruption, the image of disaster offered a means, perversely perhaps, both to allude to such excess, but in doing so also to redeem the image of the Company as a 'family' embodying commerce in the way Jonas Hanway had envisaged it, as 'the link by which men are united in love'.[42]

Through the sentimental image of the family, the loss of the *Halsewell* was firmly connected to the moralized discourse on commerce, and to discourses of luxury, nationhood and imperial decline, whereby the idea of the national significance of the East India Company as a metaphor for the fortunes of the nation is again firmly reinforced. We must view the images of shipwreck of East Indiamen as informed by such moralized codifications, which extend the significance both of the individual disaster beyond the commercial confines of the Company, and also of the corresponding visual imagery beyond the scope of localized textual illustration, towards the more philosophical weightiness of the 'grand style'. It is an irony that what was lost when Pierce and his daughters went down with the *Halsewell*, according to one commentator, was 'worth, honor, skill, beauty, amiability, and bright accomplishments'.[43] For these are surely precisely the values which an image such as Smirke's – itself provoked by the commercial activity of the East India Company and produced as part of a

---

[40] *An Interesting and Authentic Account*, p. 27.
[41] *Monody*, pp. 12–13.
[42] See note 2, above.
[43] *A Circumstantial Narrative*, p. 40, repeated verbatim in both *An Interesting and Authentic Account* and Thomas, *The Shipwreck of the Halsewell*, p. 18.

wide-ranging, speculative, commercial artistic venture, in an open and competitive market for art – proclaimed as the marks of civilization created by commercial society: the material evidence for which would be the subject of his own picture, an East Indiaman, and its refined artistic treatment.

India and the East India Company in the Public Sphere of Eighteenth-Century Britain[1]

JEREMY OSBORN

This essay begins with two examples which illustrate the diverse ways in which English men and women in George III's Britain engaged with India. The first is an extract from a little known and rarely performed play by Fanny Burney, entitled *A Busy Day; Or, An Arrival from India*. Written in 1801, the play centres around the fortunes of an heiress who has recently returned to her family in London after a childhood spent in India under the protection of a wealthy nabob. The play juxtaposes the urbane manners of Eliza, a young heiress, with the vulgar manners of her long-lost and stay-at-home sister, Miss Watts.

> MISS WATTS. Pray, Sister Eliziana, where did you get that pretty travelling dress?
> ELIZA. It was made in Calcutta.
> MISS WATTS. La! can they make things there? I thought they'd been all savages.
> MR WATTS. Yes, yes, they can make pretty good things there, I promise you! I suppose there's more hundred thousands made in Calcutta than in all the known world besides.
> MISS WATTS. Pray, Sister, do the Indins do much mischief?
> ELIZA. Mischief?
> MISS WATTS. What kind of look do they have? Do they let'em run about wild? Wa'n't you monstrous frightened at first?
> ELIZA. Frightened? The native Gentoos are the mildest and gentlest of human beings.
> MISS WATTS. La, nasty black things! I can't abide the Indins. I'm sure I should do nothing but squeal if I was among'em.
> MR WATTS. There's no need for you to go among'em now, my dear, for I can give you as handsome I war'nt me, as the Nabob gave your Sister.[2]

India had a private as well as a public dimension in George III's Britain. My second example comes from the less raucous and more private pages of the eighteenth-century betting books of various Oxford colleges. Here one finds

---

[1] This paper is based on my recent DPhil thesis. J.R. Osborn, 'India, Parliament and the Press under George III: A Study of English Attitudes Towards the East India Company and Empire in the Late Eighteenth and Early Nineteenth Centuries' (Oxford Univ. DPhil thesis, 1999).

[2] From *A Busy Day*, Act I; *A Busy Day*, by Fanny Burney, ed. T.G. Wallace (New Brunswick, NJ, 1984), p. 47.

evidence, for example, that a couple of the Fellows of Lincoln College made a bet with one another that one of their absent colleagues would not decorate his rooms 'before the taking of Seringapatam when Tippoo was killed'.[3] The bet was lost and the topic forgotten for some years until the winner, who was licking his lips for the bottle of port which had been wagered, remembered his good fortune. In itself this bet is of little significance but it was not alone, and scanning the frayed pages of other betting books from Oxford senior common rooms one finds additional references to Indian topics. The Fellows of Corpus Christi College also had a flutter over Tipu Sultan and the fall of Seringapatam, betting one another 'whether Seringapatam was taken before the first of March 1792' and whether 'the intelligence of the capture of Seringaptram [sic] is confirmed within three days'.[4] Some years later the Fellows of University College bet one another 'that Mango Pickle is chiefly brought from the East Indies' and 'that all the Indian Nabobs are Mahometans'.[5]

The links should be considered between representations on stage of a returning heiress from India and the informed bets of a group of Oxford dons. Miss Watts's total ignorance of India and her peoples was a means, of course, by which Fanny Burney could portray wealth and commerce as vulgar, and the harbinger not of understanding but of prejudice. But the scene is also comical and the comedy would only have worked if her intended audience had known that Indians were no more nor less mischievous and frightening than any other group of civilised peoples who were being drawn into the sphere of the British empire at the turn of the nineteenth century. The Oxford betting books, on the other hand, are rather good barometers for measuring the level of knowledge and interest in India and the East India Company amongst well-educated and intelligent people in late eighteenth-century England. Why should a handful of Oxford dons have had the slightest interest in the affairs of the East India Company at home and abroad during this period? Although none of them appear to have been shareholders in the Company, they may, of course, have had relatives and friends in the service of the Company who sent them letters filled with news about India and British military progress across the sub-continent. But it is most likely that they and other dons gained their knowledge about India from reading the newspapers which most senior common rooms subscribed to on a regular basis by this period. Presumably the fellows of Lincoln College and of Corpus Christi College were following the rumours and reports of the Third Mysore War in the London press, or through the paragraphs of the metropolitan

---

3   Lincoln College Senior Common Room Betting Book, June 1809 to August 1842. See Appendix II of V.H.H. Green's *The Commonwealth of Lincoln College, 1427–1877* (Oxford, 1979), p. 714.

4   Corpus Christi College Senior Common Room Betting Book, 1795–1810. Buckland vs Williams, 28 April 1792; Wake vs Guard, 28 April 1792; Putt vs Williams, 28 April 1792; Stretch vs Guard, 16 May 1792.

5   University College Senior Common Room Betting Book, 1794–1810. Gent vs Stapylton [1809]; Rowley vs Gent, 11 July 1809.

newspapers distilled into *Jackson's Oxford Journal*. It is the accessibility of information about India through the newspapers in the late eighteenth century which
links Fanny Burney's intended theatre audience with these Oxford dons: for without
a relatively broad and popular engagement with India through the newspapers
neither the comedy of *A Busy Day* nor the wagering of bottles of port would have
made much sense.

The newspapers and monthly periodicals were probably the most important
means by which information and speculation about India and the East India
Company were disseminated to large numbers of people in London and the provinces. The hackneyed and sentimental 'Newsman's Verses', printed in *Felix Farley's
Bristol Journal* in December 1786, convey a palpable sense of the excitement with
which news from London, in this example of Indian nabobs and their wealth, was
received in the provinces:

> Attentive silence seals up every tongue –
> With voice, air, accent all his own, he reads.
> Domestic Knights! – of Nabobs too he reads –
> Of jewels wond'rous rich! by stealth convey'd –
> That shed no lustre on the British Crown – [6]

The English press had reprinted news about the East India Company and its
territorial expansion across India on a regular and frequent basis since at least
the Seven Years War (1756–63). A systematic analysis of the English press in the
late eighteenth century reveals a steady and inexorable rise in the volume of information reprinted about empire, India and the East India Company. This was
no doubt partly a function of the growth of the late eighteenth-century press and
of the lifting of censorship on Parliamentary reporting after the Middlesex elec-
tion in 1768. In addition, after the American War of Independence there was less
competition with news from America, which allowed Indian news to hold centre
stage in the theatre of imperial politics. Most significantly, however, there was
greater information about India and the East India Company in the English
press during the period of the Revolutionary Wars with France in the 1790s than
during the Seven Years War in the 1750s because there was greater public interest
in, and demand for, news from the East. This in itself suggests that large numbers
of people in England engaged on a regular basis with imperial affairs in the
sub-continent by the end of the eighteenth century.

This article will briefly describe some of the ways in which India was drawn
into the private world and the public sphere of Britons in the late eighteenth
century. The engagement of Oxford dons with the news of military victories in
India, and the consequent mixing of imperial affairs with domestic concerns, is
indicative of wider shifts in attitudes towards the East. They fluttered on imperial
affairs and displayed an informed interest in news from India because it was

---

6   *Felix Farley's Bristol Journal*, 23 Dec. 1786.

topical, fashionable and interesting to do so. Improvements in communications and the growth of the press under George III had made the peripheries of the Second British Empire accessible to the imaginations of late eighteenth-century Britons. It was easier than ever for interested Britons after the Seven Years War to read about the creation of an empire of conquest in India, the subjugation of the peoples of the sub-continent, the appropriation of the natural resources of the East and the harnessing of native skills and technologies to the commercial profit of the East India Company. Part of the reason for this was the accessibility of newsprint.

Rather than offering a detailed historiographical criticism of the nature of late eighteenth-century public opinion, this article will take the form of a whistle-stop tour of some of the diverse ways in which Georgians engaged with India during the last third of the eighteenth century, and of the ways in which a public debate about an empire in India was presented in the public prints. The relationship between newspapers and public opinion has now been well established by historians such as Jeremy Black, Bob Harris, Hannah Barker and others, whose work suggests that, in the absence of MORI and Gallup polls, newspapers offer one of the most penetrating insights into the nebulous concept of eighteenth-century public opinion. Their argument runs, in essence, that newspaper publishers vied with one another in a highly competitive market for the attention of a limited audience who could afford the money to buy a newspaper or the leisure time in which to read it; and that in order to survive financially in this cut-throat business the editors of the newspapers needed adequately to respond to the interests of their readers. It would be fair to argue that newspapers both reflected and shaped public opinion during this period. However, one should bear in mind that newspaper editors were also won over to Government through 'gifts' from the Secret Service Fund, that wealthy men such as Robert Clive and Warren Hastings befriended men in the press with their ill-gotten gains from India, and that powerful institutions such as the East India Company also had a vested interest in planting well-timed information in the newspapers artificially to raise and lower the price of the Company stock. There is, however, a sufficient volume of news about India in the English press during this period to correct the aberrations created by intrusions such as these.

Considerable ground-work has also been laid by historians such as Arthur Aspinall, G.A. Cranfield and John Brewer on the circulation figures of eighteenth-century newspapers. Qualitative and quantitative evidence derived from private letters, diaries, advertisement duty, Stamp Tax figures and the loud trumpet blasts blown by the editors of the newspapers themselves suggests that the newspapers were read by a broad cross-section of eighteenth-century English society. Although many readers would have fitted into the social category of the aristocratic elite and the urban middle-class, it is also likely that newspaper readership penetrated the ranks of the tenant farmers, artisans and the more fortunate labourers. César de Saussure, an astute foreign observer during the reigns of George I and George II, commented that:

all Englishmen are great newsmongers. Workmen habitually begin the day by going to coffee-rooms in order to read the daily news. Nothing is more entertaining than hearing men of this class discussing politics and topics of interest concerning royalty.[7]

It is clear, moreover, that eighteenth-century newspapers had more readers than purchasers. Addison famously wrote in *The Spectator* for 12 March 1711 that a readership of 20 for each newspaper was 'a modest Computation', and the *Westminster Review* recorded more than a century later that every London newspaper was read by an average of 30 people.[8] Newspaper readership increased significantly after mid-century, particularly during the years of the American War of Independence (1775–83). As the experience of the Allied bombing of Afghanistan in 2001 demonstrates, warfare always sells news, and this was as true in the 1770s and the 1780s as it was in the 2000s. Indeed, John Brewer has calculated that in 1775 almost 35,000 newspapers were sold each day to individual purchasers, private subscribers, barbers shops, taverns and coffee-houses. When this figure is multiplied by the 20 of Addison's claim, one is able to calculate that upwards of half a million people out of a total population of seven million might well have read the London or provincial newspapers on a regular basis. An historical consensus is emerging from recent work that in the late eighteenth century probably one-third of the metropolitan population, and at least 7 percent of the population of England as a whole, may well have had regular access to newspapers.[9]

Through their newspapers Britons had access to a range of information about empire, India and the East India Company. New worlds of knowledge opened up with the expansion of the Second British Empire in the late eighteenth century. Yet men and women in England experienced India in many diverse ways during the reign of George III. They engaged with India not only in their imaginations but also through their experience of the products of the East, principally cotton textiles, which were transported back to England. One London coffee house, for example, was selling curry to its customers as early as the winter of 1773,[10] and,

---

7   Quoted in G.A. Cranfield, *The Development of the Provincial Newspaper, 1700–1760* (Oxford, 1962), pp. 187–8.

8   *The Spectator*, x, 12 March 1711; *Westminster Review*, X, April 1829, 478–9. The *Westminster Review* assumed that every London newspaper was read by an average of 30 people whilst every provincial newspaper by an average of 7–8 people, and calculated that this made an average of 25 readers for each English newspaper. 'If we allow that throughout Great Britain every copy of a newspaper is read by only twenty-five persons (and perhaps it would not be fair to take a higher average for the whole kingdom, for many of the Provincial Newspapers are not read by more than seven or eight persons), we shall find that of the gross population, about one-eightieth part are readers of news-papers.'

9   H.J. Barker, *Newspapers, Politics and Public Opinion in Late Eighteenth-Century England* (Oxford, 1998), pp. 115–17.

10 J.M. Holzman, *The Nabobs in England: A Study of the Returned Anglo-Indian, 1760–1785* (New York, 1926), p. 90. The Norris Street Coffee House, Haymarket, advertised its curry dishes in the *Public Advertiser*, 6 Dec. 1773. I have been unable to track down a copy of this edition.

as has been suggested above, the fellows of University College, Oxford, were almost certainly served mango chutney on their high table in the 1800s. The senses of quite ordinary people in late eighteenth-century Britain were stimulated with increasing frequency by the luxury manufactured goods of the sub-continent, and by the exotic animals and plants of India and the East Indies. Such animals brought back from India and then displayed in the public world of travelling menageries and the more private world of stately homes will now be considered. Through the ways in which Britons responded to these animals one can gauge the excitement surrounding the incorporation of India into the imperial vision of a polite and commercial people.

Animals from India were exhibited as the exotic prizes of the Second British Empire in the parks of several of the great houses of southern England, where menageries and more permanent caged exhibits anticipated the first zoos of the nineteenth century. The accessibility of these animals to an interested public was further broadened through the paintings, prints and cartoons of them. It is known, for example, that during the spring of 1772 great excitement was caused in Oxford by the arrival of a travelling menagerie, where, amongst other animals, a porcupine, a lion, a leopard and a panther were all exhibited. 'The famous Marlborough Tyger' was also on display, and *Jackson's Oxford Journal* described how the tiger had lodged for six years at Blenheim Palace after Lord Clive had brought him over from India. The tiger 'is a very striking Part of the Animal Creation', the editor of the newspaper explained. 'His body is finely ornamented with variegated Stripes, from the Point of the Nose to the very Extremity of the Tail.'[11]

The animals of India and Africa were popular amongst an English middle class that was busy experiencing the new and unusual products of the Second British Empire. The desire to consume imports from the East, and the topicality of tales of the ruling dynasties of India, are suggested by the frequency with which horses were given notably 'Oriental' names. There was a horse racing in Newmarket in 1786 called 'Hyder Ally';[12] a horse of a similar name had raced some years earlier on the same circuit,[13] and examples have been found of horses called 'Bamboo',[14] 'Mogul'[15] and 'Muslin'.[16] The East India Docks in London periodically echoed with the trumpets, roars, hissings and squawkings of Indian animals and birds as they were unloaded from the Company's ships after their long voyage from the East, along with the chests of tea from China, the spices from the East Indies, and the bales of cotton and packages of muslins from India. The *London Chronicle*, for example, reported in the summer of 1772 that 'a most beautiful Tyger, a curious Hyena, and a Civit Cat' were on board the *Ponsborn*

---

11 *Jackson's Oxford Journal*, 4 April 1772.
12 *Jackson's Oxford Journal*, 29 April 1786.
13 *London Chronicle*, 2 May 1772.
14 *London Chronicle*, 25 July 1772.
15 *London Chronicle*, 3 Sept. 1772.
16 *St. James's Chronicle*, 17 Oct. 1772.

Indiaman when it docked in London.[17] The animals of the Second British Empire functioned not only as entertaining side-shows in the public sphere of Georgian Britain but also as metaphors by which the weaknesses of the Royal Family could be ridiculed. For example, Warren Hastings's gift of an Indian hyena to the Prince of Wales in 1786 was interpreted by the editors of the London newspapers as a reflection of the rapacious and licentious habits of the young prince.

The Tower of London and Windsor Palace were well stocked with Indian animals. Robert Clive sent the Duke of Cumberland's uncle a wild cat from India, which was known in the East as the 'siyah-ghush', the Persian for 'fine ears'. There was considerable interest in this cat at both a popular and a scientific level, and articles about it appeared in the London Magazine,[18] the Philosophical Transactions of the Royal Society of London[19] and the Gentleman's Magazine.[20] The London Magazine was the first off the mark when it included a print of the animal and recorded in November 1759 that 'a very beautiful and uncommon animal, lately arrived from the East-Indies' had been 'lodg'd in the Tower'. The cat, which was considered a great rarity in India, had originally been sent as a present from the Nawab of Bengal to George III, along with an animal keeper who was sent over from the sub-continent to look after it. The London Magazine recorded that

> it seems to be a beast of prey; yet very docile, and so tame, any one may touch it. The keeper is an Indian, and servant to the Nabob of Bengal: When he speaks to it in the Indian language, it will do any thing he bids it. A cock coming into the room where it was, he seized it immediately, and killed it. The Nabob has one to go a hunting with him (tho' they are extremely scarce in that country) which shews it is capable of being taught any thing: In short, it is a very beautiful beast.[21]

James Parsons, the author of the article in the Philosophical Transactions, which was reprinted in full in the Gentleman's Magazine, included a sketch of the cat which showed its body taut, as if ready to pounce on its prey, and its long and slender ears, because he believed that the print in the London Magazine bore little resemblance to the animal.

Responses in Britain to the arrival of a wild cat from India encapsulate several of the arguments of this essay. Clearly different audiences engaged for different reasons with the siyah-ghush, some probably because it was an unusual animal which aroused their curiosity, others because it could be slotted into the systems

---

17 London Chronicle, 11 June 1772.
18 London Magazine, Nov. and Dec. 1759.
19 James Parsons, 'Some Account of the Animal sent from the East Indies, by General Clive, to his Royal Highness the Duke of Cumberland, which is now in the Tower of London', Philosophical Transactions of the Royal Society, 51 (1759–60), 648–52.
20 Gentleman's Magazine, June 1761.
21 London Magazine, Dec. 1759.

of classification by which the natural world was being ordered. Bound up with descriptions of the physical appearance of the cat were stories about its role in courtly life in India, which may well have given it a fashionable appeal similar to the vogue for reading eastern travel writing. Moreover, descriptions of the cat's hunting agility would probably have appealed to the sportsmen who read periodicals such as the *London Magazine* and the *Gentleman's Magazine*.[22]

It is intriguing to note that many of these animals were accompanied to England by Indian animal keepers. In addition to the regular traffic in bulk and luxury cargo from India in the late eighteenth century there was also a less voluminous passage of Indians voyaging to northern Europe. It is known, for example, that the French East India Company had brought over 50 Indians from the Coromandel Coast to work in a muslin factory in Versailles in 1786.[23] It is also evident that there were Indian sailors starving in the streets around Covent Garden during the winter of 1786. J.M. Holzman has demonstrated that there were even occasional advertisements in the London newspapers for East Indian footmen and servants.[24] The presence in England of animal handlers from the sub-continent is, however, particularly interesting because it shows that many Indians would have been walking the streets of London, and through the parks attached to the palaces and great houses of England, in the last third of the eighteenth century. They remind us that by dispensing dole to the starving lascars in London some Englishmen and women would have had contact with the peoples of India as well as her products. We still know too little, in fact, about the number or the role of Indians in eighteenth-century British society, which is in marked contrast to our knowledge of the Africans of this period.[25]

Information about India was diffused amongst interested Britons principally through the newspapers and monthly periodicals. In March 1772 Samuel Johnson commented that, 'the mass of every people must be barbarous where there is no printing, and consequently knowledge is not generally diffused. Knowledge is diffused among our people by the news-papers.'[26] The way in which news from India was recorded in the periodical press changed significantly in the last third of the eighteenth century. There was rarely a shortage of news about India during the three years which have been studied in depth – 1772, 1786 and 1804 – and information sprang from a variety of sources. The

---

[22] *The English Encyclopædia* for 1802 described the hunting ability of the siyah-ghush under a more general article about cats. 'These animals inhabit Persia, India, and Barbary; where they are often brought up tame, and used in the chace of lesser quadrupeds, and the larger sort of birds, such as cranes, pelicans, peacocks, &c. which they surprise with great address. . . . They are said to attend the lion, and to feed on the remains of the prey which that animal leaves.' *The English Encyclopædia*, 10 vols (London, 1802), III, 469 and plate 24.

[23] *Morning Chronicle*, 5 Oct. 1786.

[24] Holzman, *The Nabobs in England*, p. 91.

[25] See, for example, D. Dabydeen, *Hogarth's Blacks: Images of Blacks in Eighteenth-Century English Art* (Manchester, 1987), and N. Myers, *Reconstructing the Black Past: Blacks in Britain, 1780–1830* (London, 1996).

[26] *Boswell's Life of Johnson*, ed. G.B. Hill, 6 vols (Oxford, 1934–50), II, 170.

principal providers of information to the editors of the London newspapers were, unsurprisingly, the Court of Directors of the East India Company and Parliament. The Directors fed the London press with the crisply written dispatches of the governor-generals of India and the heads of the army, along with accounts of the General Court of Proprietors and the state of the Company's finances. Parliamentary debates, select committees and secret committees were another major source of information and opinion about the East India Company. The *de facto* lifting of restrictions on the reporting of Parliamentary debates in 1771 opened the floodgates to the more extensive and more regular reporting of Indian affairs.

Official news was supplemented by excerpts from private letters written by servants of the Company and their families in India to friends and relatives in Britain. In many ways these letters are the most interesting and revealing of all the sources of information in the English press because they reflect the views of ordinary men and women involved in the Company's commercial and territorial expansion across India, and it is clear from reading these that the currents of public and private opinion flowed along similar courses in the late eighteenth century. Foreign newspapers, particularly those of the Netherlands, France, Spain and Portugal, along with the newspapers produced by the British in the three presidencies in India, were all regularly pillaged for news about India and the exploits in the East of the various European companies trading there. The last major sources of information and speculation about India and the East India Company were gossip and hearsay, picked up by the editors of the newspapers in the coffee houses, taverns and streets of London. Indeed, the London newspapers were peppered with witty, scandalous and probably libellous rumours about the Company and its servants throughout this period. A 'Patriotic Paragraph' in the *Public Advertiser* in the spring of 1772 was typical of many: 'We hear that 500,000*l.* have lately found their way from Leadenhall-Street to a certain old House in Westminster. *Perhaps the Bengal Plunderers may bring an* OLD HOUSE *about their Ears* NOTWITHSTANDING.' [27]

There were two major developments in the ways in which India was written about in the English press in the late eighteenth century. The first was a substantial increase in the volume and regularity of news from India and the East Indies; the second was greater differentiation in the editorial ordering of this information. It is problematic to explain convincingly why there should have been an increase in the amount of Indian news in the metropolitan press. This was probably caused in part by the general expansion in the number of newspapers in London and the provinces, which provided new sources from which editors could copy and plagiarise news from the East. Whereas in 1760 there had been only nine or ten London newspapers, this figure had risen to 23 by 1790 and to 52 by 1811.[28] The growth of the press provides a partial but not a sufficient

[27] *Public Advertiser,* 25 April 1772.
[28] Figures quoted in J. Black, *The English Press in the Eighteenth Century* (Aldershot, 1991), p. 14.

explanation for this increase in news about India. A second explanation may be that the channels by which information and opinion about the East India Company reached London were more deeply entrenched by the 1800s than they had been in the 1770s. News from the East may have travelled more efficiently by sea and by land to Britain under Wellesley's governor-generalship than under Clive's. Certainly the servants of the Company and their families learnt how to find the press for themselves and how to appropriate newspapers when it suited them. A further explanation may be that the editors of the London and provincial newspapers were responding to the demands of their readers by allotting greater space in their publications to Indian affairs: that is to say, that an increasing volume of news about India was a function of public demand for it. Why should this have been so? In 1772 and 1786 the reading public was still coming to terms with the changes wrought to the parameters of the Second British Empire by the Seven Years War and the American War of Independence. This made information, opinion and speculation about India and the East Indies novel and exciting. Moreover, in 1804 Britain was fighting a world war against Napoleonic France and then, as now, warfare sold news. Whilst most newspapers and periodicals printed a steady undercurrent of news and comment about the Second British Empire during the reign of George III, this swelled into a torrent during moments of particular tension and crisis. The water-level of this current rose steadily during the last third of the eighteenth century.

The second major change one observes in the reporting of news from India and the East Indies is greater differentiation in the ways in which it was ordered in the press. In the early 1770s Indian news was usually mixed up indiscriminately with news from London and abroad. By the 1800s, however, there was much greater editorial differentiation, and it became the usual practice to organise Indian news under leading headlines such as 'East Indies' or 'India'.[29] By this period the map of the Second British Empire was more firmly fixed in the mind's eye of newspaper editors and readers than it had been at an earlier stage. This was also the most practical way of ordering the information connected with the Napoleonic Wars after hostilities resumed in 1803.

If one turns now to a more detailed analysis of the English newspapers for 1772 it is clear that both the spectacular victories of the British in India during the Seven Years War, as well as the substantial gains wrested from the French by the Treaty of Paris in 1763 and secured to the East India Company, seemed long distant to many people in England. The honeymoon that follows success in a world war, when soldiers and citizens alike can bask in the triumphs of victories won on the battlefield, had become sour by the early 1770s when news began to filter home about the devastating Bengal famine of 1769–70 and of the enormous abuses committed by Company servants in India. A close reading of the press for 1772 demonstrates that public opinion in England about the creation of an Indian empire crystallised slowly after the battles of Plassey (1757) and

---

[29] See, for instance, the *London Chronicle*, 5 Jan. 1804 and 28 April 1804.

Buxar (1764). The sudden transformation of the British in India from traders to rulers after Robert Clive's acquisition of the *diwani* of Bengal and her adjacent territories in 1765 was being debated even many years after the event in the English press. Many of the editors of the metropolitan newspapers and their correspondents were still unsure in 1772 about the benefits that the State and the Company would derive from the administration of these territories. After 1765 the East India Company ruled indirectly over millions of Hindus and Muslims in north-east India, and it was the unique nature of British rule over 'civilised' non-Europeans which was central to the debate in the metropolitan press in 1772.

The Treaty of Paris effectively destroyed French political (but not military) power in the sub-continent, and made the British the dominant European force in Indian politics. It is no surprise, therefore, that these cataclysmic events should have been debated for many years afterwards in the English press. During the last third of the eighteenth century India became accepted as a fact of public life in England, and a dimension not only of imperial affairs but also of domestic politics. Throughout 1772 there was a vigorous and informed debate in the metropolitan and provincial newspapers about empire, India and the East India Company. Historians of eighteenth-century Britain have long recognised that by the 1770s the London press had become a legitimate arena in which Company directors, proprietors and servants played out their factional rivalries and fought for the spoils of office.[30] Their analysis of the metropolitan press, however, has tended to focus only on the most visible and obvious newspaper paragraphs about the East India Company and the passage of Lord North's East India Regulating Bill in 1772–73. I have adopted, by contrast, a more rigorous methodological approach in which I have looked for references to India and the East India Company in every paragraph of every page of the newspapers with which I have worked. I believe that this approach provides a more accurate picture of the prevalence of Indian imagery and metaphors in the English press under George III. In November 1772, for example, the anti-ministerial newspaper the *Public Advertiser* satirised an account in the *London Gazette* of a grand banquet hosted at this time by the Ministry. 'The Devil,' it announced, 'in Honour of the present joyous Prospect of Things, gave a grand Entertainment to his Officers of State, Imps, and Choice-spirits.' The 'Bill of Fare' of the banquet described the dishes of the feast, each one analogous of the weaknesses of North's ministry:

> Tongues, but no Brains with them.
> A Ministry roasted whole.
> An opposition boiled away to Rags.
> A King smothered with Fools.

---

30 J.P. Thomas, 'The British Empire and the Press, 1763–1774' (Oxford Univ. DPhil thesis, 1982).

Thus far the menu appeared to represent a conventional critique of Government by an anti-ministerial publication. But what is interesting is that the next succulent dish to be handed around at the Devil's feast was 'The Hen with the golden Egg: Killed in India', which is perhaps a reference to the Company's resentment towards the State's regulation of its activities in India. This was followed by dessert where 'Nabob's Plums' were offered to the ministerial guests.[31] This metaphor can be read on a number of levels: it may refer to the extreme wealth of many returning Anglo-Indians;[32] it may refer to the diamonds that were a popular means of remitting money from India to Britain; or it may be a crude sexual metaphor for the State crushing the testicles of nabobs under the pressure of Parliamentary regulation of the Company. It is references like this to the East India Company and wealthy nabobs, hidden within a lengthy satire of the corruption and cronyism of Lord North's ministry, that have passed generally unnoticed by historians of late eighteenth-century Britain. I am not arguing that by themselves these stray references are significant, but that cumulatively they demonstrate that India and the East India Company were topics of daily concern and of some interest for newspaper editors and readers in George III's Britain.

The consistency with which news about the Company and the sub-continent was reprinted in the English press throughout 1772 demonstrates that India was a part of the daily newspaper diet of many Britons in London and the provinces. Newspaper editors and their correspondents garnered information and proffered opinions about the East India Company, its servants, and Britain's expanding territorial empire in the East on a regular basis. Daily and weekly newspapers were cheap, but even so they may well have been read cover to cover before being handed onto the next person in line. A reader of newspapers in 1772 would have had to be particularly selective not to have assimilated from them some knowledge, however rudimentary, of the East India Company and India. It would appear that by 1772 the newspapers were a legitimate arena in which the political debates and the factional struggles of Parliament and East India House were continued and fought out. Whilst it is certain that men like Robert Clive, Lawrence Sulivan and George Colebrooke would have paid editors in 1772 to have inserted favourable paragraphs in their newspapers, as discussed below, it would seem unlikely that every article in the English press was written by a hack journalist in the pay of a wealthy Company servant. There were, after all, thousands of articles about the East India Company and India in the newspapers and periodicals of 1772, and these represent only a handful of the available historical sources.

The daily, weekly and monthly press of London and the provinces helped many Britons to construct their view of the world and to contextualise the events in India and the East Indies. The information available in the press about India

---

[31] *Public Advertiser*, 24 Nov. 1772.

[32] In the late eighteenth century a 'plumb' was a sum of money worth £100,000. 'A custom has prevailed of writing *plumb*, but improperly . . . [In the cant of the city.] The sum of one hundred thousand pounds.' Samuel Johnson's *Dictionary* (London, 1785).

and the East India Company would probably have been read at several different levels by consumers of newsprint from varying social, educational and regional backgrounds. The newspapers and periodicals may well have helped many Britons to perceive the inter-connectedness of an empire of trade and territory in both the West and the East in the 1770s. The public prints gave the Parliamentary regulation of the East India Company and the victories over the French in India a wider significance. Battle for the control of the Company was not only about corruption in the presidencies and stock-fixing at home, but was also a question of the sanctity of chartered rights and the corrupting influences of eastern wealth and principles. Battle for military supremacy in the sub-continent was not only about containing and channelling the aggression of Indian rulers but also about carving out victories over the French in a far corner of the world as part of an Anglo-French struggle for global supremacy which had been raging for most of the eighteenth century. At times India was championed as a potential panacea for the spiralling costs of the National Debt; at other times she was portrayed as a *bête noire* who would embroil Parliament in the difficult responsibilities of ruling an empire of non-Europeans far from Westminster.

The newspapers and periodical press demonstrate that English public opinion about an empire in India was remarkably ambivalent in 1772. The triumphalism of the mid-1760s, after British victories over the French during the Seven Years War, sits uneasily with the anxieties many Britons evidently felt in the 1770s about the responsibilities of ruling an empire of conquest thousands of miles from the metropolis. Some feared that the East India Company's vast source of patronage would become a honey-pot on which the civil and military servants of the Company, as well as their family and friends, would gorge, intoxicated by its sweetness and profuseness, until there was nothing left; others feared that the Crown would achieve financial independence from Parliament if it was given greater control over the East India Company, and that it would then pack the House of Commons with MPs whose daily bread and butter was derived from positions within the East India Company.

The London and the provincial press of 1772 played a significant role in framing a public debate about the Second British Empire. Discourses of imperialism were not confined to the hallowed chambers of Westminster Palace but extended out into the metropolitan boroughs and provincial shires. This debate was no less vigorously and tenaciously fought in the London and periodical press than in Parliament and India House. Sir George Colebrooke, the newly elected chairman of the East India Company, angrily informed a General Court of proprietors in August 1772 that, 'News-paper attacks were weapons he never dealt in; he despised them when used by his enemies, he abhorred them when used by his friends.'[33] Colebrooke may well have been lying, but the fact that he felt obliged to state publicly that he had never appropriated the newspapers for his own political ends indicates the importance of the press in creating a body of

---

[33] *London Chronicle,* 27 Aug. 1772; *St. James's Chronicle,* 27 Aug. 1772.

informed opinion about empire and the East India Company. Robert Clive was clearly anxious about his public image and reputation in the press when he complained to the House of Commons in March 1772, at the opening of the Parliamentary enquiry into his conduct in India, that:

> The press has, for some time past, teemed with so many reflections upon the servants of the East India Company, and particularly upon me, that, were I not first to remove the bad impressions thus made, I am afraid any observations I could make upon the present subject of your deliberations would have little or no effect, except perhaps to my own prejudice.[34]

This example well illustrates the perceived impact of the late eighteenth-century press: the depth of Clive's fears is less significant than the fact that he believed, or at least claimed to believe, that his reputation had been publicly tarnished in the press long before the opening of the Parliamentary session for 1772. Newspapers could and did influence the outcome of debates in Westminster and the activities of the State in the last third of the eighteenth century.[35] This may explain why Edmund Burke referred to the 'public' in May 1789 as 'the ultimate judges under God of all our actions'.[36] It is evident from the London and the provincial press for 1772 that the public debate about India and empire was different in kind from that to be seen in 1786 or 1804. It was narrowly focused around the necessity of reining in a chartered company that seemed determined to run away with the spoils of imperialism after the military victories of the Seven Years War.

In 1786 a poem was published in a variety of newspapers during the New Year which provided a vision of British political authority rooted in monarchy and commercial empire. In this poem Britain's expanding economic dominion converges with the expanding political authority of George III, and distant areas of the world are incorporated into Britain's imperial sphere through commerce and trade.

> She speeds, at GEORGE'S sage command,
> Society from deep to deep,
> And zone to zone she binds;
> From shore to shore, o'er every land,
> The golden chain of commerce winds.[37]

Interestingly, the tension that had existed between the authority of the Crown in India and the power of the East India Company since Pitt's India Act (1784) is suppressed in this poem. This poem is symptomatic of other paragraphs in the

---

[34] *London Chronicle*, 4 April 1772; *London Magazine*, 'Debates of a Political Club', May 1772.

[35] See, for example, P. Langford, 'William Pitt and Public Opinion, 1757', *English Historical Review*, 88 (1973), 54–80.

[36] Quoted in P.J. Marshall, 'The Impeachment of Warren Hastings' (Oxford Univ. DPhil thesis, 1962), p. 129.

[37] 'Ode for the New Year' in the *Gentleman's Magazine*, Jan. 1786; *London Chronicle*, 5 Jan. 1786; *Felix Farley's Bristol Journal*, 7 Jan. 1786.

English newspapers of this period. The evidence of the newspapers for 1786 demonstrates that Britons were more comfortable than they had been in 1772 with the East India Company's territorial expansion in India and more confident in the Company's ability to sustain its rule in its newly conquered territories. Such confidence was probably inspired by the favourable terms of the Peace of Versailles, which ended the hostilities of the American War of Independence in September 1783 and which helped to entrench the British in India at the expense of the French.

Newspaper editors in London were well aware of the commercial, strategic and territorial importance of India to Britain's future supremacy in global politics both during and after the American War of Independence. Warfare in India was described in the *Annual Register* of 1783, for example, as one of the principal events of the year. In the 'Preface' to the periodical the editor wrote that, 'The conclusion of the war in the East Indies has necessarily claimed our utmost attention in the History of the present year.' This appears to have been one of the first occasions in the public prints when British expansion across India was represented so prominently as an object of State policy and not just as the concern of the East India Company and its shareholders. 'Exclusive of the great national importance of that arduous contest, and the vast stakes which were played for by all the parties,' the editor continued,

> the number and variety of military events, both by sea and land, of which it was so unusually productive, together with the superior abilities and extraordinary exertions of the principal leaders on all sides, must ever render the late war in India peculiarly interesting.[38]

It is significant that the editor of the *Annual Register* – a periodical which was considerably influenced by Edmund Burke, who became one of its first editors in 1759 – chose to single out warfare in India as one of the major episodes of a year in which there were many other significant political events, such as the fall of the Fox–North coalition after the disastrous passage of Fox's East India Bill in December and the rise of William Pitt's new ministry under the patronage of the King. It was already apparent that Britain's destiny as an imperial power lay in the East, as compensation for the loss of America in the West. This should come as no surprise, given the fact that most English newspapers had abandoned America as a lost cause as early as the summer of 1778, and had then begun to replace news from America with news from Europe, the West Indies and Africa.[39] Moreover, after Cornwallis surrendered Yorktown in 1781, it was clear to informed observers in England that the revolutionaries in America would undoubtedly succeed in their aim of political and legislative independence from Britain. The perceived inevitability of the outcome to the war probably reduced

---

[38] 'Preface' to the *Annual Register*, 1783.
[39] For a detailed discussion of British newspapers and the American War of Independence, see T.O. Bickham, 'Sympathising with Sedition? Portrayals of George Washington and the American Congress in the English Press, 1774–1783' (Oxford Univ. MPhil thesis, 1997).

consumer demand in England for news from America, and thus liberated space in the metropolitan newspapers for information about India and the East India Company at a time when the British were fighting critical battles with the French and her allies in the East.

There is good reason to believe that India was part of the imperial world-view of many informed people in Britain by 1786. Almost every day there was news and information about India in the English newspapers, which swelled when Parliament was in recess and whenever the Company's ships returned from the East. The editors of the English newspapers were also beginning to categorise information about India more systematically under its own heading, such as 'Indian News', rather than always including it under the more general heading of 'Foreign News'.[40] The complexity of these daily reports and articles about India demonstrates that the editors of the English newspapers assumed that there was a reasonably sophisticated understanding amongst the readers of their publications of the relationship between the domestic politics of the Indian princes, the success of the East India Company and the prosperity of Great Britain. The English newspapers created a world-view for their readers in which the Second British Empire was becoming as significant to Britain's political, strategic and economic interests as the First British Empire had been and, to a large extent, continued to be even after the American War of Independence.

The newspapers helped to contextualise the changes and continuities of Indian politics, whilst at the same time aiming to educate and entertain their readers. The opening of the impeachment of Warren Hastings in 1786 was a flash-point for the debate in the press about Britain's empire of conquest in India. The London newspapers, it should be remembered, rarely confined themselves to reports of recent events in the global imperial arena, and as a matter of course referred back to significant victories (and occasionally defeats) which had happened many years earlier in India and the East Indies. This probably helped consumers of newsprint to perceive more easily the interconnectedness of the First with the Second British Empire, and to understand more clearly why the British fought the French for global supremacy with as much commitment in the East as they did in the West. The trial may well have acted like a catalyst in the minds of many Britons, encouraging them to confront the broader problems associated with the administration of their eastern empire.

The opening of the impeachment of Warren Hastings sparked a renewed interest amongst English polite society in India and the Second British Empire, interest which had flagged during the early stages of the American War of Independence. For at least the first few weeks of the trial, the gallery of the debating chamber was packed with fashionable audiences who squashed together to catch a glimpse of Warren Hastings or to hear a snippet of the opening speeches of Edmund Burke and Richard Sheridan.[41] Fanny Burney was filled with admira-

---

40 *London Chronicle,* 19 Aug. 1786.
41 See, for instance, the *General Evening Post,* 6 April 1786; *General Evening Post* and *London*

tion for Hastings when she first met him in May 1786. 'He spoke with the utmost frankness of his situation and affairs, and with a noble confidence in his certainty of victory over his enemies, from his consciousness of integrity and honour, that filled me with admiration and esteem for him.'[42] For many authors writing in the 1780s, however, 'Hastings and his wife were regarded as the perfect exemplars to illustrate the crimes of the newly-moneyed, of their luxury, extravagance, and upstart pretension.'[43] Although the formal politics of Hastings's trial have been studied exhaustively, the opening of Hastings's impeachment has not yet been placed within the context of a public debate about India.[44] This is particularly significant in the light of Peter Marshall's observation that Edmund Burke believed that the trial only stood a real chance of success if it continued to attract the attention of the public.[45] 'If we proceed under the publick eye,' Burke wrote in the winter of 1787 to Henry Dundas, who had voted for Hastings's impeachment the year before, 'I have no more doubt than I entertain of my existence, that all the ability, influence and power that can accompany a decided partiality in that tribunal can [not] save our criminal from a condemnation followed by some ostensible measure of justice.'[46] The Managers of the impeachment hoped that the majority of MPs would be sufficiently susceptible to public opinion to disregard the legal deficiencies of their case. As is well known, English public opinion about Indian affairs played a significant role in the fall of the Fox–North coalition in December 1783, and had clearly become an element of national political life which MPs ignored at their peril.[47]

The debate about India in the London and the provincial newspapers for 1786 ranged across a broader territory than the immediate issues raised by the impeachment of Warren Hastings. Amongst many other articles on India, there

---

Chronicle, 2 May 1786; *Felix Farley's Bristol Journal*, 6 May 1786. The attention of Anglo-Indians in the Company's presidency towns towards the impeachment is demonstrated by the *Calcutta Gazette*'s claim to have reprinted in June 1787 one of Sheridan's speeches from the trial. See the *Calcutta Gazette*, 23 Aug. 1787. Reprinted in *Selections from Calcutta Gazettes of the Years 1784–1823*, eds W.S. Seton-Karr and H.D. Sandeman, 5 vols (London, 1864–9), I.

[42] *Diary and Letters of Madame d'Arblay*, 4 vols (London, 1876), II, 60.

[43] J. Raven, *Judging New Wealth: Popular Publishing and Responses to Commerce in England, 1750–1800* (Oxford, 1992), p. 225.

[44] S. Suleri and K. Teltscher have employed the new tools of literary analysis in their reading of Warren Hastings's impeachment, which they both see as an arena in which British guilt over the colonization of India was given form and expression. Their books do not, however, fully place the trial within the context of the debate in the press about the foundation of an empire of conquest in India. See S. Suleri, 'Reading the Trial of Warren Hastings', in her *The Rhetoric of English India* (Chicago, 1992), pp. 49–74; and K. Teltscher, ' "Geographical Morality": The Trial of Warren Hastings and the Debate on British Conduct in India', in her *India Inscribed: European and British Writing on India, 1600–1800* (Delhi, 1997), pp. 157–91.

[45] P.J. Marshall, *The Impeachment of Warren Hastings* (Oxford, 1965), pp. 70–1.

[46] *Ibid.*, p. 71.

[47] P.J. Marshall, *Problems of Empire: Britain and India, 1757–1813* (London, 1968), p. 42; L.G. Mitchell, *Charles James Fox* (Oxford, 1992), pp. 63–71.

was considerable information in the press about the savings and reforms being
made by the East India Company at home and in its presidencies abroad, the
Maratha Wars and the alliance of Tipu Sultan with the French, the expanding
European knowledge of the sub-continent's useful plants and animals, and the
pernicious influence of returning nabobs in the political and social life of
Britain. The impeachment in Parliament was echoed in the debate 'without
doors' which the newspapers encouraged by their editorials and the letters they
chose to print. The successes, and the manifold failures, of British rule in India
were discussed as passionately in the public prints as they were in Parliament. It
is not unreasonable to suppose that Britons of some education probably continued to engage throughout 1786 with news about the Second British Empire,
as they had done since at least 1772, and to consider the difficulties and
dilemmas of imperial rule through their newspapers. Indeed, continuity and
change in concepts of imperialism and the destiny of Britain were expressed
through the responses of these people in the English press to the territorial
expansion of the East India Company in the East.

'A mathematical survey was lately made of our territorial possessions under
the patronage of Governor Hastings', reported many metropolitan and provincial newspapers in April 1786, which showed that

> the English interest in that part of the globe . . . contained a tract of country
> equal to England, Ireland, and France, taken together; besides tracing the
> outline of near 2000 miles of sea-coast, and a chain of islands in extent 500
> more.[48]

Whatever 'absence of mind' Victorian historians might later identify in England's experience of expansion, none of the Georgian readers of these articles
could have missed the point that Britain's Asian interests now encompassed vast
territories and not merely commerce. This essay has argued that it was during
the last third of the eighteenth century that a fundamental change took place in
English attitudes towards an empire of conquest in India. Expansion had a domestic as well as an Eastern frontier: territorial empire in India, mapped with the
precision of trigonometry, was a fact of the domestic history of Britain, as well as
of South Asia.

In Asia, the new boundaries of British power had been set as early as 1763,
when the Seven Years War ended with the East India Company as the dominant
European presence in the sub-continent. It took a generation, however, for the
scope of this power to be appreciated at home. In 1772 the English press was
deeply critical of the East India Company and its servants, particularly of Robert
Clive, accusing them of plundering India of her wealth and of creating the
conditions which led to the devastating famine in Bengal. There was widespread

---

[48] *Gentleman's Magazine*, April 1786; *General Evening Post*, 4 April 1786; *London Chronicle*, 6
April 1786; *Felix Farley's Bristol Journal* and *Jackson's Oxford Journal*, 8 April 1786.

hostility in England at this time towards the creation of a territorial empire in India by a private company of merchants, most of whom were considered to be inept, corrupt and self-seeking. It was believed that fortunes made in India would erode the balance of the British constitution by allowing the Crown and wealthy individuals to purchase political support in Britain. It is evident that by 1786 attitudes in England were beginning to soften, and that India, even in the hands of Hastings's critics, had become a space in which British virtue might find its highest expression. By the end of the century the integration of India into national life, from the agitations of Evangelicals to the architecture of Royal Pavilions, would be complete.

Why did public opinion shift so dramatically in such a short time, the 30 years between 1770 and 1800? The loss of America in 1783 provides only part of an explanation. The answer lies as much in changing attitudes towards the East India Company and British dominion over non-European peoples as it does in changing attitudes towards the expanding authority of the British State. These two elements – the domestic and the international – are a consistent feature of the ways in which India was represented in the English press in the late eighteenth century. Informed Britons were becoming increasingly knowledgeable about India and the East Indies, and they derived their information from a variety of sources: parliamentary debates, newspapers, periodicals, books, pamphlets, cartoons and plays. It was evident to many people during this period that India was rapidly being drawn into Britain's system of worldwide trade, and that events in the sub-continent, as well as the activities of the East India Company's servants there, directly affected the material prosperity of large numbers of people in Britain. Although public opinion in 1786 remained largely ambivalent about the power of the East India Company, increasing numbers of people were beginning to argue in the press that a land-based empire in India was necessary and desirable in the context of Britain's rivalry with France for global imperial supremacy. There were also significant changes occurring to the language with which Britain's expanding empire in India was described in the press. The triumphalism and sense of military superiority which characterised British reactions to the Company's victories over Tipu Sultan in the Third Mysore War (1789–92) were reiterated even more strongly in the 1800s.

Britain's military and naval struggle with France for global supremacy was a core feature of the debate in the press about Britain's empire in the East. The British had come so close to being driven out of India by the French during the Second Mysore War (1780–4) that it became imperative to demonstrate, in the press if nowhere else, that the East India Company and the Royal Navy had regained the whip hand in the imperial stakes. This was all the more pressing given the fact that the English newspapers were widely available on the Continent and were swiftly dispatched to the courts of the European monarchs when they contained important items of news. James Boswell, for instance, wrote of the *London Chronicle* in 1756 that, 'from what I observed, when I was abroad, [it] has a more extensive circulation upon the Continent than any of the [other]

English newspapers'.[49] India was represented in the English press not as a distant and exotic land, filled with unfamiliar peoples, but as a political extension of Europe. India's importance to Western states in the eighteenth century was more contingent on European financial schemes and political priorities than it was on those of South Asia and the Far East. In the English press the sub-continent and the Spice Islands were integrated into European priorities and concerns, and orientated towards a Western vision of the world. All of the major European wars of the second half of the eighteenth century and of the turn of the nineteenth century – the Seven Years War, the American War of Independence, the Revolutionary Wars and the Napoleonic Wars – were fought out in India as well as in Europe, the West Indies and America. It was thus possible for the editors of the press to represent British victories in India, particularly during the Third Mysore War, as the delivery of Indians from French tyranny into English liberty.

India was a fact of British social and cultural life throughout the last third of the eighteenth century. Lascars starved to death on the streets of London, representatives of the Indian princes were occasionally sent to the Court of St James to improve relations with the East India Company, animals from the sub-continent toured the country in travelling menageries, and seeds and plants from the East filled the herbariums and hothouses of the capital. Furthermore, images of the sub-continent and of her peoples were consumed in Britain as readily as the textiles, dyes and spices of the East. Key events of the East India Company's engagement with India were seared into the nation's collective memory, and were retold as dreadful warnings of the fickleness of Indian princes and of the selfishness of Company servants. The Bengal famine acted as the moral antithesis of the Black Hole of Calcutta (1756), demonstrating that British administrators could match the depraved behaviour of Indian princes. There can be no doubt that informed Britons became increasingly familiar with the sub-continent and her peoples after 1772. Whilst the ruler of Mysore, Haidar Ali, was a distant figure to many people in Britain in the 1770s, his son, Tipu Sultan, was well known in the 1780s and 1790s through his appearances in cartoons and paintings accessible in London. Representations of Tipu Sultan in English newspapers and cartoons confirm Kate Teltscher's observation that he was closely allied with the French in the imagination of many Britons, and that his rule was considered to be the epitome of tyranny. Napoleon's self-elevation as Emperor of the French in 1804 was often described as a Western version of Tipu Sultan's kingship in India. 'As the Government of the tyrant TIPPOO is extinguished,' wrote *The Times*, 'his brother of the Western world need not give himself much trouble about ensigns and emblems; let him take Tippoo's *tyger* for his standard. BUONAPARTE will, however, far surpass even the Despot of Mysore, in the multitude of his *devices*.'[50]

In the spring of 1804 the English newspapers reported the news that General

[49] *Life of Johnson*, I, 318.
[50] *The Times*, 29 Sept. 1804.

Wellesley had marched triumphantly into Delhi and taken the old, blind emperor, Shah Alam, hostage.[51] It was the first time in its history that Delhi had fallen to a European army. The London newspapers lauded the fact that the British had penetrated deeper into India than Alexander the Great and his Greek army had ever achieved. The confidence displayed by the English newspapers in the relentless progress of the British armies across northern Indian manifests itself in an article in the *London Chronicle*: 'If we persevere in success,' argued its editor, 'we shall, either by conquest or alliance, have the same command of all North Western India, that we have now of Bengal, Bihar, and Orissa.' A comment such as this in the English newspapers of 1772 would have undoubtedly provoked considerable public criticism. 'On that supposition,' the *London Chronicle* continued, 'immense sources of mines, riches, and revenue, are opening to Britain.' In little more than one generation the creation of the British empire in India had become the national concern of the British State and people, rather than the narrow concern of the stakeholders in the East India Company. By 1804 English public opinion had turned decisively in favour of an extensive territorial empire in India, administered and protected by a public–private partnership of the East India Company and the State. The *London Chronicle's* article captured the mood of the Maratha Wars of the 1800s when it ended confidently: 'Should we continue in our course, there is a moral probability that we shall be as well acquainted, in a short time, with the Banks of the Indus, for many hundred miles, as we are now with the Banks of the Ganges.'[52] 'Little England' was far behind.

---

[51] See, for instance, the *London Chronicle* and *The Times*, 5 April 1804.
[52] *London Chronicle*, 7 April 1804.

Afterword: the Legacies of Two Hundred Years of Contact

P.J. MARSHALL

In their prospectus for this conference the organisers stated that it would 'focus on the development and operations of the East India Company as a maritime-based trading company, exploring the impact of its commercial activities on the cultural, economic and social lives of Britain and Asia'. 'Asia' has of course to be interpreted as 'maritime Asia', around the Indian Ocean and South China Sea, with an overwhelmingly strong emphasis on India. The task of an afterword must therefore be to try to assess the contribution made by the proceedings of the conference to our understanding of how contact with certain parts of Asia influenced Britain and how those parts of Asia were influenced by contact with Britain in the period from 1600 to 1833.

Any attempt to assess the impact of increased contact between societies has to begin with questions about the underlying differences and similarities between them. Most Europeans, both in the age of the East India Company and subsequently, assumed that there were fundamental differences between Britain and Asia. Collectively, however, the papers in this volume tend, like much recent work on Eurasian history in the early modern period, to bring out similarity, convergence and complementarity rather than stark difference.[1] We are not dealing with the cataclysmic consequences that marked the encounters between the British and native Americans in the seventeenth century or those of the first white settlers and the peoples of the Pacific, beginning with the landing of the first fleet in Australia in 1788. In such cases, where societies and cultures had been cut off from one another in historic times and had developed in very different ways, first contacts had spectacular consequences, most notoriously the

---

[1] See, for instance, the essays in *Modern Asian Studies*, 31 (1997), especially pp. 463–546, Victor Lieberman, 'Transcending East–West Dichotomies: State and Culture Formation in Six Ostensibly Disparate Areas', and pp. 735–62, Sanjay Subrahmanyam, 'Connected Histories: Notes Towards the Reconfiguration of Early Modern Eurasia'; the essays of Frank Perlin collected in *'The Invisible City': Monetary, Administrative and Popular Infrastructures in Asia and Europe, 1500–1900* (Aldershot, 1993), *The Unbroken Landscape: Commodity, Category, Sign and Identity: Their Production as Myth and Knowledge* (Aldershot, 1994); and on India specifically, the essays of David Washbrook, notably, 'South Asia, the World System and World Capitalism', in *South Asia and World Capitalism*, ed. Sugata Bose (Delhi, 1990), pp. 40–84. There is a vigorous exposition of this view in André Gundar Frank, *ReOrient: Global Economy in the Asian Age* (Berkeley, 1998).

decimation of population by the transfer of diseases. Influences and legacies are therefore easy to trace. Where, as was the case with Europe and Asia, contact has been maintained for centuries, leading to at least a limited exchange of influences over a very long period, an intensification of contact is likely to have speeded up the process of mutual adjustment rather than to have produced dramatic changes. Such adjustments are less easy to chart. This is the case with the increased contact between Europe and Asia in the three centuries following the Portuguese rounding of the Cape of Good Hope in 1498. It took place within a framework of essential similarities rather than of fundamental differences. This book is about interactions between two sides who already shared much in common.

To make such a point is to contradict ancient and tenacious beliefs that East was East and West was West. Such beliefs were embodied in powerful British stereotypes about Asia. The dominant stereotype for the seventeenth and much of the eighteenth century was that of an exotic Asia, far removed from the common experience of Europe. Non-Islamic Asian societies were presumed to be dominated by otherworldly systems of religious or secular beliefs: Hinduism, Buddhism (in as far as contemporary Europeans could identify it) or Confucianism. They and the Muslim states were thought to be despotically ruled by courts of almost unimaginable wealth and luxury which exercised a ruthless control over subjects deprived of all rights against the state. A rather different stereotype was also present even in the seventeenth century and became much more pronounced in the later eighteenth century. This stressed decadent decay as characteristic of Asian regimes rather than exotic grandeur. There was some recognition of the achievements of Asian societies in the past. Yet in the opinion of those who were increasingly using models of historical evolution through certain clearly defined stages, if India and China had reached the advanced stage of 'commercial' societies a long time ago, they had stuck there. Unlike western societies, they had ceased to progress. Both intellectually and in vital practical concerns, such as the development of technology or political and military organisation, they had atrophied. Sanjay Subrahmanyam shows how seventeenth-century English ambassadors were already affecting to despise Mughal despotism and the military weakness of the empire.[2]

Both these stereotypes about the East assumed that increased contact with Europe would be a vehicle for dramatic, if largely one-sided, changes. Britain, it was supposed, had little to learn from Asia in practical matters, although a few expected that its cultural life might be enriched by awareness of exotic civilisations, even to the point perhaps of bringing about what was later to be called an 'Oriental Renaissance' to match the classical renaissance of the fifteenth century.[3] By the end of the eighteenth century, it was axiomatic that Asia had much to learn from Britain in all respects. Whether it would resume the course of prog-

---

[2]   See above, pp. 69–96.
[3]   This is the title in translation of a book by Raymond Schwab, *La renaissance orientale* (Paris, 1950), which dealt primarily with France and Germany.

ress that was the natural expectation of humanity, was thought ultimately to depend on whether it could learn its lessons, if need be under the stern tuition of colonial rule.

The material in this volume does little to support ancient stereotypes about an exotic Asia. Representations of Asia, exotic or not, do not feature at all in the chapter on visual art by Geoff Quilley, whose focus is on the aspirations and values embodied in the many striking images of East India Company shipping produced in the later years of the Company.[4] Contributions on the work of the numerous British painters who went to India, or in a few cases to China, in the later eighteenth century would no doubt have revealed a rather deeper engagement with Asia. Although most of the artists were concerned with portraying European or Indian princely sitters for handsome fees, ideals of the picturesque were to be applied to Indian scenes by painters from William Hodges onwards.[5] Contributions on the Company and literature would certainly have shown a preoccupation with the exotic in the stimulus given to the poetry of such as Robert Southey, Thomas Moore or Lord Byron by the translations made under the Company's patronage from Persian, Arabic or Sanskrit by men such as Sir William Jones or Charles Wilkins.[6]

The majority of the contributions to this book deal with mundane activities, trade, manufacturing, the sailing of ships or political negotiations. Here the similarities on the Asian and British sides are much more marked than any differences. The terms of reference seem to have been essentially the same for both, and there is little evidence that an allegedly static and immobile Asia was at a marked disadvantage in any of them before the nineteenth century. Indeed, the evidence tends to the contrary, suggesting change and adjustment on the Asian as well as the British side.

Until the later eighteenth century, trade was the *raison d'être* of the East India Company and the main vehicle of contact between Britain and Asia. As Om Prakash writes, 'Along with its rival organization in the Netherlands, the Dutch East India Company, [the English East India Company] stood out as the most remarkable edifice of commercial capitalism.'[7] The way in which the British Company came to eclipse the Dutch, if much more slowly and uncertainly than is often assumed, is the theme of Femme Gaastra's contribution.[8] There was no indigenous commercial organisation in Asia that even remotely approached the Company's modes of operation. It was able to fund its trade on a scale that no Asian merchant combine could possibly match and its permanent joint stock was a device unknown in Asia. It conducted its operations through an elaborate organisation with echelons of salaried employees and intensive record and

---

4   See above, pp. 183–99.
5   G.H.R. Tillotson, *The Artificial Empire: The Indian Landscape of William Hodges* (Richmond, 2000).
6   Nigel Leask, *British Romantic Writers and the East: Anxieties of Empire* (Cambridge, 1992).
7   See above, p. 1.
8   See above, pp. 49–65.

account keeping, based on London but reaching out to many Asian ports, of a size and sophistication that some contemporaries thought was superior to any British government department. Huw Bowen's essay argues persuasively that, although the elements of continuity in the Company's history can be over-exaggerated, a structure for administering an empire could be built with relatively little adaptation on the commercial organisation of the Company. When it became 'an imperial agency', the 'Company's structures and systems remained essentially those of a commercial organization', he writes.[9] In Asia the organisational structures for conducting the Company's trade could also be adapted to its later military and administrative roles without fundamental changes. Even in the seventeenth century, the Company armed its trading ships and fortified and garrisoned some of its trading posts, thus becoming a quasi-naval or military power in a way that was totally alien to Asian traders.

This great company, clear forerunner of modern world-wide enterprises, was not, however, operating in a pre-capitalist Asia. As K.N. Chaudhuri has written, 'what happened in Western Europe' that made possible the launching of maritime expansion 'may not have been quite so unique after all. One can find parallel developments . . . in many areas of the Indian Ocean.' These included the rise of 'commercial capital' in the hands of merchants and the exercise of increased control by them over producers.[10] A process that we would now recognise as globalisation was taking place from the sixteenth century onwards, and the East India Company was to have an important role in this. Bruce Lenman's chapter, for instance, shows illuminatingly how the traders in precious stones operated on a world-wide basis.[11] David Hancock reveals that a global trade in wine existed in the eighteenth century, and thus 'the Madeira wine traders brought India into the Atlantic'.[12] This process of globalisation should, however, be seen not so much as the 'incorporation' and subordination of Asia within a western world economy, as the closer integration of economic systems which had long been developing along roughly similar lines.

In the ports of India and China or around the Red Sea and the Persian Gulf there had long been rich merchants, able to borrow extensively in local money markets, to remit funds by bills of exchange and to insure their ships and their cargoes. The production of the commodities in which the British wished to trade, such as Indian textiles, Indonesian spices or Chinese tea, was undertaken on a small scale by artisans or farmers, but was organised and financed by local merchants who sold the goods to the Company at the principal ports or more commonly received contracts from it to deliver them by a certain date in return for advanced payments.

However much the Company itself may have been an innovator as a trading

---

9   See above, pp. 28–9.
10 K.N. Chaudhuri, *Trade and Civilisation in the Indian Ocean: An Economic History from the Rise of Islam to 1750* (Cambridge, 1985), pp. 208–9.
11 See above, pp. 97–109.
12 See above, pp. 153–68.

body, it is important to remember that much British trade in Asia was conducted not by the Company's agents on behalf of their employer, but by them and by other British people on their own behalf. From 1661 the Company decided largely 'to withdraw from inter-Asian trade and concentrate its energies and resources on Euro-Asian trade'.[13] This left the way clear for individual British people to seek their fortunes trading from one part of Asia to another. The leading Company servants in particular became deeply involved in shipping goods out of Indian ports to markets in the Middle East, South-east Asia or China. In these operations they became part of an Asian trading world. They went into partnership with Asian merchants, borrowed money from them or from Asian bankers, carried goods on freight for their Asian owners and sailed Asian-built ships with largely Asian crews. They were competing for their share in a long-established pattern of maritime trade with Asian merchants over whom they had no pronounced advantages, at least until the rise of British colonial power late in the eighteenth century. The individual British merchant only gave way to the private British companies, the so-called houses of agency, the ancestors of Jardine Matheson and its peers of recent times, at the beginning of the nineteenth century. Even then, the early houses of agency were still part of an essentially Asian commercial world.

The Company's own trade, let alone that of private individuals, was conducted for most of the period without direct control over production. Chinese tea, Indian cotton cloth, silk or indigo, Arabian coffee, Javanese pepper all came to the British through Asian intermediaries, such as the brokers of Surat, the Bengal *dadni* merchants or the Hong guild at Canton. Sumatran pepper plantations were an early example of direct control over production, but as Anthony Farrington shows, there was wide scope at Bengkulu for Chinese enterprise.[14] In India direct control over production was only established after the rise of British political power in the later eighteenth century on the Coromandel Coast and in Bengal.[15]

Acting through Asian intermediaries without significant direct control over the output of any major commodity, the British took only a limited part of what was being produced for a wide variety of markets. Om Prakash estimates that increased British and Dutch demand for textiles in Bengal, the area most able to meet the new European enthusiasm for Indian cotton cloth, created about 100,000 full-time jobs among weavers, spinners and other artisans, a figure that would amount to some 10 percent of the total workforce.[16] This figure has, however, been contested by a scholar who regards it as too high and argues that Asian demand for Bengal textiles was always greatly in excess of what the Euro-

---

[13] See above, p. 4.
[14] See above, pp. 111–17.
[15] See above, pp. 8–9.
[16] See above, p. 7.

peans bought before the establishment of British political control.[17] Outside the coastal areas, which specialised in production for export, there were huge numbers of Indian weavers working for local markets and entirely unaffected by European demand. The very buoyant British demand for tea from Canton in the later eighteenth century may still have only have amounted to 15 percent of the annual crop, the rest supplying a vast internal market.[18]

Demand on such a scale was clearly not sufficient to bring about the introduction of new methods of organising production or new technology. The expansion of output of Indian textiles seems to have been achieved by artisans devoting more of their time to weaving or spinning, presumably therefore devoting less time to agriculture, and working within specialised artisan communities.[19] The establishment of colonial rule brought little change in the way in which textiles were manufactured, apart from innovations in the manner of reeling raw silk. European devices were introduced which required the reelers to work together under the same roof in what were virtually factories, called filatures.[20] The extent to which European demand for so-called 'export' porcelain produced the great concentration of production at Ching-tê Chêng near Nanking, where some three thousand kilns were said to be working in the early eighteenth century, is unclear but it is unlikely to have been significant.[21]

The pre-industrial British artisan or craftsman and his Asian counterpart seem to have worked in similar ways under much the same conditions. They worked for the most part in their own homes for distant merchants. It has recently been argued that the real wages of Indian weavers may actually have been higher than those of British ones.[22] In precision metalwork British artisans seem to have commanded skills that Asians could not match: in producing fine cottons or porcelain Europeans only slowly came up to Asian standards. There was thus a complementary global division of skills. British demand produced an increase in output in certain articles and introduced limited technological change in Asia. The impact of vast Asian imports on British manufacturing is hard to assess, but the obvious potential domestic and export demand for cotton cloth and hard-paste porcelain that the scale of these imports revealed was no doubt a powerful stimulus to the rise in Britain of machine-produced textiles and of potteries whose ware could compete in the home market with the Chinese. With industrialisation from the later eighteenth century, the balance of

---

[17] Sushil Chaudhury, *From Prosperity to Decline: Eighteenth-century Bengal* (New Delhi, 1995).

[18] Susan Naquin and Evelyn S. Rawski, *Chinese Society in the Eighteenth Century* (New Haven, 1987), p. 104.

[19] See above, pp. 6–7.

[20] N.K. Sinha, *The Economic History of Bengal from Plassey to the Permanent Settlement*, 2 vols (Calcutta, 1956–62), I, 189–99.

[21] K.N. Chaudhuri, *The Trading World of Asia and the English East India Company, 1680–1760* (Cambridge, 1978), p. 409.

[22] Prasannan Parthasarathi, 'Rethinking Wages and Competitiveness in the Eighteenth Century: Britain and South India', *Past and Present*, 158 (1998), 79–109.

advantages tilted decisively in favour of Britain. Nevertheless, high transport costs meant that the Indian artisans only slowly lost their Asian markets. Lancashire cloth did not make deep inroads into India until the 1830s. The high level of skills of Indian artisans also meant that the transfer of western industrial technology was a very slow process, limited to steamships on the Ganges and a few steam-powered mills in the lifetime of the East India Company.

Until the 1830s the exchange of manufactured goods between Britain and Asia was overwhelmingly in Asia's favour. The exchange of agricultural produce was almost totally in Asia's favour and remained so. Britain exported virtually nothing of her own growth in return for Asian spices and pepper, coffee, indigo and some other dyestuffs and the tea which became so dominant at the end of the period. There was very little transfer of farming techniques or crops, by comparison with the American case where there were huge shifts in both directions: maize, potatoes or turkeys to Europe; sugar cane and a great range of European plants and domestic animals to America. At the end of the period, the British established botanical gardens in their main settlements in India and made some efforts to encourage plant transfer, mostly from one part of Asia to another.[23] The early efforts were very limited in effect, the great development of tea in north-eastern India not coming until after 1833. With encouragement from the Company, potatoes became a part of the diet of some in its Indian provinces. There was a small reverse flow of plants from Asia to Europe. Some rich British servants of the East India Company tried to acclimatise Asian plants and trees in their gardens on their return home.

Early in the period, Asian agriculture, especially that of China, was generally regarded as a triumph of human ingenuity and industry. Under colonial rule, opinion shifted against Indian farming methods. Nevertheless, significant innovations were not attempted. Under the Company, there were no equivalents of the new world plantations under European management. Crops which Europeans wished to export, such as indigo, were grown for them by Indian peasant farmers, using their own techniques. British sponsored irrigation projects were limited to restoring those of earlier rulers.

For two centuries after the arrival of Vasco da Gama, Europeans in Asia were primarily people of the sea. In the construction and navigation of ships and above all in their ability to mount guns on them, the Portuguese had clear initial advantages over any Asian competitor. By the time of the first voyages of the English East India Company the gap had begun to close a little. Indian shipbuilders, working at Surat on the west coast, at ports in the south-east or in Burma, were incorporating western features into their ships. From 1736 Parsi shipbuilders were working under British protection in the Company's settlement at Bombay.[24] By the end of the seventeenth century the merchant fleets owned by

---

23 David Mackay, *In the Wake of Cook: Exploration, Science and Empire, 1780–1801* (1985), Chapter 7.
24 See above, p. 143.

the great Indian merchants of Surat[25] or by the British 'country' traders of Madras or Calcutta seem to have been essentially interchangeable, a kind of hybrid of European design and Indian shipbuilding methods. This tradition found its fullest flowering in the Bombay country ships that carried private trade to China in the early nineteenth century.[26] Armed ships from Aceh in Sumatra or from the Arab states of the Persian Gulf had begun to contest the sea with the Portuguese by the end of the sixteenth century. The British were later to complain of 'piracy' by the gunned ships of west Indian maritime states or of the Gulf Arabs, even though the warships of the Royal Navy never faced any serious Asian challenge. The Portuguese reported that compasses and cross-staffs were being used by Asian pilots in the Indian Ocean. As Andrew Cook shows, British mariners deployed new navigational skills and hydrographical knowledge embodied in maps, charts and sailing directions.[27] The extent to which such knowledge was absorbed by *nakhodas*, Indian or Arab sailing masters, on ships where European officers were not employed, is unclear.

Around the Indian Ocean by the early nineteenth century, for all their ability to adapt from Europeans, purely Asian-owned and operated ships had shrunk into a subordinate role on largely short-haul voyages. The ships of the Bombay Parsis were the obvious exception. Great fleets of Chinese junks were, however, still plying between South-east Asia and the ports of southern China. The extent to which European elements had been incorporated into their design or modes of operation has yet to be elucidated.

For understandable reasons, the convenors of the conference on 'a maritime-based trading company' did not commission any papers on armies and military technology. Yet any attempt to separate the commercial and the maritime from the military and the political would be misleading. 'The English Company, from its very inception, was not merely a commercial but a political actor', as Subrahmanyam points out,[28] and fortifications and garrisons had long been a prop of the Company's trade in India. From the mid-eighteenth century it became a huge military power; by far the largest number of British people in its service in Asia were thereafter to be soldiers. Even before then, Indian powers had begun to absorb military lessons from the Europeans, including the British. How they did so was highly characteristic of the whole range of Eurasian interactions in our period.[29]

There was essential common ground on military matters between Europe and Asia well before the first maritime incursions of the Portuguese. Firearms were in wide use throughout Asia by the fifteenth century. The Ottoman Turks honed

[25] Ashin Das Gupta, *Indian Merchants and the Decline of Surat, c. 1700–1750* (Wiesbaden, 1979), p. 90.

[26] Anne Bulley, *Bombay Country Ships, 1790–1833* (Richmond, 2000).

[27] See above, pp. 134–6.

[28] See above, p. 70.

[29] Geoffrey Parker, *The Military Revolution: Military Innovation and the Rise of the West, 1500–1800* (2nd edn, Cambridge, 1996), Chapter 4, is the standard account.

their military methods in conflict with European powers and their techniques were no doubt absorbed by other Asian powers. In addition to the cavalry that was their particular pride, Mughal emperors had large forces of infantry armed with muskets and a most formidable artillery train, including pieces obtained from and serviced by Europeans.[30] Aggressive moves by the British and French in the 1740s and 1750s demonstrated the limitations in adaptation by post-Mughal Indian powers to 'the European military revolution in field warfare'.[31] Carefully drilled infantry, including Indian sepoys in European formations, supported by field artillery, dispersed their armies with ease. Processes of adaptation continued, however. The armies of Mysore, the Maratha powers and later the Sikhs trained their infantry along European lines, acquired or constructed their own field artillery and, with the exception of Mysore, hired European officers. They could not turn the tide of British territorial expansion, but the price of victory over forces that were not qualitatively different to its own could be very high for the East India Company.

At a superficial level there was a deep gulf between the political world of the servants of the East India Company and that of the Asian rulers from whom they solicited favours. British people considered that they were dealing with 'despotic' regimes. In the canon of European political thought since Aristotle, despotism, that is rule without law, was a perverted political system. It was the opposite to the balanced constitution with limited representation and legally guaranteed rights under which early-modern Englishmen in particular believed that they lived. The equation of eastern government with despotism was as old as the Greeks, but the concept of 'oriental despotism' had been powerfully revived in the seventeenth and eighteenth centuries, largely by French writers on the Ottoman, Persian or Mughal empires, and by theorists, above all by Montesquieu. Sanjay Subrahmanyam shows how enthusiastically seventeenth-century Englishmen spouted the discourse of Asian despotism.[32] To Asians of any political consequence the East India Company's servants must have seemed to be no more than merchants, who were useful people, to be cherished and protected in return for good behaviour, but who could by definition have no political role. They had none of the qualities that fitted a man for such a role. In theory only men of learning and sanctity or of military prowess were so fitted, not those engaged in the accumulation of wealth. Occasionally Asian rulers encountered royal ambassadors who were not merchants. Subrahmanyam describes such encounters between Sir Thomas Roe, ambassador of James I, and the Mughal emperor, Jahangir, and later between Sir William Norris and the court of Aurangzeb. Jahangir evidently found 'little of interest in Roe'.[33] At the

---

[30] Iqtidar Alam Khan, 'Nature of Gunpowder Artillery in India during the Sixteenth Century: A Reappraisal of the Impact of European Gunnery', *Journal of the Royal Asiatic Society*, 3rd ser., 9 (1999), pp. 27–34.

[31] Parker, *Military Revolution*, p. 131.

[32] See above, pp. 77–8 and 90–2.

[33] See above, p. 83.

end of the eighteenth century the Quianlong emperor of China also encountered a British royal emissary, Lord Macartney. The emperor concluded that Macartney was irredeemably 'ignorant'.[34]

Subrahmanyam's paper is an acute analysis of the possibilities of mutual understanding between English and Mughal noblemen on political matters. He rejects extreme interpretations. Mughal principles of governance were not beyond the comprehension of Englishmen, but they did not 'translate' easily into their idioms either. Seventeenth-century Englishmen could not escape from an antagonistic framework of belief that they were dealing with a despotic regime akin to the ancient enemy, the Ottoman Turks.[35] Yet for all their disdain for despotism, the British Company servants had to recognise that they traded with a tolerable degree of security under the aegis of a government that maintained an order in which property rights were protected. Moreover, from the mid-eighteenth century, as Indian states passed under their control, the British began to govern provinces through the institutions of the despotic regimes that they so derided.

Historians are increasingly coming to recognize that by then, in spite of the wide ideological gulf between British and Indian ideals of statecraft, certain similarities had been developing between eighteenth-century western European and post-Mughal Indian states. The concept of a 'fiscal-military' state, that is of a state which was shaped by its commitment to maintaining powerful armed forces and to raising the money needed to sustain those forces, was forcibly applied to eighteenth-century Britain by John Brewer in his 1989 book called *The Sinews of Power*.[36] Eighteenth-century Indian states have also been described as 'fiscal-military' ones.[37] In response to the example and to the increasing threat of the Europeans, some of them began 'modernising' their forces. The contingents raised by Mughal *mansabdars* from their revenue grants were replaced by what seemed to resemble European standing armies, that is by professional troops under mercenary captains directly paid by the state. To pay for these forces, tax yields were boosted by leasing out to moneyed men rights to collect revenue or to exercise monopolies over the distribution of certain commodities. State supervision over the raising of taxes was increased by the employment of more local officials directly under the state's authority. As in western Europe, Indian states borrowed extensively in advance of their revenue receipts from bankers, who came to play a role in supporting the state that reminded British people of that of the Bank of England.

These were foundations on which the East India Company could build once it

---

[34] James L. Hevia, *Cherishing Men from Afar: Qing Guest Ritual and the Macartney Embassy of 1793* (Durham, N.C., 1995), p. 185.

[35] See above, p. 95.

[36] John Brewer, *The Sinews of Power: War, Money and the English State, 1688–1783* (London, 1989).

[37] Burton Stein seems to have been the first person to apply the phrase in that context, see 'State Formation and Economy Reconsidered', *Modern Asian Studies*, 19 (1985), 387–413.

had taken political power. It too needed large armies to defend its provinces and to implement the ambitious policies of its governors. The soldiers of the successor states to the Mughals were easily recruited into the new Native Infantry regiments of the Company under British officers. To support its armies and sustain an enlarged commerce, the Company needed to maximise its revenues. In Bengal and in parts of the south it inherited systems of revenue extraction which produced high yields with only limited British intervention. The Company too went into partnership with Indian bankers from whom it raised loans in anticipation of its revenue and who enabled it to transfer money to support its armies in the field or from one presidency to another by their bills of exchange. Thus early East India Company regimes seem to provide yet more examples of the genus fiscal-military state.[38] They were, however, undeniably despotic regimes without representative institutions and applying systems of Hindu or Islamic law to which British concepts of the right of the individual against the state embodied in the common law seemed to be largely alien.

If British people were perforce willing to operate the institutions of a despotic state, some important Indians were also perforce willing to give their services to a state dominated by unbelieving *farangis*, who were nominally merchants. To realise the revenue now due to them, the British urgently needed the expertise of the officials who had served previous regimes in district administration or in the central treasuries. In Bengal until 1772 the Company delegated the running of the *diwani* revenue administration almost entirely into Indian hands. Thereafter for a long time to come, even though the Company had 'stood forth' as directly engaged in the collection of the revenue and made increasing use of its European servants, Indian *diwans*, *sarristadars* and *mutasaddis* remained indispensable to the running of the system. To staff the courts of justice, now the Company's responsibility, it required the services of Muslim law officers and Hindu pandits. Not only were such people willing to accept employment, but they were willing to contribute their knowledge and to seek to implant right ideas of governance in their ignorant masters. Muhammad Reza Khan, who bore almost the entire responsibility for the revenue administration in the early years of the *diwani*, wrote treatises aimed at instructing the British in the principles of Mughal state-craft. As his biographer has put it, the Mughal empire had always recruited its elite from a wide variety of sources: 'Room had been found in the past for all nationalities in the imperial service; there was no reason why the English should not be found a place.'[39] They were awarded honorific Mughal titles and a few, among whom Clive was conspicuous, were given imperial *jagirs* or grants of revenue rights. A number of treatises on revenue administration were written by experienced Indian revenue officials in response to British inquiries. In adminis

---

38 See, for instance, C.A. Bayly, 'The British Military-Fiscal State and Indigenous Resistance: India 1750–1820', in *An Imperial State at War: Britain from 1689 to 1815*, ed. Lawrence Stone (London, 1994), pp. 322–54.

39 Abdul Majed Khan, *The Transition in Bengal, 1756–1775: A Study of Sciyid Muhammad Reza Khan* (Cambridge, 1969), p. 16.

tering Hindu or Muslim law, the British sought guidance from codes and digests provided for them by pandits and *maulavis*. These were translated from Arabic, Persian or Sanskrit for the benefit of British judges by great luminaries like Nathaniel Halhed, Sir William Jones or Henry Thomas Colebrooke. Those who gave the British access to texts were not necessarily selling their culture for the Company's shilling or simply providing the pretexts for their masters to indulge in orientalist fantasies. What they offered was no doubt corrupted in some degree by the Europeans who translated it and sought to render it more systematic, but even so, the early British–Indian legal texts seem to have involved a genuine intellectual exchange in which the Indian participants took a full part. Like Muhammad Reza Khan, the Hindu pandits recognised a duty to instruct their masters and to facilitate the due administration of justice, whatever the nature of the regime.[40]

In ideological terms British and Asian people no doubt inhabited different political worlds. To the British, most Asians lived as slaves under despotism. To Asians who thought about them, the British probably appeared to be devoid of moral principles and corrupted by the unrestrained pursuit of material gain. Nevertheless, events in certain parts of India showed that these worlds could converge. In the working of the newly conquered Company provinces, Indian and British officials showed that they shared common preoccupations in the running of tax systems, the maintaining of order and the administration of justice. They could even debate meaningfully with one another about the ends of government.

The East India Company operated widely across maritime Asia at various times in its history. In most areas, however, it was a limited and peripheral presence. This would be true, for instance, of the Company in the Moluccas, Japan, the Persian Gulf or the Red Sea. In western Sumatra the Company had long-established coastal settlements. In China it carried on a very large-scale trade over a long period, but one that was virtually confined to the single port of Canton. There is therefore little reason to expect that the Company should have left deep and lasting legacies even in Sumatra and China. India was, however, quite another matter. From the mid-seventeenth century the Company's trade had increasingly been focused on India and an Indian territorial empire had begun to be created in its name from the mid-eighteenth century. By 1833 the Company ruled huge areas and exercised a commanding influence over those

---

[40] This emerges from the studies of Rosane Rocher: 'The Career of Radhakanta Tarkavagisa, an Eighteenth-Century Pandit in British Employ', *Journal of the American Oriental Society*, 109 (1989), pp. 27–33; 'British Orientalism in the Eighteenth Century: The Dialectics of Knowledge and Government', in *Orientalism and the Postcolonial Predicament*, eds Carol A. Breckenridge and Peter van der Veer (Philadelphia, 1993), pp. 215–49; 'Weaving Knowledge: Sir William Jones and his Indian Pandits', in *Objects of Enquiry: The Life, Contributions and Influences of Sir William Jones (1746–1794)*, eds Garland Cannon and Kevin R. Brine (Philadelphia, 1993), pp. 51–79.

rulers that survived elsewhere. Only the polities of Sind and the Punjab in the northwest lay outside its control for the time being.

Yet even for India, the chapters in this book show that patterns of change that can be attributed to the Company are not distinct and that the legacies of the Company are not very readily identifiable. This essay has tried to offer reasons why this might have been so. The India in which the Company began its trade in the seventeenth century was not a world totally removed from Europe; it was part of the same world. The Company's servants and the Indians with whom they dealt shared common preoccupations in commerce, manufacturing, agriculture, navigation, the waging of war and the effective practice of government. Their approaches to these preoccupations had much in common. The technology and methods of organisation available to them were essentially similar. As a result the exchanges remained relatively equal. Om Prakash concludes of the trading phase of the Company's operations before it acquired political power that Indian merchants, certainly, and Indian artisans, probably, both gained from increasing European demand. Thus 'there can be very little doubt that the English East India Company and other European trading companies' commercial operations in the subcontinent represented a distinctly positive development from the perspective of the Indian economy'.[41] Rulers were no doubt aware of this when they conceded trading privileges to Europeans. Even the processes of conquest were brought about through Indian alliances or with the eager participation of Indians seeking their own advantage. The new British regimes were built on the foundations of the Indian states that had been consolidated in the eighteenth century, and many important Indians committed their expertise and their knowledge to them. Without this expertise, the loyalty of Indian soldiers, and the acquiescence of huge sections of the population, these regimes could not have taken root. In their early stages they were inevitably mixed Indo-British regimes, reflecting the aims and ideals of both sides. Om Prakash points out that there is evidence of a 'reasonably vibrant agricultural sector and rural economy' under early British colonial rule even in Bengal, long assumed to have been the victim of ruthless British revenue extraction and commercial exploitation.[42]

At least by 1833, but probably some years earlier, more or less equal exchange was giving way to outright British domination. A greater degree of control was being exercised over more of the Indian economy.[43] The Company's regime now felt little need of Indian expertise in the higher ranks of its government or the guidance of Indian knowledge. Through the new schools and colleges promoted under the Company's aegis by private groups like missionary societies and by the Indian and British citizens of large towns, 'new' knowledge was confidently being disseminated. Indian knowledge was becoming a matter of curiosity, not of practical use, the concern only of the self-confessed orientalist.

---

41 See above, pp. 7–8.
42 See above, p. 16.
43 See, for instance, the discussion in D.A. Washbrook, 'Progress and Problems: South Asian Economic and Social History, c.1720–1860', *Modern Asian Studies*, 22 (1988), 57–96.

Thus the legacy of the East India Company to India perhaps worked itself out over two phases. In the first phase, throughout the seventeenth century and for nearly all the eighteenth, the Company operated in an Indian milieu that it could not dominate. In its trade and even in its wars and state-building it achieved Indian purposes as well as its own. Its legacies were therefore to facilitate the development of certain trends that were already established in India, increasing commercialisation and the rise of regional states. By the end of this first phase, however, changes in Britain and the increasing power at the Company's disposal were leading to domination. Continuities were being broken and India was being subjected to a new colonial regime, whose legacies, for better or for worse, are much more clear cut.

The legacies of the Company to Britain were also part of the terms of reference set for the conference. Bringing about a widening of British consumption patterns was one of the major contributions made by the Company. Turning Indian calicoes into a common item of dress or decorative fabrics from the later seventeenth century was one of two great revolutions in consumption brought about by the Company. Turning tea into a drink for almost the whole of British society from the mid-eighteenth century was the other one.

Other legacies by the Company to Britain are no more clear cut than are the Company's legacies to India. The Company's activities were part of a wide pattern of overseas expansion bringing wealth to Britain from the seventeenth to the nineteenth centuries. By comparison with trade and empire across the Atlantic, the East India Company's contribution was somewhat circumscribed. Transatlantic trade enriched west-coast ports from Glasgow to Bristol as well as London. The Company's trade was confined to the port of London. A very large volume of imports by the Company flowed through London to the profit of the government's customs, of the Company's shareholders, of those who worked in the port or of the merchants who bought at the Company's sales and distributed the goods to the domestic and the re-export markets. Indigo in particular provided an important dying material for the British textile industry, and much of the Company's imported white cloth was printed in Britain. On the other hand, the volume of shipping used was comparatively small, for all the great size of the Company ships, and the contribution to the development of British manufacturing was limited by comparison with the Atlantic trades. Whereas by the mid-eighteenth century there were over 2 million consumers of British goods in the 13 North American colonies and large foreign markets for these goods in Spanish America, Brazil and West Africa, Asian countries were largely self-sufficient in manufactures. Selling even small quantities of woollens and metal goods in Asia was an uphill task for the Company.

A buoyant demand for European labour in North America and until late in the seventeenth century in the West Indies attracted large flows of British migrants across the Atlantic. By the eighteenth century the white population of British America was generally enjoying a higher standard of living than those in Britain. There were, however, few opportunities for British people to better themselves in Asia. Asian labour was skilled and abundant. Soldiers apart, the

British population in India, even in the later eighteenth century, could be numbered in hundreds. Some in that small population were, however, among the richest individuals anywhere in the British world. Great fortunes were being made out of trade or later out of the profits of wars and political coups. Below these conspicuous individuals by the end of the eighteenth century were well-paid civilian and military officers who were employed in the new empire created by the Company.

The Company certainly generated wealth, but the spread of those who benefited was narrow by comparison with the wealth generated by the Atlantic. Geographically, London was a major beneficiary as was Scotland, which supplied many recruits for the Company's service. The English outports or the manufacturing districts were generally less deeply involved in India. The Company was no more capable of bringing about the transformation of Britain than it was of India. Until at least the end of the eighteenth century, however, it was the channel through which both sides could adapt from one another in relatively equal exchange.

INDEX

Printed and bound by CPI Group (UK) Ltd, Croydon, CR0 4YY

16/04/2025

14658570-0001